# Twenty Years of the *Journal of Historical Sociology*

# Twenty Years of the *Journal of Historical Sociology*

## Volume 1 – Essays on the British State

Edited by **Yoke-Sum Wong** and **Derek Sayer**

**Blackwell** Publishing

BLACKWELL PUBLISHING
350 Main Street, Malden, MA 02148-5020, USA
9600 Garsington Road, Oxford, OX4 2DQ, UK
550 Swanston Street, Carlton, Victoria 3053, Australia

Library of Congress Cataloging-in-Publication Data

Twenty years of the Journal of historical sociology / edited by Yoke-Sum
Wong and Derek Sayer.
    p. cm.
  Includes bibliographical references and index.
  ISBN 978-1-4051-7933-1 (pbk. : alk. paper)  1. Historical
sociology.   2. Social history.   I. Wong, Yoke-Sum.   II. Sayer,
Derek.   III. Journal of historical sociology.

  HM487.T94 2008
  301.09–dc22
                                                    2008004417

Set in 10 on 12pt Bookman
by SNP Best-set Typesetter Ltd., Hong Kong
Printed and bound in Singapore
by Markono Print Media Pte Ltd.

For further information on Blackwell Publishing, visit our website:
http://www.blackwellpublishing.com

# Contents

# Contents

*The Ghost of Max Weber*

# Preface: A Curious Little Magazine

"Curiouser and curiouser!" cried Alice (she was so much surprised, that for the moment she quite forgot how to speak good English).

Lewis Carroll, *Alice's Adventures in Wonderland*

"A curious little magazine" is how one distinguished historical sociologist, who shall remain nameless, is reported to have once described the *Journal of Historical Sociology*. It is a characterization we can happily live with, though we are no longer quite so little. Twenty years after the *JHS* was launched on a wing and a prayer the journal is available in over 2500 libraries worldwide. The range of material we have published certainly stretches the accepted bounds of what historical sociology is supposed to compass. We have by no means ignored the traditional terrain of "big structures, large processes, huge comparisons" (to quote Charles Tilly) that for many *is* historical sociology, as variously exemplified in the work of Tilly himself, Barrington Moore, Theda Skocpol, Perry Anderson, John Hall, Alan Macfarlane, or Michael Mann. The exchange between Patrick Karl O'Brien and Michael Mann over the latter's *Sources of Social Power*, reproduced in the present collection (Volume 1), is one case in point. We have carried commentaries on acknowledged founding figures of historical sociology – Max Weber and Emile Durkheim among them – in our "Schools and Scholars" section. But much of what we have published falls under neither of these rubrics, and a fair selection of our contents, including many of the articles reprinted in this anthology, subverts the intellectual and professional boundaries and identities they define, not to say police. What makes the *JHS* "curious" – to some – is this abrasion between what the title *Journal of Historical Sociology* connotes, and what, year in year out, we have actually published. We could, of course, have changed the title. We preferred instead to challenge the field.

We believe that historical sociology should be more than a sub-discipline in which, for the most part, sociologists mine historians' findings in pursuit of large-scale comparative generalizations. We are not convinced that the grand narratives that result from such endeavors are the best, let alone the only form in which either the diverse socialities of the past or the past's multiple hauntings of the present can be apprehended. Undoubtedly they have their place: which is, we would contend, less to provide *über*-explanations of the course of human history than to provoke thought, reorient research, and raise questions about what should be studied and how. A goodly number of historians, including some of those represented in this collection, find sociologists' reflections on their subject-matter illuminating – even as they frequently chafe at their colleagues' disdain for the niceties of detail and disregard for the particularities of time and space. To have an honored place in a field, though, is not – or should not be – the same thing as to define it. Our starting-point was broader. In the words of Philip Abrams (in his posthumously published *Historical Sociology*), which we quoted at the head of our opening editorial in Volume 1, Issue 1, "In my understanding of history and sociology there can be no relationship between them because, in terms of their fundamental pre-occupations, history and sociology are and always have been the same thing. Both seek to understand the puzzle of human agency and both seek to do so in terms of the process of social structuring [. . .] It is the task that commands the attention, and not the disciplines."[1]

Our *Author Guidelines* spell out how we interpret that task. "The *Journal of Historical Sociology*," they state, "was founded in 1988 on the conviction that historical and social studies have a common subject-matter. We welcome articles that contribute to the historically grounded understanding of social and cultural phenomena, whatever their disciplinary provenance or theoretical standpoint. We are open as to topic, period, and place, and seek to be as international as possible in both the content and the authorship of articles." Adopting a deliberately catholic policy as to authors' disciplinary affiliations, theoretical orientations, and methodological preferences, we have sought the widest possible range of contributions that might *variously* advance our understanding of what Abrams's "same thing" might be. We did not set out to be "interdisciplinary" in the impoverished sense that term has since taken on as a fashionable mantra of research funding councils and university administrations. We have always recognized that different disciplines provide *different* perspectives and insights, whose clashes can often be as intellectually fruitful as any forced collaborations. We have carried articles whose authors are located in anthropology, geography, political science, literature, law, classics, and science and technology studies, not to mention food writers and even one zoologist, as well as historians and sociologists. We have also more than delivered on our promise to publish work that covers an astonishingly wide range of times, places, and topics, and is truly international in its authorship. This variety contributes, *diversely*, to demonstrating what a historical sociology that is not

[1] "Editorial," *JHS* Vol. 1, No. 1, 1988, 1.

confined by the classical questions that have constituted it as a sub-discipline of sociology might accomplish.

Indeed, it could be argued that the breadth of what we have published reveals the traditional preoccupations of that sub-discipline – the rise of "the West," the origins of capitalism, the distinctiveness of modernity, to name some of the most recurrent – to be distinctly parochial, not to say abidingly Eurocentric concerns; with the caveat, as Teodor Shanin (whose original idea it was to establish the *JHS*) was fond of saying, that in this mindset North America is Europe and Bulgaria is not. Antoinette Burton makes just such a case vis-à-vis "British History" in her essay in this collection (Volume 1). The conceptual geographies and historical periodizations that give the "classical" questions their salience would look very different from the vantage points of Michael Taussig's shamans or Brackette Williams's Dutchman ghosts (Volume 2). They seem equally curious when viewed from the perspective of Patrick Wormald's Anglo-Saxon or John Gillingham's Anglo-Norman England (Volume 1), which like many of the terrains our contributors have explored over the last twenty years confound conventional sociological wisdoms about what is and is not definitively "modern". Some of the most radical work we have published, in fact, has been by "traditional" historians whose obstinate attention to empirical detail has uncovered many a ticking time bomb waiting to explode.

The theoretical and methodological diversity, empirical richness, and cross-disciplinary intellectual challenge of the historical sociology encouraged by the *JHS* over the last twenty years will, we hope, be apparent from the thirty or so contributions gathered in these two volumes. The idea for the collection was the late Daniel Nugent's, and its possible composition was a frequent topic of discussion among the journal's editors (Derek Sayer, Philip Corrigan, Gavin Williams, Daniel Nugent, Martha Lampland, and Leon Zamosc) in the later 1990s. Dan used to refer to it as the "*JHS* Greatest Hits." The result is not quite that: our selection has been guided not by statistics of most frequent citations or downloads but by our judgment of what mix of contributions would best convey the spirit of the journal. Many other articles might equally well have been chosen, and some have been left out with considerable regret. While we have kept to Daniel's original plan for two volumes, the first focusing on English (and sometime British) state formation and the second displaying the journal's attempt to broaden the subject matters and methodologies of historical sociology beyond its traditional limits, the selection of contents is the personal choice of the present *JHS* Managing Editors, Derek Sayer and Yoke-Sum Wong. A full list of what we have published since 1988 may be found on the *JHS* website at www.blackwell-synergy.com.

"Our hallmarks, we hope, will be openness, exploration, and diversity," proclaimed that same opening editorial in March 1988.[2] We offer these volumes not only as a sampler of how far the *JHS* has come in realizing those objectives during the first twenty years of its existence but also as an invitation to all those who suffer, like Lewis Carroll's Alice, from the fatal disease of a surfeit of curiosity, to keep the submissions coming. Daniel Nugent would have made a particular point of extending this invitation to those he called "the undoctored and the untenured," for whom he was always insistent on making space. That insistence was typical of him. By training Dan was a Chicago anthropologist, but by vocation he was a historical sociologist in the generous sense we have tried to give the term in the pages of the *JHS*. One of his last writings, whose topic is shit in high places and low, is included here (Volume 2). Daniel was not one to mince his words. Passionate, cussed, quirky, awkward, ill at ease in polite academic company, disordered and disorderly – and withal a superb and committed scholar, he epitomized everything we ever wanted the *Journal of Historical Sociology* to be. We affectionately dedicate this collection to his memory.

Derek Sayer
Yoke-Sum Wong

[2] "Editorial," *JHS* Vol 1, No. 1, 1988, 3.

# An Introduction: Volume 1, Essays on the British State

There are more things in heaven and earth, Horatio,/Than are dreamt of in your philosophy. – William Shakespeare, *Hamlet*, Act 1, Scene 5

A piece of advice often given by *JHS* editors to contributors is to dispense with the elaborate introduction that tells readers how to read what follows, and not waste too much time situating their article in relation to existing literature in the field – a footnote will usually do. Cut to *the substance*: what is new in what you have to say, and why it matters. "A typical *JHS* article," say our *Author Guidelines*, "will contain little by way of extended literature review (which we are prone to edit out), will say something substantial and new about its empirical subject matter, will be aware of the theoretical implications of its topic without turning into an abstruse discussion of pure theory, and will be of interest to readers beyond a specialist geographical or disciplinary audience." These somewhat unconventional rules of thumb do not stem just from our concern to use a limited page budget to maximum effect or our disinclination to provide summaries of conclusions that professors in a hurry can skim in lieu of a full perusal of the evidence upon which they rest. We are trying, in our small way, to resist a species of what Philip Corrigan and I long ago called "moral regulation."[1]

Like much else in contemporary scholarly life – consider the way what counts as "research" is regulated in the forms that have to be filled in for granting agencies – the form of the academic article has increasingly been *standardized*, explicitly so in the style guidelines of most journals and more insidiously and pervasively in their editors' expectations, in support of a Faustian (or should we perhaps say Foucauldian?) bargain through which professional credibility and academic authority are purchased. The price of the mess of pottage is renunciation of many of the communicative possibilities of language. Insofar as our subject matter and its subjects are constituted in language, and language abounds in metaphor, ambiguity, and allusion, slipping and sliding down

---

[1] See Philip Corrigan and Derek Sayer, *The Great Arch: English State Formation as Cultural Revolution*, Oxford: Blackwell, 1985; Philip Corrigan, *Social Forms/Human Capacities: Essays in Authority and Difference*, London: Routledge, 1990.

Lacanian chains of signification and freighted with Derridean traces that can never be excised, this self-denying ordinance – which like the inner-worldly asceticism of Max Weber's Protestants is a refined technology for fashioning and empowering an active subject – may turn out to be a very bad deal for historical sociology.

Several of the writings reprinted in this collection demonstrate the perils and pleasures as well as the profits to be gained from venturing beyond this disciplined pale, most notably the contributions of Colin Richmond and Allen Shelton in Volume 2, whose uncanny ability to capture and communicate the histories and socialities with which they deal cannot be severed from their poetic qualities because the currency in which they trade is the poetry of the everyday. Like the novelist and short story writer Richard Ford or the ethnographer Kathleen Stewart,[2] who should be right up there on any historical sociologist's reading list alongside Marx, Weber, and the Annales School, they write beautifully – and effectively – because they have learned the languages and listened to the speech of the times and places about which they are writing. They convey the complexities of lives in all their fragmentariness, rather than reducing them to orderly abstractions.

We should surely by now have learned that *not* everything that is worth saying can be said within a single literary form – if the academic article, at least in the oxymoronically named social sciences, any longer deserves to be called that. *What* is said is inseparable from *how* it expressed. But no. The "linguistic turn" that has swept the humanities in recent years seems to have had little or no impact upon the writing requirements of academic journals – including, all too often, those journals that regard themselves as champions of avant-garde literary and social theory. To actually *write* in a manner that shows any sensitivity to post-structuralist insights into how language works is usually to invite a swift rejection, buttressed by complaints from reviewers that the argument is not sufficiently clear or the concepts wanting in precision. What is required is *clarity*, not the muddled and muddying thickness of description; the reassuring singularity of a narrative that has clear beginnings, middles, and ends, not the open-ended anarchy of a collage. Meaning must be made *transparent* – as if such a thing were possible. We should not be altogether surprised by this disjunction between our theories and

---

[2] See Richard Ford, *Rock Springs*, New York: Random House, 1996; *Women with Men*, New York: Vintage, 1998; Kathleen Stewart, *Ordinary Affects*, Durham: Duke University Press, 2007; *A Space on the Side of the Road*, Princeton: Princeton University Press, 1996.

our practice. The academy is not some Archimedean point that stands outside the world it studies. These are the disciplinary mechanisms that construct not only academic subjects but academic subjectivities too. The bottom line is that there is too much to lose.

Any text – and (to open a still bigger can of worms) whatever reality may or may not lie behind the archives, artifacts, oral testimonies, or interviews with surly ghosts[3] to which the text is complicatedly connected – *exceeds* any introductory gloss its author, let alone an editor, might put upon it. A text comprises more than its argument, and a summary of an argument, of the sort one usually finds in an introduction, is not the same as the argument itself. In the passage from the one to the other the McDonalds on the corner too easily reduces to (just) another instance of global capitalism, and (to anticipate some of what is debated in the present volume) a myriad of activities from collecting taxes to registering births, marriages, and deaths too smoothly coalesce into something (but is it a thing? asks Philip Abrams) called The State. Unless we are very careful these second-order abstractions then become the terms which debate is conducted, usurping the place of the wealth of particulars from which they were drawn. The standard article format colludes in this slide by tacitly suggesting that the *essence* – as distinct from the substance – of any text is capable of being summarized in an introduction and recapitulated in a conclusion. The *reductio ad absurdum* is the (aptly named) one-hundred-word Abstract, of which we are not especially fond at the *JHS* either. We accept that abstraction may sometimes be necessary. But abstraction is *always* violent. Something has *always already* changed in the discursive shift from the one register to the other. It is impossible to summarize without ordering and prioritizing. And it is equally impossible to summarize without remainder.

Introductions do far more, as well as a good deal less, than tell us what is to come in a text. They frame it. And too cumbersome a frame, as we all know, may distract attention from the details of the picture it encloses, just as too clear a signposting may discourage readers from venturing down roads less traveled – particularly when the signs direct us along routes we already know. In the case of the academic article, the usual convention is to provide a lens for reading that situates what is said in relation to the state of the field as defined by past authority and current intellectual fashion, and foregrounds the author's own interpretation of the significance of

[3] We refer here to Brackette Williams's article in Volume 2 of this collection, pp. 106–138.

the material with which he or she is dealing rather than leaving the reader to decide for her or himself what it means. The latter expectation has become so ingrained that a text that simply presented its findings without placing them in the context of an argument or drawing any conclusions – an article that refused to *interpret*[4] its findings – would strike most journal editors as unpublishable. We might pause to reflect where such a requirement might leave Walter Benjamin's "One-Way Street" (or indeed the whole of his Arcades Project).[5]

But as Roland Barthes long ago reminded us, a text can never be reduced to its context – or to its author's conscious intentions – because it is written in a language that transcends both and is the property of all.[6] Words come freighted with multiple significations, and meanings are never singular. Talking about photographs, Barthes distinguishes between what he calls the *studium*, the field of vision that makes an image immediately intelligible within the cultural preoccupations of its time and place, and a "second element" in *the photograph itself* that is more akin to a found object, in the sense the surrealists gave that term:

The second element will break the *studium*. This time it is not I who seek it out (as I invest the field of the *studium* with my sovereign consciousness), it is this element that rises from the scene, shoots out of it like an arrow, and pierces me. A Latin word exists to designate this wound, this prick, this mark made by a pointed instrument: the word suits me all the better in that it also refers to the notion of punctuation, and because the photographs I am speaking of are in effect punctuated, sometimes even speckled with these sensitive points; precisely, these marks, these wounds, are so many points. This second element that will disturb the *studium* I shall call *punctum*; for *punctum* is also: sting, cut, little hole – and also a cast of the dice. A photographer's *punctum* is that accident which pricks me (but also bruises me, is poignant to me).[7]

The distinction applies equally well to the written text. The *substance* of an article is not identical with its Abstract. It is *puncta* that shatter paradigms, and for these one needs to be able to see the whole picture, preferably unencumbered by any frame at all.

[4] See, in this context, Susan Sontag's classic essay "Against Interpretation," in her *Against Interpretation and Other Essays*, New York: Picador, 2001.

[5] Walter Benjamin, "One-Way Street," in *Walter Benjamin: Selected Writings Volume 1, 1913–1926*, ed. Marcus Bullock and Michael W. Jennings, Cambridge: Belknap Press of Harvard University Press, 1996; *The Arcades Project*, Cambridge: Belknap Press of Harvard University Press, 1999.

[6] Roland Barthes, "The Death of the Author," in his *Image, Music, Text*, New York: Hill and Wang, 1977.

[7] Roland Barthes, *Camera Lucida*. New York: Hill and Wang, 1981, 26–27.

This invocation of Barthes, Derrida, and Lacan by way of preface to an anthology of articles on the state by (mostly) British historians may seem as surreal as Lautréamont's famous chance encounter of an umbrella and a sewing machine on a dissection table, and provide yet further evidence of what a curious little magazine the *JHS* is. But as it happens, one of the more striking features of the journal has been the readiness of some of Britain's most eminent historians to publish in its pages side by side with authors who have been heavily influenced by post-structuralist thought, and not only in the person of Michel Foucault. This first volume of this anthology, whose subject is the state in general and the state in Britain in particular, is a sampling of their work. Like, perhaps, more things in heaven and earth than many historians and most sociologists – though Robert Merton was an unexpected exception[8] – are prepared to admit, this happy confluence had its beginnings in pure serendipity, a throw of the dice.

We are, of course, a scrupulously peer-reviewed journal – excepting "Issues and Agendas" pieces, which are intended to provoke, texts of lectures and the like that we wish to publish *verbatim*, and certain of the imaginative histories of Colin Richmond,[9] where reviewing would simply be absurd. We have occasionally been known to carry articles, especially from younger scholars, against reviewers' advice if we think them sufficiently challenging and the author is able to persuade us that she or he can answer the reviewer's criticisms. (Another *JHS* editorial rule of thumb is to remember that those best qualified by their expertise to review a piece may also be the ones with the biggest axes to grind and the greenest turf to protect.) Nevertheless, like most academic journals, we have our networks, both formal (the Editorial Board) and informal, through which many a prized submission has initially reached us. One of the most productive of these, which has provided us with reviewers as well as contributors over the last twenty years, has been the Discussion Group on the State that met annually at St Peter's College, Oxford, from 1982 to 2001. A majority of the papers in the present volume began life as presentations to that group. The journal owes DGOS an enormous debt of gratitude. We would like in particular to thank Steve Hindle, who was a co-convenor of the

---

[8] See Robert K. Merton and Elinor Barber, *The Travels and Adventures of Serendipity: A Study in Sociological Semantics and the Sociology of Science*, Princeton: Princeton University Press, 2006.
[9] Apart from essays published in the *JHS* and *Common Knowledge*, see Colin Richmond, *The Penket Papers*, 1996.

group in its later years, for his help in selecting the writings that make up this volume.[10]

Readers will understand, we hope, why we are reluctant to use this introduction to summarize their contents or otherwise frame what they have to say. The articles, conference papers, and exchanges collected here will speak for themselves, doubtless in as many ways as they have readers. Having considered various fancy or fanciful titles for the volume, we settled in the end for the straightforward *Essays on the British State*. But, of course, "the" "British" "state" is not straightforward at all. Suffice it to say that between them, and, again, variously – for their authors by no means speak with a single voice – these essays reveal their subject to be anything but a straightforward object or category of analysis. If you want to know more, cut to the substance, and read the book.

Derek Sayer

---

[10] More on DGOS can be found in my brief piece "Gerald Aylmer and DGOS," below, pp. 272–275, which was written as a preface to the *JHS* publication of all the papers presented at the twentieth and last DGOS meeting in 2001, whose topic was "When/What was the English State." Two other contributions to that symposium, by Colin Richmond (pp. 276–286) and Patrick Collinson (pp. 287–293) are also included in this volume.

# Notes on the Difficulty of Studying the State (1977)*

## PHILIP ABRAMS (1933–1981)

**Abstract** The state is not the reality which stands behind the mask of political practice. It is itself the mask which prevents our seeing political practice as it is. There is a state-system: a palpable nexus of practice and institutional stucture centred in government and more or less extensive, unified and dominant in any given society. There is, too, a state-idea, projected, purveyed and variously believed in in different societies at different times. We are only making difficulties for ourselves in supposing that we have also to study the state – an entity, agent, function or relation over and above the state-system and the state-idea. The state comes into being as a stucturation within political practice: it starts its life as an implicit construct: it is then reified – as the *res publica*, the public reification, no less – and acquires an overt symbolic identity progressively divorced from practice as an illusory account of practice. The ideological function is extended to a point where conservatives and radicals alike believe that their practice is not directed at each other but at the state; the world of illusion prevails. The task of the sociologist is to demystify; and in this context that means attending to the senses in which the state does not exist rather than to those in which it does.

*****

"When the state itself it is danger", Lord Denning said in his judgment yesterday, "our cherished freedoms may have to take second place, and even natural justice itself may have to suffer a setback".
"The flaw in Lord Denning's argument is that it is the government who decide what the interests of the state should be and which invokes 'national security' as the state chooses to define it", Ms Pat Hewitt, director of the National Council for Civil Liberties, said yesterday.

*The Guardian*, 18.2.77

When Jeremy Bentham set out to purge political discourse of the delusions and fantasies generated by the many "alegorical contrivances" through which self-interest and sectional power are masked as independent moral entities, the notion of the state did not enjoy wide currency in English political or intellectual life. Had it done so he would surely have included it along with "government" "order" and "the contsitution" as one of those terms peculiarly apt to foster "an atmosphere of illusion" – a fallacy of confusion at best, an "official malefactor's screen" at worst, giving spurious concreteness and reality to that which has a merely abstract and formal existence.[1] By 1919, however, the combined efforts of hegelians, marxists and politicians had wrought a change: "nearly all political disputes and differences of opinion", Lenin could then observe, "now turn upon the concept of the state" – and more particularly upon "the question: what is the state?"[2] At least among sociologists his observation seems to be still very largely correct; fifty years of asking the question have not produced any very satisfactory or even widely agreed answers. At the same time the sort of invocation of the state as an ultimate point of reference for political practice voiced by Lord Denning, and the sort of objection to such invocations voiced by Ms. Hewitt, have become steadily more commonplace. We have come to take the state for granted as an object of political practice and political analysis while remaining quite spectacularly unclear as to what the state is. We are variously urged to respect the state, or smash the state or study the state; but for want of clarity about the nature of the state such projects remain beset with difficulties. Perhaps a new Benthamite purge is opportune?

## 1. The Problem in General

Political sociology, according to W. G. Runciman, springs from the separation of the political – and more especially the state – from the social. It is constructed as an attempt to give a social account of the state with the latter envisaged as a concrete political agency or structure distinct from the social agencies and structures of the society in which it operates, acting on them and acted on by them. It is, we are told, this "distinction . . . which makes possible a sociology of politics".[3]

Marxism, sociology's only serious rival in the search for a contemporary theory of the state, builds, superficially at least, on a very similar distinction. Most varieties of marxism assume that adequate political analysis must, as Marx put it, proceed on the basis of "the actual relation between the state and civil society, that is, their separation".[4] Within that framework the crucial issue in marxist political analysis then becomes the question of the degree of actual independence enjoyed by the state in its relations with the principal formations of civil society, social classes. Even when marxist writers, such as Poulantzas, overtly reject this framework they do so only to substitute for the separation of state and civil society a problematic formulated as "the specific autonomy of the political and the economic" within the capitalist mode of production. And the resulting problem about the nature and function of the state is to be resolved through analysis of the relations of the state to the field of class struggle by way of an unmasking of the autonomy of the former and the isolation of the latter. Here, too, the problematic envisages the state as in effect a distinct entity and the task is to determine the actual forms and modes of dependence or independence that relate it to the socio-economic.[5]

Yet this common context of analysis, extant and agreed for over a century, has not proved very fruitful. Political sociology is rich in agendas: "the major empirical problem of political sociology today would seem . . . to be the description, analysis and socio-logical explanation of the peculiar social structure called the state", "political sociology starts with society and examines how it affects the state". But it is noticeably poor in performance. The fact that Dowse and Hughes find hardly anything implementing such agendas to include in their textbook accurately reflects the state of the field.[6] The sociology of the state is still best repre-sented by the fragmentary observations of Max Weber. And the striking feature of Weber's political sociology is that it is, as Beetham has so clearly shown, at its best a highly *ad hoc*, historically specific, analysis of complex systems of class politics with little or no provision for the state as something separate from class politics.[7] For the rest, the intellectual separation of society and the state in sociology seems in practice to have meant the exclusion of the state from the political – distinctive notions such as the "polity" serve to collapse the identity of the state rather than to clarify it.[8]

Marxist writers have attended to the analysis of the state more thoroughly and explicitly but, with the possible exception of the analysis of Bonapartism, not on the whole all that much more conclusively. The great debate on the relative autonomy of the state, which looked so promising when it was launched, ended with a sense that its problems had been exhausted rather than resolved. The main protagonists turned their attention to other issues. By 1974 Ralph Miliband was urging political sociologists "from a marxist point of view" not to dissipate their energies in further studies of our speculations about the state but to embrace an alternative problematic couched in terms of wider and differently conceived processes and relationships of domination.[9] Meanwhile, Nicos Poulantzas moved from the opaque conclusions of his struggle to clarify a marxist theory of the state – "the state has the particular function of constituting the factor of cohesion between the levels of a social formation" – not to attempt a more exact clear and empirically specific formulation of such ideas, but rather to the study of particular regimes and to the larger problem of the class structure of capitalism.[10] The only agreed results of the debate appeared to be a mutual recognition of a number of important features of the presumed relationship of state and society which could not, as yet anyway, be adequately demonstrated. Thus, the credibility of the notion of class domination is saved – but then it is of course *given* in all varieties of marxism – but the demonstration of such domination in the context of particular states remains unaccomplished. At this level the state once again succeeds in defying scrutiny.

It seems necessary to say, then, that the state, conceived of as a substantial entity separate from society has proved a remarkably elusive object of analysis. Aridity and mystification rather than understanding and warranted knowledge appear to be the typical outcomes of work in both the traditions within which the analysis of the state has been regarded as a significant issue in the recent past. Possibly this bafflement has to do with the way both traditions have conceptualised the state. In fact of course the marxist problem with the state is quite different from the sociological problem with the state and they must be explored independently. Before doing that, however, we should note the way in which commonsense constantly reinforces the taken for granted wisdom of both traditions.

## 2. The Problem in Particular

The everyday life of politics suggests forcibly that the conception of the state offered in marxism and political sociology is – whatever the difficulties of operationalising it – well-founded. Commonsense impels us to the inference that there is a hidden reality in political life and that that reality is the state. Either way, the search for the state and the presumption of its real, hidden existence are highly plausible ways of "reading" the way the public aspects of politics are conducted. The naive research experience of sociologists who have attempted to study what they regard as the workings of the state or any of its presumed agencies is our most immediate store of commonsense in this respect. Anyone who has tried to negotiate a research contract with the Home Office or the Department of Health will be aware of the extreme jealousy with which such agencies instinctively protect information about themselves. The presumption, and its effective implementation, that the "public sector" is in fact a private sector about which knowledge must not be made public is all too obviously the principal immediate obstacle to any serious study of the state. The implementation of the claim takes a variety of ingenious forms. One of the most familiar is the combination of bland public assurances that state agencies would welcome "good" research into themselves, coupled with the apologetic but quite effective mutilation or vetoing of almost all actual research proposals on grounds of defective or inappropriate methodology or other "technical" considerations. It is a nicely disabling technique of knowledge control to claim that it is the procedural defects of the proposed investigation rather than its object that justifies the refusal of access. Nor can there be many who have been through this type of experience who doubt that "good in such contexts means supportive – a sociology of decision not a sociology of criticism. Again, there is the blocking or warping of research on grounds of the need to protect an undefined public interest or, more brazenly, the interests of subjects. Attempts to study topics as diverse as the behaviour of officers of the Supplementary Benefits Commission and the attitudes of army wives have in my own experience foundered on such rocks. And if one approaches the more serious levels of the functioning of political, judicial and administrative institutions the control or denial of knowledge becomes at once simpler and more absolute of course: one encounters the world of official secrets.

Any attempt to examine politically institutionalised power at close quarters is, in short, liable to bring to light the fact that an integral element of such power is the quite straightforward ability to withold information, deny observation and dictate the terms of knowledge. It would be a substantial service to the sociology of the state simply to collect, document and try to make sense of sociologists" experiences in this respect. Until that is done it seems only reasonable in the face of such elaborate efforts at concealment to assume that something really important is being concealed – that official secrecy must take the blame for many of the current shortcomings of both sociological and marxist analyses of the state.

But can it? Perhaps we have here only a spurious difficulty. So often when the gaff is blown the official secrets turn out to be both trivial and theoretically predictable.[11] More often still when the state papers are opened and the definitive scholarly work is done it only serves to affirm or add detail to the interpretations read from the surface of events by sharp-eyed and theoretically informed observers thirty years earlier.[12] Let us enter a note of doubt about the importance of official secrecy before going on.

For meanwhile commonsense in all its forms dulls such scepticism. *Private Eye* finds its existence imperilled by even trivial flirtations with the task of political research. The *Sunday Times* provokes a public crisis by its attempts to publish the gossipy and unrevealing secrets of Richard Crossman's *Diaries*. And Philip Agee and Mark Hosenball find themselves deported because, they and we are told, their knowledge might endanger the lives of employees of the "state" – unknown and unknowable actual people whose existence as "state's-men" is really jeopardised by what is presumably the truth about their activities. Simultaneously Joe Haines reports the persistent, covert and devious management of knowledge by Treasury officials in their battle to impose a statutory incomes policy on elected politicians pledged to fight such a policy.[13] And Tony Bunyan finds himself in the odd situation of being able to demonstrate the existence of a highly effective and repressive political police in this country in the 1930s while having his suggestion that such agencies still exist in the 1970s dismissed as "unconvincing" because, in effect, he had failed to break through the dense and hazardous barrier of contemporary police secrecy.[14] The fact that someone can impose secrecy is surely evidence both that that person has power and that he has something to hide – commonsense infers.

In sum, the experience if not the findings of both academic and practical political research tends towards the conclusion that there is a hidden reality of politics, a backstage institutionalisation of political power behind the onstage agencies of government; that power effectively resists discovery; and that it may plausibly be identified as "the state". In other words it remains reasonable to assume that the state as a special separate and autonomous entity is really there and really powerful and that one aspect of its powerfulness is its ability to prevent the adequate study of the state. We seem to have evidence that the state itself is the source of the state's ability to defy our efforts to unmask it.

## 3. An Alternative

I want now to suggest that this whole involvement with the problem of the state may be in an important sense a fantasy. We have, I shall argue, been trapped both in political sociology and in marxism by a reification which in itself seriously obstructs the effective study of a number of problems about political power which ought to concern us – even though the weight of post-Hegelian received ideas probably made the entrapment inevitable. The difficulty we have experienced in studying the state springs in part from the sheer powerfulness of political power – the ability of Mr. Rees to deport Mr. Agee and give no reason for doing so other than the interest of the state is a fact and does need explaining. But it is perhaps equally a consequence of the way we have presented that problem to ourselves.

In trying to reconstitute the issue I shall begin by suggesting that the difficulty of studying the state can be seen as in part a result of the nature of the state, but in an equally large part must be seen as a result of the predispositions of its students. In both respects the business of "studying the state" seems to be shot through with highly Benthamite fallacies. And we might do better to abandon the project in those terms and study instead something which for the moment and for want of a better term I will call politically organized subjection. In other words I am suggesting that the state, like *the* town and *the* family, is a spurious object of sociological concern and that we should now move beyond Hegel, Marx, Stein, Gumplowicz and Weber, on from the analysis of the state to a concern with the actualities of social subordination. If there is indeed a hidden reality of political power a fist step towards discovering it might be a resolute refusal to accept the legitimating account of it that political theorists and political actors so invitingly and ubiquitously hold out to us – that is, the idea that it is "the state". My argument, in sum, is that we should take seriously the remark of Engels – one of the few classical sources of the marxist theory of the state *not* cited in *Political Power and Social Classes*, incidentally – to the effect that, "the state presents itself to us as the first ideological power over man". Or the notion presented so forcibly in *The German Ideology* that the most important single characteristic of the state is that it constitutes the "illusory common interest" of a society: the crucial word there being "illusory".[15]

Before developing that argument it will help to look a little more closely at the difficulties of marxism and political sociology in their contemporary intellectual dealings with the state.

## 4. The State of Political Sociology

Despite the constant assertion by political sociologists that their discipline is constituted as an attempt to give a social explanation of the state, the state is in practice hardly considered at all in the normal conduct of political sociology. What has happened instead is that the notion of the polity, or in Daniel Bell's most recent writing, "the public household" has absorbed the notion of the state.[16] The sociological explanation of the state is replaced by the sociological reduction of the state – an observation made trenchantly by Sartori as long ago as 1968.[17] Nevertheless, this transformation is not entirely unprofitable. In advancing their case for making the polity the central concept of political sociology Parsons, Almond and Easton, the principal advocates of that project, had at least one strong card in their hand. This was of course the claim that the important thing to study was not structures but functions.[18] In effect they were going back on the proclaimed agenda of political sociology to the extent of arguing that the distinctiveness of the state, or the political was a matter of processes not of institutions: that the state was a practice not an apparatus. That claim still seems to me, as a principled revision of the agenda, entirely sound. But if we go back to the models of the polity that functionalist writers offered us in the 1960s and then compare them with the empirical work that has actually been done by political sociologists in the last twenty years an odd discrepancy appears. Many of the formal accounts of the polity proposed in the pioneering days of political sociology took the form of input-output models.[19] In those models the commonsense functions of the state – the determining and implementing of goals, the enforcement of law, the legitimation of order, the expropriation and allocation of resources, the integration of conflict -were all characteristically assigned to the output side of the political process. There is of course an absurdly mechanistic quality about such models. Nevertheless, what must strike one about the body of work political sociologists have actually produced since their field was defined in this way is that almost all of it has been concerned with input functions not output functions. Even after its functional reconstitution the state has not really been studied. Here again, Dowse and Hughes reliably represent their colleagues.[20] What has been studied is political socialisation, political culture, pressure groups (interest-articulation), class and party (the aggregation of interests), social movements including the Michels' thesis about the oligarchic degeneration of social movements, riots, rebellion and revolution.[21] Overwhelmingly, attention has been paid to the grass-roots processes of the polity and not to the coordinating, power-deploying central functions. Why should this be?

A simple answer would be that political sociologists, like their colleagues in other fields are, in organising their research interests in this way – in studiously averting their eyes from the state and attending instead to its subjects – merely displaying the timorous and servile opportunism rightly and variously trounced by Andreski, Nicolaus, Gouldner, Schmid, and Horowitz but still it seems rampant in the normal determination and selection of social science research projects.[22] The temptations of the "eyes down, palms up" mode of research organisation are compelling and reductive, not least for people who are themselves in positions of privilege which might not withstand much scrutiny from below.

Nevertheless, my own feeling is that venality is not the whole of the story, or even in this country a large part of it. Nor, I think, can we blame the types of occupational time-serving and semiconscious identification with power of which Nicolaus and Horowitz make so much in the United States. British sociology and certainly its professional association are much less implicated, happily, with the institutions of power than their American counterparts. One advantage of not being perceived as useful is that one is left relatively free as an academic to do the work one wants to do. To that extent the failure of political sociologists to attend to the state, even within their own problematic, must be explained in terms of their intellectual rather than their material proclivities. There is perhaps a strictly professional pathology of political sociology which defines the important and researchable problems of the discipline away from the state. The most obvious aspect of this pathology is methodological. The distinctive methods of political sociology, *from* public opinion polling onwards, are adapted to studying the attitudes and behaviour of large, accessible and compliant populations and are not adapted to studying relationships within small inaccessible and powerful networks. Conversely consider what happened to the efforts of American political sociologists to study even the modest power structures of local communities: the whole field was at once transformed into a swamp of virulent accusations of methodological ineptitude. More generally, from the publication of *The Power Elite* onwards all attempts by political sociologists to examine the authoritative or repressive functions of the polity have suffered this methodological reduction. The line from Dahl to Bachrach and Baratz, to Lukes, to Abell marks a steady retreat from talking about political practice to talking about how one might talk about political practice: an obsession with good method: better to say nothing than to risk being charged with muck-raking.[23] The notion that a sufficiently large accumulation of methodologically impure forays into the description of power in the manner of Mills might add up to something convicing does not seem to have been considered.

Over and above the methodological prohibition, however, there is a more substantial theoretical obstacle within political sociology that serves to discourage attention to what political sociologists themselves claim is the central problem of their field.

Two main difficulties can be identified here. First, the functional translation of the notion of the state effected by Easton, Almond, Mitchell and others and generally accepted as a crucial defining strategy of political sociology has left political sociologists with a curiously nebulous, imprecise notion of just what or where their supposed principal explicandum is. A vague conception of the functions being performed – "goal attainment", "rule adjudication" and so forth – necessarily opens the door to a vague conception of the structures and processes involved in their performance. It is clear for example, to take the case of Almond and Coleman, that even under the conditions of high specificity of structure attributed to "modern" polities no one-to-one relation between "governmental" structures and the "authoritative" functions is going to emerge. Thus, although "the analytical distinction between society and polity" continues to be insisted on by these authors the structural identification of key phases of the polity, let alone their relation to society, defeats them.[24] Suzanne Keller is quite in line with the mood of her colleagues therefore when she abandons the concept of the state in favour of the more inclusive, and less committing, notions of "a social centre, a core, a fulcrum", settling in the end for the idea of "unification around a symbolic centre".[25] The idea of the centre preserves the conception of state functions in principle but leaves all questions to do with the execution of such functions disastrously wide open. Moreover, it inhibits both empirical and conceptual analysis of the relevant processes by drastically reducing the specificity of the functions themselves. As indicated already the real tendency of political sociology is perhaps not to explain the state at all but to explain it away.

The second problem has to do with the persistence within political sociology of an initial interest in a particular type of substantive issue, the question of the entry into the arena of political action of previously quiescent subject populations. Within the broad intellectual framework of the field, the separation of state and society, this became the compelling practical problem for almost all of the pioneers whose work was taken as effectively defining what political sociologists did. There were many reasons for this concentration of interest, some radical, some conservative, but its overall consequence is clear. In practice political sociology became a body of work centred on such themes as "the extension of citizenship to the lower classes", "working class incorporation", "conditions for stable democracy". In almost all of this work the state, or some equivalently real, institutionalised nexus of central power was virtually taken for granted – either because it was thought of as historically given or because it was assumed to be a dependent variable vulnerable to the impact of the external social forces which were the immediate object of concern. Accordingly although a sense of the state was there the state was not treated effectively as part of the problem to be investigated. What makes studies like Peter Nettl's analysis of the German Social Democrats *so* exceptional as contributions to political sociology is that they do treat the problem of the entry of new groups as a genuinely two-sided matter involving both state and society in active interaction.[26]

Taken together, these theoretical and substantive inclinations of political sociology go a fair way to explain why its concern with the state has remained – for all its importance in principle – so rudimentary in practice. Insofar as it *has* been developed, moreover, it has been largely as an unexpected result of studies of the presumed "input" functions and processes of the polity such as political socialisation and not a consequence of a direct assault on the central issue. That is to say, the best of the socialisation studies have found that sort of input to be rather strongly shaped by powerful downward actions and influences emanating from "the centre".

The study of political socialisation, one of the most flourishing branches of political sociology, itself makes good sense within the general pattern of interest in the problem of "new groups". The issue posed by new groups is simply extended to include the taming of what Parsons has called the "barbarian invasion" of infants as well as the control of what Lipset has termed the "populist excesses" of more mature invaders. Nevertheless, work in this area has in an odd way tended to "rediscover" the state: and it is to that extent one of the more creative and promising features of contemporary political sociology – see, for example, Dawson and Prewitt's discussion of the business of "learning to be loyal", or David Easton's demonstration of the way children are led to confuse parents, presidents and policemen in a single package of benign authority.[27]

Of course, it is true that such studies discover the state in only a rather special aspect. What is perceived is a rather powerful agent of legitimation. Those sociologists attracted to a Weberian conception of politics, of whom Daniel Bell is perhaps the most interesting contemporary representative and for whom, in Bell's words "the axial principle of the polity is legitimacy", will conclude that real progress is being made by research on political socialisation.[28] Those who envisage the state as an altogether more forcible agency of control and coordination will find such a conclusion bland and inadequate if not vacuous. But the question is, can sociologists of this second persuasion demonstrate that a state of the kind they believe in actually exists? What the socialisation studies have done – along with other work more explicitly focussed on legitimation processes, such as that of Mueller – is to establish the existence of a managed construction of belief about the state and to make clear the consequences and implications of that process for the binding of subjects into their own subjection. Furthermore, they have shown that the binding process even if not effected by the state proceeds in terms of the creation of certain sorts of *perceptions* of the state. From Stein's claim that "the King is the embodiment of the pure state idea" to the American child's belief that "the President is the best person in the world" is hardly any step at all.[29] The discovery that the *idea* of the state has a significant political reality even if the state itself remains largely undiscovered marks for political sociology a significant and rare meeting of empiricism and a possible theory of the political.

In other words the state emerges from these studies as *an ideological* thing. It can be understood as the device in terms of which subjection is legitimated: and as an ideological thing it can actually be shown to work like that. It presents politically institutionalised power to us in a form that is at once integrated and isolated and by satisfyIng both these conditions it creates for our sort of society an acceptable basis for acquiescence. It gives an account of political institutions in terms of cohesion, purpose, independence, common interest and morality without necessarily telling us anything about the actual nature, meaning or functions of political institutions. We are in the world of myth. At this point the implications for political sociology of my suggested alternative approach to the study of state perhaps become clear. One thing we can know about the state, if we wish, is that it is an ideological power. Is it anything more? Myth is of course a rendering of unobserved realities, but it is not necessarily a correct rendering. It is not just that myth makes the abstract concrete. There are senses in which it also makes the non-existent exist. From this point of view perhaps the most important single contribution to the study of the state made in recent years is a passing observation of Ralph Miliband's at the start of chapter 3 of *The State in Capitalist* Society to the effect that: There is one preliminary problem about the state which is very seldom considered, yet which requires attention if the discussion of its nature and role is to be properly focused. This is the fact that the "state" is not a thing, that it does not, as such, exist."[30] In which case our efforts to study it as a thing can only be contributing to the persistence of an illusion. But this brings us to the point where it is necessary to consider the implications of my alternative approach to the study of the state for marxism.

## 5. The State of Marxist Theory

The most remarkable feature of recent marxist discussions of the state is the way authors have both perceived the non-entity of the state and failed to cling to the logic of that perception. There seem to be compelling reasons within marxism for both recognising that the state does not exist as a real entity, that it is at best an "abstract-formal" object as Poulantzas puts it, and for nevertheless discussing the politics of capitalist societies as though the state was indeed a thing and did "as such, exist".[31] Of course, Marx, Engels and Lenin all lend their authority to this ambiguity, assuring us that the state is somehow at one and the same time an illusion and "an organ superimposed on society" in a quite non-illusory way: both a mere mask for class power and "an organised political force" in its own right.[32] Accordingly, instead of directing their attention to the manner and means by which the *idea* of the existence of the state has been constituted, communicated and imposed, they have come down more or less uneasily in favour of the view that the existence of the idea of the state does indicate the hidden existence of a substantial real structure of at least a state-like nature as well. There is an imperceptible but far-reaching slide from the principled recognition of the state as an abstract-formal object only to the treatment of it as a "real-concrete" agent with will, power and activity of its own. Even Miliband, notably the least mystified of marxist analysts of the of the state, moves along that path to a point where we find that the state does, for example, "interpose itself between the two sides of industry – not, however, as a neutral but as a partisan", and has a "known and declared propensity to invoke its powers of coercion against one of the parties in the dispute rather than the other".[33] And Franz Oppenheimer who in 1908 made a valiant attempt to demonstrate that the concept of the state was no more than "the basic principle of bourgeois sociology" and to expose the realities of forcible political appropriation, or as he put it "robbery" behind and underpinning that principle, found himself talking of the state as "itself the robber; he unmasks the state as one sort of real-concrete object only to reconstitute it as another.[34] But the most complex and ambiguous version of this distinctive marxist ambiguity is of course that of Poulantzas.

Before attempting an account of Poulantzas" dealings with the state, however, it is worth considering why marxism generally should have proved so susceptible to this sort of ambiguity. I think it results from an unresolved tension between marxist theory and marxist practice. Marxist theory needs the state as an abstract-formal object in order to explain the integration of class societies. In this sense I can see little real discontinuity between the young Marx and the old or between Marx and marxists: all are hypnotised by the brilliant effect of standing Hegel the right way up, of discovering the state as the political concentration of class relationships. In particular the class relationships of capitalist societies are coordinated through a distinctive combination of coercive and ideological functions which are conveniently located as the functions of the state. Conversely, political institutions can then be analysed from the particular point of view of their performance of such functions within the general context of class domination. At the same time marxist practice needs the state as a real-concrete object, the immediate object of political struggle. Marxist political practice is above all a generation of political class struggle over and above economic struggle. To that extent it presumes the separateness of the economic and the political: separate political domination is to be met by separate political struggle. And one can easily see that to propose that the object of that struggle is merely an abstract-formal entity would have little agitational appeal. The seriousness and comprehensiveness of the struggle to conquer political power call for a serious view of the autonomous reality of political power. Paradoxically, they call for a suspension of disbelief about the concrete existence of the state. In effect to opt for political struggle thus becomes a matter of participating in the ideological construction of the state as a real entity.

Maintaining a balance between the theoretical and practical requirements of marxism thus becomes a rather intricate matter. It is achieved in *The German Ideology* but not often elsewhere: "every class which is struggling for mastery, even when its domination-
. . . postulates the abolition of the old form of society in its entirety and of mastery itself, must first conquer for itself political power in order to represent its interest in turn as the general interest, a step to which in the first moment it is forced; . . . the practical struggle-
. . . makes practical intervention and control necessary through the illusory "general interest" in the form of the state".[35] More commonly, the requirement for a unity of theory and practice works itself out by the theoretical acceptance of the state as a genuine, extant, "organised political force" acting in its own right; theory then becomes a matter of deciphering the relationship between the actions of that force and the field of class struggle. The ambiguity of many marxist accounts of the state may thus be understood not so much as a matter of doctrinal error but rather as expressing a conflation and confusion of theory and practice instead of a true unity.

Both Miliband and Poulantzas very nearly escape from this difficulty. But neither quite succeeds. Miliband, having recognised the non-entity of the state, substitutes a fairly familiar political scientists" alternative which he calls the "state-system", a cluster of institutions of political and executive control and their key personnel, the "state-elite": "the government, the administration, the military and the police, the judicial branch, sub-central government and parliamentary assemblies".[36] Plainly, these agencies and actors do exist in the naive empirical sense as concrete objects and it is perfectly possible, desirable and necessary to ask how they relate to one another – what *form* of state-system they comprise – and how they, as an ensemble, relate to other forces and elements in a society – what *type* of state is constituted by their existence. These are in effect just the questions that Miliband does pursue. The claim that, taken together, these agencies and actors "make up the state", is a perfectly sound analytical proposition and serves to differentiate the state as an abstract object quite clearly from the political system as a whole. But there are other crucial questions about the nature and functions of that object in relation to which Milibands approach is less helpful. The difficulty comes to the surface when at the end of *The State in Capitalist Society* Miliband tells us that "the state" has been the "main agent" that has "helped to mitigate the form and content of class domination".[37] The conclusion we might have expected, that political practice or class struggle has mitigated class domination by acting on and through politically institutionalised power or the state system is not forthcoming; instead the state reappropriates a unity and volition which at the outset the author had been at pains to deny.

Far from unmasking the state as an ideological power the more realistic notion of the state system serves if anything to make its ideological pretentions more credible. And thus a key task in the study of the state, the understanding and exposure of the way in which the state is constructed as an "illusory general interest" remains both unattempted and if anything harder to attempt on the basis of this type of realism. A striking feature of the two long chapters in which the legitimation of capitalist society is discussed by Miliband is the virtual absence of the state from them. Not only does he see legitimation as occurring mainly outside the state system ("the engineering of consent in capitalist society is still largely an unofficial private enterprise"), through political parties, churches, voluntary associations, mass media and "capitalism itself, but the legitimation of the state system itself as *the state* has no place in his account. If the construction of the state does indeed occur independently of the state to such a degree – the principal exception is naturally education – and can be attributed to agents with a quite immediate and concrete existence perhaps other political processes, such as the mitigation of class domination, could also be explained in this more immediate and concrete manner. In any event it is odd that in a work written at the culmination of a period that had seen an ideological reconstruction of the state – as the "welfare state" – as thorough as anything attempted since the 17th century that sort of link between domination and legitimation should have been ignored. Could it have anything to do with a failure to resolve the dilemma that marxism, knowing the state to be unreal "for purposes of theory" needs it to be real "for purposes of practice"?

Like Miliband, Poulantzas begins by proclaiming the unreality of the state. It is not for him a "real, concrete singular" object, not something that exists "in the strong sense of the term".[38] Rather, it is an abstraction the conceptualisation of which is a "condition of knowledge of real-concrete".[39] My own view is rather that the conception of the state is a condition of ignorance, but more of that shortly. Consistently with this view of the problem he at once adopts a functional rather than a structural account of what the state is: by the state we are to understand the cohesive factor within the overall unity of a social formation. But actually, factor is an ambiguous word implyng both function and agency. And functions are of course institutionalised. The slide begins. The function of cohesion is said to be located in what Poulantzas calls "a place"

– the place in which the contradictions of a social formation are condensed.[40] The particular point of studying the state is thus to elucidate the contradictions of a given system which are nowhere so discernible as in this particular site. And secondly, to apprehend just how the system in question is rendered cohesive despite its contradictions.

The idea of the state or the political as "the factor of maintenance of a formation's unity" is in itself quite banal and conventional in non-marxist political science and therefore, apart from the way in which the definition directs attention to process rather than to structure in the first instance little special value can be claimed for this aspect of Poulantzas" analysis. The more specifically promising element has to be the claim that the maintenance of unity involves the creation of "a place" within which contradictions are condensed – in other words the suggestion that an empirically accessible object of study is brought into being which, if studied aright will reveal to us the modalities of domination within given social systems. The question is, what sort of place is it – abstract-formal or real-concrete? A consistent functionalism would of course propose only the former. Poulantzas, however, appears to speak of the actual political-juridical structures of "the state", of "the political structures of the state", the institutionalised power of the state", "the state as an organised political force" and so forth.[41] Suddenly we are in the presence of the real state again. And in this case the reappearance is quite explicitly linked to considerations of political practice: "political practice is the practice of leadership of the class struggle in and for the state".[42]

So function becomes place and place becomes agency and structure – the specific structures of the political. The crux of the analysis appears to be this: we are interested in the performance of a particular function, cohesion, and we postulate that that function is performed in a particular place, political structures, which we call the state: the empirical question to be answered concerns the relationship of the state to class struggles, what, then, is gained by introducing and insisting upon the state as meaning both the name of the place and the agent of the function? Does the naming not serve to make spuriously unproblematic things which are necessarily deeply problematic? I am not seeking to belittle what is in many ways a pioneering and important analysis of the political processes of class societies. But I think we do need to ask whether the centrality given to the state in that analysis is really a service to understanding. That there is a political function of cohesion effected repressively, economically and ideologically in class societies is plain enough and calls for elucidation. To identify it as "the global role of the state" seems to me, by introducing a misplaced concreteness, to both oversimplify and over-mystify its nature.

The difficulty is compounded by the fact that Poulantzas clearly recognises that large parts of the process of cohesion, and of the condensation of contradictions, are not performed within common-sensically "political" structures at all but are diffused ubiquitously through the social system in ways which make any simple equation of the state and political structures of the kind proposed by Miliband untenable if the functional conception of the state is to be seriously pursued.[43] The danger now is that the notion of the global functionality of the state will lead one into a forced recognition of the global structural existence of the state – a sense of its imma-nence in all structures perhaps. Certainly, the move is towards an abstract understanding of the state which is so structurally unspe-cific as to seem either to make the conception of the state redun-dant, or to substitute it for the conception of society. It seems that the key political functions cannot be definitively assigned to any particular personnel, apparatuses or institutions but rather "float" with the tides of class power.[44]

And the same difficulty of location dogs the attempt to treat the problem from the structural side. Poulantzas adopts a familiar distinction between institutions and structures, a distinction in which institutions are already abstract-formal objects, normative systems rather than concrete agencies. Class power is exercised through specific institutions which are accordingly identified as power centres. But these institutions are not just vehicles of class power: they have functions and an existence more properly their own as well. At the same time a structure, an ideologically hidden organisation, is constituted out of their existence. This hidden structure of power centres appears to be what is meant by the state.[45] And the task of studying the state would thus seem to be primarily a matter of lifting the ideological mask so as to perceive the reality of state power – class power – in terms of which the structuring is achieved: and secondly, a matter of identifying the apparatuses – functions and personnel – in and through which state power is located and exercised. Neither task is unmanageable in principle: but the management of both presupposes a fairly determinate conception of state functions. And this, I have sug-gested, is what Poulantzas, for good reasons declines to adopt.

So functions refuse to adhere to structures, structures fail to engross functions. The particular functions of the state, economic, ideological and political, must be understood in terms of the state's global function of cohesion and unification. The global function, eludes structural location. Perhaps it would be simpler to dispense with the conception of the state as an intervening hidden structural reality altogether?[46] If one abandoned the hypothesis of the state would one then be in a better or a worse position to understand the relationship between political institutions and (class) domination?[47]

Before considering that possibility we should note the existence of a less drastic alternative. It would be possible to abandon the notion of the state as a hidden structure but retain it to mean simply the ensemble of institutionalised political power – much in the manner of Miliband. On page 92 of *Political Power and Social Classes* and at frequent intervals thereafter Poulantzas appears to favour this alternative. We are now offered the idea of institutionalised political power (that is, the state) as "the cohesive factor in a determinate social formation and the nodal point of its transformation".[47] Here, too, we have a perfectly manageable basis for the study and understanding of the state. But unfortunately in the light of Poulantzas" correctly comprehensive sense of how cohesion is achieved – which is, of course, supported by Miliband's analysis of legitimation – the attribution of that function simply to institutionalised political power is plainly inadequate. Either the state is more than institutionalised political power or the state is not on its own the factor of cohesion.[48] We may therefore want to consider seriously the first possibility; the possibility of abandoning the study of the state.

## 6. The Withering Away of the State

In his Preface to *African Political Systems*, A.R. Radcliffe-Brown proposed that the idea of the state should be eliminated from social analysis.[49] He found it a source of mystification and argued that the concepts of government and politics were all that was needed for an adequate conceptual grasp of the political. My suggestion is not as radical as that. I am proposing only that we should abandon the state as a material object of study whether concrete or abstract while continuing to take the *idea* of the state extremely seriously. The internal and external relations of political and governmental institutions (the state-system) can be studied effectively without postulating the reality of the state. So in particular can their involvements with economic interests in an overall complex of domination and subjection. But studies proceeding in that way invariably discover a third mode, dimension or region of domination – the ideological. And the particular function of the ideological is to mis-represent political and economic domination in ways that legitimate subjection. Here, at least in the context of capitalist societies, the *idea* of the state becomes a crucial object of study. In this context we might say that the state is the distinctive collective misrepresentation of capitalist societies. Like other collective (mis)representations it is a social fact – but not a fact in nature. Social facts should not be treated as things.

Since the 17th century the idea of the state has been a cardinal feature of the process of subjection. Political institutions, the "state-system", are the real agencies out of which the idea of the state is constructed. The problem for political analysis is to see it as an essentially imaginative construction, however. Engels – admittedly only the young Engels – came as near to understanding the issue in this way as anyone has done. As early as 1845 we find him arguing that the state is brought into being as an idea in order to present the outcome of the class struggle as the independent outcome of a classless legitimate will. Political institutions are turned into "the state" so that a balance of class power – which is what Engels means by "society" – may masquerade as unaffected by class. But, and here we return to the present modes of analysing the state, "the consciousness of the interconnection" between the construction of the state as an independent entity and the actualities of class power "becomes dulled and can be lost altogether". More specifically, "once the state has become an independent power vis-à-vis society, it produces forthwith a further ideology" – an ideology in which the reality of the state is taken for granted and the "connection with economic facts gets lost for fair".[50] My suggestion is that in seeking to dismantle that ideology it is not enough to try to rediscover the connection with economic facts *within* the general terms of the ideology as a whole, the acceptance of the reality of the state. Rather, we must make a ruthless assault on the whole set of claims in terms of which the being of the state is proposed.

The state, then, is not an object akin to the human ear. Nor is it even an object akin to human marriage. It is a third-order object, an ideological project. It is first and foremost an exercise in legitimation – and what it being legitimated is, we may assume, something which if seen directly and as itself would be illegitimate, an unacceptable domination. Why else all the legitimation-work? The state, in sum, is a bid to elicit support for or tolerance of the insupportable and intolerable by presenting them as something other than themselves, namely, legitimate, disinterested domination. The study of the state, seen thus, would begm with the cardinal activity involved in the serious presentation of the state: the legitimating of the illegitimate. The immediately present institutions of the "state system" – and in particular their coercive functions – are the principal object of that task. The crux of the task is to over-accredit them as an integrated expression of common interest cleanly dissociated from all sectional interests and the structures – class, church, race and so forth – associated with them. The agencies in question, especially administrative and judicial and educational agencies, are made into state agencies as part of some quite historically specific process of subjection; and made precisely as an alternative reading of and cover for that process. Consider the relationship between the acceptance and diffusion of John Locke's account of political obligation and the reconstitution of government on the basis of private accumulation in 18th century England.[51] Or consider the relationship between the discovery of the civil service as an integral element of the state and the scale of operations achieved by capitalist production and marketing in the last quarter of the 19th century.[52] Not to see the state as in the first instance an exercise in legitimation, in moral regulation, is, in the light of such connections, surely to participate in the mystification which is the vital point of the construction of the state.

And in our sort of society at least mystification is the central mode of subjection. Armies and prisons are the back-up instruments of the burden of legitimacy. Of course what is legitimated is, insofar as it is legitimated, real power. Armies and prisons, the Special Patrol and the deportation orders as well as the whole process of fiscal exaction – which Bell shrewdly sees as "the skeleton of the state stripped of all misleading ideologies" – are all forceful enough.[53] But it is their association with the idea of the state and the invocation of that idea that silences protest, excuses force and convinces almost all of us that the fate of the victims is just and necessary. Only when that association is broken do real hidden powers emerge. And when they do they are not the powers of the state but of armies of liberation or repression, foreign governments, guerilla movements, soviets, juntas, parties, classes. The state for its part never emerges except as a claim to domination – a claim which has become so plausible that it is hardly ever challenged. Appropriately enough the commonest source of challenge is not marxist theory or political sociology but the specific exigency created when individual revolutionaries find themselves on trial for subversion, sedition or treason. It is in documents like Fidel Castro's courtroom speech – and almost uniquely in such documents – that the pretensions of regimes to be states are unmasked.[54]

The state is, then, in every sense of the term a triumph of concealment. It conceals the real history and relations of subjection behind an a-historical mask of legitimating illusion; contrives to deny the existence of connections and conflicts which would if recognised be incompatible with the claimed autonomy and integration of the state. The real official secret, however, is the secret of the non-existence of the state.

## 7. Deciphering Legitimacy

The form of misrepresentation achieved by the idea of the state in capitalist societies is incisively and thoroughly grasped by Poulantzas even though he fails to grasp the full extent to which it *is* a misrepresentation.[55] It seems to me that this combination of insight and failure of vision is directly attributable to his principled objection to historical analysis – and here we come to a serious practical question about the study of the state. He sees perfectly clearly what the idea of the state does socially but because history is not permissible in his scheme of analysis he can only explain how it is done by assuming that it is done by the state. The state has to exist for him to explain his own observations. Only a very careful investigation of the construction of the state as an ideological power could permit a recognition of the effects he observes in combination with a denial of the notion that they are effects of the state.

In capitalist societies the presentation of the state is uniquely pervasive, opaque and bemusing. Centrally it involves the segregation of economic relationships from political relationships, the obliteration within the field of political relationships of the relevance or propriety of class and the proclamation of the political as an autonomous sphere of social unification. Poulantzas perceives all this admirably and with a clarity not achieved in any previous text: "by means of a whole complex functioning of the ideological the capitalist state systematically conceals its political class character at the level of its political institutions".[56] His analysis of the "effect of isolation" which is the special and pivotal mirage of the idea of the state in capitalist societies is wholly compelling. And yet, having come this far he cannot accept that the idea of the state is itself part of the mirage. Rather, he insists that the structures of the state must not be reduced to the ideological: "the state represents the unity of an isolation which, because of the role played by the ideological is largely its own effect".[57] His argument appears to involve both the claim that the state is an ideological fraud perpetrated in the course of imposing subjection and the belief that the state has a nonfraudulent existence as a vital structure of the capitalist mode of production.

I suggest that the former can be shown clearly to be the case and that the latter is an undemonstrable assertion making sense only within a closed theoretical system but having no independent warrant or validity. Once again one can only be impressed by the narrowness of the miss. Again and again he comes within an inch of wholly unmasking the state; again and again his theoretical presuppositions prevent him from following his own argument to its proper conclusion. Thus: "the role of ideology . . . is not simply that of hiding the economic level which is always determinant, but that of hiding the level which has the dominant role and hiding the very fact of its dominance".[58] Ideology in other words displaces power from its real to an apparent centre. But even this does not lead to the conclusion that in the capitalist mode of production where "the economic . . . plays the dominant role" and where accordingly "we see the dominance of the juridico-political region in the ideological", the state might be primarily an ideological power, a cogently effected misrepresentation.[59] What he really needs is two distinct objects of study: the state-system and the state-idea. We come, then, to a fundamental question. We may reasonably infer that the state as a special object of social analysis does not exist as a real entity. Can we agree with Radcliffe-Brown that it is also unnecessary as an abstract-formal entity – that it does nothing for us in the analysis of domination and subjection? Obviously my own conclusion is that we can. Indeed, that we must: the postulate of the state serves to my mind not only to protect us from the perception of our own ideological captivity but more immediately to obscure an otherwise perceptible feature of institutionalised political power, the state-system, in capitalist societies which would otherwise seize our attention and prove the source of a trenchant understanding of the sort of power politically institutionalised power is. I refer to the actual disunity of political power. It is this above all that the idea of the state conceals. The state is the unified symbol of an actual disunity. This is not just a disunity between the political and the economic but equally a profound disunity within the political. Political institutions, especially in the enlarged sense of Miliband's state – system, conspicuously fail to display a unity of practice – just as they constantly discover their inability to function as a more general factor of cohesion. Manifestly they are divided against one another, volatile and confused. What is constituted out of their collective practice is a series of ephemerally unified postures in relation to transient issues with no sustained consistency of purpose. Such enduring unity of practice as the ensemble of political institutions achieve is palpably imposed on them by "external" economic, fiscal and military organisations and interests. In the United Kingdom for example, the only unity that can actually be discerned behind the spurious unity of the idea of the state is the unity of commitment to the maintenance, at any price, of an essentially capitalist economy. This sort of disunity and imbalance is of course just what one would expect to find in an institutional field that is primarily a field of struggle. But it is just the centrality of struggle that the idea of the state – even for marxists – contrives to mask.

My suggestion, then, is that we should recognize that cogency of the *idea* of the state as an ideological power and treat that as a compelling object of analysis. But the very reasons that require us to do that also require us not to *believe* in the idea of the state, not to concede, even as an abstract formal-object, the existence of the state. Try substituting the word god for the word state throughout *Political Power and Social Classes* and read it as an analysis of religious domination and I think you will see what I mean. The task of the sociologist of religion is the explanation of religious practice (churches) and religious belief (theology): he is not called upon to debate, let alone to believe in, the existence of god.

## 8. Towards a Recovery of History

The obvious escape from reification, the one rejected by Poulantzas and neglected by Miliband is historical. The only plausible alternative I can see to taking the state for granted is to understand it as historically constructed. Even so, the unmasking is not automatic as Anderson's analysis of Absolutism makes clear.[60] The argument of *Lineages of the Absolutist State* shows very clearly how a particular presentation of the state was constructed historically as a reconstitution of the political modalities of class power. Yet even this author is not able to shake off the notion of the state – indeed "the State". Every time he uses that word, others – regime, government, monarchy, absolutism – could be substituted for it and the only difference would be to replace an ambiguously concrete term with ones of which the implications are unambiguously either concrete or abstract. But it is not just a semantic matter. Anderson's treatment reveals two processes of political construction. The first is the centralisation and coordination of feudal domination – the "upward displacement of coercion" as he rather oddly puts it – in the face of the declining effectiveness of local control and exaction. This was a reorganisation of the apparatus of feudal administration on a basis which enhanced the possibility of political control of the underlying population in the interests of the nobility but did so in a way that also created the possibility of more effective political coercion in the political process among the nobility.[61] Nevertheless, the nature of the construction as a whole is plainly demonstrated; a shift from individualised to concerted coercive subjection of rural populations to noble domination through the invention of new apparatuses of administration and law. Law provides the common ground in which the first aspect of the construction of absolutism meets the second. This was the *ideological* construction of the "Absolutist State" as the panoply of doctrine and legitimation under which the reorganisation of feudal domination proceeded and in terms of which it was presented. The essential elements of this ideological construction were, Anderson argues, the adoption of Roman law as a legitimating context for centralised administration and the formulation in European political thought from Bodin to Montesquieu of a general theory of sovereignty providing a still higher-level rationale for the administrative reconstruction that was taking place.[62] The idea of the state was created and used for specific social purposes in a specific historical setting – and that is the only reality it had. Everything else is more precise.

It could be said that Anderson does not quite do justice to the turbulent nature of these processes of political construction. Early modern European history should perhaps be seen rather more definitely as a struggle within the European nobilities to hammer out or grasp a basis for generalisable renewed noble domination – a struggle in which the kings tended to prevail because the available bases both institutional and ideological could be secured by them as kings in a uniquely effective way. Quite apart from killing their rivals the royal victors could both impose and legitimate noble domination better than the vanquished nobility. Similarly, one might want to add to Anderson's analysis of the persistent feudal bias of these regimes in their dealings with bourgeois groupings rather more emphasis on the way in which the manner of the reconstitution of feudal domination in this period *permitted* certain types of bourgeois activity to flourish: the crisis of the aristocracy was solved by the creation of juridical, political and ideological frameworks which both saved the aristocracy and tolerated the bourgeoisie; among the unfavoured they were uniquely favoured.[63] However, such modifications would not impair recognition of the masterly nature of Anderson's work as a whole. For this particular historical context he does demonstrate just how the idea of the state as a "veil of illusion" is perpetrated in the course of an entirely concrete institutional reconstruction of domination and subjection. Even his own uncritical use of the term "the state" to indicate relations and practices he persistently shows to be much more precisely identifiable than that, although it weakens the impact of his argument, does not wholly undermine the historical demonstration he achieves.

If that sort of radical unmasking of the state is possible for absolutism, why not for more recent political arrangements? Of course there is a certain brutal candour and transparency about absolutism which subsequent constructions have not reproduced. "L'état, c'est moi" is hardly an attempt at legitimation at all; it so plainly means "I and my mercenaries rule – O.K.?" Yet on balance I think it is not the devious cunning of more recent political entrepreneurs that has deceived us but rather our own willing or unwitting participation in the idea of the reality of the state. If we are to abandon the study of the state as such and turn instead to the more direct historical investigation of the political practice of class (and other) relationships we might hope to unmask, say, the Welfare State as effectively as Anderson has unmasked the Absolutist State. The state is at most a message of domination – an ideological artefact attributing unity, morality and independence to the disunited, amoral and dependent workings of the practice of government. In this context the message is decidedly *not* the medium – let alone the key to an understanding of the sources of its production, or even of its own real meaning. The message – the claimed reality of the state – is the ideological device in terms of which the political institutionalisation of power is legitimated. It is of some importance to understand how that legitimation is achieved. But it is much more important to grasp the relationship between political and nonpolitical power – between in Weber's terms class, status and party. There *is* no reason to suppose that the concept, let alone belief in the existence, of the state will help us in that sort of enquiry.

In sum: the state is not the reality which stands behind the mask of political practice. It is itself the mask which prevents our seeing political practice as it is. It is, one could almost say, the mind of a mindless world, the purpose of purposeless conditions, the opium of the citizen. There *is* a state-system in Miliband's sense: a palpable nexus of practice and institutional structure centred in government and more or less extensive, unified and dominant in any given society. And its sources, structure and variations can be examined in fairly straight-forward empirical ways. There *is*, too, a state-idea, projected, purveyed and variously believed in in different societies at different times. And its modes, effects and variations are also susceptible to research. The relationship of the state-system and the state-idea to other forms of power should and can be central concerns of political analysis. We are only making difficulties for ourselves in supposing that we have also to study the state – an entity, agent, function or relation over and above the state-system and the state-idea. The state comes into being as a structuration within political practice: it starts its life as an implicit construct: it is then reified – as the *res publica*, the public reification, no less – and acquires an overt symbolic identity progressively divorced from practice as an illusory account of practice. The ideological function is extended to a point where conservatives and radicals alike believe that their practice is not directed at each other but at the state: the world of illusion prevails. The task of the sociologist is to demystify; and in this context that means attending to the senses in which the state does not exist rather than to those in which it does.

## Notes and References

* This paper was first delivered at the 1977 British Sociological Association annual conference. The revised version published here was delivered to the sociology staff/graduate seminar at the University of Durham on November 9, 1977. We are grateful to Mrs Sheila Abrams for permission to publish this paper.

[1] Jeremy Bentham. *The Handbook of Political Fallacies*, edited by H. A. Larrabee, Harper and Brothers, New York 1962.

[2] V. I. Lenin, "The State", *Selected Works*, vol. ll, New York, 1943, p. 639.

[3] W. G. Runciman, *Social Science and Political Theory*, Cambridge, 1963, p. 32.

[4] *Ibid.*, p. 33, citing *Marx-Engels Gesamtausgabe*, I, p. 492, "Aus der Kritik der Hegelschen Staatsrecht".

[5] Cf., N. Poulantzas, *Political Power and Social Classes*, New Left Books, London, 1973, pp. 130–37 and 150–53.

Incidentally I find Poulantzas' attempt to discredit other varieties of marxism in this respect – especially the work of Lefebvre and the Italian School – as resulting from "a play on words" in the reading of Marx, quite unconvincing. On the contrary, what Lefebvre, Della Volpe and others have done is to read the key passages of Marx literally – if anything, too literally.

[6] P. Orleans and S. Greer. "Political Sociology" in R. L. Faris (ed.) *Handbook of Modern Sociology*, Rand McNally, New York, 1964, p. 810 is the source of the first agenda and R. Bendix and S. M. Lipset, "Political Sociology: an Essay and Bibliography", *Current Sociology*, 1957, vi, p. 87 of the second. And see R. E. Dowse and J. Hughes, *Political Sociology*, John Wiley and Sons, New York, 1972, for the general dearth of appropriate subsequent work.

[7] D. Beetham, *Max Weber and the Theory of Modern Politics*, Allen and Unwin, 1973.

[8] I have enlarged on this theme in *Political Sociology*, Allen and Unwin (forthcoming); and the point is also made by Poulantzas, *Political Power and Social Classes*, pp. 40 and 266.

[9] R. E. Dowse, *Report* of a Conference on Political Sociology sponsored by the Political Science Committee of SSRC, Social Science Research Council, London, 1974.

[10] Poulantzas, *Political Power and Social Classes*, p.44; the question of the nature of the state is of course returned to at some length in two of this author's later works, *Fascism and Dictatorship*, New Left Books, 1974 and *Classes in Contemporary Capitalism*, New Left Books, 1975, but the problem of precisely identifying and locating the functions of the state is not advanced.

[11] Almost any of the endless series of political autobiographies, private papers, diaries and so forth that flow from the pens of retired politicians or end up in those collections of family papers eventually released to historians will confirm this point; what is revealed is that the egotism of politicians is always more inflated than one might have imagined and that the interpersonal politicking had a sharper edge than one could have guessed. It is very rare indeed for accounts of this sort, however

well-informed, to significantly alter the publicly available and previously established sense of the essential character and power structure of a regime. The explanation of "events" may be changed but not the understanding of "states". It is at the level of the ephemera rather than the necessities of political life that the revelation of the backstage world of politics is startling; the most obvious recent British example is R. H. S. Crossman, *Diaries of a Cabinet Minister*, Longman, London, 1976.

[12] The "school" of history represented by the work of Maurice Cowling is quite important in this respect. The most exhaustive scrutiny of the most minute evidence leads only to the conclusion that *The Impact of Labour* (M. Cowling, Cambridge University Press, 1971) or *The Impact of Hitler* (M. Cowling, Cambridge University Press, 1976) was to intensify political infighting, re-shuffle the personal alliances and opportunities of individual politicians and clarify in the minds of political actors the class and other alignments of political power which had already been understood by informed journalists and uninformed historians. Once again the surprises prove to be all at the level of events not of structures.

[13] Joe Haines, *The Politics of Power*, Hodder & Stroughton, London, 1977; it is of course symptomatic of the way political realities are masked in advanced capitalist societies that the public reception of this book should have been almost entirely in terms of the author's comments on personal political relationships and that his highly perceptive and informed analysis of an institutional structuring of power should have been virtually ignored.

[14] Tony Bunyan, *The Political Police in Britain*, Quartet, 1976 and cf., the review of this book in *Rights*, I, i, 1976.

[15] F. Engels. *Ludwig Feuerbach and the End of Classical German Philosophy* in (e.g.) L. Feuer (ed.) *Marx and Engels: Basic Writings on Politics and Philosophy*, Doubleday, New York, 1959, p. 236: K. Marx and F. Engels, *The German Ideology*, Lawrence and Wishart, London, 1965, p. 42 – although it must be admitted that the crucial statements of this view were marginal additions by Engels to the main text of the collaborative work; which possibly confirms a view I have long held that to have done himself full justice Engels should have collaborated with Durkheim rather than with Marx.

[16] D. Bell, *The Cultural Contradictions of Capitalism* Basic Books, New York, 1976.

[17] G. Sartori. "From Sociology of Politics to Political Sociology" in S. M. Lipset (ed.) *Politics and the Social Sciences*. Oxford University Press, 1969.

[18] Cf., T. Parsons, "Voting and the Equilibrium of the American Political System", in E. Burdick and A. Brodbeck (eds.) *American Voting Behaviour*, Free Press, 1959: D. Easton, *A Systems Analysis of Political Life*, John Wiley & Sons, New York. 1965: G. Almond and J. Coleman, *The Politics of the Developing Areas*, Princeton University Press, New Jersey, 1960; W. Mitchell, *The American Polity*, Free Press, 1966. The net perception of political process achieved by this school of analysis could perhaps be formalised in something like the following manner:

### *Political Systems*

Social systems have common *functional problems*:

> adaptation
> integration
> pattern-maintenance
> goal-attainment

Functional problems are handled by *functional sub-systems*:

> economy
> household
> culture
> polity

Polities (political systems) perform common *functions*:

> selection and specification of goals
> allocation of costs and values
> authorisation

The performance of these functions involves:

> creation of a *political role-structure* within
> which binding decisions can be made

Political role-structure is generated through sets of *interchanges* between the polity and other social sub-systems:

Input:   demands     role structure/        Output:   decision
         support     decision-making                  implementations
         resources                                    controls

The *communications* involved in these interchanges generate also a *political culture*: political culture operates as a medium of feedback from output to new inputs, etc.

The social *processes* central to the operation of political systems may be further specified:

Input:   political socialisation          Output:   legitimation
         recruitment                               promulgation
         articulation and aggregation              administration
         of interests.

All political systems have *structure*: but not common items of structure. All political structure may be analysed in terms of common *organisational properties and levels*:

> levels:       government – regime – community
> properties:   external differentiation – internal differentiation
>               and functional specificity of roles – visibility –
>               formalisation – institutionalisation of competition
>               for leadership roles – stratification of influence –
>               balance of formal and informal structures.

The *style* of action of all political structure may be evaluated along four value-dimensions (pattern variables):

> ascription vs. achievement
> particularism vs. universalism
> effectivity vs. affective neutrality
> diffuseness vs. specificity

All real-world political structure is multi-functional; the style of all political performance is "mixed".

Plainly, such a conception has neither operational nor theoretical need for the concept of the state. The state has not been explained; but it has been explained away.

[19] The best known of course is that suggested by David Easton, *op. cit.*

[20] Dowse and Hughes, *op. cit.*, but note especially the *absences* in their chapter 5, "Structures of Power in Industrial Society".

[21] This pattern was already evident in the bibliographies of the field produced in the 1950s – for example, Lipset and Bendix, *op. cit.* – and is no less so in the 1970s; consider the "Further Reading" proposed by Dowse and Hughes.

[22] S. Andreski, *Social Science as Sorcery*, Deutsch, London, 1972, M. Nicolaus, "The Professional Organisation of Sociology; a View from Below", in R. Blackburn (ed.) *Ideology in Social Science*, Fontana, London, 1972; A. Gouldner, "The Sociologist as Partisan", in *For Sociology*, Allen Lane, London, 1973; I. Horowitz *Professing Sociology*, Allen Lane, London, 1972.

[23] R. Dahl, *Who Governs?*, Yale University Press, New Haven, 1961; N. Polsby, *Community Power and Political Theory*, Yale University Press, New Haven, 1963, and "Pluralism in the Study of Community Power", *The American Sociologist*, iv. 2, 1969, p. 118; P. Bachrach and M. S. Baratz, *Power and Poverty*. Oxford University Press, 1970; S. Lukes, *Power: A Radical View*, Macmillan, London. 1974; P. Abell, "The Many Faces of Power and Liberty", *Sociology*, xi. 3. 1977 p. 3.

[24] Almond and Coleman, *op. cit:* compare especially the promise of the Introduction with what is actually offered in the Conclusion.

[25] Suzanne Keller, *Beyond the Ruling Class*, Random House, New York, 1963, p. 34.

[26] Peter Nettl, "The Social German Democratic Party as a Political Model" *Past and Present*, 1965.

[27] K. Dawson and J. Prewitt, *Political Socialisation*, Little Brown, Boston, 1971 : D. Easton et al., *The Development of Political Attitudes in Children*, Aldine, Chicago, 1967; F. Greenstein, "The Benevolent Leader", *American Political Science Review*, liv, 1960, p. 934: and generally, Dowse and Hughes, *op. cit.*, ch. 6.

[28] Daniel Bell. *The Cultural Contradictions of Capitalism*, Heinemann, London, 1976, especially pp. 220–232.

[29] L. von Stein, *Das Koenigturn* Leipzig. 1850, cited in E. Schraepler, *Quellen zur Gesichte der sozialen Frage in Deutschland*, Musterschmidt Verlag, Goettingen. 1960, p. 130; J. Hess and D. Easton, "The Child's Changing Image of the President", *Public Opinion Quarterly*, xxiv, 1960, p. 632.

[30] R. Miliband, *The State in Capitalist Society*. Weidenfeld and Nicolson, London, 1969, p. 49.

[31] In a comment on an earlier version of this paper Dr. P. R. D. Corrigan makes the point very forcefully, "that the state is both illusory and there – indeed, its 'thereness' is how the illusion is sustained" and again that the state is "an illusion in the sense that its claim to be what it appeared to be is invalid; it is not illusory in the sense that it is not a logical error, a problem with our vision, or a conjuring trick that sustains it but precisely those powers and relations which its claim to be what it appears to be conceals". It could also be said, however, that whether or not the state is really there marxist analysis has to treat it as really there in order to locate key phases of the integration of class power which otherwise remain elusive: this seems to be especially the case in Poulantzas. *Classes in Contemporary Capitalism*, pp. 155–58.

[32] See the discussion of these dualities in the work of Marx, Engels and Lenin in S. W. Moore, *The Critique of Capitalist Democracy*, A. M. Kelley, New York, 1969.

[33] R. Miliband, *op. cit.*, p. 81.

[34] F. Oppenheimer, *The State*, Bobbs Merrill, New York, 1914.

[35] *German Ideology.* part I, p. 53.

[36] R. Miliband. *op. cit.*, p. 54.

[37] *Ibid.*, p. 266.

[38] N. Poulantzas, *Political Power and Social Classes*, p. 12; "It can be said that in the strong sense of the term, only *real, concrete, singular* objects exist. The final aim of the process of thought is knowledge of these objects: e.g. of France or England at a given moment of their development". Quite apart from the epistemological shakiness of the distinction as illustrated by the example we are left with a situation in which all the tools of thought – mode of production, class, state and so forth – are in the strong sense agreed to be unreal and the task of thought is to use them without reifying them. My suggestion is that it is precisely when these tools are least useful that the danger of reification is greatest; in that sense "mode of production" is an effective tool, "the state" is not.

[39] Poulantzas, *op. cit.*, p. 39.

[40] *Ibid.*, pp. 45, 47–51; and cf., *Classes in Contemporary Capitalism*, pp. 158–9.

[41] *Political Power and Social Classes*, pp. 44, 93, 132.

[42] *Ibid.*, p. 43; Poulantzas is here citing the "completely acceptable" words of J. Verret, Théorie *et Politique*, Paris, 1967, p. 194. The problem for this sort of analysis is naturally especially evident in any consideration of political practice. For purposes of practice the state is treated as primarily a structure – and indeed the most obvious and delimited structure, political institutions ("the state as a specific level of structures in a social formation" p. 43). For purposes of theory the state is primarily a set of functions – of cohesion, condensation of contradictions, isolation, and so forth. And the trouble is that the functions manifestly do not reside in the structures; the structures are simply not the "place" where the functions are performed. So the state begins to be redefined as some more abstract, generalised, impalpable sort of structure.

[43] Poulantzas makes this point against Miliband very effectively in the debate between the two authors originally published in the *New Left Review* and re-printed in R. Blackburn *op. cit.*, pp. 238–63, see especially pp. 251–2. Conversely, Miliband very effectively makes the point about the structural elusiveness of the state in Poulantzas' conception, see especially, p. 256. Both criticisms are of course entirely well taken and appropriate.

[44] This is especially evident in Poulantzas' discussions of the relationship between the state and the dominant class in capitalism; cf., *Political Power and Social Classes*, pp. 296–307 and *Classes in Contemporary Capitalism* pp. 156–62 where we are told, for example, that the state has a "specific role" in "elaborating the political strategy of monopoly capital" only to find that that role is never in fact either specified or located by this author and indeed cannot be because as a matter of principle the state "does not have its own power but . . . forms the contradictory locus of consideration for the balance of forces that divides even the dominant class itself". For all its apparent precision the term "the state" actually indicates chaos.

[45] *Political Power and Social Classes*, pp. 115–17; but once again any sense of concreteness, of a defined empirical referent for what one is talking about is quickly dissipated; "the state", in the sense of political institutions is only one among a cluster of power centres, companies, cultural institutions and so forth being cited as others: yet it is via the *ensemble* of power centres that functions of the state are executed.

[46] Alternatively one could in order to focus the mind on its abstract-formal character try to conceive of the state not as an agent, object or structure but as a relationship. This is indeed the solution favoured by Poulantzas in *Classes in Contemporary Capitalism* ("the state is not a thing but a relation", p. 161). But unfortunately this formulation proves as unstable as all those that have gone before it; the relation turns out to be "more exactly the condensation of the balance of forces" within the dominant class and between that class and others. Although this is in principle an empirical claim it is not in fact pursued as such. Meanwhile the relationship increasingly turns back to an agent. Although in any sort of common sense usage relationships would be said to have functions rather than ends Poulantzas seems driven to attribute independent volition to the relationship. Thus, the state "takes responsibility for the interests of the hegemonic fraction, monopoly capital" (p. 157): and again, it "takes responsibility for the interests of monopoly capital as a whole" (p. 158). Relationships, however do not act in this sense: marriage does not take responsibility for the interests of men in relation to women, though it could well be said to function to that end. In practice Poulantzas does not "avoid the false dilemma in which contemporary discussion of the state is trapped, between the state as a thing and the state as a subject" by regarding it as a relationship. His understanding of the dilemma is correct but the effort to treat the state consistently and exclusively as a relationship defeats him; instead of going on to ask what sort of relationship and between whom? he reverts to the sterile issue of the "relative autonomy of the state . . . inscribed in its very structure".

[47] The point to be emphasised here is that domination is a crucially important problematic and that trying to deal with it by thinking about the state really seems to have proved extraordinarily unprofitable. I am not suggesting that if we think away the state we shall do away with domination – I would hate to be accused of that sort of Young Hegelianism. But it does begin to seem possible that the real relations of domination within the state-system and between it and other interests and institutions and groups might be seen more clearly were it not for the apparent problem of the state.

[48] This was of course the nub of the debate between Miliband and Poulantzas referred to above; and it was their inability to agree on a locus for the factor of cohesion other than institutionalised political and governmental power (Miliband's state-system) which mainly explains the inconclusive and slightly demoralising way in which that debate ended.

[49] A. R. Radcliffe-Brown, "Preface", M. Fortes and E. E. Evans-Pritchard (eds.). *African Political Systems*, Oxford University Press, 1940.

[50] F. Engels, *Ludwig Feuerbach and the End of Classical German Philosophy*, in (e.g.) L. Feuer, op. cit., pp. 236–7.

[51] C. B. Macpherson. *The Political Theory of Possessive Individualism*, Oxford University Press, 1962.

[52] A valuable analysis of this connection is provided by P. R. D. Corrigan, *State Formation and Moral Regulation in 19th. century Britain*, Ph.D. dissertation, University of Durham, 1977.

[53] D. Bell, *The Cultural Contradictions of Capitalisrn*, p. 220, quoting Rudolf Goldscheid.

[54] M. Alexandre (ed.) *On Trial*, Lorrimer Publishing, London, 1968.

[55] N. Poulantzas, *Political Power and* Social *Classes*, pp. 195–223.

[56] *Ibid.*, p. 133: but note that the state even here is an agent as well as a mystification; this author simply cannot escape from the veil of illusion created by the idea of the state even though he knows it to be a veil of illusion.

[57] *Ibid.*, p. 134.

[58] *Ibid.*, pp. 210–211.

[59] *Ibid.*, p. 211.

[60] Peny Anderson, *Lineages of the Absolute State*, New Left Books, London, 1974.

[61] *Ibiid.*, pp. 12–22, 429–30.

[62] *Ibid.*, pp. 24–30, 424–6.

[63] This point is indeed conceded *en passant* by Anderson, *op. cit.*, p. 23, but figured very prominently in the various writings of Engels: cf., *Anti-Dühring*. Foreign Languages Publishing House, Moscow, 1947, p. 126, and of course the famous passage in *The Origin of the Family, Private Property and the State*, Marx, Engels, *Selected Works*, Foreign Languages Publishing House, Moscow, 1962, "By way of exception, however, periods occur in which the warring classes balance each other . . . . . . ." etc.

*Editorial note*: It is important to repeat that this paper was *written in 1977*, before the publication of Poulantzas's *State Power, Socialism* (London, New Left Books, 1978) Part 1 of which ("The institutional materiality of the state") could have led Philip Abrams to modify somewhat his commentary on Poulantzas. That this last work of Poulantzas draws from Foucault is another marker for an explainable absence in Abrams's text.

# The Genesis of American Capitalism: an Historical Inquiry into State Theory

## CLAUDE DENIS

**Abstract** We usually think that we know what "the state" is, even when we embark on a theoretical quest for it. Somehow, the state is closely associated with Government – including bureaucracy and army. Or we sometimes think of it differently, in terms of city-state or nation-state. I had the first notion in mind when I started to research the socioeconomic context of the making of the U.S. constitution. But the historical research forced me to face the vagueness of the concept, and to recognize that it is not only useless, but actually harmful in our understanding of modern societies. This paper is made-up of three parts: the historical narrative of U.S. constitution-making is sandwiched between, first, a deconstruction of the concept of state and, third, an attempt at establishing a new concept of state. I discard along the way the dichotomies of state/civil society and base/superstructure. And I argue for a close integration of theory and history in social analysis.

## 1. The State?

The state is, of course, the focus of much political analysis. And we all seem to know pretty much spontaneously what "the state" *is*. We may argue about whether or not, in capitalist societies, it is "the executive committee of the bourgeoisie"; or whether or not one should adopt a Weberian definition of it; and so on. But in the end, we all know what beast we are after: some version of "the Government", to be counterposed to civil society, the market and the family.

Certainly, this is what I had in mind when I undertook the historical inquiry that ultimately yielded this paper: an analysis of what class biases may have been inscribed in the American constitution when it was written in 1787. I was trying to explicate what the relation has been between capitalism and the state in the United States: could we speak of a capitalist state, inherently biased against socialist politics, or were we merely dealing with "a state in a capitalist society"? I was struggling with the question of what kind of theoretical animal a "capitalist state" might be. All the while assuming that I knew what a "state" is: I simply borrowed a very sensible, Weberian, definition positing that the state is

a set of organizations invested with the authority to make binding decisions for people and organizations juridically located in a particular territory and to implement these decisions using, if necessary force.[1]

But by the time I finished the historical research, I was not so sure of what "the state" is, anymore. As I went along, I became increasingly uneasy with the general conceptual framework that underpins the definition I adopted, and that opposes the state to civil society. In liberal discourse, this opposition between the state and civil society produces the knowledge that politics and economics are separate spheres. In the political economy tradition, the state performs important economic functions in addition to its repressive attributes, but the basic notions remain that the state-as-Government is a sector of society, separate from civil society, and that the market is a theoretically independent domain.

The deep consensus on the meaning of "state" as Government is particularly striking when it maintains its hold upon political theorists concerned with the state as a "contestable concept". John Hoffman debates whether the state belongs at the heart of a theory of politics. But he never puts into question the basic notion of the state-as-Government. This often results in an awkward logic. For instance: "If defining the state is . . . a difficult and uneasy task, this is because, as I have argued above, the state itself is a difficult and uneasy institution."[2] How can one know before defining it, that the state is an institution, and a difficult and uneasy one at that? In their *Dictionnaire critique de la sociologie*, French sociologists Raymond Boudon and François Bourricaud also fall prey to the power of common sense. They begin a comparatively long article on "L'Etat" with the disclaimer that "Defining the state is an almost impossible task." But they always operate from within the definition of the state-as-government.[3]

And yet, there is another sense in which "state" is widely understood, usually in a different context: the history of international relations. Here, "state" is often used as an equivalent for "country" – a territorial political unit "conceived as autonomous from any external and superior power" and whose authority recognizes no rival jurisdictions in its territory.[4] Closely associated with this use are "nation-state" and "city-state". It is of such "states" that traditional political historians often wrote. Otto Hintze, for example:

All the great empires of ancient times and of the non-European world were despotic in their form of government. So far as historical experience goes, free constitutions emerged only where a number of states existed next to each other on equal terms, the independence of each one being recognized by the others. Today we are inclined to consider this the normal and natural condition in the life of states; but this is not the case. Such a society of states has always been the exception.[5]

We, as readers, are generally spared widespread confusion on which sense is invoked, on the basis of the context in which "state" is used, but only because we are thoroughly familiar with both senses of the term. Because, indeed, we are so familiar with them that we do not seem to need to choose between usages.[6] The utter familiarity of "state" is so great that the conventional wisdom maintains its hold on Anthony Giddens, a theorist who usually is highly self-conscious, and not adverse to reformulating long-accepted notions. Giddens does identify the two senses of "state", but sees no theoretical problem with the instability: "State" has two senses in ordinary language, but the ambiguity is not a particularly worrying one for social theory". He goes on however to replace the term by, on the one hand, "state apparatus" and, on the other hand, "culture" and "society" – two concepts. Giddens adds, that "have their own ambiguities".[7] In so doing, he indicates a discomfort with "state" that ought to be taken seriously.

Finally, what should we think of Robert Alford and Roger Friedland's attempt to theorize the state when, after four hundred pages of *The Powers of Theory*, they end up admitting: "Although it has organized our entire argument, [the concept of the state] remains a remarkably ambiguous one"?[8] Could it be that the state as usually thought of cannot be conceptualized rigorously? But I am getting ahead of myself.

So, following in so many footsteps, I naively plunged into my historical inquiry of the social underpinnings of the American constitution. Building from the theoretical outline of the state-as-Government-separate-from-civil-society, students of the history of the United States have formulated what amounts to an American axiom: from its inception the American state was weak and, thanks in good part to constitutional "checks and balances" on Government, civil society has thrived and made the country rich and powerful. Weakness of the state, vitality of civil society . . .

As I investigated the processes surrounding the adoption of the 1787 constitution, I became convinced that this thinking was not only inaccurate, it was also fundamentally wrongheaded. So, I tried to outline an alternative. Since my theoretical musings were inspired by an historical investigation, I will present in the next section my historical analysis of the genesis of the American constitution; it brought about the theoretical discomfort introduced above, and was written *before* I outlined a theoretical alternative.[9]

## II. The State, Economic Interests, and Incipient Capitalism in the United States

To some extent, this historical account takes the form of a reassessment of Charles A. Beard's contribution to our understanding of the socio-economic history of the constitution.[10] We are now two hundred years removed from the writing of the constitution, and

whatever cognitive access we have to its circumstances is constituted not only by the availability of the "sources", but also by the
mountains of studies it has elicited.

I consider the events surrounding the adoption of the constitution to represent a prime episode of "state making", and that this
historical concept provides much of the cement binding together
the other elements of explanation common in the literature. I will
characterize this episode of state-making as establishing the institutional forms of the first mode of development of American capitalism – a development particularly important for the problem of
working class formation. In this perspective, the industrial working
class can be said to be a late comer in American capitalism, which
grew out of an alliance between the state and early merchant
capitalists. As this alliance was quickly outgrown, the emerging
working class was dealt a hand from a stacked deck.

An analysis such as this promotes an understanding based on
the political-economic dynamism of history, rather than on unme-
diated socio-economic factors or the narrow political factors of
liberal theory. With regard to the substantive questions at hand, it
warns against what seems to be one of the most obvious contributions to American exceptionalism: the alleged importance of the
electoral system (understood as the "single-member-district plurality system", further biased against third-parties at the national
level by the nation-as-a-single-constituency phenomenon created
by the Electoral College). Indeed, the actual import of this factor
probably lies in its discursive dimension (the fact that people
believe in its importance and act accordingly) rather than in its
systemic impact. This is not to say that the electoral system is not
biased against socialist politics, but rather that its importance has
been systematically overestimated, probably as a result of the
hegemony of liberal discourse. Historically produced political-
economic factors that become inscribed and then reproduced in the
institutions, on the other hand, have been gravely underestimated.

In *An Economic Interpretation of the Constitution* (1913), Charles
Beard proposed a thesis, whose general thrust was simple and
provocative, and which quickly proved to be very popular among
the "progressive historians" of his time: he maintained that the
constitution was drafted by members of the upper class to serve the
interests of a privileged minority, and was ratified through an
undemocratic process. More specifically, Beard contended that it
was the commercial faction of the upper class, wealthy merchants
and public security holders,[11] as against the landed faction who, by
writing this new constitution, produced a document that protected,
served, and furthered their class interests. For the better part of
this century, Beard's work has been a central pole of attraction for

constitutional scholars, and for all intents and purposes has set the research agenda. In this respect, Beard's thesis should be seen as the organizing principle around which we may come to understand the socio-economic history of the constitution.

As an organizing principle, Beard's thesis has a heuristic value not only for the phenomena it highlights, but also for those that it keeps in the dark. Of particular interest among the latter should be a theme that once was a mainstay in the interpretation of the constitution, but has fallen into disrepute: the geo-political situation of revolutionary America between the declaration of independence and the adoption of the constitution in 1789. As well, a missing link in the literature is a consideration of America's situation in the international political economy, and an articulation of internal/external dynamics.

Most importantly, the question of the role of slavery in revolutionary America and in the debates surrounding the constitution was very much neglected by Beard. Although the politics of slavery often weighed very heavily at the Philadelphia convention,[12] they did not square with Beard's particular economic emphasis. It may also be because of this very contentiousness on the floor of the convention that the slavery issue was played down by Beard, whose case for an anti-democratic conspiracy among the framers might have been weakened by the display of their divisions. In any case, the framers may have found a viable long-term framework for the nurturance of commerce – as we shall see below – but they certainly did not produce an equivalent answer to the question of slavery.

The early, positive, reaction to Beard's argument stemmed from its same inherent radicalism that dimmed Beard's star in the 1950s, and that to this day keeps him in a virtual netherworld. In recent years, a partial and often unacknowledged rehabilitation of Charles Beard's work has occured, but it has yet to produce a synthesis on the question of the origins of the constitution.

If the debate is cast in broad terms, highlighting dichotomies such as socio-economic equality/inequality, democracy/elitism, or even the founding fathers' concern for national/class interests, much of Beard's thesis is vindicated by recent research. On the other hand, his description of class cleavages is highly deficient, and his neglect of all but economic phenomena has been the single most important cause of his thesis's demise.

This mixed verdict (Is the glass half-full or half-empty?) explains why analysts such as Diggins, who focus on the importance of political ideology, tend to come down hard on Beard. Others like McGuire and Ohsfeldt, who studied the economic interests of the founding fathers and of delegates to the ratifying conventions, call for his "rehabilitation".[13]

Towards a New Constitution

When the founding fathers convened in Philadelphia, Americans lived under the authority of the Articles of Confederation, written by a committee of Congress in 1777 and ratified by the thirteen states between 1777 and 1781. Under the Articles, Congress alone had power of war and peace, of entering into treaties and alliances, coining money, and maintaining the army and navy;[14] when compared with the previous political order in revolutionary America, the Articles represented an increase in the centralization of power.[15]

Extensive debates had produced many drafts of the Articles with much dispute on what would constitute a reasonable degree of centralization. Whereas the first draft called for much centralization, the following drafts toned it down. The end result produced "a central confederation . . . , something new in political history – a divided and multiple sovereignty".[16] In the new confederation, the states retained their sovereignty and Congress depended upon them for the execution of measures it adopted. Congress had no direct access to the citizens, and vice versa. "Furthermore, in three major areas its powers were absent: Congress could not lay taxes; it could not regulate commerce; and there was no authority in the Congress so far as the western lands were concerned".[17]

These constraints on Congress proved to be a significant hindrance for the nation's ability to fight the War of Independence. The war effort entailed considerable expense. This was met by the states and Congress by the issuance of paper money and public securities. Because of its inability to generate revenue, and because of its dependence on the states, Congress rapidly became paralyzed and fell into insolvency.[18]

As early as 1780, which was "in many ways the most discouraging year of the war",[19] it had become apparent to a number of national leaders that reforms were needed if America were to retain its independence, let alone prosper: Congress had to be strengthened.[20] The Nationalist movement of 1781–83 undertook to do precisely that. Their aim was for Congress to be able to impose taxes, enabling it to fund the debt already incured through the emission of securities.

In 1782, Robert Morris submitted to Congress a plan to fund the debt that included the creation of a federally sponsored bank, and which was certain to create domestic capital. What Morris was proposing was a new system where political and economic goals were organically merged. In other words, "the drive for political reform was associated with changes in economic policies".[21] Although it was clear that such a programme would have reinforced America's position in the struggle against Britain, Morris' proposal fell through and the Nationalist movement faded. But the problems remained.

If there were good reasons to strengthen the national government, there were also good reasons to resist centralization. Many harboured philosophical concerns for democracy, while others plainly feared tyranny. And, in keepingwith Beard's line of argument, E.J. Ferguson has noted that "any political change appealed to some persons more than to others and could be expected to have differential effects upon various groups of the population".[22] Like Beard before him. Ferguson thus recognized that in addition to the national interest, class or other group interests were involved.

But Beard's more specific claim of an opposition between realty and personalty – the landed vs the commercial interests – within the upper classes has not aged well. Recent research shows that, among the rich, various types of property were quite integrated. The one notable exception to the integration of various types of property was slave-holding, concentrated in the South as it was, but widely distributed among the citizenry – from the great planters who owned hundreds of slaves to the relatively poor freeholders who may own a few.

"Great landowners in all geographical sections of the North American colonies were by the mid-eighteenth century typically involved in additional economic affairs".[23] All combinations of merchant-planters, landowner-speculators, landowner-commercial developers, etc. could be found. Merchants lived mostly in seaport towns, and made fortunes as middlemen from import/export throughout the colonial period and the war years. As rich farmers diversified their activities, non-farmers invested in land: for instance, A.H. Jones's data show that "the average values of land held were highest for the merchants in New England and for 'esquires, gentlemen and officials' in the other two regions".[24]

A large majority of the white male population were small subsistence farmers, owned little property, and lived between poverty and "at best, modest property".[25] A great many farmers had to incur debts in order to acquire their farms, equipment, livestock, etc. without at the same time being involved in commercial agriculture – which would have provided the means to pay back the debt in "hard" money. Consequently, paper money was "an attractive solution to the farmers' financial problems".[26]

Merchants were among those relatively few people who held public securities and had a direct interest in the way Congress handled its debt. According to E.J. Ferguson, in 1790 the 280 largest public security holders had $7.88 million worth of securities – nearly two thirds of all securities that can be traced with certainty. The top one hundred holders had $5 million.[27] This group, writes J.R. Nelson, "consisted mainly of well established merchants who accumulated their fortunes trading with the British empire during the colonial period and after the revolution."[28]

With respect to this general situation, where did the members of the 1787 constitutional convention stand? There is little controversy here: they were, writes Pessen, representative of "the lightly populated but extremely influential and relatively wealthy upper levels of the social order". Robert E. Brown, who remains Beard's main critic, agrees with Pessen's evaluation of the framers, but he goes on to say that they "represented property in general and were interested in a government which would protect property".[29] Arguably, this concern was shared by most Americans because most white men owned some property. Then as now, however, the community of interests between small and large property owners has its limits; and the question remains as to whether the framers catered primarily to the shared interests of all property owners, or to the specific interests of their class.

It is clear that the political and economic situation under the Articles was inherently unstable: Congress had exclusive jurisdictions, but no autonomous means of enforcing its decisions. Each state had its own commerce regulations which, due to their disparities, impeded the trading capacity of numerous merchants who, as a socio-economic group, wielded considerable power and influence. Similarly, the tendency of the state legislatures to issue paper money quite freely was a constant threat to the stability of the confederation's economy – not to mention the soundness of merchants' credit. And indeed, if small farmers found paper money to their liking, many merchants regarded it as a destabilizing factor in the economy.

Finally, the war years had left a legacy of economic disruption that could not be dealt with by an impotent Congress and state legislatures concerned more with the local good than with an emergent national interest. Reflecting on the problems in which Congress was embroiled under the Articles, Thomas Jefferson wrote to the Governor of Virginia, on January 16, 1785 of "the urgent need for action on a federal level and the extreme difficulty of accomplishing anything within the existent governmental framework".[30] The shortcomings of the governmental system were compounded by a worsening economic situation during the 1780s. As different people expected different things from the government, the debate intensified.[31]

It is impossible to give here a detailed enough account of the lines of cleavage in the debt debate, which was central to the question of what form the confederation should take. But, drawing upon Jackson Turner Main's presentation of the period, which has not been substantially challenged, a summary picture can be sketched. Debates centered on two types of debts: the federal debt, to which was tied the issue of Congress' power of taxation, and private debts, which were very common among farmers, and to which was tied the issue of paper money.[32]

We have already seen that the creditors of both types of debt were relatively few, and that many of them were merchants. These people stood to profit from a stronger Congress capable of levying taxes in order to pay its debts, while the large majority of people who did not hold securities would have to pay taxes: "Critics asserted that the mass of the people were being taxed to benefit few . . .".[33] Main's general conclusion, in accordance with Staughton Lynd,[34] is that the significant opposition of interests in the debate on centralization was between commercial and non-commercial interests (essentially subsistence farmers) – as opposed to the realty/personality opposition proposed by Beard.

Pressure had been building throughout the 1780s to bring changes to the Articles, but the debate came to a head in 1786–87, in the wake of Shays's Rebellion, a populist revolt in Massachusetts against the financial double-binds plaguing small farmers: "Upon the outbreak of Shays's Rebellion, the almost universal reaction among men of means was to crush it", and the drive for a stronger government was accelerated.[35] The specific reasons that caused Congress to call for a constitutional convention instead of adopting a series of amendments remain unclear;[36] but it is safe to say that by 1786, when the wheels were set in motion for a convention, the situation was ripe for change.

When the convention assembled, only a few of its members opposed a strong government:[37] most Antifederalists were either preempted, or considered the Convention so biased as to render participation useless. And, as we have seen earlier, a large majority represented to varying extents the "commercial interests". As it soon became clear that "the delegates intended to establish a strong government, the Antifederalists, one by one, drew back".[38] Left to themselves, the Federalists got to write the constitution they wanted.

They had, however, to contend with the divisions arising from the status of slavery, which according to Deep South delegates, had the potential to destroy the Union. In the end, compromises were struck that reinforced the legal standing of slavery but that failed to set ground rules for its expansion or reduction in the future. Seventy years of uneasy ad hoc compromises would ensue, finally bringing the Union to the breaking point of the Civil War.[39] Agreements came quickly among the framers on economic questions other than slavery – the regulation of commerce, taxation, etc.

The question "Who did the Federalists work for?" can now be tackled directly. It will be addressed by pinpointing three issues: (1) the choice that had to be made between favoring the commercially oriented sectors of the population, or the non-commercial sectors – what Lee Benson has called the alternative between the commercial society and the agrarian society;[40] (2) the question of how to deal with the public securities issue: (3) the intention behind the system of checks and balances in government. This intention has been interpreted by Beard as anti-democratic, mostly on the basis of an analysis of *The Federalist Papers*, and by others as expressing a great concern for democracy, also partly on the faith of *The Federalist*.[41]

Choosing Commercial Society

There is no doubt that one of the intentions of the framers was to favor the expansion of commerce. Relying, like Beard, on *The Federalist* as an expression of the will of the founding fathers, Martin Diamond recalled "how large a portion of *The Federalist* deals with the improvement in commerce made possible by the new constitution", and the emphasis put by *The Federalist* on "the role of government in nurturing" commerce.[42]

In examining "the powers conferred upon the federal government", Beard started of course by considering the "taxation power, (which) was the basis for all other positive powers". One of these was the capacity to "raise and support military and naval forces" – instruments of defence against "the commercial and territorial ambitions of other countries"; these forces "may be used also in forcing open foreign markets".[43] But the most important power relating to commerce was that "the Constitution vests in Congress plenary control over foreign and interstate commerce".[44] Needless to say, interstate commerce was to be favored, as Hamilton showed in *The Federalist* #11.

With respect to foreign commerce, Beard refers to #35 and seems to interpret Hamilton's text as saying that "protective and discriminatory laws", made possible under the constitution, would favor American interests[45]. But, as I read it, Hamilton's *Federalist* #35 argues against high tariffs, and for moderation in all forms of taxation if one wants a healthy economy:

All extremes are pernicious in various ways. Exorbitant duties on imported artic-les . . . tend to render other classes of the community tributary, in an improper degree, to the manufacturing classes, to whom they give a premature monopoly of the markets.[46]

This, writes Hamilton, is bad for commerce. According to Beard, however, the clause in the constitution allowing protectionism represented a victory for those mercantile and manufacturing interests that had been asking for protection.[47] Hamilton's tenure as the first Secretary to the Treasury under the new constitution, does not support Beard's claim: while it is true that Hamilton was besieged by manufacturers seeking protection from imported goods, he always refused to satisfy them, praising the benefits of free trade.[48]

Beard's more general claim does have validity: nobody denies that the founding fathers were interested in "nurturing" commerce – but through ways other than protectionism, in Hamilton's case at least. As Benson points out, in the context of the period this overriding concern for commerce was not a foregone conclusion:[49] a small minority of Americans were involved primarily in commercial activities, while more had secondary ties to commerce. But it could hardly be said that a majority of the population (or of the electorate) would have felt or been vitally attached to the state of commerce. Given the choice between strengthening commerce and the central state on the one hand, or small farms and local institutions on the other, it is quite possible – to say the least – that a majority of farmers would have chosen the second alternative. But those who could have argued the point were not present at the convention.

It must then be clear that the framers did make a choice. By opting for the "commercial society" model, they favored their class interests, overruling those of subsistence farmers. Still, it is possible that in context these class interests merged with a broader national interest, insofar as a stronger national state would reinforce the nation's position internationally.

In any case, the decisions of the framers transformed profoundly the American political economy: they codified the first regime of accumulation of American capitalism, for until then the activities of merchants had grown despite some key institutional features of American society (barriers on interstate commerce, a weak monetary system). From then on, commercial capitalism would grow by leaps and bounds, abetted by custom-made institutional forms.

The issue of the public securities, tied to the funding of the debt and taxation powers, is in some ways intractable: for instance, it is not known who among the founding fathers owned securities at the time of the convention. In another way, it was not even an issue, in the sense that by 1787 nearly everyone agreed that Congress needed some taxation power.[50] In yet another way, it can be tentatively identified as a launching platform for American capitalism. It is all but certain that many delegates to the convention were security holders. More generally, they were socially akin to holders of large amounts of securities and they knew the effect that their proposal would have on the value of these securities. They were not alone in knowing the economics of the new constitution: their adversaries constantly accused them of catering to their own economic interests – Beard's argument was not anachronistic after all, despite what many of his critics have claimed.[51]

When Robert Morris had tried in 1782 to set up a plan to fund the debt, Alexander Hamilton was Morris' tax receiver. In 1789, as the constitution took effect, Hamilton as Secretary to the Treasury implemented a debt-funding plan that was very similar to Morris's plan of eight years earlier.[52] As was the case for its predecessor, Hamilton's plan was as political as it was economic. It led the nation in a new direction – although one may dispute that the direction was a matter of historic necessity, as Ferguson believes.[53]

The first consequence of Hamilton's plan was that, "since the securities were held by propertied men, the gains from an increase in security values would go to persons in a position to use them not for consumption but for investment".[54] Hamilton built on this possibility for accumulation of capital and in 1791 proposed a series of measures meant to "advance the cause of the business class",[55] starting with the creation of a federally supported bank (the Bank of the United States). The goal was to "stabilize credit and divert capital from the agricultural sector of the economy to the industrial and mercantile sectors".[56] The next measure was the imposition of an excise tax on farmers.

In itself, Hamilton's program (four years after the constitutional convention) says nothing of the intent of the framers in Philadelphia, even though it is entirely consonant with what Hamilton wrote in *The Federalist*. But it does shed light on the political agenda of some of the leading framers – who quickly found themselves at the head of the new state. Indeed, rather than nurturing an obsession with the framers' "original intent", we should focus on what the leading framers did with their consututional tools once they were adopted. Hamilton effectively created a state machinery that would exponentially increase the ability of American capitalists to accumulate capital.

Finally, the debate on the framers' conception of democracy brings us to Beard's claim that the adoption of the constitution was undemocratic, and to his most fundamental weakness: his unwillingness to examine the ideology of the period and, more generally, to consider the ideological dimensions of the phenomena studied. As he assumed that the majority of the American people would not have voted against its own interests, Beard found it necessary to claim that the process was undemocratic. To prove his point, Beard focused on the manner in which the delegates to the constitutional convention were selected, and on the property qualifications used by the states to exclude "the injection of too much popular feeling"[57] in the ranks of the members of legislatures in general and of the convention in particular. In addition, Beard investigated the process of the ratification of the constitution.

The confrontation of Beard's arguments with subsequent research deals Beard his most severe blows. It is here that we encounter Beard's most fundamental weakness: by refusing to stray from a purely economic interpretation in which material interests dictate political manipulation by the framers, he denied himself the ability to recognize the oligarchical character of the polity during the revolutionary years. An elitist political system, where "common men" are expected to surrender the running of the affairs of the Polis to men of the "better sort", would produce exactly the kind of political process and electoral results that were displayed at the constitutional convention and during the process of ratification.[58]

The emerging picture shows that the new constitution was adopted through a process that was legally democratic, but thoroughly controlled by members of the upper class. These men had the strength to use the political process to serve their own class interests; they were also in a position that allowed them to strengthen or weaken democracy. What, then, was the political system that they got the new nation to adopt?

Studying "the underlying political science of the constitution" and "the structure of government or the balance of powers",[59] Beard analyzed closely a few of *The Federalist* papers. He concluded with a significant degree of justification that the purpose of the system of checks and balances built by Madison was to keep the majority of the population from exerting its authority upon the hitherto privileged minority of merchants and other wealthy men. But here, as in other occasions before, while Beard had a case, he tried to prove too much, with too little conceptual depth.

Following another tack, J.R. Pole has suggested that Europe's tradition of constitutionally separating the "orders" (in England the House of Lords and the Commons; in Ancien Régime France the nobility and the "tiers état". etc.) may well have found its way into the framers' insistence on checks and balances. This is a perspective that rather downgrades the founding fathers' democratic drive and highlights the elite character of their project, for they were building "a carefully ordered hierarchy, under the aegis of which power and authority related to a conscientiously designed scale of social and economic rank, both actual and prospective".[60]

In a way that is oddly compatible with Pole's argument, R.E. Brown has questioned Beard's placing so much significance on Madison's *Federalist* philosophy, on the grounds that Madison's reasons for wanting a system of checks and balances were not necessarily the other delegates' reasons for wanting the same thing. Drawing from the Records of the convention, Brown insists that delegates had a whole set of various rationales to adopt the system of checks and balances.[61] Discussing this claim would take more space than is available here. Brown is half-convincing, and Pole provides an attractive alternative (or supplement) to *Federalist* exegesis. And yet it is my impression, based partly on Brown's own account, that Madison's writings do express feelings of distrust and fear very close to, even if more intellectualised than, those of many delegates. In this respect, Madison's contribution to The *Federalist* does constitute a valuable proxy for the framers' intent,[62] and could even be reconciled with Pole's "feudal" thesis.

Madison's writings on the checks and balances in *The Federalist* have been subject to varying interpretations. And they are the mainstay of radical critics of the framers, who see in this system the main cause of the working class's lack of political representation. Of particular interest are papers #10, #47 and #51. In #10, there is no ambiguity: the separation of powers aims at keeping a faction (quite possibly the majority) from gaining control of all the government organs at once, thus protecting minorities against the possibility of tyranny. If elective terms are of different lengths, the majority of one year may not be the majority of a year or two later.

Paper #47 appears to guard against the danger to liberty represented by the state itself, if all power is concentrated in the same hands. By refering to Montesquieu, Madison hints at the kind of tyranny known in Europe – the tyranny of the very few over the many. And in #51, Madison articulates the two perspectives of #10 and #47: "In framing a government which is to be administered by men over men, the great difficulty lies in this: you must first enable the government to control the governed; and in the next place oblige it to control itself".[63]

Beard chose to interpret the two perspectives as one and the same, and used a questionable method to make his point: he started a long quote from Madison's #51, about the second perspective, skipped a part of the text and resumed the quote at a point where Madison talks about the first perspective. The two halves of the quote are three pages apart in Madison's text[64], but the impression is given that only one perspective exists. Could it be, however, that despite his questionable method, Beard may have been right?

The means of control of government are the same for the two problems posed by Madison, and the perspective presented in #47 might have had a purely political purpose: disarming Antifederalist hostility toward a stronger state. Beard's interpretation amounts to this: Madison's articles in The *Federuaist* were written to gain political support, and were not necessarily candid statements of his beliefs. If one considers the ideology of the period, however, Beard is skating on very thin ice. It was a widely held belief during the eighteenth century that government had to be checked, as it stemmed from man's bad nature.[65] Madison's concern about the tyranny of government and the consequent need for a separation of powers was totally in line with that fear.

Madison, apparently influenced by Hume and Hobbe,[66] innovated when he introduced his fear of the tyranny of the majority. This innovation, in a sense, is only a special case of the general proposition that government must have built-in features that protect it from being overtaken by one group, or even one individual (king, despot), and being turned into an instrument of tyranny. But it is a special case with much political weight, the significance of which has not been missed by radical critics of the founding fathers. And yet, the very obviousness of the class character of this twist may have done its critics a disservice.

Over the years, the electoral system has made it difficult for third parties to become institutionalized, but it does not make it impossible: powerful sociological trends have produced changes in the party systems, from the era of the Federalists and Whigs to that of the Democrats and Republicans. Certainly, the growth of such a massive industrial proletariat as the American should have been a powerful enough trend to overcome the obstacles of the electoral system.

Much more problematic for the working class are other features of the American political economy, at work not only in the electoral sphere, but every day in every facet of social life. It is the general power balance between the American bourgeoisie and the working class that accounts for the latter's failure to organize politically (and to a considerable degree in labour unions).

Models of relative class power have emphasized factors (or variables) that tend to relate to a group's inherent resources and characteristic.[67] Absent from such a model's theoretical formulation are the state and other institutions that often define the forms taken by social relations. It has been the ambition of this paper to show that such institutional forms are not neutral and that, therefore, their full impact ought to be considered in an analysis of relative class power.

If the American working class is weak, it is because the American bourgeoisie is strong. It grew and became strong, even before the birth of an industrial proletariat, after some of its members succeeded in redefining the state and other key institutions according to its interests. The gap between the founding fathers' era and the period when a socialist party could have emerged presents us with a new question, well beyond the scope of this paper: to what extent did the ruling class retain control over the state in the decades that followed the adoption of the constitution? The problems encountered in the establishment of the Federal Bank indicate that struggles were going on, and that the advocates of Capital did not always prevail.

In a sense, and with respect to economic policy,[68] the bourgeoisie did not have to actively retain control over the state, so long as the institutional form given to it in 1787–89 was not imperiled or, alternatively, did not become dysfunctional under new historical conditions. A regime of accumulation was in place, which in its fundamental thrust was a catalyst to the growth of capitalism: commerce had been unbound, and financial and monetary institutions had been created, actively promoting commerce. In this light, the notion that the American state was indeed used to thwart the growth of working class organizations in general and of a political party in particular is but one (instrumental) expression of its truly constitutive role as catalyst of capitalism.

In the end, what can be said of the intentions of the framers when they established the system of checks and balances? Did they want to serve, or to curb democracy? Diggins argues fairly convincingly that they wanted to do both: "the Revolution aimed to resist tyranny, while the creation of the new federal government aimed to control democracy".[69] J.R. Pole notes with typical and piercing skepticism, however, that:

> The American Revolution was certainly a war for self-determination, but self-determination and democracy are not interchangeable terms ( . . . ). A society need not be democratic in order to achieve a high degree of internal unity when fighting for self-detemination.[70]

But even granting Diggins's point of a "controlled democracy": Once we add that the control in question is a class control, we get a picture of the American political system that shows the state form to be truly capitalist in character. A capitalist state, that is, before the advent of the working class, and before the rise of industrial capitalism.

### III. The State as Society

In the very last stages of researching this paper, after discontent with the conventional wisdom on the state had set in and led me to search for and formulate an alternative, I encountered an article by the late Philip Abrams. An extraordinarily stimulating and provocative article. In a self-described "ruthless" mood, Abrams called for an end to studies of "the state" because that object, he claimed, does not exist. The idea of "the state" however is another story:

> My suggestion, then, is that we should recognize that cogency of the idea of the state as an ideological power and treat that as a compelling object of analysis. But the very reasons that require us to do that also require us not to believe in the idea of the state, not to concede, even as an abstract formal-object, the existence of the state.[71]

If reification of the idea of the state is to be avoided, wrote Abrams, "the only plausible alternative I can see to taking the state for granted is to understand it as historically constructed". We should, then, "abandon the study of the state as such and turn instead to the more direct historical investigation of the political practice of class (and other) relationships".[72]

The personal history of my study of the American constitution vindicates Abrams's plea for historical work, if in an unintended kind of way – but that is the beauty of it: I started with a naive, reified notion of the state, which historical inquiry swiftly deconstructed. I followed with a search for alternatives, thereby abandoning the reified state. But alternatives proved to be elusive.

Abrams proposed to simply abandon the state as an operative concept. Ruthless indeed. But, in a way, not ruthless enough, for I believe there may yet be a use for a concept of state – a very different concept than the one targeted by Abrams. The hint that there may be an escape from Abrams's "ruthless" attack is provided by his odd neglect of Gramsci's work on the state – a neglect made all the more surprising by his sustained consideration of the Gramsci-influenced writings of Nicos Poulantzas.

It seems that, in this century, Antonio Gramsci has come closest to providing an alternative to the conventional wisdom on the state. In dealing with Gramsci's work, looking for a fresh understanding of the state, we must face a double difficulty: first, not surprisingly, he alternates between at least two senses of "state": second, he provides hints of an alternative, rather than a coherent conception. The key hint – the object of enough exegesis to indicate that there is a problem with the conventional wisdom[73] – is that "in actual reality civil society and State are one and the same":[74] and, civil society "is the State itself".[75]

Gramsci is groping his way out of the state/civil society opposition, which also implies breaking down the state/government identity. Thus, he writes that the identification of State and government is a representation:

> . . . of the confusion between civil society and political society. For it should be remarked that the general notion of State includes elements which need to be refered

back to the notion of civil society (in the sense that one might say that State = political society + civil society, in other words hegemony protected by the armour of coercion).[76]

Gramsci's notion of the "general state", although original in terms of the modem debate on the state, undoubtedly owes much to Marx and Hegel. Hegel's model, saddled with much normative weight, is found in his philosophy of right: the state is conceived as that society where men are subject to the rule of law. Hegel thus proposed a concept of "state" sharply different from that of state-as-Government.[77] Unfortunately, this construct remained unstable, for Hegel adduced to it a theory of the "powers of the state"[78] to which the citizens are subjected, which appeals to the sense of state-as-Government – unless we think of it as the powers that a society exercises upon itself.

Beyond this instability, Hegel never questioned the compatibility of this construct with his own previous construction of the dichotomy state/civil society. And he certainly did not abandon the latter. This is a double inheritance that his great pupil, Karl Marx, never shook: on the one hand, he sometimes used the concept of "the state as a whole"[79] – the state as society – and on the other, he reversed and maintained the relationship between state and civil society.

Marx so maintained the state/civil society dichotomy, writes French philosopher Jean-Francois Corallo, that he built his theory of Capital on its basis, whereby "the state exists outside of the mechanisms of civil society, which is structured by Capital".[80] Corallo's interpretation is bolstered by a rather stunning admission by Marx in a letter to Kugelmann, cited by Derek Sayer:

Marx himself acknowledged in the 1860s that 'the relations of the different state forms to the different economic structures of society' was something he did not deal with adequately in *Capital*, and others might find it difficult to do on the basis provided there.[81]

What would happen to the theory of Capital, "which is, in a sense a theory of the separate civil society", Corallo asks, if we were to overcome the state/civil society separation? This is an important question, that we must face. Corallo seems to think that abandoning the dichotomy would doom Marx's theory. It seems to me, however, that jettisoning this separation would allow us to enhance the historical character of Marx's socioeconomic theory; and to correct the "inadequacy" of *Capital*.

In a sense, this is what a number of French political economists – the "Regulation School", also thought of as a certain "neoinstitutionalism" – have been doing in the last fifteen years or so. As a prime example and source of this approach, Michel Aglietta's theoretical analysis of the socio-economic history of the United States[82] goes a long way in reconciling theory with history, relations of production with institutions and struggle. The conceptual reinsertion initiated by Aglietta of economic processes within the social space will provide us with the first tools to find our way out of the state/civil society quagmire.

Approaching the same meta-theoretical problem from a different angle, Philip Corrigan and Derek Sayer's *The Great Arch* effectively shatters the splendid isolation of "the state" from "civil society". An historical essay on English state and society, *The Great Arch* shows through a daring "longue durée" narrative how deeply intertwined are the histories of the English state, English culture and English capitalism. Following Abrams, and showing a debt to Michel Foucault, Corrigan and Sayer provide the historical grounding to the claim that:

> What is made to appear as 'the State'are regulated forms of social relationships; forms, as we quoted Philip Abrams at the start, of politically organized subjection. The enormous power of 'the State' is not only external and objective; it is in equal part internal and subjective, it works through us.[83]

Abrams's point that the idea of the state is systematically reified – thus giving rise to the notion that such a thing as "the state" exists – has been generalized and systematized by Sayer in *The Violence of Abstraction* (1987), a work of social theory that, largely through a rereading of Marx, explicates several theoretical stands more or less implicit in *The Great Arch*.[84] While Abrams focused his attention on the state, Sayer's more general argument brings the question of the relationship of the state to civil society "back in".

Just as Abrams marvelled at how close Poulantzas and Perry Anderson came to unmasking the state without actually getting there, I find it extraordinary how Corrigan and Sayer's historical work and Sayer's critique of the separation of civil society and the state goes almost all the way: if these two notions – bound up with that of their separation – are reifications, ideological products of capitalist social relations, why in the world should we retain them as analytic concepts, or even as "weak" concepts just good enough as abbreviations in an historical narrative?

In *The Great Arch*, Corrigan and Sayer show eloquently how to study the state and civil society as one and the same. But they fail to reconcile this practice with their frequent use of the expression "the state" in a common-sensical manner. The depth of their analysis, as well as the residual problem of naming "the state" are well illustrated in this claim, which highlights the state's strong hold on our societies:

The social classifications of capitalist civilization are actively – often forcibly – regulated by the state, and made palpable in its routine functioning. What counts as a 'real' property right, as between, say, rights in conquest, custom, law, is defined by state practices, legitimating certain forms of claim, outlawing others. A relation between two people is only a marriage if contracted according to certain forms, religious or civil, solemnized in definite, licensed places, and recorded in specific registers. The same is true of what constitutes a household, a trade union, a political organization, a school, a university . . .[85]

Like Abrams, I believe that we must study the ideas of the state and of civil society, but we must not believe that they exist – whether or not their reified selves are supposed to operate independently and separately, or together in some organic relation. We must not even allow ourselves to use the expression "the state" as a convenient abbreviation for all manners of government agencies and other such institutions.

It is a sad irony that bourgeois ideology scored a decisive point against Marx when, unable to free himself in practice from the state/civil society dichotomy, he enclosed *Capital* within civil society – opening the door for generations of Marxists to misconceive laws and governmental institutions as a "superstructure". The dichotomy itself, no matter how its elements are articulated, fosters separate accounts of the economy and of the polity. Which is what most Marxists have been doing for years, in close parallel to liberal economists and political scientists.

Let me now try something else, diversely inspired by Hegel and Marx, Gramsci and Foucault, Abrams, Sayer and Corrigan. Discarding the state/civil society aspect in the thoughts of Hegel, Marx and Gramsci, I will hold on to the "general state" idea. If the state includes the government and private organisms, if it includes "spontaneous consent given by the great masses of the population", two capital questions must be asked, and answered: What does the state not include? How can it be grasped in a unitary fashion? (We may also ask, if the state/civil society opposition disappears, why should we even retain a concept of civil society?)

The first question is also relevant to the work of Althusser and Poulantzas, in a more practical way because of their influence upon Marxists – we need only think of the use made of the concept of "state ideological apparatuses". The problem has been perceived acutely by Abrams, with respect to Poulantzas's work:

The danger now is that the global functionality of the state will lead one into a forced recognition of the global structural existence of the state – a sense of its immanence in all structures perhaps. Certainly, the move is towards an abstract understanding of the state which is so structurally unspecific as to seem either to make the conception of the state redundant, or to *substitute it for the conception of society*. It seems that the key political functions cannot be definitively assigned to any particular personnel, apparatuses or institutions, but rather 'float' with the tides of class power.[86]

Despite its difficulty, the notion of a general, or global, state deserves to be explored. Its fate will essentially depend on our ability to answer the second question, reconciling the globality of the concept with a necessary definitional boundedness. If such a reconciliation can be achieved, the problem of "civil society" will, so to speak, take care of itself.

What I propose here is a conceptual reorganization that will take me away from the state vs civil society tradition. I propose that *"states" are a historically specific type of society, whose institutions take the legal-constitutional discursive form which has enabled capitalism to rise* – a state is not in (or above) society, a state is a society. In consideration of Abrams's concern, I should note that the state here is not substituted for society, it specifies it historically.

In such a state/society, economic institutions perform, quite literally, within the terms set for them by Government. Thus, laws give form to socio-economic space, a form enforced by hegemony – the legitimacy of "the rule of law" – and, when necessary, by military acts themselves dependent upon legislation.

Given the conception of the state-as-government that I am trying to get rid of, and the central role that law plays in my model, I must make explicit the relation in which government and law stand to the state-as-society. This should take care of Abrams's more important apprehension, that of the unspecificity of a global concept of the state. Government and law are both state institutions, form-giving institutions, at two different levels of analysis. Government (and the bureaucracy) makes laws and regulations. Laws are empirical objects of a discursive nature, which are binding on the practices of social agents – in any field of social life that we wish to look at; because they are binding, they embody the "policing" function of state institutions, on the basis of their claim to legitimacy. If statute laws and regulations fail to enforce through hegemony the form that they define, government may be called to revert to coercion, which itself is to be justified on the basis of constitutional law.

The state institutions thus "tvrap" society in discourse, giving it form. A society that is shaped by juridico-legal discourse is a state. Indeed, if state institutions sometimes use physical violence against people in situations of "unrest", if they often repress "deviants", they mostly always talk. The key political functions lamented by Abrams, then, do not "float" in some disembodied world of ideas, but on the contrary find a material existence in the discursive realm, at the heart of state institutions. And given that laws and regulations are omnipresent in an "advanced" society, a concept of the state must be global or cannot be.

At this point, I should make explicit the relation between my empirical inspiration (constitution-making in the U.S.A.), my theoretical model of the state, and a more general, transhistorical model into which the historically specific "state" would fit. I am trying to develop *the theoretical model of a type of society* whose empirical source is modern, capitalist and democratic (in the liberal sense). The question of the relevance of this model to other societies, through the construction of other types on the basis of the same metatheoretical principles, goes well beyond both the motivating force and the means of this article.

The general theoretical task, then, would be to construct a typology of societies, whose dynamic principle is the historical process, and whose internal constitution is the relationship between form and content. That is to say, each type of society is characterized by a specific institutional and discursive form, and socioeconomic content, and by the relationship between the two. This relationship, internal to each type, is shaped by history, which also accounts for the transformation of societies from one type into another.

For my initial theoretical block, the state as society, I started from two substantive insights, derived from the analysis of the genesis of the U.S. constitution. The first one is that the form taken by American society – *society*, not government – in the last two-hundred years has been defined to an extraordinary degree by the 1787 constitution. Indeed, I shall say that this constitution discursively defines the general form of American society, making it a state.

This theoretical claim provides an underpinning for the second insight: the realization that economic institutions such as free internal markets (or national markets) are created and maintained by acts of sovereign Governments – in this case, under pressure from what we have called "the commercial interests" in revolutionary America. In this sense, in societies similar to the United States, markets (and other socioeconomic institutions) exist within the boundaries set for them by Government, through the language of laws and regulations. The empirical insight that the forms taken by markets are dependent upon acts of Government is banal, and has been a commonplace among historical scholars for decades;[87] but it has received scant theoretical attention, especially among Marxist scholars hell-bent on preserving the legacy of Marx's "pure" analysis of capital,[88] including the deeply damaging conventional view of the base/superstructure.

The theoretical object that I propose, the state, is capitalist in content and juridico-legal in form; its two dimensions cannot be understood apart from each other. Economic and political-legal dimensions of society are thus unified through juridico-legal discourse, which articulates power relations with the presentation that society gives of itself.

This conception, obviously indebted to Michel Foucault (although in a way of which he may not have approved), takes me some way from what we usually understand by "Marxism". But in a curious way, a way I did not anticipate, this model may be substantially faithful to Marx's project, at least as interpreted by Derek Sayer. It is worth quoting him at length:

> Marx's analysis of legal and political 'superstructures', I believe, hinges upon two key points, both of which are very subversive of 'traditional historical materialism'. First, he seeks to establish that the regulative agencies of state and law are substantially internal to capitalism's 'base' itself. That is to say, they are but forms of the social relations within and between classes – division of labour and labour/ capital relation – upon which the possibility of capitalist economy is predicated. Their appearances of independence notwithstanding, state and law are in reality 'the form in which the individuals of a ruling class assert their common interests, and in which the whole civil society of an epoch is epitomised' [Marx and Engels, *The German Ideology*]. Marx insists, moreover, that state and law are necessary forms of bourgeois rule . . .[89]

The historical narratives generated by the model proposed here will present an account such as this: At a given time in a statist society (i.e. a society that take the form of a state), social relations are pursued on the basis of a certain balance of power between individuals and groups. These social relations, and the balance of power on which they rest are expressed in the dominant discourses by "the law of the land".

In the course of historical struggle, agents that adopt reformist strategies will try to further their interests against each other's, by speaking the language of the state, via the changing of laws and regulations – hence the struggles around the formation of labour regimes (the Wagner Act vs Taft-Hartley), tax rates, deregulation, abortion laws, etc.

When a reformist agent is successful and gets a law or regulation passed or modified that "fits" its interests, the form of society is altered by the introduction, enhancement or reversal of a bias, which must then be enforced. To the extent that the bias is enforced, via hegemony and/or coercion, the relative balance of power between agents is altered.[90] And even failure to enforce a new bias, an indication of a current balance of power, results in such an alteration.

When, on the other hand, at least one historical actor explicitly rejects the legal mediation of struggle, refusing to speak the state's language, that actor may be termed revolutionary. But even revolutionary subjects are forced to define themselves in relation to the state's language, with very little chance of escaping it, for this is the language that we are raised into. Which is why it is so difficult to imagine what could replace the universalist "rule of law" in this social world where "From each according to his\her capacities, to each according to his/her needs". The difficulty in escaping the state's language is underscored by the implications of the "linguistic turn" in European social theory. For if we, the human species, live in a language, or rather in languages, the language that we, North Americans and Western Europeans, live in, is the state.

Great as it may be, the difficulty in escaping a dominant language – in this case the state – need not be thought of as absolute. As a general point, I should emphasize that I conceive the relationship between form and content as inherently problematic in the sense that – to put it simplistically – we should expect content to resist the form imparted by institutions, and vice versa.

The methodologically built-in empirical tension between form and content, the efforts by Governments and Churches to resolve it, and the practices of resistance of subjects, are (part of) the stuff of history. And they are the stuff of the study of history. From insider trading and moonlighting to rape and murder, laws are not always obeyed and moral codes are not always effective. (This is even the case within the form-giving institutions – recent spectacular examples of this, range from attempts by "Reagan's junta"[91] to subvert the American constitutional process, to several sex scandals in the U.S. and Canada involving "televangelists" and ordinary priests.) On the other hand, law-makers, whether secular or religious, often resist reformist impulses coming from "below".

It should be clear, then, that I am not reverting to idealism,[92] and that I am not suggesting that form causes content. I am not succumbing either to the power of liberal discourse, by reemphasizing the role of law. Indeed, the question is not whether we should retain certain bourgeois categories, but which ones, and in what capacity. I suggest that capturing "the rule of law" as a legitimating and empowering discourse organically linked to social relations, and submitting it to such a critique is more enlightening than retaining the traditional concepts of state and civil society.

### Acknowledgements

I wish to thank Robert J. Brym, Len Guenther and Dominique Jean, as well as the editors and anonymous readers of *JHS* for their comments and suggestions. The research and writing of this article were conducted while I was receiving funding, in the form of a Doctorate Fellowship, from the Social Science and Humanities Research Council of Canada.

## Notes

[1] D. Rueschemeyer and P. Evans "The State and Economic Transformation" in P. Evans, D. Rueschemeyer and T. Skocpol (eds) *Bringing the State Back In*, Cambridge University Press 1985, pp. 46, 47.

[2] J. Hoffman *State, Power and Democracy*, Brighton: Wheatsheaf 1988, p. 37.

[3] R. Boudon and F. Bourricaud *Dictionnaire critique de la sociologie*, Paris: Presses Universitaires de France 1982, pp. 220–30.

[4] Quentin Skinner, cited A. Pizzorno "Politics Unbound" in C.S. Maier (ed.) *Changing Boundaries of the Political*, Cambridge University Press 1987.

[5] O. Hintze "The Formation of States and Constitutional Developments" [1902] in F. Gilbert (ed.) *The Historical Essays of Otto Hintze*, New York: Oxford University Press 1975. p. 164.

[6] Pizzorno, in "Politics Unbound", feels free to use "state" in both ways a few paragraphs apart without blinking. See his references to Hegel followed by a paraphrase of Skinner, at pp. 30, 31. It could be argued that the two senses of "state" I identify are one, by noting that the governments of independent countries recognize each other's sovereignty without referring to the societies ruled by these governments. The second sense of "state" would thus be absorbed by the first. I do not find this argument convincing. When, for instance, a government is overthrown by a revolution or a palace coup, the governments of other countries have to decide whether or not to "recognize" the new one; this decision does not usually put into question the independence of the country whose government changes. It is indeed the "nation-state" that is involved in Hintze's quote, not "the government".

[7] A. Giddens *The Nation-State and Violence. vol. 2: A Contemporary Critique of Historical Materialism*, Berkeley and Los Angeles: University of California Press 1987, p. 17.

[8] R. Alford and R. Friedland *Powers of Theory*, Cambridge University Press 1985, p. 400.

[9] I have abridged the account somewhat, but I have not modified its perspective, especially with regard to "the state", after starting to outline a theoretical alternative to the standard vision of the state. This means that the view of the state that I now consider unsatisfactory permeates the whole historical narrative. Indeed, it is its inability to deal theoretically with the historical process that I was describing which led me to look deeper.

[10] See C. A. Beard *An Economic Interpretation of the Constitution of the United States*, New York: Free Press 1966. This historiographical detour should not be mistaken for the purpose of the journey, which is a substantive one: understanding the circumstances of this episode of state-making and its consequences for the future of American capitalism.

[11] To finance the war of independence against Britain, the states had emitted securities, of which large amounts were held by relatively few men as we will see below.

[12] See W. M. Wiecek *The Sources of Antislavery Constitutionalism in America, 1760–1848*, Ithaca: Cornell University Press 1977, pp. 62–83.

[13] J.P. Diggins "Power and Authority in American History" *American Historical Review* 86, 1981; R. McGuire and R. Ohsfeldt "Economic Interests and the American Constitution" *Journal of Eonomic History* 44, 1984. In light of Maguire and Ohsfeldt's work, McCann's quick dismissal of Beard's "instrumentalist economic theory" requires some rethinking. See M. W. McCann "Resurrection and Reform: perspectives on property in the American constitutional tradition" *Politics and Society* 13, 1984.

[14] H. Aptheker *Early Years of the Republic*, New York: International Publishers 1976, pp. 5.6.

[15] Aptheker *Early Years of the Republic*, p. 12.

[16] Aptheker *Early Years of the Republic*, p. 8.

[17] Aptheker *Early Years of the Republic*, p. 6.

[18] E.J. Ferguson "The Nationalists of 1781–83 and the Economic Interpretation of History" *Journal of American History* 56, 1979, p. 243.

[19] Ferguson "The Nationalists of 1781–83" p. 241,

[20] Ferguson "The Nationalists of 1781–83" p. 241; Aptheker *Early Years of the Republic*. p. 8; Diggins "Power and Authority in American History" p. 711.

[21] Ferguson "The Nationalists of 1781–83" p. 242.

[22] Ferguson "The Nationalists of 1781–83" p. 242.

[23] E. Pessen "Wealth in America Before 1865" in W.D. Rubinstein (ed.) *Wealth and the Wealthy in the Western World*, London: Croom Helm 1980, p. 169.

[24] Alice Hanson Jones *Wealth of a Nation To Be*, New York: Columbia University Press 1980, p. 210, and "Wealth and Growth of the Thirteen Colonies" *Journal of Economic History* 44, 1984. The other two regions were the "middle colonies" and the South. Jones's methodology in studying wealth inequality probably underestimated the degree of inequality because she distributed evenly throughout the population the people whose belongings had not been probated following their death. If one assumes, however, that the non-probated descendents were at a low end of the distribution of wealth, then inequality would have been greater than Jones found. I thank Lars Osberg who brought this bias to my attention. For a detailed analysis of Jones's bias, see L. Osberg and F. Siddiq "The Inequality of Wealth in Britain's North American Colonies: the importance of the relatively poor" *Review of Income and Wealth*, Series 34, 2, 1988, pp. 143–64.

[25] Pessen "Wealth in America Before 1865" p. 168.

[26] J.T. Main *The Antifederalists: Critics of the Constitution*, Chapel Hill: University of North Carolina Press 1961, pp. 6, 7.

[27] E.J. Ferguson "The Nationalists of 1781–83" p. 260.

[28] J.R. Nelson "Alexander Hamilton and American Manufacturing: a reexamination" *Journal of American History* 65, 4, 1979, p. 973.

[29] E. Pessen "Social Structure and Politics in American History" *American Historical Review* 87, 5, 1982, p. 1309; R. E. Brown *Charles Beard and the Constitution*, Princeton University Press 1956, p. 90.

[30] Cited Aptheker *Early Years of the Republic*, p. 22.

[31] Main *The Antifederalists*, p. 56.

[32] Main *The Antifederalists*, pp. 6, 7, 71.

[33] Main *The Antifederalists*, p. 58.

[34] S. Lynd *Class Conflict, Slavery and the United States Constitution*, Indianapolis: Bobbs-Merrill, pp. 15, 16.

[35] Main *The Antifederalists*, pp. 61, 62, 64.

[36] M. Jensen *The New Nation*, New York: Knopf 1950. pp. 4–9, 420.

[37] Main *The Antifederalists*, p. 116.

[38] Main *The Antifederalists*, p. 1 17.

[39] Wiecek *The Sources of Antislavery Constitutionalism*.

[40] L. Benson *Tuner and Beard*, New York: Free Press 1960.

[41] Brown *Charles Beard and the Constitution*, pp. 30, 98; G.W. Carey "Separation of Powers and the Madisonian Model" *American Political Science Review* 72. 1. 1978; R.L. Morgan "Madison's Analysis of the Sources of Political Authority" *American Political Science Review* 75.3, 198 1. For recent reaffirmations of the Beard argument, see Greenberg "Class Rule under the Constitution" in R.A. Goldwin and W.A. Schambra (eds.) *How Capitalist is the Constitution?* and Parenti "The Constitution as an Elitist Document" in Goldwin and Schambra (eds.) How *Democratic is the Constitution?*, both Washington D.C.; American Enterprise Institute for Public Policy Research.

[42] M. Diamond "Democracy and *The Federalist*" [1959], in *The Reinterpretation of the American Revolution 1763–1789*, New York Harper & Row, 1968, p. 510. Laissez-faire is not necessarily the "natural" ideology of early capitalists: "It is commonly thought that in the eighteenth and nineteenth centuries men of property preferred a laissez-faire government, one that kept its activities to a minimum. In actuality, they were not against a strong state but against state restrictions on business enterprise. They never desired to remove civil authority from economic affairs but to ensure that it worked for, rather than against the interests of property. This meant they often had to work toward new and stronger state formations." (Parenti "The Constitution as an Elitist Document" p. 29).

[43] Beard *An Economic Interpretation*, pp. 170, 171, 173.

[44] Beard *An Economic Interpretation*, pp. 175.

[45] Beard *An Economic Interpretation*, pp. 175.

[46] A. Hamilton "The Federalist #35" in R.P. Fairfield (ed.) *The Federalist Papers*, New York: New American Library 1961.

[47] Beard *An Economic Interpretation*, pp. 40–49, 175.

[48] Nelson "Alexander Hamilton" p. 973.

[49] Benson *Turner and Beard*, p. 218.

[50] Jensen *The New Nation*, pp. 417–8.

[51] Diggins "Power and Authority" p. 720.

[52] Ferguson "The Nationalists of 1781–83" p. 248: Aptheker *Early Years of the Republic*. p. 34.

[53] Ferguson "The Nationalists of 1781–83" p. 260.

[54] Ferguson "The Nationalists of 1781–83" p. 248 [My emphasis].

[55] Albert Fried (ed.) *The Jeffersonian and Hamiltonian Traditions in American Politics*, New York: Anchor Books/ Doubleday 1968. p. 5.

[56] Fried *The Jeffersonian and Hamiltonian Traditions*, p. 5.

[57] Beard *An Economic Interpretation*, p. 65.

[58] On this question, see J.R. Pole "Historians and the Problem of Early American Democracy" [1962] in Pole *Paths to the American Past*, Oxford University Press 1979.

[59] Beard *An Economic Interpretation*, pp. 156, 159.

[60] Pole "Historians" p. 243 and *passim*.

[61] Brown *Charles Beard and the Constitution*, pp. 97–100.

[62] This whole discussion may be thought of as a concession to the "original intent" perspective, and in a sense it is. The point of it is, on the one hand, to assess whether the framer's goal was to serve democracy or to curb it: and on the other hand, understanding the framer's purposes in creating their system of checks and balances should help us understand the political dynamics embedded in the system itself, at least in its early years. This last element seems to me at once pragmatically sound and philosophically fragile. I also think that a consideration of "original intent" in historical discussions such as this one belongs in an altogether different class of statements than appeals to original intent in the context of contemporary (i.e. Reagan and after) political debate and judicial decision-making.

[63] *The Federalist Papers*, p. 160.

[64] *The Federalist Papers*, p. 159–61.

[65] Aptheker *Early Years of the Republic*, p. 7.

[66] Diggins "Power and Authority" pp. 708–12.

[67] See, for instance, R.J. Brym "Anglo-Canadian Sociology" *Current Sociology* 34, 1, 1986, p. 54.

[68] As opposed in particular to slavery, a problem which was not solved by the new constitution and that came to a head with the Civil War, after almost a century of tensions, conflicts and ad hoc compromises.

[69] Diggins "Power and Authority" p. 711.

[70] Pole "Historians" p. 232.

[71] P. Abrams "Notes on the Difficulty of Studying the State" [1977], *Journal of Historical Sociology* 1.1, 1988, p. 79; also p. 76.

[72] Abrams "Studying the State" pp. 80–1.

[73] See for instance B. Jessop *The Capitalist State*, Oxford: Martin Robertson 1982, p. 147; J. Hoffman *State, Power*, Democracy, pp. 44, 45 who actually misquotes Gramsci on the subject; and P. Hamel.and J.-F. Léonard *Les organisations populaires, l'Etat et la démocracie*, Montréal: Nouvelle Optique 1983, pp. 161–170.

[74] A. Gramsci *Selections from the Prison Notebooks*, New York: International Publishers 1971, p. 160.

[75] Gramsci *Prison Notebooks*, p. 261.

[76] Gramsci *Prison Notebooks*, pp. 262–3.

[77] I translate from my copy of G.W.F. Hegel *Propédeutique philosophique*, Paris: Gonthier, Bibliothèque Médiations 1964, p. 46: "L'Etat est la société d'hommes soumis a des rapports de droit . . ." The paragraphs that articulate this conception are from #24 to #27.

[78] Hegel *Propédeutique philosophique* # 28 and #29, pp. 48–50.

[79] For instance, in "The Jewish Question" [1843], quoted D. Sayer *The Violence of Abstraction*, Oxford: Basil Blackwell 1987, p. 100.

[80] J.-F. Corallo "Etat-société civile" in *Dictionnaire critique du marxisme*, Paris: Presses Universitaire de France 1982.

[81] Sayer *Violence of Abstraction*, p. 97. Marx's letter is dated 28 December 1862.

[82] M. Aglietta *Régulations et crises du capitalisme: l'expérience des Etats-Unis*, Paris: Calmann-Levy 1976. For a critical overview of ten years of research by one member of the "Regulation School", see R. Boyer *La théorie de la régulation*, Paris: La Découverte, coll. Agalma 1986.

[83] P. Corrigan and D. Sayer *The Great Arch*, Oxford: Basil Blackwell, 1985, p. 180.

[84] Sayer argues convincingly that Marx has been widely misunderstood in the formulation of his key concepts, among them "ideology" and the

"basesuperstructure" metaphor. I fear that, just as Marx has been misunderstood, the full import of Abrams's and Sayer's revisionisms will be gutted by the same cognitive processes that Sayer unmasks. There may just be an "iron law of ideology" operating here that all but ensures reification.

[85] Comgan and Sayer *The Great Arch*, pp. 196–7.

[86] Abrams "Studying the State" p. 74 [my emphasis]. The term global should be understood here and in the following pages at the level of a whole society, not that of the entire capitalist international economy.

[87] See for instance *The Historical Essays of Otto Hintze*, pp. 427–8.

[88] See Corallo "Etat-société civile".

[89] Sayer *Violence of Abstraction*, p. 190.

[90] In formal terms, the relations between form and content look like this:

The form, F, of statist society, S, is expressed by a body of laws, L, that claims hegemonic status, i.e. the monopoly of legitimate force, and the elements of which are constitutional laws, statute laws, and regulations (L-1, L-2, L-3 . . . ); the degree to which hegemony is enforced is an empirical question.

The content, C, of S is made up of individuals and their activities, the social relations in which they enter and which constitute them as groups, and the power relations between these groups.

\* No cognitive access to C by analysts and/or participants is possible without its insertion in F. In other words, if we are to understand C, we must do it via its expression in F.

The organic link between F and C is constituted by the expression by L of power relations in C. This expression is the resultant of struggle between groups X, Y, Z in C. When struggle in C is expressed in the language, L of S, it is reformist. When at least one of C's groups refuses to express its struggle in L, it puts into question at once the legitimacy of L, F and S: we have a revolutionary struggle.

So we set up this situation: In S, at time t-1, groups X, Y and Z are engaged in social relations within a given pattern of power relations: this is expressed in general form by F, the specifics of which are found in L. At time t, X tries to reinforce its position in the social relations, a dimension of C, by transforming L-2, so that it becomes $L-2^1$. In so doing, X, Y and Z act upon the specific character, L, of F, in the very language, F, of S. If X is successful, L at t + 1 will be altered to $L^1$, expressing X's punctual victory in the legal struggle. And to the extent that elements of $L^1$ are binding upon C via hegemony and/or coercion, Xs victory in L at t will be in effect in C, starting at t + 1 for an undetermined period. L will have been altered to some degree, along with C, by struggle carried out in the language, F, of S, thus ensuring the maintenance of that type of society.

[91] I borrow the phrase from T. Draper "Reagan's Junta" *New York Review of Books* 29 January 1987.

[92] On the question of idealism, I cannot do better than follow Sayer's lead: "I am not trying to restore idealism. Law or morality were never, for Marx, independent of people's 'materialistic connection.' The point is that for him law was not a superstructure, as tradition understands the term, external to and causally determined by the economy, either. Rather, it is one of the myriad forms the social relations which premise that economy empirically take." (*Violence of Abstraction* p. 145).

# Issues and Agendas

# Who Needs the Nation? Interrogating "British" History[1]

## ANTOINETTE BURTON

**Abstract** This paper pursues the question "who needs the nation?" which was first posed by Kobena Mercer, the Black British cultural critic, in *Welcome to the Jungle* (1994). It interrogates not just the proposition of who needs the nation as a fixed referent, but who can afford to be content to be contained by its disciplinary boundaries. These are questions of interest to practitioners committed to understanding what the ramifications are for national histories in the wake of postcolonial studies and work around diasporic communities and subjects. Who writes – who even sees – the histories of subjects exiled from the "national body", those refugees (deliberate or otherwise) from national history and its disciplinary regimes – before the 20th century, in the European context? Who questions the apparent naturalness of the nation as an analytical framework in western histories? And, finally, what does this question mean for the sovereignty of Greater Britain, whose historiography has traditionally been one of the technologies of the national state and which is in the process of being challenged and refigured through the analytics of culture, postcolonialism and feminism?

*****

In his 1964 essay "Origins of the Present Crisis", Perry Anderson argued that British colonialism had made "a lasting imprint" on English life because of the historically imperial basis of mercantile capitalism. As interlocutors of capitalism from J.A. Hobson to E.P. Thompson have done (on those rare occasions when they have addressed the impact of empire on domestic English culture at all), Anderson focused his attention on the working classes – who, he argued, were "undeniably deflected from undistracted engagement with the class exploiting them. This was the real – negative – achievement of social-imperialism", according to Anderson. "It created a powerful 'national' framework which in normal periods insensibly mitigated social contradictions and at moments of crisis transcended them" (Anderson, 1967).

Although Anderson touched but briefly on empire, he was rare among his left academic contemporaries in suggesting that Britain's colonial enterprises had a constitutive effect on working-class and indeed on English life as a whole in the modern period – despite the fact that the expropriation of colonial rent and resources was, historically, one of the two major pillars of primary capital accumulation in the west (Habib, 1995). Eric Williams' 1944

*Capitalism and Slavery* had posited both empirical and ideological connections between the plantocratic practices of empire and domestic British politics and society, though its impact outside of Caribbean history or slavery/emancipation studies was arguably limited for decades.[2] It is tempting to stop here and talk about the relative invisibility of empire in British marxist analyses, at least in the 1960s and 1970s. Eric Hobsbawm's *Industry and Empire* (1968) is an important exception, though it does not deal with the cultural or even political ramifications of empire for "domestic" culture and society. The consequences of historical amnesia in British historiographical traditions have been variously explored by Gauri Viswanathan's critique of Raymond Williams, E.P. Thompson's remarkable monograph, *Alien Homage*, and the introduction to Catherine Hall's *White, Male and Middle Class* – all of which grapple with the ramifications of such willful blindness in different ways and for different ends (Viswanathan, 1991; Thompson, 1993; Hall, 1992; Trivedi, 1995; see also Gregg and Kale, forthcoming). What I want to focus on here is Anderson's observation about the "national" framework created through the appropriation of imperial discourses and politics by elites and populists because it signals, I think, a nostalgia for the nation which is often articulated even and perhaps especially by ostensible critics of empire. For Anderson as for others interested in the relationship of imperial culture to British history, what was regrettable about empire was in many respects enabling for the nation – insofar as the fact of colonialism provided what, in Anderson's own estimation, was the very grounds for "national culture". In light of Anderson's 1967 essay, "Components of the National Culture" – which argues that Britain produced no "overall account of itself" because a classical sociology originating "at home" failed to emerge – what empire achieved for the nation is hardly insignificant. Taken together Anderson's two essays imply that it was colonialism which provided the opportunity for Britons of all classes to conceive of the nation and to experience themselves as members of a "national culture".[3]

Such an observation runs the risk of seeming almost pedestrian, especially given the burgeoning of work in the last ten years on the imperial dimensions of Victorian, and to a lesser degree twentieth-century British, society. As a participant in and critic of these developments, I want to register my unease at the some of the conservative effects of this remapping of Britishness, historically conceived. I want to suggest that among the subjects being implicitly and perhaps unconsciously conserved in current debates is the nation and its integrity, in part because there is nothing inherently destabilizing to the nation in critical attention to empire as a constitutive part of "British" history and society – either in Anderson's time or now. Moreover, I want to argue here that one tendency in current responses to "imperial studies" is to shore up the nation and re-constitute its centrality, even as the legitimacy of Great Britain's national boundaries are apparently under question. What is at stake in these debates is not just the nation per se, but the territorialized domains of the social versus the cultural and with them, the complicity of history-writing itself in narratives of the "national" citizen-subject as well. And despite traditional British historians' almost pathological fear of contamination by literary studies via the linguistic turn, it is actually anthropology and the "ethnographic" turn which places the sovereignty of British history at risk.[4]

It would require a herculean effort in 1996 to gainsay Edward Said's claim that "we are at a point in our work when we can no longer ignore empires and the imperial context in our studies" (Said, 1993). As Peter Hulme has pointed out, the enduring purchase of Said's work – its "irritative process of critique" – lies in its insistence that what is at risk from attention to orientalism is the integrity of the European "heartland" itself, because "the principal motifs and tropes of . . . European cultural tradition, far from being self-generated, were the product of constant, intricate, but mostly unacknowledged traffic with the non-European world" (Hulme, 1989).

Recent scholarship in British history has documented the traces of empire that were everywhere to be found "at home" before World War I – in spaces as diverse as the Boy Scouts, Bovril advertisements, and biscuit tins; in productions as varied as novels, feminist pamphlets, and music halls; and in cartographies as particular as Oxbridge, London, and the Franco-British Exhibition.[5] And either because they were part of permanent communities with long histories and traditions in the British Isles, or because they were travelers or temporary residents in various metropoles and regions throughout the United Kingdom, a variety of colonial "Others" circulated at the very heart of the British empire before the twentieth century. They were, as Gretchen Gerzina has recently noted, a "continual and very English presence" from the Elizabethan settlement onward (Gerzina, 1995; Hesse, 1993; Fryer, 1987; Visram, 1986; Holmes, 1988; Burton, 1997). If there is little consensus about the significance of empire's impact on Britain's domestic cultural formations, primary evidence of its constitutive role nonetheless abounds, and scholars of the Georgian, Victorian and Edwardian periods are at work to re-map Greater Britain as an imperial landscape using a variety of evidentiary bases and techniques (Mackenzie, 1995; Marshall, 1993). Empire was, in short, not just a phenomenon "out there", but a fundamental part of

English culture and national identity at home, where "the fact of empire was registered not only in political debate . . . but entered the social fabric, the intellectual discourse and the life of the imagination" (Parry, 1993).

If these claims would seem to make good historical sense, they have met with an opposition so determined that it would be easy to imagine that they pose some kind of threat to national security. While it is undoubtedly true that there are important recent voices – Catherine Hall, Bill Schwarz, Laura Tabili and Mrinalini Sinha among them – taking issue with the siege mentality of British history, I have chosen to focus here on the battlements, and more specifically, on how and through what kinds of referents they have been drawn and defended. Studies which seek to rematerialize the presence of non-white Britons in the United Kingdom before 1945 have attracted the most censure, in part because, as Paul Gilroy has argued with regard to the emergence of black history in Britain, they are perceived as "an illegitimate intrusion into a vision of authentic national life that, prior to their arrival, was as stable and peaceful as it was ethnically undifferentiated" (Gilroy, 1993). Accusations by a British government minister in 1995 that the elevation of historical figures like Olaudah Equiano and Mary Seacole to the status of British heroes constituted a "betrayal" of true British history and "national identity" certainly testify to the political contests that representation has the power to set in motion.[6] But recent attention to empire's influences at home has provoked a response even when the topics are commodities and aesthetics, ideologies and politics, rather than an "alien" presence. Whether by a calm, cool refutation of claims about empire's centrality (as exhibited by Peter Marshall's essay in the *Time Literary Supplement*, "No Fatal Impact?") or via the impassioned denunciations of Said (articulated in John Mackenzie's recent monograph, *Orientalism: History, Theory and the Arts*), those in charge of safe-guarding Britain's national heritage, from Whitehall to the Senior Common Room, have raised the standard in defense of the nation's impenetrability to outside forces. Although a number of scholars are beginning to track empire's constitutive impact on metropolitan society as the starting point for new critical geographies of British imperial culture, empire cannot be viewed as having made Britain "what it was" for Professor Marshall because it was so centrifugal and uneven – and by implication, perhaps, untraceable – in its impact.[7] This kind of response worries me because it seems to echo J.R. Seeley's infamous quip that the British empire was acquired in "a fit of absence of mind" (a phrase later amended to "a fit of absence of wives" by Ronald Hyam). John Mackenzie's role in this debate is perhaps the most puzzling and intriguing, since his now

twenty-plus volume series, "Studies in Imperialism", has arguably
advanced our understanding of the myriad ways in which empire
was, to quote his 1984 monograph, "a core ideology" of national
culture (Mackenzie, 1984).

Clearly the persistent conviction that home and empire were
separate spheres cannot be dismissed as just any other fiction.[8]
Because history-writing is one terrain upon which political battles
are fought out, the quest currently being undertaken by historians
and literary critics to recast the nation as an imperialized space –
a political territory which could not, and still cannot, escape the
imprint of empire – is an important political project. It strikes at the
heart of Britain's long ideological attachment to the narratives of
the Island Story, of splendid isolation, and of European exceptionalism. It materializes the traffic of colonial goods, ideas and people
across metropolitan borders and indeed throws into question the
very Victorian distinctions between Home and Away that defined
the imagined geography of empire in the nineteenth century –
helping to challenge the equally Victorian conviction that "England
possesses an unbroken history of cultural homogeneity and territorial integrity" (Lindeborg, 1994). And yet what it potentially leaves
intact is the sanctity of the nation itself as the right and proper
subject of history. It runs the risk, in other words, of remaking
Britain (itself a falsely homogeneous whole) as the centripetal origin
of empire, rather than insisting on the interdependence, the
"uneven development", as Mrinalini Sinha calls it, of national/
imperial formations in any given historical moment.[9] And – perhaps
most significantly – it leaves untouched the conviction that
"national" history can be tracked through a linear chronological
development (with empire added in) rather than as "a set of relations that are constantly being made and remade, contested and
refigured, [and] that nonetheless produce among their contemporaneous witnesses the conviction of historical *difference*" (Wilson,
1995). Anne McClintock, in her recent book, *Imperial Leather*, for
example, tends to see empire and nation precisely as *two*, and in a
sequential relationship at that: for example, "as domestic space
became racialized", to quote from *Imperial Leather*, "colonial space
became domesticated" (McClintock, 1995). Here not only is the
binary reinstantiated, not only is the "nation" represented as a
privileged and cohesive subject, but empire follows nation in a fairly
conventional linearity.[10] The fact that this relationship is a classi-
cally *imperial* concept of nation-empire relations should be our first
clue to the limits of its critical usefulness (not to mention its
historically specific constructedness). Rather than emerging as an
unstable subject-in-the-making, the nation is in danger of functioning as a pretext for post-modern narrative in the same way it

functioned as the foundation for post-Enlightenment historicism. Such a coincidence implicates them both, though differently, in the metanarrative(s) of western imperial discourse, where the nation has historically served as the sovereign ontological subject.[11]

Despite the veritable explosion of work in the field, few have been willing to embrace or even engage the notion of deracinated, mobile subjects posed by Paul Gilroy's *Black Atlantic* (a text that has been woefully under-engaged by British historians, at any rate). Britain – and England within it – tends to remain the fixed referent, the *a priori* body upon which empire is inscribed. Even when it is shown to be remade by colonialism and its subjects, "the nation" often stands as the mirror to which imperial identities are reflected *back*.[12] This is perhaps because not many historians are willing to fully countenance the notion that the nation is not only *not* antecedent to empire, but that as both a symbolic and a material site the nation – as Judith Butler has argued for identity and Joan Scott for gender and experience – has no originary moment, no fixity outside of the various discourses of which it is itself an effect. And so, to paraphrase Anna Marie Smith, the fiction of a pre-existing England is left largely unchallenged (Smith, 1995; Butler, 1992; Scott, 1992). Rarely is the starting point of the newly imperialized British history the "precarious vulnerability" of imperial systems, as Ann Stoler has strenuously argued for the Dutch East Indies context (Stoler, 1995; Stoler and Cooper, 1989). Indeed, the very concept of Britain, and of England within it, seems to have a "fantasy structure" that is more resilient and more resistant to its own displacement than almost any other "national" imaginary today (Salecl, 1993). Even the naming of Britain as an imperial space – a maneuver which challenges the colonial status quo by implying that "home" was not hermetically sealed from the colonies – potentially works to naturalize the distinctions between "home" and "empire", when it seems clear that the nineteenth century is one particular historical moment during which such discursive categories were being affirmed (if not invented) and circulated as evidence of "modernity" and civilization in the first place. Perhaps this is a question of emphasis. In the case of McClintock, at any rate, I think the emphasis is not placed carefully enough.

One of the many queries that follows from such observations is this: if the fixity of nation is in fact being conserved in some new imperial studies projects, why has opposition to them been so fierce? I think this is a matter for discussion and debate. For my part, I believe that the terms upon which such critiques are articulated – both in print and in public – reveal a lot about the stakes involved. John Mackenzie, for example, takes Said and all those have who ever footnoted him to task because their work is not sufficiently historical. Here "History" (capital H) is a convenient stick with which to berate the un- or under-disciplined and the great "unwashed" – literary critics, yes, but feminists and post-modern sympathizers as well (Mackenzie, 1995). Rarely is the disciplinary power of history so blatantly on display – though other examples may be gleaned through a perusal of the pages of the book review section of the *American Historical Review* for past decade, where the "Real History" stick is routinely used to discipline authors of postmodern or cultural studies works, especially those interested in "discourse" or textual analysis.[13] It might be argued that this is evidence that traditionalists are fighting a losing battle, since the book review is not a particularly effective or enduring site of protest.[14] And yet it also suggests that the re-fashioning of Britain's conceptual borders and indeed, of British history's "mission" itself, is by no means a fait accompli. Clearly, one of the purposes of a discipline is to discipline. The necessity of disciplinary action may seem especially urgent in an historical moment like this one when disciplinary boundaries are said to be dissolving – and their perceived dissolution is producing what Judith Allen aptly calls historically unprecedented "spatial anxieties" as well (Allen, 1992). The impulse to discipline may also be an indication of how invested some professionals in Britain and the United States are in the historicist (and implicitly, empiricist) models which are at least partly responsible for their material and political hegemony, historically if not also today (Ermarth, 1992). But an equally powerful purpose of "disciplinary action" is also, surely, to enculturate – a project historically bound up with the mission to produce "a certain sort of cosmopolitan liberal subject" among educated citizens and, especially, among university students. If disciplinarity is in fact a kind of cultural artifact, historians' attempts to patrol their own shifting boundaries may be read as an historically intelligible fear that literary studies and cultural studies more generally are in the process of stealing "culture" itself (Appadurai, 1996).

I want to be clear here that I am not unappreciative of Said's limits, oversights, or glosses, and that I find the materialist critique of *Orientalism* articulated by Mrinalini Sinha, Benita Parry and others to be helpful guides to a more politically engaged, rigorously historical approach to texts and contexts. Nor would I deny that the emergence of "a new, multivocal historical discourse" may serve in part "to hide stasis or even further segregation at the level of social relations" (Brown, 1996). But I do think that recourse to arguments about the truest, "most historically" historical method like those invoked by Mackenzie runs parallel to the desire for a return to the truest, purest nation – one not entirely untouched but certainly not centrally defined by empire, its institutional practices and its political legacies. "Why the need for nation?" – a question posed, significantly, by the contemporary black British cultural critic, Kobena Mercer – is not, therefore, a rhetorical question (Mercer, 1994). Those who need it tend to require that their historical subjects be national at heart – not only fixed by borders but equally unfragmented and coherent, as stable as the rational post-Enlightenment subjects which postcolonial studies, feminist theory and postmodernism together have revealed as a kind of self-interested, if historically intelligible, modernist western fantasy. Nostalgia for and attachment to the nation are thus connected with regret for the passage of that historical moment when the subjects of history were as yet uncontaminated by the critical apparatus set in motion by decolonization, the women's and other social movements and the gradual, if glacial, democratization of the western academy over the past quarter century (Appleby et al., 1994). As historians of American women in the 1950s have argued, one historically engaged response to such nostalgia is to remind its advocates that the power of her image not withstanding, there never was a June Cleaver [the famous postwar TV mom] – or, rather, that she was a fiction, the invention of a cultural moment which has continued to displace and obscure the material conditions under which such iconography (like that of the nation) emerged (Meyerowitz, 1994). This is not to say that we should disregard the historical "fact" of nation, but rather to suggest that in our attempt to understand its historical significance, we need to pay more attention to the question of who needs it, who manufactures the "need" for it, and whose interests it serves. In this sense, my initial interrogatory, "who needs the nation?" might profitably be imagined as a question of "who can afford to be sanguine about (or oblivious to) needing the nation?" – thus guaranteeing that social class, material dispossession and political disenfranchisement will inform historical narratives about imperial culture.[15] If, as Homi Bhabha claims, "the western metropole must confront its postcolonial history . . . as an indigenous or native narrative internal to its national identity", then this kind of refiguration requires us to ask how – that is, through what kinds of practices – is it possible to practice "British" history so that it does not continue to act as a colonial form of knowledge? (Bhabha, 1997; Cohn 1996)

The fact that arguments about the boundaries of the nation and the integrity of the citizen-subject are increasingly advanced by *social* historians who are simultaneously enmeshed in debates about the merits of *cultural* history/studies is surely significant. The coincidence of debates about empire with debates about the legitimacy of both culture as an object of historical inquiry and the tools used to unpack it (i.e., deconstruction) suggests that History, the Nation, and the category of the Social are being recuperated as endangered species in need of protection from a variety of "others". Susan Pederson, who gave a keynote address on gender and imperial history at the Anglo-American Conference in London in the summer of 1995, constructed just such an identity of interests when she asserted that practitioners of history are, have been, and always will be interested in "political outcomes" and as a result, the kinds of textual analyses performed by feminists and others in the field of gender and cultural history are not finally useful to Historians (capital H). A similar kind of argument, offered as a lament in the context of an essay basically sympathetic to new narrative forms in history-writing, was articulated recently by Dorothy Ross, who claimed that cultural history's contributions are limited because it cannot address what for her represents historians' "real" concern: change over time (Ross, 1995). Nor is this debate limited to the west, as animated discussions of the way subaltern studies has been corrupted into "bhadralok" and "Bankim" studies in India testify (Guha, 1995; Chakravarty, 1995; Guha, 1996). On offer in cultural history, of course, is the promise of new possibilities for "the political narrative", through a set of analytical techniques that juxtaposes social history's commitment to history from the bottom up with a commitment to history from the side in, if you will – this is the turn to the ethnographic to which I alluded at the start, where the ethnographic allows for a vertical rather than an exclusively horizontal vision.[16] Projects concerned with public representation, material culture and historical memory – like Raphael Samuel's *Theatres of Memory*, James Vernon's *Politics and the People*, Judith Walkowitz's *City of Dreadful Delight*, Patrick Joyce's *Democratic Subjects* or Laura Mayhall's work on the Suffragette Fellowship – are good examples of how insights drawn from anthropology can give historical thickness to cultural forms and reshape our notion of the domains of the political, the social and the cultural – as well as challenge our convictions about their separability – in the process (Samuel, 1994; Vernon, 1993; Walkowitz, 1992; Joyce, 1994; Mayhall, 1995). They also interrogate the convention that change over long periods of time is the "real" interest of historians by emphasizing the local and the quotidian (two characteristics of ethnographic work). Despite the fact that it remains largely bounded by traditional conceptions of the nation, hardly touching on imperial culture at all, the success of this kind of scholarship is due in part to the fact that its authors do not insist that one historical technique must displace another, or even that one technique for recovering the past is more properly historical than the other. With the possible exception of Joyce, these authors do not operate as if the Whig interpretation of progressive evolution – and extinction – really obtained (Eley and Nield, 1995). In fact, crucial to their approach is a critique of the very self-fulfilling, liberal narrative of progress that gave rise to, and continues to sustain, the idea of the autonomous, originary nation to begin with. In this sense, in the British context at least, such work threatens the sovereignty of a nation whose very sanctity is, historically and culturally, bound up with Victorian notions of progress, mission, and historical destiny – the very hallmarks of nineteenth imperial ideology itself – because it questions claims about the primacy of temporality that are at the heart of modern historical narrative practices.

As Elizabeth Ermarth has so persuasively argued, these claims appear to be so commonsensical that they continue to masquerade as "a condition of nature" rather than as "a convention and a collective act of faith" – not just among historians, but throughout western culture as well (Ermarth, 1992). Britain is not, therefore, an exceptional case – though, as a French observer has remarked, "no country [is] more consistently bent upon differing from others" than Britain, and England within it (Lowenthal, 1994). The tenacity of the nation in debates about re-making British history signals an historically and culturally specific kind of attachment to the project of linear progress – even as it dramatizes how imperial traditions have shaped that investment and, finally, how and tenuous the stability of "national" culture really is. That these debates occur while a post-Thatcher Tory government tries to negotiate a place in the post-colonial European Union indicates how crucial it is to see imperial and continental histories as equally implicated in the uneven development of "British" history and society.[17] I hasten to add that the aim of such multi-perspectival practices is not identical with liberal multicultural inclusion, which can tend to reinscribe identities in the process of politicizing them. Nor is its end "a more cosmopolitan and sophisticated parochialism" – unless it is a less geographically fixed and, by implication, a less permanently realized version than the kind of parochialism to which we have become accustomed (Goodman, 1994). The kinds of new practices that are being resisted help to make this kind of imaginary possible by unmasking the fictionality of conventional historical narrative and exposing the fictions of an apparently insular "British" culture – by insisting, in other words, that narratives of the nation (like all stories) are never "found" in nature but are always construed by historians for implicit and explicit political purposes and in discrete historical circumstances (Curthoys and Docker, 1996). And yet this remains the intriguing and unsettling paradox of the "new" imperial history and studies: for the work of unmasking, however valuable, can and often still does leave the nation in pride of place, rather than staging it as precarious, unmoored and in the end, finally unrealizable.

It would be fair to say that the model of a performative, rather than a prescriptive, nation is one that has scarcely been explored in any national history.[18] Following Carlo Ginzburg (1976) and Emmanuel Le Roy Ladurie (1974) in the 1970s, there seemed to be a moment when some European historians were willing to recognize the historical precariousness of nation-state formation. But a monograph like Eugen Weber's *Peasants into Frenchmen* (1976) looks now like a kind of one-off production, rather than the beginning of a revisionist trend which took the artificiality of national categories and the coercive power of their normalizing regimes as its point of departure. In the English case, Philip Corrigan and Derek Sayer's *The Great Arch* (1985) – subtitled, significantly, "English state formation as *cultural* revolution" – posited the state itself as an cultural effect in a series of essays which, in retrospect, look not just way ahead of their time, but like a model still waiting to be fully utilized, at least by British historians. The combination of historical analysis and politically engaged skepticism about the naturalness of the modern state which their book enacts represents a model to which we might profitably return, not least because of its emphasis on the state and with it, the nation, as something *always* in the process of *becoming*. Or, to use language that draws as much on Bernard S. Cohn as it does on Greg Dening and Judith Butler, they managed to stage the state as an historically pliable ideal always being performed through repetitive and ritualized acts, but never fully achieved (Dening, 1996; Butler, 1990; Cohn, 1983). Here I want to note that historians of the early modern and early Victorian period have been more interested in exploring how the nation was as such "forged", a phenomenon that suggests how much work is yet to be done to subject the later nineteenth-century state to scrutiny in order to understand that it too was by no means a fait accompli but was also always in the making (Bayly, 1989; Colley, 1992).[19] Yet it is equally important to underscore that the burden of representing fragmentation, diaspora and community-making as operations of nation-building would seem to have fallen disproportionately on ex-colonies and postcolonial nations, the United States included. Significantly, when national history is challenged there, it tends to be by those interested in the anti-citizens of modernity – slaves, African-American freed men and women, white suffragists, Native Americans and, most recently, gays and lesbians – many of whom are said to inhabit, à la George Chauncey's *Gay New York*, a kind of anti-national subculture, *even* (and perhaps especially) when they aspire to national belonging (Chauncey, 1994). Not incidentally, this unequal burden is one of the lingering effects of the kind of asymmetry that is foundational to colonialism and its cultural productions. At the same time, concern about the disciplinary regimes imposed by history is articulated rarely enough, even as interdisciplinary work abounds and threatens, in quite concrete and salutary ways, to remake epistemologies at the heart of the liberal tradition – especially where "discipline" works in opposition to the "playfulness" of subjects when they end up exceeding conventional boundaries. Clearly the politics of who or what is the subject of a "national" history begs the question of how such a subject becomes nationalized, as well as what kind of disciplinary action such a process requires.

I am not sure that I would go as far as Catherine Hall does in calling for Britain to be conceptualized as a "post-nation" – one that is not ethnically pure but "inclusive and culturally diverse" (Hall, 1996; see also Alexander and Mohanty, 1997). This not because there is something inherently destabilizing to civil society in going "beyond the nation", as Partha Chatterjee fears, but rather because I am keenly aware of the persistent operations of "the citizenship machinery" deployed by the contemporary transna-tional state (as I'm sure Hall is as well) (Chatterjee, 1997). Nor would I like to suggest that critics of national history are always or completely impervious to the romance of nation-building that seems to haunt all of the modern disciplines. Historians of women, of blacks and of other "others" have often sought inclusion for their subjects in the narrative of the nation-state – trying to make them, in W.E.B. Dubois' wonderfully ambivalent phrase, "the ward[s] of the nation" (Dubois, 1989). Even Ruth Behar and Deborah Gordon, the feminist anthropologists who recently edited *Women Writing Culture*, ground their attempt to remake the discipline in the hope that the new feminist anthropology will have "no exiles" (Behar and Gordon, 1995). It is admittedly possible to read their call as an attempt to frustrate traditional structures of the nation-state – to argue that no one should have to be an exile in the sense of being prohibited from a place.[20] And yet even this generous reading tends to obscure the question of why critics of the regu-latory power of their own discipline seek to reformulate it as some kind of idealized nation – that is, one with no exiles. Who writes – who even sees – the histories of subjects exiled from the "national body", those refugees (deliberate or otherwise) from national history and its disciplinary regimes, especially before the twentieth century? (Kale, 1994; Malki, 1995; Lavie and Swedenburg, 1996). Feminist historiography, which works at the boundaries of a variety of disciplines, as well as at the intersection of the academy and the community, should be one site for this kind of interroga-tory work. But as Ien Ang has observed, feminism, no less than the discipline of history, "must stop conceiving itself as a nation, a 'natural' political destination for all women, no matter how multi-cultural" (Ang, 1995; Murdolo, 1996). Indeed, the rhetorics of des-tination, of arrival and of home itself have provided "sentimental story lines" not just for women's national imaginaries, but for nation-states operating via transnational capital as well (George, 1996; Ong, 1993; Rafael, 1996). What we need is conceptual work that turns "on a pivot" rather than on the axis of inside/outside – an image which suggests not just a balancing act but the kind of counter-clockwise historicizing maneuver such "subjects" require in an era when national histories, unlike the pivot, seem unwilling or unable to budge (Lewis, 1995).

Why social history and cultural studies must necessarily do battle is, frankly, a puzzlement – except that this is an age when resources are scarce, when all histories can evidently lay claim with equal success to the notion that they are embattled, and when the social darwinist presumptions of the social science disciplines still apparently have some appeal for those who would have the strong triumph over the weak. Read in this context, Sherry Ortner's piece on "Theory in Anthropology since the 1960s" – where she traces the clearly national divisions between American attachment to explanatory frameworks that privilege culture, versus British insis-tence on "society" as the crucial analytical component – suggests that the contest for British history may well be about who should be permitted to write it, and from what ideological perspectives (Ortner, 1984). Clearly this is an age-old battle with historically specific meanings which tell us as much about the political economy of the western academy as they do about the crisis of Britishness, culturally speaking. The brouhaha in Britain over Roger Louis (an American) being chosen as the editor of the new Oxford History of the British Empire is more indication of how easily these (again highly naturalized) nationalistic lines can be drawn in the sand (Sinha, 1997). And yet if we revisit Stuart Hall's equally compelling account of the rise of cultural studies paradigms in Britain, we see that the tensions between culture and the social as analytical premises are not merely lineaments of national dif-ference, but have long and fraught legacies not just inside modern disciplinary practices like history-writing or anthropology, but at the heart of interdisciplinary projects as well (Hall, 1980). The fact that the category of "culture" has traditionally been used to legiti-mate imagined communities either on the move or outside the west (as a substitute for nation-ness, if you will) may in part explain why metropolitan historians are loathe to see that category applied to the center. In many ways, using culture rather than the nation or even the social as a primary historical tool means exoticizing the grand narratives of British history and de-familiarizing the naturalness of its ideological corollary, imperial greatness. Indeed, given its historic relationship to colonialism (Dirks 1992), the analytic of culture may threaten to de-naturalize, if not to corrupt, the apparent coherence and purity of nation-ness of an always already fragmented and multicultural entity like the "United Kingdom" – though cultural studies of the Celtic fringe in opposition to Englishness have not proven much more successful than colonial histories in challenging the presumptive originality of "Britain" and with it, "England" as the heart of the empire, except perhaps to revive the "four nations" impulse in domestic British historiography. This is an exception which is often as frustrating as it is interesting, in so far as it represents more of an additive than a reconstitutive position with regard to the construction of ideas about nation and national cultures (Kearney, 1989; Jeffery, 1996).

That social history is characterized as the strong and cultural history as the weak "historical" approach bears some scrutiny. And the fact that the struggle between the social and the cultural is being played out on the terrain of empire should command our attention no less actively than the flowering of production on empire and imperial culture itself. Although the struggle is often framed as a manichean battle between the empiricists and the deconstructionists – those who believe in coherent nations, subjects, and histories versus those who don't – this is a red herring designed to throw us off the scent of other compelling issues. Chief among these is the fact that modern history-writing (and not just in the west) has historically been a "narrative contract" with the territorially bounded nation-state (Kaviraj, 1993). Prying the nation from that contract is nothing less than a struggle to reorganize and reconstitute the spatial bases of power (Harvey, 1990). Few can escape the struggle over geography, and British history in an age of postcoloniality is no exception. If narratives of geography are at stake in narratives of history (Carr, 1994) then undoing the narrative contract may mean displacing nation-states like Britain from center-stage. It may call for an analytic frame which recognizes that "the imperium at the heart of the nation-state" was "not an entity *sui generis*" (Breckenridge, 1989). It may even require a cultural map which is "all border" as well – especially since the nation itself has historically served as "the ideological alibi of the territorial state" (Boyce Davies, 1994; Appadurai, 1993). This work involves more than just challenging the parameters of "British" history or studies. It means unmasking the complicity of history-writing in patrolling the borders of national identity as well.

Casting the project of an unstable "British" history may well end up letting let the nation in through the back door, though such is not my intention. Such a result may in the last analysis be a testimony to how difficult it is to escape the grasp of national investigative frameworks even when one attempts a highly self-conscious and, hopefully, principled critique of the allure of nation-ness for "British" historians. Admittedly in this paper I offer more of a diagnosis than a prognosis, in part because I think that the question "who needs the nation?" still rings hollow for many. The extent to which we will succeed in displacing the nation from center stage depends in the end on our willingness to take seriously the ramifications of the claim that a nation is never fully realized, but always in-the-making – and to interrogate the ways in which our own narrative strategies may help fetishize one of history's most common explanatory frameworks, if not its most seductive inves-tigative modality. This is, hopefully, a practice worth imagining: for it suggests that one does not have to give up on history in order to interrogate the narrative strategies of its practitioners or to fight for (and about) its unstable meanings.

## Notes

[1] This essay owes much to Bernard S. Cohn, for whose generosity of mind and spirit I have long been grateful. A number of friendly critics–including Nadja Durbach, Rob Gregg, David Goodman, Ian Fletcher, Madhavi Kale, Dane Kennedy, Philippa Levine, Laura Mayhall, Maura O'Connor, Fiona Paisley, Doug Peers, Minnie Sinha, Susan Thorne and Angela Woollacott – have helped to strengthen my arguments, for which I of course bear the final responsibility. Herman Bennett's long-term invest-ment in this piece has made all the difference. I am equally indebted to Peter Marshall's energetic engagements. And finally, I greatly appreciate the feedback I received at presentations for the Australian Historical Association (Melbourne, 1996) and the Workshop on State Formation in Comparative Historical and Cultural Perspectives (Oxford, 1997), espe-cially from Ann Curthoys, Philip Corrigan, Marilyn Lake, Vinay Lal, Derek Sayer, and Sudipta Sen.

[2] Eric Williams, *Capitalism and Slavery* (Chapel Hill: University of North Carolina Press reprint, 1994). See especially Colin Palmer's intro-duction to this edition, where he unearths the critical response to the manuscript before it was accepted for publication, followed by its review history (pp. xi–xxii). Perry Anderson does not cite Williams, though his argument in "Origins of the Present Crisis" echoes much of what Williams had meticulously advanced in *Capitalism and Slavery*. Thomas C. Holt's *The Problem of Freedom: Race, labor and Politics in Jamaica and Britain, 1832–1938* (Baltimore: Johns Hopkins University Press, 1992) is also relevant here.

[3] In this sense it was petit bourgeois as well, though Anderson does not take this up explicitly. See his, "Components of the National Culture", in *English Questions*, pp. 52 and 103. For an instructive colonial take on the question of "national" culture, which was contemporaneous with Anderson's (but to which he does not allude, even in the 1990s reprint), see Frantz Fanon, "On National Culture", in *The Wretched of the Earth*

(Penguin: Harmondsworth, 1967). This chapter is also reprinted in Patrick Williams and Laura Chrisman, eds., *Colonial Discourse and Post-Colonial Theory: A Reader* (New York: Columbia University Press, 1994), pp. 36–52. For evidence of the continued search for explanations about why Britain failed to produce a "native" sociology see José Harris, "Platonism, Positivism and Progressivism: Aspects of British Sociological Thought in the Early Twentieth Century", in Eugenio F. Biagini, ed., *Citizenship and Community: Liberals, Radicals and Collective Identities in the British Isles, 1865–1931* (Cambridge University Press, 1996), pp. 343–60.

[4] For a recent response to the literary turn which engages this phenomenon see Dane Kennedy, "Imperial History and Postcolonial Theory", *Journal of Imperial and Commonwealth History* 24, 3 (September 1996): 345–363. The fact that the linguistic turn and the ethnographic turn are related is often overlooked; for a recent discussion of their historical connections see Sara Maza, "Stories in History: Cultural Narratives in Recent Works in European History", *American Historical Review* 101, 5 (December, 1996): 1497 and ff.

[5] John M. Mackenzie's editorship of the multi-volume series, "Studies in Imperialism", is responsible for much of the wealth of historical material now available on the impact of empire on domestic British culture. See for example his *Imperialism and Popular Culture* (Manchester University Press, 1986) and *Propaganda and Empire: The Manipulation of British Public Opinion, 1880–1960* (Manchester University Press, 1984). Other relevant monographs include Jenny Sharpe, *Allegories of Empire: The Figure of Woman in the Colonial Text* (University of Minnesota Press, 1993); Firdous Azim, *The Colonial Rise of the Novel* (Routledge, 1993); Catherine Hall, *White, Male and Middle Class: Explorations in Feminist History* (Routledge, 1992); Vron Ware, *Beyond the Pale: White Women, Racism and History* (Verso, 1992); Antoinette Burton, *Burdens of History: British Feminists, Indian Women, and Imperial Culture, 1865–1915* (University of North Carolina Press, 1994); Annie E. Coombes, *Reinventing Africa: Museums, Imperial Culture, and Popular Imagination* (Yale, 1994); Mrinalini Sinha, *Colonial Masculinity: The "Manly Englishman" and the "Effeminate Bengali" in the Late Nineteenth Century* (Manchester: Manchester University Press, 1995); and Anne McClintock, *Imperial Leather: Race, Gender and Sexuality in the Colonial Contest (New York: Routledge, 1995).*

[6] Olaudah Equiano was a slave from Benin who purchased his freedom in 1766 and wrote his life story (*The Interesting Narrative of the Life of Olaudah Equiano*) in 1789; Mary Seacole was a Jamaican nurse who served in the Crimean war and wrote an account of it (*The Wonderful Adventures of Mrs. Seacole in Many Lands*); see Paul Edwards and David Dabydeen, eds., *Black Writers in Britain, 1760–1890* (Edinburgh University Press, 1991). For newspaper coverage of the Major government's response to their inclusion in British history texts, see "The 'Betrayal' of Britain's History", *Daily Telegraph*, September 19, 1995; "Heroic Virtues" and "History Fit for (Politically Correct) Heroes", *The Sunday Telegraph*, September 24, 1995. I am grateful to Audrey Matkins for these references.

[7] See Bill Schwarz, ed., *The Expansion of England: Race, Ethnicity and Cultural History* (New York: Routledge, 1996); Catherine Hall's "Histories, Empires and the Post-Colonial Moment", in Iain Chambers and Lidia Curti, eds., *The Post-Colonial Question: Common Skies, Divided Horizons* (New York: Routledge, 1996), pp. 65–77; and P.J. Marshall, *The Cambridge Illustrated History of the British Empire* (Cambridge, 1996). Professor

Marshall agrees with two of the OED's definition of "constitutive" as 1) "having the power of constituting; constructive" and 2) "that which goes to make up; constituent, component", but cannot agree with its third: "that which makes a thing what it is". Private correspondence, 15 September, 1996.

[8] I am grateful to Catherine Hall for pressing this point in conversation; see also her *White, Male and Middle Class*, p. 1 and her "Rethinking Imperial Histories: The Reform Act of 1867", *New Left Review* 208 (1994): 3–29.

[9] See Sinha, *Colonial Masculinity*. For one example of how this false homogenization works to obscure the role of the Celtic fringe in empire see Dipesh Chakrabarty's discussion of how crucial Dundee was in the history of the jute mills in Calcutta; *Rethinking Working-Class History* (Princeton, 1989), chapter 2.

[10] I am aided in these observations by Prasenjit Duara's *Rescuing History from the Nation: Questioning Narratives of Modern China* (University of Chicago Press, 1995).

[11] See Elizabeth D. Ermarth, *Sequel to History: Postmodernism and the Crisis of Representational Time* (Princeton University Press, 1992), pp. 18, 21. She is not concerned with the imperial contexts of modern western discourses but her characterizations of historical convention are extremely useful nonetheless.

[12] I am aided in this observation by Kim F. Hall's reading of Richard Hakluyt in *Things of Darkness: Economies of Race and Gender in Early Modern England* (Ithaca: Cornell University Press, 1995), p. 48.

[13] See for example Harold Perkins' review of José Harris' *Private Lives, Public Spirit: A Social History of Britain, 1870–1914, American Historical Review* 100, 1 (February 1995): 164 and Bruce Kinzer's review of James Vernon's *Politics and the People: A Study in English Political Culture, c. 1815–1867, American Historical Review* 100, 3 (June 1995): 900.

[14] Most recently, Gilroy's *Black Atlantic* has been up held in a review essay by Frederick Cooper as an example of a "transcontinental" study that requires proper historical work to fill in its "gaps". See Cooper, "Race, Ideology, and the Perils of Comparative History", *American Historical Review* 101, 4 (October, 1996): 1129.

[15] Although the exiles I have in mind in this particular formulation (and in this essay in general) are people of color and ex-colonial migrants in Britain, it must also be said that working-class men and women have a differently ambiguous and though equally painful relationship to the nation and its ideological apparatus, the state. As Carolyn Steadman writes so poignantly in her autobiography, *Landscape for a Good Woman* (New Brunswick: Rutgers University Press, 1987), "I think I would be a very different person now if orange juice and milk and dinners at school hadn't told me, in a covert way, that I had a right to exist, was worth something" (p. 122). I am grateful to Nadja Durbach for this citation and for how it compelled me to refigure the question of "who needs the nation?"

[16] I am aided in this conceptualization by Greg Dening's "P 905 .A512 × 100: An Ethnographic Essay", *American Historical Review* 100, 3 (June 1995): 864.

[17] I am grateful to Maura O'Connor for urging me to appreciate this point, and for sharing her essay, "Imagining National Boundaries in the Nineteenth Century: English Travelers, Diplomats and the Making of Italy", paper presented at the North American Conference of British Studies, Chicago, 1996.

[18] Herman Bennett's forthcoming book, *Strategic Conjugality: Race, Ethnicity and Creolization in the Making of Colonial Mexico's African Diaspora* which posits the performative model, is a particularly promising exception.

[19] This is especially challenging, I think, in light of how powerful late-Victorian rhetoric about the long history of the English nation-state was in the wake of more recent Italian and German unification, not to mention the challenges posed by Irish Home Rule and the Indian National Congress.

[20] Thanks to Darlene Hantzis for suggesting this possibility to me.

## References

Alexander, M. Jacqui and Chandra Talpade Mohanty, eds. (1997). *Feminist Genealogies, Colonial Legacies, Democratic Futures.* New York: Routledge.

Allen, Judith A. (1992). "Feminist Critiques of Western Knowledges: Spatial Anxieties in a Provisional Phase?" in K.K. Ruthven, *Beyond the Disciplines: The New Humanities.* Canberra: Papers from the Australian Academy of the Humanities Symposium, pp. 57–77.

Anderson, Perry (1967). "Components of the National Culture" in *English Questions.* London: Verso (1992), pp. 48–104.

———. (1964). "Origins of the Present Crisis" in *English Questions.* London: Verso (1992), pp. 15–47.

Ang, Ien (1995). "I'm a Feminist, But . . . 'Other' Women and Postnational Feminism" in Barbara Caine and Rosemary Pringle, eds., *Transitions: New Australian Feminisms.* New York: St. Martins, pp. 57–73.

Appadurai, Arjun (1996). "Diversity and Disciplinarity as Cultural Artifacts", in Cary Nelson and Dilip Parameshwar Gaonkar, eds., *Disciplinarity and Dissent in Cultural Studies.* New York: Routledge, pp. 23–36.

———. (1993). "The Heart of Whiteness", *Callaloo* 16, 4: 796–807.

Appleby, Joyce, Lynn Hunt and Margaret Jacobs (1994). *Telling the Truth About History.* New York: W.W. Norton.

Azim, Firdous (1993). *The Colonial Rise of the Novel.* New York: Routledge.

Bayly, C.A. (1989) *Imperial Meridian: The British Empire and the World 1780–1830.* London: Longman.

Behar, Ruth and Deborah Gordon, eds. (1995). *Women Writing Culture.* Berkeley: University of California Press.

Bennett, Herman. *Strategic Conjugality: Race, Ethnicity and Creolization in the Making of Colonial Mexico's African Diaspora*, forthcoming.

Bhabha, Homi K. (1997). "Life at the Border: Hybrid Identities of the Present", *New Perspectives Quarterly* 14, 1 (Winter): 30–31.

Boyce Davies, Carole (1994). *Black Women, Writing, and Identity: Migratory Subjects.* London: Routledge.

Breckenridge, Carol (1989). "The Aesthetics and Politics of Colonial Collecting: India at World Fairs", *Comparative Studies in Society and History* 31 (Spring): 195–216.

Brown, Kate (1996). "The Eclipse of History: Japanese America and a Treasure Chest of Forgetting" (with photographs by Gary Oliveira), *Public Culture* 9: 69–92.

Burton, Antoinette (1997). *At the Heart of the Empire: Indians and the Colonial Encounter in Late-Victorian Britain.* Forthcoming, Berkeley: University of California Press.

———. (1994). *Burdens of History: British Feminists, Indian Women and Imperial Culture, 1865–1915.* Chapel Hill: University of North Carolina Press.

Butler, Judith (1992). "Contingent Foundations", in Judith Butler and Joan Scott, eds., *Feminists Theorize the Political.* New York: Routledge, pp. 3–21.

————. (1990). *Gender Trouble.* New York: Routledge.

Carr, Robert (1994). "Crossing the First World/Third World Divides: Testimonial, Transnational Feminisms, and the Postmodern Condition", in Inderpal Grewal and Caren Caplan, eds., *Scattered Hegemonies: Postmodernity and Transnational Feminist Practices.* Minneapolis: University of Minnesota Press, pp. 153–172.

Chakravarty, Anita (1995). "Writing History", *Economic and Political Weekly,* December 23, p. 3320.

Chakrabarty, Dipesh (1989). *Rethinking Working-Class History.* Princeton: Princeton University Press.

Chatterjee, Partha (1997). "Beyond the Nation? Or Within?" *Economic and Political Weekly* (January 4–11): 30–34.

Chauncey, George (1994). *Gay New York: Gender, Urban Culture, and the Making of the Gay Male World, 1880–1940.* New York: Basic Books.

Cohn, Bernard S. (1996). *Colonialism and its Forms of Knowledge: the British in India.* Princeton: Princeton University Press.

————. (1983). "Representing Authority in Victorian India", in Eric Hobsbawm and Terence Ranger, eds., *The Invention of Tradition.* Cambridge University Press, pp. 165–209.

Colley, Linda (1992). *Britons: Forging the Nation, 1707–1837.* New Haven: Yale University Press.

Coombes, Annie E. (1994). *Reinventing Africa: Museums, Imperial Culture, and Popular Imagination.* New Haven: Yale University Press.

Cooper, Frederick (1996). "Race, Ideology, and the Perils of Comparative History", *American Historical Review* 101, 4 (October): 1122–1138.

Corrigan, Philip and Derek Sayer (1985). *The Great Arch: English State Formation as Cultural Revolution.* Oxford: Blackwell.

Curthoys, Ann and John Docker (1996). "Is History Fiction?" *The UTS Review: Cultural Studies and New Writing,* 2, 2 (May): 12–37.

Dening, Greg (1995). "P 905 .A512 × 100: An Ethnographic Essay", *American Historical Review* 100, 3 (June): 854–864.

————. (1996). "The Theatricality of History Making and the Paradoxes of Acting", in *Performances.* Chicago: University of Chicago Press, pp. 103–127.

Dirks, Nicholas B. (1992). *Colonialism and Culture.* Ann Arbor: University of Michigan Press.

Duara, Prasenjit (1995). *Rescuing History from the Nation: Questioning Narratives of Modern China.* Chicago: University of Chicago Press.

Dubois, W.E.B. (1989). *The Souls of Black Folk.* New York: Penguin Books edition.

Edwards, Paul and David Dabydeen, eds. (1991). *Black Writers in Britain, 1760–1890.* Edinburgh: Edinburgh University Press.

Eley, Geoff and Keith Nield (1995). "Starting Over: The Present, The Post-Modern and the Moment of Social History", *Social History* 20: 355–364.

Ermarth, Elizabeth D. (1992). *Sequel to History: Postmodernism and the Crisis of Representational Time.* Princeton: Princeton University Press.

Fanon, Frantz (1967). "On National Culture", in *The Wretched of the Earth.* Harmondsworth: Penguin.

Fryer, Peter (1987). *Staying Power: The History of Black People in Britain.* London: Pluto Press.

Gerzina, Gretchen (1995). *Black London: Life Before Emancipation*. New Brunswick: Rutgers University Press.

George, Rosemary Marangoly (1996). *The Politics of Home: Postcolonial Relocations and Twentieth-Century Fiction*. Cambridge: Cambridge University Press.

Gilroy, Paul (1993). *The Black Atlantic: Modernity and Double Consciousness*. Cambridge: Harvard University Press.

Goodman, David (1994). *Gold Seeking: Victoria and California in the 1850s*. Sydney: Allen and Unwin.

Gregg, Robert and Madhavi Kale. "The Empire and Mr. Thompson: The Making of Indian Princes and the English Working Class", forthcoming in *Economic and Political Weekly*.

Guha, Ramachandra (1996). "Beyond Bhadralok and Bankim Studies", *Economic and Political Weekly*, February 24, pp. 495–496.

————. (1995). "Subaltern and Bhadralok Studies", *Economic and Political Weekly*, August 19, pp. 2057–2058.

Habib, Irfan (1995). "Capitalism in History", *Social Scientist* 23, nos. 7–9 (July–September): 15–31.

Hall, Catherine (1996). "Histories, Empires and the Post-Colonial Moment", in Iain Chambers and Lidia Curti, eds., *The Post-Colonial Question: Common Skies, Divided Horizons*. New York: Routledge, pp. 65–77.

————. (1994). "Rethinking Imperial Histories: The Reform Act of 1867", *New Left Review* 208: 3–29.

————. (1992). *White, Male and Middle Class: Explorations in Feminist History*. London: Routledge.

Hall, Kim F. (1995). *Things of Darkness: Economies of Race and Gender in Early Modern England*. Ithaca: Cornell University Press.

Hall, Stuart (1980). "Cultural Studies: Two Paradigms", in Nicholas B. Dirks, Geoff Eley and Sherry B. Ortner, eds., *Culture/Power/History: A Reader in Contemporary Social Theory*. Princeton: Princeton University, pp. 520–538.

Harris, José (1996). "Platonism, Positivism and Progressivism: Aspects of British Sociological Thought in the Early Twentieth Century", in Eugenio F. Biagini, ed., *Citizenship and Community: Liberals, Radicals and Collective Identities in the British Isles, 1865–1931*. Cambridge University Press, pp. 343–360.

Harvey, David (1990). *The Condition of Postmodernity*. Oxford: Blackwell.

Hesse, Barnor (1993). "Black to Front and Black Again", in Michael Keith and Steve Pile, eds., *Place and the Politics of Identity*. London: Routledge, pp. 162–182.

Holmes, Colin (1988). *John Bull's Island: Immigration and British Society 1871–1971*. London: Macmillan.

Holt, Thomas C. (1992). *The Problem of Freedom: Race, labor and Politics in Jamaica and Britain, 1832–1938*. Baltimore: Johns Hopkins University Press.

Hulme, Peter (1989). "Subversive Archipelagos: Colonial Discourse and the Break-Up of Continental Theory", *Dispositio* 14, 36–38: 1–23.

Jeffery, Keith, ed. (1996). *An Irish empire? Aspects of Ireland and the British Empire*. Manchester: Manchester University Press.

Joyce, Patrick (1994). *Democratic Subjects: The Self and the Social in the Nineteenth Century*. Cambridge University Press.

Kale, Madhavi (1994). "Projecting Identities: Empire and Indentured Labor Migration from India to Trinidad and British Guiana, 1836–1885", in

Peter van der Veer, ed., *Nation and Migration: The Politics of Space in the South Asian Diaspora*. Philadelphia: University of Pennsylvania Press, pp. 73–92.

Kaviraj, Sudipta (1993). "The Imaginary Institution of India", in Partha Chatterjee and Gyanendra Pandey, eds., *Subaltern Studies VII: Writings on South Asian History and Society*. Delhi: Oxford University Press, pp. 1–39.

Kearney, Hugh (1989). *The British Isles: A History of Four Nations*. Cambridge: Cambridge University Press.

Kennedy, Dane (1996). "Imperial History and Postcolonial Theory", *Journal of Imperial and Commonwealth History* 24, 3 (September): 345–363.

Lavie, Smadar and Ted Swedenburg, eds. (1996). *Displacement, Diaspora and Geographies of Identity*. Durham: Duke University Press.

Lewis, Earl (1995). "Turning on a Pivot: Writing African Americans into a History of Overlapping Diasporas", *American Historical Review* 100, 3 (June): 765–787.

Lindeborg, Ruth H. (1994). "The 'Asiatic' and the Boundaries of Victorian Englishness", *Victorian Studies* (Spring): 381–404.

Lowenthal, David (1994). "Identity, Heritage and History", in John R. Gillis, ed., *Commemorations: The Politics of National Identity*. Princeton, pp. 41–73.

Mackenzie, John M. (1986). *Imperialism and Popular Culture*. Manchester University Press.

———. (1995). *Orientalism: History, Theory and the Arts*. Manchester University Press.

———. (1984). *Propaganda and Empire: The Manipulation of British Public Opinion, 1880–1960*. Manchester University Press.

Malki, Liisa H. (1995). *Purity and Exile: Violence, Memory and National Cosmology among the Hutu Refugees in Tanzania*. University of Chicago Press.

Marshall, P.J. (1996). *The Cambridge Illustrated History of the British Empire*. Cambridge: Cambridge University Press.

———. (1993). "No Fatal Impact? The Elusive History of Imperial Britain", *Times Literary Supplement* (March 12), pp. 8–10.

Mayhall, Laura (1995). "Creating the 'Suffragette Spirit': British Feminism and the Historical Imagination", *Women's History Review* 4, 3: 319–344.

Maza, Sara (1996). "Stories in History: Cultural Narratives in Recent Works in European History", *American Historical Review* 101, 5 (December): 1493–1515.

McClintock, Anne (1995). *Imperial Leather: Race, Gender and Sexuality in the Colonial Contest*. New York: Routledge.

Mercer, Kobena (1994). *Welcome to the Jungle: New Positions in Black Cultural Studies*. New York: Routledge.

Meyerowitz, Joanne, ed. (1994). *Not June Cleaver: Women and Gender in Postwar America*. Philadelphia: Temple University Press.

Murdolo, Adele (1996). "Warmth and Unity? Historicizing Racism in the Australian Women's Movement", *Feminist Review* 52 (Spring): 69–86.

O'Connor, Maura (1996). "Imagining National Boundaries in the Nineteenth Century: English Travelers, Diplomats and the Making of Italy", paper presented at the North American Conference of British Studies, Chicago.

Ong, Aiwha (1993). "On the Edges of Empires: Flexible Citizenship among Chinese in Diaspora", *positions* 1, 3: 745–78.

Ortner, Sherry (1984). "Theory in Anthropology since the 1960s", in Nicholas B. Dirks, Geoff Eley and Sherry B. Ortner, eds., *Culture/Power/History: A Reader in Contemporary Social Theory*. Princeton University Press, pp. 372–411.

Parry, Benita (1993). "Overlapping Territories and Intertwined Histories: Edward Said's Postcolonial Cosmopolitanism", in Michael Sprinker, ed., *Edward Said: A Critical Reader*. Oxford: Blackwell, pp. 19–47.

Rafael, Vincente (1996). "Overseas Filipinos and Other Ghostly Presences in the Nation-State", paper presented at the Seminar for Global Studies in Culture, Power and History, Johns Hopkins University, October.

Ross, Dorothy (1995). "Grand Narrative in American Historical Writing", *American Historical Review* 110, 3 (June): 651–677.

Said, Edward (1993). *Culture and Imperialism.* New York: Vintage Books.

Salecl, Renata (1993). "The Fantasy Structure of Nationalist Discourse", *Praxis International* 13, 3 (October): 213–223.

Samuel, Raphael (1994). *Theatres of Memory.* London: Verso.

Schwarz, Bill, ed. (1996). *The Expansion of England: Race, Ethnicity and Cultural History.* New York: Routledge.

Scott, Joan (1992). "Experience", in Judith Butler and Joan Scott, eds., *Feminists Theorize the Political.* New York: Routledge, pp. 22–40.

Sharpe, Jenny (1993). *Allegories of Empire: The Figure of Woman in the Colonial Text.* Minneapolis: University of Minnesota Press.

Sinha, Mrinalini (1995). *Colonial Masculinity: The "Manly Englishman" and the "Effeminate Bengali" in the Late Nineteenth Century.* Manchester: Manchester University Press.

———. (1997). "*Historia Nervosa*; or, Who's Afraid of Colonial-Discourse Analysis", forthcoming in the *Journal of Victorian Culture* 2, 1.

Smith, Anna Marie (1995). *New Right Discourse on Race and Sexuality.* Cambridge University Press.

Steadman, Carolyn (1987). *Landscape for a Good Woman: A Story of Two Lives.* New Brunswick: Rutgers University Press.

Stoler, Ann (1995). *Race and the Education of Desire.* Duke University Press.

——— and Frederick Cooper (1989). "Introduction: Tensions of Empire: Colonial Control and Visions of Rule", *American Ethnologist* 16: 609–621.

Tabili, Laura (1994). *"We Ask for British Justice": Workers and Racial Difference in Late Imperial Britain.* Ithaca: Cornell University Press.

Thompson, E.P. (1993). *Alien Homage: Edward Thompson and Rabindranath Tagore.* Delhi: Oxford University Press.

Trivedi, Harish (1995). *Colonial Transactions: English Literature and India.* New York: St. Martin's Press.

Vernon, James (1993). *Politics and the People: A Study in English Political Culture, c. 1815–1867.* Cambridge University Press.

Visram, Rozina (1986). *Ayahs, Lascars and Princes.* London: Pluto Press, 1986.

Viswanathan, Gauri (1991). "Raymond Williams and British Colonialism", *The Yale Journal of Criticism* 4, 2: 47–67.

Ware, Vron (1992). *Beyond the Pale: White Women, Racism and History.* London: Verso.

Walkowitz, Judith (1992). *City of Dreadful Delight: Narratives of Sexual Danger in Late-Victorian London.* Chicago: University of Chicago Press.

Williams, Eric (1994). *Capitalism and Slavery*. Chapel Hill: University of
     North Carolina Press reprint.
Williams, Patrick and Laura Chrisman, eds. (1994). *Colonial Discourse and
     Post-Colonial Theory: A Reader*. New York: Columbia University Press.
Wilson, Kathleen (1995). "Citizenship, Empire and Modernity in the
     English Provinces, c. 1720–1790", *Eighteenth Century Studies* 29, 1:
     69–96.

# The Peculiarities of the English State

## G. E. AYLMER

**Abstract** This article explores the extent of distinctiveness and of similarity between the English and other comparable states, in an historical context. The author ranges widely in space and time. He finds likenesses as well as differences between England and such other polities both near and far as Scotland, Denmark, France and Japan. In accounting for English distinctiveness, more emphasis is put on geography, climate and ethos than on more conventional political and economic factors.

## I

Is there anything to be explained? Every country's history is different from that of every other country; it therefore follows that no two "States" can be identical. And it may well be that the differences between the English state and the other states of Christian Europe whether Catholic, Protestant or Eastern Orthodox were not at any time of more significance than the differences between the various continental states themselves. Moreover the divergences among them may have been insignificant compared to those between any European states and those of the non-Christian world: the great land empires and the smaller units of Asia and the Middle East, the pre-Columban political entities of the Americas, the pre-colonial states of sub-Saharan Africa, and so on.

In order to test such broad generalisations as these, the historian and the social scientist need to agree on some minimum definitions. No doubt a whole book, let alone a single article could be devoted to this and nothing else. For my present purposes what is proposed in a recent introductory sociological text seems generally adequate. According to Hall and Ikenberry, a State can be defined as: (1) requiring a set of institutions with its own personnel, including the means of violence and coercion; (2) these being at the centre (metaphorically rather than physically) of a geographically bounded territory: and (3) enjoying a monopoly of rule-making within (that is, over the whole of) this territory.[1]

In relation to those over whom a state rules, this might be reformulated as follows. (a) The state provides protection against external and internal enemies: invasion and subversion. (b) It offers protection to persons and property, according to some normative set of values and legal code for dealing with crimes and disputes. (c) The state's role is inevitably to some extent also positive in cultural terms: it may indoctrinate, inculcate, or at a minimum merely provide a kind of protective covering for dominant groups or classes to do this within its boundaries. (d) Its other modern functions, in such areas as education, health, housing, welfare, transport and communications, and planning, have grown enormously during the last 100–150 years, though some of them have origins much further back in time. (e) In order to carry on all these activities, the state needs its subjects to provide services and/or tribute in kind or in money, often known as taxation. A pithy alternative summary was offered by V. H. Galbraith, an eminent medieval administrative historian of the last generation. In his view the state has three basic functions: (i) financial, (ii) judicial, and (iii) general administrative, including security.[2]

Obviously these definitions could be elaborated, refined and improved upon, both by other historians and by social scientists. I hope, however, that they convey enough of the essentials to be used as a set of simple criteria of statehood in the discussion which follows.

## II

What are the features of English history which might *a priori* lead us to wonder whether the English state might have been, conceivably still is, in some meaningful sense peculiar and distinctive, possibly even unique? All of them are obvious to the point of being self-evident, although some – as we shall see – are more debatable than others. To begin with, there is an extraordinarily long-lasting definition of what formed the territorial unit under a single sovereign power.

From the hegemony of the Wessex kings in the 9th–10th centuries "England" has comprised much what it does today. Wales was subjugated by stages between the 11th and 13th centuries, although not constitutionally and judicially amalgamated until somewhat later. The only internal land frontier of any consequence was the border with Scotland, which itself remained remarkably little changed for many centuries before its final disappearance as a state frontier in 1603: a rough and ready ethnic-cultural dividing line it still of course remains. In spite of successful invasions (by Danes and Normans), and dynastic changes (effected by Lancastrians, Yorkists, Tudors, Orangists) the boundaries of England as a territorial entity and the unity of the English state were very little affected. The Norman Conquest had been followed not only by a massive internal transformation but by the start of a long period of involvement in France, through links successively with Normandy, Anjou and Gascony and eventual attempts to conquer the whole country and unify the two crowns. While it would be arbitrary, if not downright absurd, to treat this whole phase (1066–1450) as an aberration, it will none the less be argued later in this article that the modem English state owes more to its ultimately unsuccessful ending than to any of its periodic more "glorious" successes. By 1603 there were no internal political frontiers, not merely within southern Britain but throughout the whole of the British Isles. In that year Scotland and England were united dynastically although, except for the brief republican forced union of 1652–1660, they formed a kind of "dual monarchy" until the legislative and fiscal (but even then not judicial) union of 1707. Wales had been finally integrated with England in the 16th century, while the English conquest of Ireland was also brought to a victorious conclusion in 1603. For practical purposes this may be called "final" in that, although there were to be hard-fought, unsuccessful wars of liberation in 1641–52 and again in 1689–93, rule by and from England was not to be ended until the early 20th century, and then over only 26 of the 32 countries of Ireland. Moreover the administrative boundaries inside England (of countries and parishes) were to be altered remarkably little from the 12th to the 19th century.

Which other European states could challenge such long-lasting territorial unity? In Spain the *reconquista* was not complete, even if we overlook the Moorish sub-kingdom of Granada, until the 13th century. Even then the degree of political as opposed to cultural distinctiveness between the realms of Aragon and of Castile much exceeded those within England and Wales. Until the dynastic union of 1479 the relationship was more like that of England and Scotland, while from that date until the Bourbon reforms of the 18th century it was comparable to that between England and Scotland from 1603 to 1707. And, as we shall see, within Iberia there were other contrasts too with England, and nearer parallels with the British Isles as a whole. At the other end of Europe, the boundaries of the Scandinavian kingdoms have certainly varied too much until modem times for any parallel to be valid. The Danish nucleus perhaps comes nearest to having had a kind of territorial stability since the Viking era, at times with, at others without Norway and/or Sweden.[3] Even setting aside the Union of Kalmar (1380–1520) – a sort of Danish *imperium* over all Scandinavia – Denmark continued to include what is now the southern Swedish province of Scania until 1660.

In this, as in most other respects, the most obvious parallel to investigate is of course with Britain's immediate southern neighbour. The *Ile de France* heartland around Paris has indeed been a political entity since Frankish times. If temporarily merged in the much larger Carolingian Empire (itself covering more or less the same geographical extent as the original European Economic Community of the 1950s–60s), its separate identity is clear again from the 10th century. But outside the north-central region, what constituted "France", has changed with bewildering frequency over the centuries, on its maritime as well as its landward borders. One has only to enumerate, in a clockwise direction, Normandy, Flanders, Burgundy, Savoy, Provence, Languedoc, Roussillon-Navarre, Gascony, Britanny, to see that the concept of "natural frontiers" on the Rhine, the Alps, the Mediterranean, the Pyrenees, and the Atlantic (the "hexagon" of post-Gaullist technological times) has been an abstraction more often than a reality. This has been true however it has been formulated by whichever French rulers – monarchical, Jacobin, Bonapartist or republican. And it is of limited use in understanding the detailed course of French history and of the French state's relations with its neighbours, whether these have been sovereign or subordinate. None the less, as a unitary monarchy ruling over an extended territory, France affords the least artificial historic parallel. The area and population under the direct control of the French kings often exceeded those of England (without the rest of the British Isles).

England's northern neighbour, the kingdom of Scotland provides another superficially plausible comparison. Scotland became a state, as we have defined this, considerably later than England, at earliest by the 11th century.[4] Apart from the abortive attempts at conquest by the English during the 13th and 14th centuries, this state can be said to have had an independent existence until 1603 and a quasiautonomous one until 1707. Paradoxically, in spite of providing the royal house (Stuart, then Hanoverian) which was to rule and then reign in a united Britain, it seems idle to deny that Scotland was swallowed up in an anglo-centric Britain, instead of England being absorbed into a polycentric one. As to the Scottish state from the later Middle Ages to the 17th century, we shall come later to assess its likenesses and differences with England. A large part of medieval and modern "British" history can be seen as a process of conquest and forcible anglicisation, extending of course to Ireland as well as to Wales and Scotland.

We should look briefly at other parts of continental Europe, if only to discard possible comparisons. It is evident at once that with the Netherlands, Germany, central Europe, the Balkans, the Italian peninsula, no sustained historical parallel exists. This is not of course to deny that, over shorter timespans there are extremely instructive comparisons to be drawn with (for example) Sweden under the Vasas, the Hohenzollern state in Brandenburg-Prussia, even with republican Venice and the United Provinces of the northern Netherlands. But this is not what is at issue here. We should,

I venture to suggest, have to go far outside the polities of Christian Europe, to an island (or strictly an archipelago) kingdom on the other side of the world, to find a closer parallel. I am not competent to measure the likenesses and differences, over a thousand years or more, between Japan and England: but at this level of generality that might well be where one would have to begin.[5] Other Far Eastern countries with long continuing territorial definition and distinctive national characteristics include Korea and Vietnam, besides China itself, some of whose peculiarities will be mentioned below.

## III

A great measure of linguistic unity, or in part of involuntary uniformity, is another feature of English distinctiveness. The southern-midland variant of "middle English" established a dominance from the 14th century: and out of this modern English has developed. Give or take regional accents and variations in usage and vocabulary, this came to extend well beyond the limits of the English state, taking in the upper social levels in Wales, the inhabitants of the Pale (or eastern coastal core) of the English lordship in Ireland, and widening areas of lowland and eastern Scotland. The Cornish language disappeared during the 16th century; the Gaelic tongues of Wales, Ireland and Scotland have none of them vanished, but all suffered in varying measure and over different periods of time the pressures of hegemonic English cultural nationalism. In the case of Ireland, from the Cromwellian reconquest until the later 19th century, the English might not unfairly be said to have practised a kind of linguistic ethnicide, as in the highlands of Scotland after 1745. For many centuries Latin remained the common language of the church, law, administration and scholarship, and it continued to be a common written language after the vernaculars had overtaken it as the spoken languages in different countries. England was a special case, in that besides this there was always a vernacular literature. The royal family and ruling elite spoke Norman-French from 1066 until the 14th century, when English triumphed over all its rivals, except legal and learned Latin. So by the 15th century at latest it had become the language of noble and courtly as well as plebeian life. Moreover there were no linguistic barriers within the realm of the English crown, except for the Celtic-speaking parts of Wales, the rest of Ireland and the highland and island zones of Scotland not being under English rule until the 17th century or later. This is in marked contrast to the Spanish kingdoms where, even if we set aside the totally different Basque language along the north coast, Catalan was more different from

Castilian than was Aragonese, and at least as much so as Portuguese. Even within the kingdom of France, as late as the 16th–18th centuries, the differences in the case of the south and parts of the west (in the areas of Provencal, Occitan, and even more so Breton) far exceeded those within England (Wales being, in this respect, broadly comparable to Britanny).

The case with Germany and Italy is, to some extent, the inverse of this. Until relatively recent times the areas inhabited by German and Italian speakers was far more extensive than the boundaries of any single state in the respective countries. The possible exceptions to this might be found briefly under the Ottonian or Hohenstaufen dynasties, although even then it does not appear that linguistic and political boundaries truly coincided. The post-Tartar period in Russian history reveals the Muscovite nucleus gradually extending to become the Great Russian state and empire, with its language and culture dominant over a vast area and numerous other peoples, as both was the case in the late Tsarist period of the 18th to very early 20th centuries, and has been in the Soviet Union since 1917. If there is a parallel to be found here, it would not be with the nuclear states of western Europe but with the Portuguese, Spanish, British and French overseas empires of the 16th to 20th centuries and their respective linguistic legacies in the Americas, southern Asia and Africa. The history of China presents yet another different relationship between language and the state. Both the historic Chinese Empire under its successive dynasties and the People's Republic of today have been held together partly by the unity of the written language, originating in north China and extending over a much larger extent of territory than has been true of any single spoken type of Chinese. Again I suspect that any closer parallel would be with Japan, despite its language too being ideographic, largely borrowed from China, with a native syllabic but not alphabetic form.[6]

Whether ethnically the English state has been more unitary than others is a harder question to answer, but fortunately perhaps a less important one. The distribution of differing blood groups in different parts of Britain may reflect the relative density of the survival either of the aboriginal stone-age inhabitants or that of the pre-Roman invaders, or of later Celtic and Romano-British elements, alternatively of Anglo-Saxon and then Danish invaders; but in any case it seems unlikely to tell us anything worthwhile about political developments. The influence of more modem immigration, from religious and racial persecution in parts of mainland Europe (16th to 20th centuries), may have been socially and culturally positive. That from Ireland back into Britain during the 19th and 20th centuries, and that from the Caribbean, Africa and Asia in our own time, may on the contrary have strengthened English nationalism through a heightened sense of distinctiveness. Members of these communities have generally shared the worst employment opportunities at the bottom of society, while the Irish like the Highland Scots were disproportionately well represented in the British armies which conquered India and much of Africa during the 19th century. The genetic significance of all this, let alone its political consequences which follow from that, may be left to dispute among biological scientists. Their bearing on the English state is too tenuous to be pursued.[7]

Two great thinkers of the past, Aristotle and Montesquieu, believed that the temperature zone in which countries were situated strongly affected their culture and politics. Since we now know that climate is not determined solely, or always even primarily by latitude, we would have to reformulate this. Is a mild, generally damp climate, seldom experiencing prolonged extreme of heat or cold, peculiar to England? Obviously not. The nearest regions to southern Britain climatically speaking are eastern Ireland, northwest France, the south island of New Zealand and British Columbia in western Canada. Historical geographers may make what they can of this, a wholly unfashionable line of argument today. Many readers will ascribe its very mention to some eccentricity on the author's part. It may, however, be unwise to discard explanations solely because they are out of fashion. Clearly being an island off the Atlantic coast of Europe and in the path of the Gulf Stream has been an underlying necessary cause of almost everything else in English and British history. Unfortunately, like other "first causes", by explaining everything, it is so general that alone it explains no individual aspect of the country's history. Yet it would be perverse to deny the importance of geography, and England's consequent relative freedom from invasion and land warfare. Moreover, when internal peace was disrupted by civil wars, in the 12th, 15th and 17th centuries, the country was not systematically ravaged by comparison with the experiences of continental Europe. England has not experienced this since William the Conqueror's "harrying of the North". And that in turn may help to explain the evident widespread reluctance to resort to arms for the settlement of intractable disputes – dynastic in 15th, constitutional in the 17th century. Even William Blake, no lackey of the Establishment, could write in what is now his best-known poem of "England's green and pleasant land".

## IV

It may be fruitful to look more closely at the political, legal, fiscal, administrative features of the English state and at the relations in general of government and society, if we are to assess where local peculiarities end and uniqueness begins.

With territorial and linguistic unity went a large measure of legal uniformity. Much of the crucial development in English common law came between the Norman Conquest and the reign of Edward I. With its later modifications this legal system was in turn to be imposed in Wales and Ireland, as well as in England's colonial empire overseas. Its origins and growth made it distinct from the Roman-law influenced judicial systems which were dominant in much of continental Europe and even in Scotland. It is difficult to define the distinctiveness of the common law without getting enmeshed in a maze of legal technicalities. Among its salient characteristics have been the jury system, the use of oral evidence not written depositions, the absence of judicial torture in ordinary civil and criminal cases, and the accused's right to silence. The common law was founded, and still rests, on a curious combination of parliamentary statutes and judge-made decisions. Its substance has sometimes seemed to outsiders to be more concerned with the protection of property than with the reciprocal rights and duties of persons, although most lawyers and legal historians would reject that generalisation.

A vital sector of state formation is that where internal and external politics interact. Here particular interest attaches to that interval of time between England's final expulsion from the European mainland (second loss of Normandy, 1450; loss of Calais 1558), and the subsequent establishment of a peacetime standing army, some units of which came to be stationed inside England – a gradual process extending from the later 17th century right through to the Victorian Age. By contrast the primacy of the navy in English strategy and military planning, and the way in which seapower was regarded by the politically dominant classes from Elizabethan times onwards is indeed something very distinctive. This is not for a moment to deny, or to wish to overlook the fact that Spain. France, latterly Germany and even Russia have had an important maritime dimension to their respective histories, and have possessed navies which have been politically and militarily important. Even so, to find a parallel to the significance of seapower in English history and the state's longlasting concern with naval strength, we should have to make comparisons with classical Athens, Viking Scandinavia, Venice, Portugal and the Dutch Republic, and perhaps here too with Japan – all of them states whose respective histories have in other respects been so different from that of England. From the 9th to 11th centuries it was usually the Vikings, Danes and Normans who were able to choose when and where to invade England from the sea. Later this was to change dramatically. In the wars which were fought primarily on land by armies, for the conquest of Scotland and Ireland, the successive invasions of France, and the much more recent campaigns in India and Africa, the use of seapower gave at least some flexibility to the deployment of England's land forces. This has been demonstrated in the case of the Lancastrians (by the early 15th century), and might be traceable further back still.[8] By the later 17th century concentration on naval strength, rather than on a land army, does seem to have made the English propertied classes readier to tax themselves as well as their compatriots than would otherwise have been the case.[9] Even so, by the 18th century the shift in emphasis from land tax to customs and excise shows them to have been readier to tax other people than themselves: by then the growth of internal and foreign trade (to which we shall return), accompanied by the extraordinary growth of London besides that of lesser towns and cities, made the potential of such revenues much greater that it would otherwise have been.

Can anything more positive be said if we turn to the institutions and personnel of government and in particular to the relations between centre and locality? As an initial hypothesis we might put forward the concept formulated by an American student of English medieval government early in the 20th century: "self-government by the King's command".[10] But this tells us little, taken in isolation, indeed could be said to obscure as much as to illuminate.

It would be an exaggeration to say that the respective royal households (or *curiae*) and their offshoots – the law and revenue institutions, in all the post-Roman successor states of Christian Europe were drawn from a single model. We do, however, know that the Anglo-Saxon kings were influenced by the Carolingians. English administrative methods show an undoubted sophistication from the 11th century both pre-and post-Conquest (use of writs, collection of danegeld, Domesday Book), while the central courts (Exchequer foremost) begin to produce a continuous series of records from the later 12th-early 13th century onwards surpassed in this only by the Papacy. Yet it would be misleading to describe this as distinctive, let alone as unique. Looking forward in time, from the 14th to the 17th century, it is worth attempting a further comparison between England and France. The two royal households were much of a size, the English one if anything proportionately a little more the expensive of the two. On the other hand, if we add together the staffs of judicial, financial and secretarial bodies at the centre and those at the regional and local levels, office-holders were far and away more numerous in France than in England, even allowing for its being about four times more populous and five or six times greater in land area. The most striking point of difference is the English crown's lack of a local bureaucracy, the absence of full-time paid functionaries stationed around the country. Until the end of the 17th and into the 18th century, the customs staff in the seaports together with bailiffs and receivers on royal estates were almost the only exceptions. In matters pertaining to defence, justice, revenue and general administration, much more was done at the local level in England by landowners under only loose central direction. Because, as officials, they were part-time and semi-amateur, we should not of course assume that such local magistrates were disinterested.

Scotland, by contrast, was more lightly governed, more thinly administered, than England, even allowing for its population being only about one fifth the size and its total national wealth an even smaller fraction than that. Scottish central government and court ceremonial were less formal, elaborate and hierarchical than English. The last separate monarch of Scotland, James VI (who reigned in his own right from the 1580s until he moved south as James I in 1603) was among the most effective in her history. James bears comparison with any of the other rulers in post-Renaissance, post-Reformation Europe. Yet the political, fiscal and judicial grasp of the state remained more tenuous than in England, the power of the nobility proportionately greater in the lowland as well as in the highland zone.[11]

One central institution, although intermittent and not in continuous session until the end of the 17th century, demands special attention. The English parliament grew concurrently with the various assemblies, estates generals, and parliaments elsewhere in Europe, between the 13th and 15th centuries. In one important respect its composition was unusual, subject to correction I think unique: the representatives of the lesser nobility (numerically much the larger part of the second estate of the realm) sat with the representatives of the third estate, the citizens and burgesses, not with the prelates and lay peers in the more prestigious upper house. As time passed, more and more boroughs came to be represented, not by genuine townsmen but by gentry landowners, who comprised the great majority of the Commons' membership from the 16th to the early or mid-19th century and perhaps for an even longer span of time than that. It took many generations for the House of Commons to establish its modem predominance: indeed historians are still arguing over when this came about. That the gentry element in its membership was crucial in this process would not, I hope, be considered controversial. There were other distinctive features too: the concept of *plena potestas* and of representation of communities (not of a numerical electorate), whereby the knights of the shire and those sent by the cities and boroughs were held to bind all the inhabitants of their respective communities.

This meant that everyone in the realm was obliged to obey laws and to pay taxes which had been duly voted in parliament, whether or not they themselves had any share in electing these representatives. Naturally there is far more to English parliamentary history than this; but if our concern is to identify what is distinctive, this is more important than the judicial, counselling or broadly political brokerage aspects of parliament. The concept was of course to be taken to absurd lengths with the theory of "virtual representation", which was used in the 18th century to justify taxing the American colonists, and from the end of the 18th to the early 20th century against those adult inhabitants of Great Britain itself who did not have the vote.

Furthermore there were no semi-independent regions or provinces in England below the national level. True, there were regional governments in Wales and the English Marcher counties and in the north of England (though excluding Lancashire and Cheshire) for part of the 16th and 17th centuries. And the same could be said of Ireland from the 14th century on, though that was surely an imperial extension of the English state, not part of its internal structure. But the Councils in Wales and the Marches of Wales and in the North could not legislate, or vote and levy taxes. Private jurisdiction, both lay and ecclesiastical, all but disappears from the 16th century. The English county was never a devolved unit of government with its own lawmaking or taxing powers. It was, however, an essential unit for the enforcement of laws and for the assessment and collection of taxes. Moreover, once the sheriff had ceased to be a royal official appointed from the centre by the king, those in charge at the local level were all natives of that locality, as royal servants temporary, amateur and part-time.[12]

Superficially the most substantial exception to this is provided by the Assize Judges. Most of England (not, however, Wales, Cheshire or Middlesex) was divided into six circuits. Two judges from the three common-law courts at Westminster rode round each of the circuits twice yearly, to hear and determine major criminal cases. Normally the judges were sent to counties of which they were not themselves natives; but the assizes were largely stage-managed by locals, notably the sheriff, and most of the cases brought to trial were heard before juries composed of local inhabitants. So this long-lasting system could be said to mark the legal supremacy of the central state, but not a centralised system of judicial administration.[13]

This is not to deny that there were some subordinate officials, such as Clerks of the Peace, who show slightly more resemblance to Weberian bureaucrats. They remain extremely few and hard to seek at least until the growth of the excise staff in the 18th century. More characteristic were the Deputy Lieutenants, nominated by the respective Lords Lieutenant with the Crown enjoying only a negative veto over their choice. In this symbiotic relationship between the English monarchy and the governing classes, both at the local level and in parliament, lay the essence of what must be meant by that phrase, "self-government by the king's command", if it is taken to mean anything at all. Nor must the relationship be romanticised. With inadequate monarchs or over-ambitious subjects it could turn sour and even break down, as it did at times in the 15th and again in the mid-17th century. The balance changed first at the national level, with the emergence by the 18th century (and after a series of violent oscillations between 1629 and 1689) of what has been called parliamentary monarchy: it might equally well be called ministerial government. At the local level the system began to break down with the massive changes in social and economic life, in particular growing urbanization, during the 18th and 19th centuries. So we see the old amateurism giving way to a new professionalism: the inspectorate, the police, the inland revenue and officials of local government. Historically the nearest parallel seems to be in the 17th century with Sweden. The Swedish territories across the Baltic (in Finland, Latvia-Esthonia. East Prussia and north Gemany) offer a further parallel of a kind with the non-English parts of the British Isles and, if this is not too far-fetched, with England's colonial empire overseas. But this comparison can only be sustained sensibly over a period of about a century. Similarities with the Netherlands, France and Prussia are visible in particular sectors, but not over the whole relationship of government and society and not for long spans of time.

In the later 15th century the Lancastrian jurist, Sir John Fortescue, drew a famous distinction between what he called a *dominium politicurn et regale* and *a dominium regale*. Some historians would prefer to use the terms mixed and absolute monarchy. He put France firmly in the latter category, England in the former. Whether this was wishful thinking, the political equivalent of an optical illusion, or the perception of a genuine and important truth, remains open to debate.[14] The English state was by no means invariably and in all major respects weaker than the French state, even though it may have been at its most peculiar, its most nearly unique in early modem times (15th to 18th, but most especially 16th and 17th centuries). As against this, some of the features which I have emphasised in this article might be expected to have exercised their influence over a much longer period of time, indeed throughout the country's history. Neither in early modem times, nor indeed in any epoch of history should we assume an identification between limited, legally bounded or "constitutional"

monarchy and a weak state. Likewise with the opposite, there is no
necessary correlation between absolutism and a strong state. The
most important single variable is the relative ability of the central
government (which means the Crown until the 18th century) to
harness national resources in a successful partnership with the
dominant social groups or classes.

## V

So far I have said little about the more strictly economic history of
England, and how this might be connected with the formulation of
the English state. It is hardly necessary to be a complete economic
determinist to suppose that such a connection is likely to exist. The
argument is over the form which it has assumed and the extent of
English exceptionalism. According to Alan Macfarlane, England
had a money economy and a free market in land by the 14th
century if not considerably earlier than that.[15] We do not need to get
involved here in the disagreements between Macfarlane and his
critics, over his use of the word "peasant", to signify strictly subsistence agriculture, and collective or familial ownership and transmission of property: if taken literally, this would exclude England
from having been a peasant society, not merely since the 13th or
14th century but probably since the Neolithic period or earlier.[16] We
do, however, need to consider more carefully what kind of state we
might expect to find in different possible types of pre-industrial
society. Two of the key questions are: (i) how did the leisured upper
class extract wealth from the labouring and producing population?,
and (ii) where did the crown, *alias* the government or the state come
into this? The means of extraction are basically threefold: by labour
services, by supplies in kind, and by money payment in the form of
tribute, rent or tax. In turn the central apparatus of government,
whether consisting of a single royal despot or some much larger,
more impersonal machine of state, can either collect its share direct
from the producers, or via the class of chiefs, lords, seigneurs, etc.
A national system of taxation is surely impossible without a certain
level of economic development. That might provide one criterion of
comparison between the political entities of medieval Europe (11th
to 13th centuries).

It is not clear whether Macfarlane sees England as having been
literally unique in these respects and, if so, over what approximate
span of time. Other histories of European agriculture suggest a
more varied regional pattern with marked chronological divergences.[17] Unless we are thinking only of forced exactions, of the
agricultural surplus as a kind of tribute, then the existence of
cities and towns whose inhabitants do not grow their own food or

produce the materials for their own clothing, shelter, heating and light, must imply some system of marketing, at a very minimum of local trade between the rural and urban sectors. Whether the marketing of the agricultural surplus is undertaken by the land-lords exploiting their demesnes, or by their tenants (or indeed by small, independent freeholders), is found to have varied even within the same country over a relatively short period of time. Many of us were taught long ago to study the legislation of Edward I if we wished to see the genesis of a market in land itself, the treatment of real property as a form of private capital. To argue from this that as much of the land of England was as easily saleable and heritable in the 13th-14th centuries as it was three or four hundred years later frankly strains credibility. Nor is it plausible to see England as having been unique in this respect.

With regard both to the marketing of agricultural produce and to the development of a market in land itself, arguments over the word "peasant" do not seem to get us much further. Possible events between the 1350s and 80s (Statute of Labourers, Poll Taxes, Great *alias* Peasants Revolt) could be said to reveal a state machine operating on behalf, or at the behest of selfish rural capitalists: or perhaps the uprising of 1381 is misnamed. By contrast, the restrictions on enclosure if it involved conversion and depopulation, and other "controls" limiting the freedom of the market, which were in force between the late 15th and early 17th century, should then lead us to the slightly paradoxical conclusion that the state had become warier of a free market, less pro-capitalist than it had been two hundred years before. Perhaps this is a case of a quasi-absolutist state, holding the balance between potentially conflicting social classes. But if that is a meaningful view of certain historical situations, it is definitely not one unique to England.

As with other monocausal explanations of historical change, Macfarlane's thesis either tells us too much to be credible or too little to be helpful. That is not to deny the originality and importance of his work and the best of his insights: nor are all the propositions involved in fact peculiar to him.[18]

## VI

Turning from structure and policies to what we may call the ethos of the state, its relationship to nationhood or nationality is one of the key variables. State and nation are not identical, yet England was (whether or not it still is) what is often called a nation-state. In the last twenty years historians have become much more aware of myth, ritual, symbol and spectacle as forms of evidence about the past. In this respect, what we might today interpret as symbols of

English nationality turn out to be very recent creations or mental constructions: for example the monarchy and the royal family as they are currently perceived, the police – unarmed, friendly and helpful, Big Ben, the Union Jack, the National Anthem. Likewise most have a strong element of myth about them, and a class specific character. For earlier equivalents we might search in Shakespeare's history plays, the demonstrations of popular xenophobia on May Day in London, the near paranoiac hostility to Rome and Spain (later to France), and sometimes to the Irish. We might need to take account too of the post Reformation English Church, simultaneously Erastian, Catholic and Protestant, with its magnificent Cranmerian liturgy and (anyway from the Wesleys' time on) some fine hymn tunes. Even so, this church has always been a source of division as well as unity. Domestic architecture and gardens, related to the climate and to the absence of excessive population pressure on the ground area, may be more enduring – as well as attractive – features of Englishness.

Thinking of intellectual and cultural influences, are we more struck by differences or similarities if we turn from the structure and policies of the English state to what may loosely be called its ethos, setting it in a European context? Much obviously was shared in common: Christianity which pre-dated political unification: the classical heritage of Greece and Rome (though with less reception of Roman law than over much of the continental mainland): the growth of wealth and population and attendant cultural blossoming of the 11th to 13th centuries, as well as the less attractive features such as the Crusades and the persecution of heretics: the demographic and epidemic crises of the 14th century and consequent commercial contraction: the intellectual movements known as the Renaissance or rise of Humanism, and then the Reformation with its attendant religious conflicts: the growing interaction with the non-European world: the beginnings of what is not unfairly called the Scientific Revolution. All of these were European phenomena in which England shared. Perhaps English development in general was stimulated by the presence of near neighbours, which in their various ways were both similar and different. By contrast, such societies as China, India and Muscovy for long stretches of their histories existed, and developed in so far as they did so, in relative isolation.

It is, however, striking that in the cases of overseas expansion and scientific advance England was behind other parts of Europe in the 15th and 16th centuries but by the 17th century had moved to the vanguard in both. Historians continue to dispute, more in the case of science than that of transoceanic trade and settlement, how far this was the consequence of social and political development. By

the later 17th century the ideals of polite society, where France set
the tone and the pace, had imparted a superficial uniformity of
manners and dress. Yet constitutionally the two states had moved
further apart. There was another different too, of both economic
and political significance. The English landlord class (peers and
greater gentry) spent more time on their country estates and took a
keener interest in agricultural improvement than their opposite
numbers in France (and probably in several other countries too).
Whether this was more a cause or an effect of political and constitutional differences again remains open to debate. I would myself
suggest interaction, with influences both ways. The commercialisation of agriculture, the growth of an internal consumer market as
well as of foreign trade, the expansion of the urban sector, the
profits of empire, the consequences of war – all help to explain the
beginnings of industrialization in the late 18th–early 19th century.
It is hard to imagine any historian who would wish to argue that it
was the nature of the English (by then the British) state which
brought about these technological and economic changes and so
produced what has been called "the first industrial nation".
Equally, it can scarcely be denied, save by the most perverse, that
the kind of state which had emerged in England, by no means
always through a smooth and peaceable process of evolution, at
least did not prevent that process.[19] There are indeed suggestions
in some recent studies that the political forms, reflecting the dominant social ethos, may have hindered rather than have helped the
development of industrial (as opposed to commercial) capitalism.[20]
This is not to be confused with the reasons which have been put
forward, to do with the social ethos and cultural norms, explaining
Britain's relative if not absolute technological and economic decline
in the last hundred years or so. This decline, which is by any
standards in danger of becoming an over-explained phenomenon,
can only in the most indirect way be related to the causes of
Britain's "rise" or emergence as temporarily dominant in the 18th
and 19th centuries.

The historian tries to describe and explain what has happened
and, in the course of doing so, may touch upon what did not
happen. But to start describing and explaining in any detail what
might have happened but did not, is something in which historians
indulge at their peril, where fantasy all too easily takes over. The
social scientist searches for regularities in human affairs, and
hence for general tendencies, whether or not these are called
"laws": the historian is stuck with uniqueness, with the peculiarity
of every human event and situation, but we must not assume from
this that every event and situation is peculiar or unique in the same
sense. Enough has been said here to suggest that the English state

has been an unusual historical phenomenon: we should not for that reason regard it as somehow being exempt from analysis, not subject to the same influences as all other human institutions including the state.

## Notes

[1] John A. Hall & G. John Ikenberry, *The State* (Open University Press, Milton Keynes. 1989), ch. 1.

[2] V. H. Galbraith, *An introduction to the use of the public records* (Oxford. 1934): *Studies in the Public Records* (London, 1948); and my own notes on his lectures, delivered in Oxford 1948–9.

[3] The early history of Denmark is ill-served by works in English, except as part of the Vikings' story. See, however, W. Glyn Jones *Denmark* (London, 1970) ch. 1; S. P. Oakley, *The Story of Denmark* (London, 1972), chs II–V.

[4] G. W. S. Barrow, *The Kingdom of the Scots: Government. Church and Society from the eleventh to the fourteenth century* (London. 1973); A. A. M. Duncan, *Scotland: The Making of the Kingdom* (Edinburgh, 1975).

[5] G. B. Sansom, *A Short History of Japan (from the earliest times to 1867–8)*, (3 vols. Stanford, Cal. 1958–63: repr. Folkestone, Kent, 1978); J. Livingston, J. Moore and F. Oldfather (eds.), *The Japan Reader*, vol. 1, *Imperial Japan 1800–1945* (New York. 1973: Harmondsworth. 1976): and, for a contrasting interpretation, Barrington Moore, Jr., *Social Origins of Dictatorship and Democracy: Lord and Peasant in the Making of the Modern World* (New York, 1966: Harmondsworth, 1967, 1969, 1973), ch. V. esp. ss. 1–2. The imperial throne's eclipse by the shogunate from the 14th to 19th centuries A.D. and the periodic existence of two rival royal courts, is one obvious, major difference from medieval and early modem England.

[6] H. Goad, *Language in Histoy* (Harmondsworth, 1958); M. T. Clanchy. *From Memory to Written Record: England 1066–1307* (London, 1979).

[7] C. D. Darlington, *The Evolution of Man and Society* (New York. 1969: London, 1971).

[8] *Navy Record Society*. vol. 123 (1982) The Navy of the Lancastrian Kings', Ed. Susan Rose; G. L. Harris led.), *Henry V: The Practice of Kingship* (Oxford, 1985), esp. C. T. Allmand's ch., p. 127.

[9] For one of the most recent and accomplished works on this, see John Brewer, *Sinews of Power: War, money and the English state 1688–1763* (London, 1989).

[10] A. B. White, *Self-Gooernment by the King's Command* (Minneapolis, 1933).

[11] Jenny Wormald, *Court, Mrk and community: Scotland 1470–1625* (New History of Scotland, vol.4. London, 1981); "James VI and I: two kings or one?", *History*, 68 (1983).

[12] I am grateful to James Campbell, Michael Clanchy, Edmund Fryde, Alan Harding, Gerald Harriss and Patrick Wormald and other participants in successive annual discussion groups on The Formation of the English State', for helping to provide the medieval background to this article, and to Victor Kieman and Derek Sayer for many helpful suggestions. Naturally none of them should be held responsible for my mistakes.

[13] See J. S. Cockburn, *A History of English Assizes 1558–1714* (Cambridge, 1972), chs. 1 & 2, pp. 1–48. Monmouth was included from 1543; London was also excluded.

[14] H. G. Koenigsberger, *Politicians and Virtuosk Essays in Early-Modern History* (London, 1981), ch. 1, originally his Inaugural Lecture at King's College, London in 1975.

[15] A. Macfarlane, *Origins of English Individualism* (Oxford, 1978).

[16] For Macfarlane's replies to some of his critics, see the essays and articles reprinted in *The Culture of capitalism* (Oxford, 1987).

[17] *Cambridge Economic History of Europe*, I, *The Agrarian Life of the Middle Ages*, ed. M. M. Postan (2nd edn. Cambridge. 1966): B. H. Slicher van Bath, *Agrarian History of Western Europe A.D. 500–1850* (London, 1963).

[18] The following may also fairly be considered celebrants of late medievalearly modem agrarian capitalism: A. R. Bridbury, in *Economic Growth: England in the Later Middle Ages* (London, 1962): Eric Kerridge in *The Agricultural Revolution* (London, 1967), and *The Farmers of Old England* (London, 1973); E. L. Jones in *The European Miracle: Environments, economies and geopolitics in the history of Europe and Asia* (Cambridge. 1981).

[19] On ethos and state formation, see P. Corrigan and D. Sayer, *The Great Arch: English State Formation as Cultural Revolution* (Oxford, 1985).

[20] P. Cain and A. G. Hopkins, "Gentlemanly Capitalism and British Overseas Expansion . . .", Parts 1 and 2, *Econ. Hist. Rev.*, 2nd ser., XL (1987), but note also M. J. Daunton. " 'Gentlemanly Capitalism' and British Industry, 1820–1914". *Past and Present*, 122 (1989), and J. Raven, "British History and the Enterprise Culture", *ibid.*, 123 (1989). Clearly the debate continues.

# *Engla Lond:* the Making of an Allegiance

## PATRICK WORMALD

**Abstract** Taking as its starting-point, Philip Abrams' celebrated perception (1988) that the state is an "ideological artefact . . . historically constructed", this essay seeks an explanation of the unrivalled longevity and durability of the English state in the fact that it was the first European political organism to exploit with complete success the model of obligatory coherence supplied by the Old Testament in the history of Israel and its relations with its Maker. This model had been applied to the early history of Anglo-Saxon Christianity by the Venerable Bede (731) in a work of unexampled literary power. The Anglo-Saxons' subsequent experience of the near-obliteration of their Christian polity by pagan Vikings lent the Biblical and Bedan messages a particular point. King Alfred and his dynasty were thus provided with an ideological blueprint which meant that their otherwise by no means unusual early medieval hegemony could command the allegiance of potential dissidents in a way that none of its counterparts were ultimately able to do.

## I Introductory

On 3rd October 1065, two hundred thegns from Yorkshire and the rest of Northumbria burst into Earl Tostig's hall at York. The earl was not at home, but they slaughtered his bodyguard and plundered his treasury. As their new earl they chose Morcar, brother of Earl Edwin of Mercia (and Lady Godiva's grandson). He led them south, attracting recruits from the north-east Midlands. At Oxford they met Earl Harold, emissary of King Edward the Confessor and Tostig's brother. A blazingly angry king was per-suaded that Tostig had to go, and Morcar was acknowledged Earl of Northumbria. The drama was soon swallowed up by the yet more spectacular events of the next year. Eight years later, the East Saxon and Thuringian nobles, with a large rural following, confronted the Emperor Henry IV at his palace of Goslar. Their demands ranged from the return of unjustly confiscated lands and the demolition of royal castles, through more regular royal residence in Saxony and more attention to Saxon advice, to better behaviour by Henry towards his wife. The rebels sought justice in the royal court, but they also had their own candidates for the crown and may even have contemplated Henry's assassination. The reverberations of this crisis lasted not for one year but for fifty; and Karl Leyser indeed traces them as far as the rise of "the backwoodsmen of Brandenburg-Prussia".[1]

English and German revolts have a lot in common. These were the most powerful – certainly the most vigorously oppressive – monarchies of later-eleventh-century Europe. Both rebellions sound a note of local resentment against intrusions by agents of royal government, including increased taxes and unacceptable judgements. Tostig was a southerner, scion of the earls of Wessex. Whatever his particular oppressions, there is good reason to think that his general offence was insufficient regard for traditional modes of northern government. Henry IV was the third emperor of the Salian (Rhineland) dynasty. His offence was to exercise his full regalities in the Saxon core of the Reich built by the Saxon Ottonians, though not himself a Saxon, and mostly in the interests of those who were not. The obvious difference between the revolts is that the Saxons pushed fellow-Saxons for the throne itself, whereas the Northumbrians merely asked the king to confirm their choice of a new earl who was not one of themselves. There is another difference however. To a real extent, 1073 sounded the knell of effective kingship in much of medieval Germany. Royal rule in the North was thereafter marginal. 1065 was the first in a string of northern English risings stretching on for 506 years. It was perhaps the only one that could claim success. Yet no more than later ones did it seriously threaten the integrity of the English state. Few English kings frequently visited the North, but their northern rule was not marginal. Why did such similar and contemporary movements have such contrasting long-term significance?

From the perspective of orthodox national historiography in the nineteenth and twentieth centuries, it was of course England that was the model and Germany the anomaly. Most European societies from Ireland to Bohemia had their histories written at one time or another as if their happy destiny (or tragic lack of it) was to emerge as states like England. Sociologists and Marxists, on the other hand, have become accustomed to regard England as exceptional, albeit fruitfully so (Sayer 1992); and historians are increasingly aware that it is indeed England's that is the *Sonderweg* (Aylmer 1990). Many modem European states first appear in roughly familiar form at some point before the year 1000. Nearly all were broken up by external assault or internal collapse, to be reconstituted only at a later (sometimes *very* much later) date. Only England has retained more or less the same form more or less continuously from its origins to the present. Whatever the present day realities, history does *not* suggest that this is in any way the "natural" form of human political association. The Ancient World organized itself for twelve hundred years either in outsize empires (such as China remains) or in city-states. Most Europeans spent most of the present millenium in city states or princely lordships. But English *histoire événementielle*, to adapt Braudel's classic distinction, has all the qualities of *la longue durée*. And readers of this journal have recently been reminded of two more peculiarities of English historical experience. In the first place, the English state was brought into, and kept in, being by a bafflingly elementary governmental apparatus (Aylmer 1990: 99–102). At no point in its pre-modern history was it sustained by anything like the cadre of professional government servants considered indispensable by states elsewhere. The mechanics of the English state have a Heath Robinsonian air: if viable, then distinctly hand-to-mouth. Second, this structure was almost as precocious in its aggression as in its generation. By the second century of the present millenium. it was persuaded of its mission to bring the blessings of civilization of its neighbours (Gillingham 1992). The English were far from the only western society to indulge expansionist appetites at this date; but they were the only ones that did so at the expense of peoples who were ostensibly Christian (Bartlett 1993).[2]

If "the only plausible alternative to taking the state for granted is to understand it as historically constructed" (Abrams 1988: 80), then historical investigation of the makings of England, the proto-type state, is, as the editors of this journal have vigorously de-monstrated (Corrigan and Sayer 1985), particularly apt. And if the state is "the opium of the citizen", an "ideological project", an "exercise in legitimation", "a bid to elicit support for or tolerance of the insupportable and intolerable" (Abrams 1988: 82, 76), then one that contrived to germinate and flower with the most unso-phisticated coercive mechanisms is likely to prove the most appo-site illustration. If, in addition, its formative ideology was considered fit for export some centuries before the date commonly allotted to the genesis of European imperialism, then its potency must have been even more prodigious than is yet appreciated. This paper seeks to show that an ideologically engendered allegiance is indeed the key to the antiquity and resilience of the English state. The argument comes in two halves. The first reviews factors that seem *un*likely to be decisive, because each was more or less avail-able to hegemonies elsewhere in Europe that did not survive. These factors are all, as it happens, structural. The second switches attention to ideological considerations. Here, it can at last be argued that there was something about England that had no European parallel.

## II Structures of Allegiance

### (i) Roman legacies

It is one symptom of the success with which the makers of English allegiance did their work, that historians have tended to detect it a lot earlier than they have any warrant to. English "unification" is a *leitmotif* of Sir Frank Stenton's book (1971), just as if there was an English identity waiting from the outset to be realized. The agency favoured for this purpose by Stenton and many others was the "*Bretwalda*". I have elsewhere given my reasons for rejecting this approach (Wormald 1983). The most important point, briefly, is that the word "*Bretwalda*" (if it is a word and not, as now suggested, a scribal slip) should mean "Britain-ruler", thus corresponding with the Latin title "*Rex Britanniae*" also found in a solitary if better attested instance. But that expression serves mainly to point a contrast between Britain and the rest of the West. It is a simple matter of fact that what had once been Roman *Britannia* was not again brought under unitary rule for over half a millenium, whereas the areas corresponding to *Italia, Hispania* and *Gallia* were marshalled comparatively quickly, if temporarily, into single hegemonies. Whatever it was that made up these Roman "provincial" identities, most historians would now agree that they had a place in the consciousness of sub-Roman aristocracies, and that, transmitted mainly through bishops, they did more to facilitate formation of the relevant political units than any residual ethnicity among western Europe's new masters, Goths, Franks and Lombards.[3] Britain's post-Roman history, however, was much more traumatic than that of most parts of the western Empire. A "*Britannia*" where neither the Church nor Romance speech survived was bound to be a more shadowy lure than "*Hispania*" or even "*Gallia*". A closer analogy with British conditions might lie in un-Roman Ireland, which certainly knew the idea of "men of Ireland", and even of a "kingship of Ireland" (focused on the remarkable prehistoric complex at Tara (Byrne 1973: 48–69. 254–74; O'Corráin 1978: 5–8). The chief exponents of these ideas were the "*filid*", descendants of Caesar's Druids and equivalents to Indian brahmin. Such classes are not given to self-effacement. The almost total silence of Anglo-Saxon sources as to any such element in their own society is therefore eloquent. In any case, the Kingship of Tara was an object of competition, not a basis for consensus. "Britain-rule" likewise promoted "unification" only in the anthropologist's sense that conflict can concentrate a society's mind on common political targets (Gluckman 1973: 27–53).

The formation of an English state was favoured neither by any imported Anglo-Saxon *wirgefühl* (to exploit a regrettably indispensable German coinage) nor by structures of coherence inherited from Roman Britain. Obsession with "unification" has in fact blinded historians to the most significant political development in the first centuries of the Anglo-Saxon period. A number, perhaps a lot, of new political entities came into existence (Campbell 1979; Bassett 1989; Yorke 1990; Kirby 1991). These constitute the "Heptarchy" long supposed to have preceded a single Anglo-Saxon Kingdom. If its lesser ingredients proved ephemeral, some of medium or larger size were sufficiently robust to linger long past their days of glory. Kent tenaciously withstood incorporation in Greater Mercia for two hundred years after the death of Æthelberht, its one great king. East Anglia put up the same sort of fight: unlike Kent, it eventually threw off Mercian rule without at the same time succumbing to West Saxon lordship. The growth of these loyalties is the English counterpart to the formation of the new Gothic or Frankish ethnicities on the continent, and they deserve more attention than they can receive here. Let it suffice to say that, if they are not even the "premature" states of Professor Strayer's model (1970: 3.9), they amount to much more than the groups given coherence by "family", "lord", "locality" or "dominant religion" which are his sole alternatives to states of more familiar type. The point for present purposes is that the stubborn refusal of the Northumbrian, Mercian, East Anglian or West Saxon kingdoms to submit to each other unanswerably rebuts the view that "England" was proceeding "logically" towards "unification". The considered reaction of St Cuthberht's community to the Viking invasion of Northumbria was to swear in one of the invaders as king using Cuthberht's relics.[4] There was considerably less in "England's" early history to indicate its future emergence than in that of comparable European states. No early Anglo-Saxon king so much as *claimed* to be "King of the English".

## (ii) Carolingian expedients

The first to do so was Æthelstan, grandson of King Alfred, in 928.[5] He ruled a realm comprising most of those by then increasingly inclined (as we shall see) to call themselves "English". The English kingdom is, along with the Carolingian realm that many nowadays see as its prototype, one of the two characterized by Professor Strayer's classic essay as "premature". His reasoning is implicitly that they did not meet his four criteria of "political units persisting in time and fixed in space, development of permanent impersonal institutions, agreement on the need for authority which can give final judgements, and acceptance of the idea that this authority should receive the basic loyalty of its subjects" (Strayer 1970: 14. 5–10). Whether either kingdom actually failed to meet any of these criteria is a distinctly open question.[6] My concern here is mainly with the fourth.

Some historians of the early English kingdom dwell on the image of a "kingdom divided against itself". To deny the relevance at this stage of England's history of what it is convenient to call "local" sentiments would be absurd. But it is not clear that it would be much *more* absurd in the tenth and eleventh centuries than at many later stages. The mould of the earlier politics naturally took time to break. When King Alfred's nephew sought Viking help in battling with his cousin for the crown, his fellow-casualties in defeat (902) included a "Byhrtsige son of the Ætheling Beornoth", who looks suspiciously like a member of the old Mercian dynasty (*Sax. Chron.*: vol. I, 92–5; *EHD*: vol. I, 207–8). Use of such scandalous allies to political ends has exact parallels among the Carolingians. in Ottonian Germany and in Ireland (Nelson 1991: 84, 111, 119; Gillingham 1971: 8; Smyth 1977: 129–53). An ambition to resurrect a Mercian kingdom is no surprise at this date, That the Archbishop of York was among those in Northumbria who backed Eric Bloodaxe in the mid-tenth century is likewise no more than one expects in a society with no tradition whatsoever of rule from the south (Whitelock 1959). Another misleading phrase beloved of Anglo-Saxon historians is "The Reconquest of the Danelaw". The overrunning of northern and eastern England by Alfred's descendants in the first half of the tenth century was a *conquest* of areas that West Saxon kings never ruled before.

Yet, given the background, it is striking how little disaffection followed. For one thing, the political and legal significance of Danish settlement (in whatever numbers) is not all that has often been supposed. Sveinn of Denmark, when marching south against Æthelred the Unready in 1014, ordered no looting until he crossed Watling St into "English" England. This at best tells us what he thought of the possibility of fifth columns. It is equally likely that he was sparing sensibilities in north-east Midland families with no cause to love Æthelred: one was that of the Northumbrian earl executed in 1006, and it was from this family that Sveinn's son Cnut took his first wife.[7] Of the three 1065 Northumbrian ringleaders, one had an English name, and two had English patronymics. The historians who stress that the "great earldoms" of pre-1066 England shared the names and some of the boundaries of ninth-century kingdoms can often be found pursing their lips in the next paragraph over the fact that the house of Godwine earl of Wessex was taking control of so many of them. The second point seriously qualifies the significance of the first.[8] Regional loyalties are manifest above all (almost only, in fact) when succession to the crown was at stake. In 924, 955–9, 975–8 and 1035–40, Mercians and West Saxons took opposite sides in succession disputes between brothers or half-brothers. But these were struggles for a single throne within a single West Saxon) dynasty. Mercian nobles hoped to enthrone princes who would gratefully favour local interests: they did not seek a king for themselves, still less one of themselves.

The 1065 Northumbrians wanted a more responsive earl, not independence. The crucial fact of late Anglo-Saxon politics is that it was factional. There was intense competition for central power and its local benefits. The anthropological insight cited earlier has yet more relevance: court manoeuvre legitimated that court's role (cf. Leyser 1979: 28–31).

Allegiance to the new kingdom of "the English" was underwritten by oath. English freemen were expected to pledge their loyalty at the age of twelve from (at least) the early-eleventh century to the latefifteenth, and perhaps (if we believe William of Malmesbury, as we should, and Blackstone's *Commentary*, as we might) from the lateninth to the early-eighteenth. Four points about this oath are particularly germane to the present argument.[9] In the first place, swearing of the oath was associated, from very early on and quite possibly from Alfred's time, with simultaneous enrolment in a tithing or frankpledge, which meant taking responsibility (including financial responsibility) for lawful behaviour by one's community as a condition of one's legal rights as a free man. Second, an elastic conception of a "king's enemy" soon, and again perhaps from the outset, stretched the meaning of disloyalty to cover the more serious of conventional crimes against the community, especially theft: thus, "felony", a word that in Old French means breach of faith with a lord, acquired by the late-twelfth century its classical Common Law sense of murder, arson, rape and robbery, as well as treason proper. Third, oaths of strikingly similar type were sworn to ninth-century Carolingian kings. Fourth, and arising from the Carolingian dimension, there is a probable connection between this oath and that sworn to William the Conqueror in 1086 at Salisbury. "All men of property in England, whosoever men they were, bowed to him and became his men, and swore loyal oaths to him against all others" (*Sax. Chron.*: vol. I, 217; *EHD*: vol. II, 168; cf. "Florence": vol. II, 19). An older generation of historians had no doubt of the importance of the 1086 oath for medieval English law's basic principle that loyalty to the king came first (Blackstone 1979: vol. I, 354–6; Pollock and Maitland 1968: vol. I, 298–300). The best modem discussion (Kienast 1952: 15–33, 173–204, 234–9, also 325, 329, 330) makes a near incontrovertible case that the Salisbury oath was not the vaunted "feudal" homage, but a loyalty oath of all substantial subjects in the Carolingian tradition. Kienast's puzzle was that he could find few traces of a Carolingianstyle oath in Normandy. He contemplated the possibility of Anglo-Saxon transmission but did not pursue it. In the light of the evidence that a general oath of wide scope was central to early English politics and government, his problem evaporates.

It is scarcely necessary to labour the significance of the fact that overriding allegiance was expected of its subjects from the very cradle of the English state. Nor will it escape notice that such an oath neatly links loyalty to a ruler with the security of ruling-class property. Potential disaffection in the aristocracy could be defused by the consideration that to threaten the power of the one implicitly threatened the wealth of the other. This introduces a second structural buttress of ruling-class solidarity: the common interests born of its widely scattered property holdings. One of the major advances in understanding of the Carolingian empire in the last half-century has been the isolation of its "*Reichsadel*" (Tellenbach 1957; Airlie 1985). These hugely rich aristocrats were almost as much the beneficiaries of the Carolingian expansion as the dynasty itself, and they had a corresponding commitment to its survival. Powerful kingship over extended areas offered their best chance of keeping their many estates together, even if backing their chosen candidate from among the warring dynasty held out the prospect of increasing their holdings at the expense of their rivals. Research has now begun to zoom in on their English equivalents (Fleming 1991: Clarke 1994). The first lesson here is how misleading it is to identify holders of the great Anglo-Saxon earldoms exclusively with interests in the territories of their ostensible rule. The houses of Godwine or Leofric may have been territorially based in Wessex and Mercia respectively, but they would have had no wish to see any ancient loyalties manifested in reborn kingdoms. A second lesson is that what applies to them is not much less true of at least twenty-five lesser lights in the Old English elite. That Norman barons had widely scattered lands whereas those of their Anglo-Saxon predecessors were territorially concentrated is simply a myth. On the contrary, it seems increasingly possible that the conquests of Alfred's descendants were accompanied by the same sort of widespread displacement of existing interests in favour of an incoming elite as 1066 itself.[10] The English had a new nobility in the early-tenth century as much as in the later-eleventh.

In England as in Francia, the existence of a *Reichsadel* has major significance for understanding how and why such states proved "premature". The historian's usual recourse is to "localism": "Royal officials tended to become leaders of autonomous local communities rather than agents of central authority" (Strayer 1970: 14). This raises awkward issues of egg and chicken, if not horse and cart. What induced acquisitive noblemen to abandon further-flung interests for more confined, if also more concentrated, power? In 887–8, with the Carolingian line in temporary abeyance, east Francia fell to one of illegitimate birth: while new dynasties, *Reichsadel* all, established themselves in Italy, Provence, Burgundy, Lorraine and northern France. The account of this development by a near-contemporary chronicler is highly pertinent: "the kingdoms which had been under [Frankish] rule broke apart, and each one settled on creating a king from its own guts: not that there were lacking persons worthy of empire by noble birth, courage and wisdom, but because none was sufficiently raised above the rest to make them willing to submit to his authority" (Regino of Prüm 1890: 278; James 1982: 178). With the final extinction of the Carolingians exactly a century later, Hugh Capet, count of Paris and great-nephew of the 887–8 north-western claimant, became king of France. His dynasty would be the eventual makers of France. But their ascendancy began by marking a precipitate decline in the power of French royalty. They were not resisted like the Salians in Saxony: merely ignored. Accepting the accession of non-Carolingian magnates asked a lot of other magnates, who might well prefer their own qualifications for the job. The bids of 887–8 simply set off emulative bids elsewhere. Localization gathered momentum once under way. Authority gained at the expense of accepted rule was itself vulnerable. The two processes familiar to medievalists in the French phrases, "*naissance des principautés territoriales*" and "*dislocation du pagus*", were interconnected. Structures in France and Italy which had survived the barbarian invasions and the coming of Carolingian power, notably the county, simply ceased to exist.[11] Ruling-class allegiance to established power in the early Middle Ages was surprisingly stable. But when competitive rivalries went beyond influencing the throne to occupying it, collapse became progressive.

Set against the pattern of the dissolution of Carolingian power, the end of the ancient royal line of Wessex with the Confessor's death should have been the moment of truth for the English kingdom. There are several parallels between the accession of Harold, Edward's senior earl, and that of Hugh Capet. One is the unsurprising fact that Harold's enthronement left Earls Edwin and Morcar with mixed feelings. Quite apart from the longer and more distinguished history of their own house, Harold might be expected to restore his brother to the northern earldom. So the sainted Bishop Wulfstan of Worcester spent spring 1066 performing one of his see's customary functions, persuading northerners to come into line (William of Malmesbury 1928: 22–3; cf. Whitelock 1959: 73–6). The signs are that he succeeded. Though Edwin and Morcar were not at Hastings, their Uncle Leofric was. He was abbot of all the monasteries most closely linked with the Mercian comital house; and he so far forgot his priestly status that he caught a fatal illness on campaign that was arguably a euphemism for a more violent misfortune (Barlow 1979: 56–7,60). Nonetheless, we may choose to think that Harold's dynasty would have become as unpopular as the Salians in Germany, and eventually as marginal as the Capetians in France. If we *so* choose, we may go on to invoke what is often adduced as the key to the survival of England as a unified state, 1066 itself (cf. Strayer 1970: 14–15). There is obvious sense in the proposition that the Norman baronage, for all its proverbial turbulence, had a newcomer's instinct for solidarity in a potentially hostile environment, *so* counter-balancing the inherent centrifuge of any early medieval elite. The trouble with this line is what it does not explain. The Conquest's immediate effect was to install a French-speaking ruling-class from a part of the world where the appartus of state power was evanescent. How was this class persuaded to accept a style of government which was in effect that of the kingdom acquired north of the Channel, and definitely not that of the kingdom left behind south of it?[12] Montesquieu and Tocqueville might not have been able to draw their contrasts between England and the *Ancien Régime* had the Normans succeeded in imposing their imported political culture. Why indeed did they so soon come to think of themselves as English? The Norman Conquest cannot have been the *making*, even if it was the saving, of England. England, as its name implies, was made already.[13]

The logic of similarities between Carolingian and English regimes is for all that inescapable. Structural allegiance did not guarantee the permanence of such hegemonies. Early medieval kingdoms could not live by oaths alone. If the kingdom of the English proved uniquely viable, the clue has got to lie where its history *contrasts* with that of its neighbours. Such a clue may be found where the ideas endorsed at the start of this paper would teach us to seek it. "Politically organized subjection" can work in a relatively unregimented society – or perhaps any society – only if it commands the assent of most of those who might otherwise successfully resist it. That it can do only by convincing them that their common interests are *not* "illusory". In the early medieval West, it was truer than ever that a state was an "ideological artefact" or in the end nothing.

### III Ideologies of Allegiance

(i) "Englishness" and its Origins

The argument can recommence where it has just been left. It is an ineluctable if startling fact that the words *"Engla-Lond"* and *"Englisc"* were being used in the eleventh century very much as "England" and "English" are used today. Popular speech was normally called "English". Cnut made law as *"ealles englalandes cyning"* for *"eall Englaland"* according to *"Engla lage"* (*Laws* 1925:

154–5. 174–5, 204–7). In a grant to Horton Abbey, the Confessor was "*Englalandes cyncg*", a title the more striking for the fact that the charter was modelled on one issued by a ninth-century "*West-saxna cyning*". Two eleventh-century leases were witnessed by thegns of Worcestershire, "both *Englisce* and Danish" (Robertson 1056: CXX, XI, XCIV. CII).[14] This is more than eleventh-century "offcialese". The same vocabulary is instinctive for the *Anglo-Saxon Chronicle* in all its versions and phases: "some thought that it would be great folly to join battle because in the two armies were most of what was noblest in *Ængla landa*"; "it was hateful to almost all to fight against men of their own *cynnes*, because there was little else that was worth anything apart from *Englisce* on either side" (*Sax. Chron.*: 175, 181: *EHD*: vol. II. 119, 125). The *Chroniclers* themselves might not unreasonably be suspected of voicing establishment attitudes. So it is instructive to find the homilist Ælfric (a man, it is true, with a Winchester education) writing of the Romano-British martyr, St Alban, that "the murderous persecution of the wicked emperor came to *engla lande*" (Ælfric 1881–5: vol. I, 414–15): thus early in its history was the English upper-class given to confusing the identities of "England" and "Britain". Nor was this cast of mind a recent growth. Already in the mid-ninth century, a Mercian royal charter was drawing an implied contrast between "riders of English race or foreigners (*Angelcynnes monna & ældeo-digra*)"; while a Kentish nobleman was expressing the hope that his testamentary dispositions would retain validity "as long as baptism in the *Angelcynnes* island" (Birch 1885–99: 488–9; Harmer 1910: X). The Mercians were admittedly "Angles" in the sense that this was their continental tribal affiliation according to Bede (*Hist. Ecl.* 1969: 50–1). But the men of Kent were by the same token "Jutes". It seems, then, that the West *Saxon* Alfred was drawing on common usage when resorting to "*englisc*" in his bid to resurrect intellectual standards among all "*Angelcynn*" (Alfred 1967: 4–7).

How is the emergence of such a well-established ethnicity to be explained, given that it had so little political basis until the first half of the tenth century? We have already seen that nearly all the "peoples" of early medieval Europe were relatively recent formations. One way in which new ethnicities were developed was by the manufacture of a common history. Irish identity (presumably not entirely new when first committed to writing) was vested in an extraordinarily elaborate cycle of myth about successive waves of Ireland's invaders (O'Rahilly 1946). Gregory of Tours, the late-sixth-century bishop of Roman aristocratic descent who wrote about Franks with mingled awe and disgust, taught them that their achievements were God's reward for the conversion of their first great king, Clovis, to Catholic orthodoxy (Thorpe 1975; Wallace-

Hadrill 1962). The early-eighth-century *Liber Historiae Francorum*, written by a Frank for Franks, further boosted their image with a Trojan origin that put them on a par with Rome, and a confrontation with Roman taxmen from which they emerged bloodied but unbowed (Gerberding 1987: 3. 159–74). The tenth-century Saxons went at least part of the way in this direction. Their descent was from Alexander's Macedonians; had not the Greeks beaten the Trojans (Leyser 1968: 29)? When it came to extending rule over other peoples with their own traditions, the most successful hegemonies of early medieval Europe began by playing on the common fear of a common enemy – preferably an infidel who thereby posed an even greater threat to the common interests and values of the potentially disaffected than the new hegemony itself. Carolingians could claim to be rescuing the Christians of Gaul from advancing Islam. The Lechfeld triumph of the Ottonians freed German believers from the pagan Magyars. For the purposes of such ideological posturing, a more inviting role-model than Greeks or Trojans was Gods original Chosen Race of Israel, itself a tribal and warrior people, and with a very special relationship to the God of Battles. Letters of admonition and liturgies were by the seventh century identifying Franks and their kings with Israel (Wallace-Hadrill 1971: 48–50). By the ninth, the ideals of Rome and Israel had merged into the concept of a Christian Empire of all those under Carolingian rule, whether or not they thought themselves Franks. For one apologist, Bishop Agobard of Lyons, its resonance was Pauline: "there is no gentile and jew, circumcision and prepuce, barbarian and Scythian, *Aquitainian and Lombard, Burgundian and Alaman*, slave and free, but all in Christ and Christ in all" (Agobard 1889: 159).

What goes for oaths or *Reichsadel* evidently applies too to most of the Barbarian West's "ideological artefacts". "Frankish", "Saxon", even "Irish" identities did not suffice to join together what other pressures were putting asunder. One can see why. Franks might be a holy *gens*; but for two centuries yet, the cultivated inhabitants of southern Gaul confined the term to the "barbarians" of the North (Werner 1970). "Aquitainian and Lombard, Burgundian and Alaman" were no more the same things than "circumcized and prepuced". Specifically Saxon ambitions faced the same problem: while the very success of the later diffusion of *Deutsch* as an ethnic badge would far outreach any medieval organizational grasp. The Learned Class that fostered the notion of the "Men of Ireland" also preserved the terminology of Ireland's prehistoric polity, to the extent that the Uí Néill warlords who might otherwise have capitalized on an Irish consciousness had to be accommodated within the immemorial "Fifths" of Ulster and Meath. Most early medieval political ideologies either lacked the dynamic to compel acceptance of political change, or had it in a form that cut across the scope of the change envisaged.

It is in this respect that England's experience was so crucially different. My argument of 1983 was that historians of the "advance of English unification" should give more heed than they usually have to the point that the word is indeed "English". According to Bede, Britain had been invaded by Saxons and Jutes as well as Angles, and there were certainly others besides. The Angles were *perhaps* the most numerous and powerful ingredient in the mix. But much more important was that theirs was the name that captured the attention of the founder of Anglo-Saxon Christianity. Unlike any other known Latin-speaker in the sixth-century Continent, Gregory the Great invariably described the pagans to whom he despatched his mission as "Angles". As a result, those distinguished by Germanic speech and heathen convictions from Britain's indigenous inhabitants became children of the mother Church of the "English" founded by Gregory's disciples at Canterbury. Anyone laying claim to an ethnic origin on the far side of the North Sea by that token acquired a common Christian identity: so all were "*Angelcynn*". "of English race". There is thus even more significance than is generally appreciated in the wellknown fact that a single English kingdom was anticipated by a single English Church. The very name of "English" was one of its fruits. Another side-effect of more than merely spiritual moment was the remarkably consistent festal cycle celebrated throughout the Anglo-Saxon Church by the tenth and eleventh centuries (Wormald 1934, though cf. Dumville 1993: 39–65). It was in the nature of "Dark Age" saintly activity that its resonance was mainly local.[15] Cults were powerful centres of local gravity: the 1065 rebellion had began with exposure of the relics of a "martyred" seventh-century Northumbrian king. But there is not all that much variation between ritual calendars from different parts of pre-conquest England, even as regards saints like Cuthberht and (King) Oswald, whose original *locus* had been the far North. On the contrary, a list of "the Saints of God who rest in *Engla lond*", apparently modelled on similar guides to the shrines of Rome, was intended to guide the steps of pilgrims to the most efficacious cults (Rollason 1978; cf. Rollason 1989: 133–63). These Anglo-Saxon saints were more than focuses of local sentiment. They were a heritage all "*Angelcynn*" shared. In the eleventh century, there was still some competition between devotees of the greatest French saints, as to who was entitled to the palm of "Apostle of Gaul". There was no such debate in England. Celebration of the festivals of Saints Gregory and Augustine, apostles of the English, had been prescribed since 747.

All the same, it may be doubted whether ecclesiastical authority would on its own have sufficed to instil a new ethnicity into Britain's Germanic-speaking inhabitants. Its impact was, however, reinforced by a supreme masterpiece of the world's historical literature. The contrasting fortunes of Europe's early medieval polities are strikingly mirrored in the nature of their contemporary historiographical monuments. Gregory of Tours did not call his masterpiece "The History of the Franks", nor were Frankish activities its primary concern. If he and the *Liber Historiae Francorum* between them contrived to give the Franks a sense of their unique status, intensified by Carolingian focus on the Old Testament, the message was lost on the many subjects of Carolingian kings who did not yet see themselves as Franks. The herald of ascendant German monarchy called his book The Deeds of the *Saxons*'. It was indeed much more a Saxon than a German history, and one too that nursed a sympathy for aristocratic rebellion against an imperious crown that German historiography never quite subsequently lost; on neither count was it likely to foster Saxon compliance with rule from elsewhere in the *Reich*. The Venerable Bede, by contrast, consciously entitled his work "*An Ecclesiastical History of the English People*".[16] Bede, as it happens, was himself an Angle. But that is not why he wrote about a "*gens Anglorum*". Among the various English churches whom he thanked in his preface for their guidance, Canterbury was clearly pre-eminent; and his conception of the "Angles" was that of the Canterbury church and of its papal founder.

But behind Bede's vision of the English lurked a deeper and weightier inspiration. He came to the writing of his own people's history after a lifetime spent studying that of Israel as told in the Old Testament. The pattern of God's dealings with his original Chosen People remains Bede's underlying theme. Thus the *Ecclesiastical History* begins with a geographical survey of Britain as effectively another land of Milk and Honey. Its opening chapters are thereafter devoted to an account of how the lands original inhabitants, the Britons, proved unworthy of the Roman and Christian civilizations that were brought to them. Once the Romans had withdrawn, the unbridled wickedness of the Britons had been faithfully chronicled by Gildas, "their own historian" (as Bede revealingly called him). Contemptuous alike of his warnings and of a first "scourging" by Anglo-Saxon invaders, they were eventually abandoned by God, who transferred their heritage to a new favourite. Rome came again to Kent, in the person of Augustine, not Julius Caesar. The English fell heirs to what the Britons had lacked the grace to deserve. The concluding notes of Bede's history are seemingly triumphalist. But they convey a severe warning, which

cannot have been far from Bede's mind, given that a letter written
to the bishop of York shortly afterwards laid into the shortcomings
of the Church in his own lime (*EHD*: vol. I, 799–810): were the
English to follow the Britons down the same sinful path, they would
surely meet the same fate. The "*gens Anglorum*" too was a people of
the Covenant. Its destiny was indissolubly bound up with its duty
to its Maker. And in presenting the Anglo-Saxons with such an
image of their past and future, Bede gave their would-be unifiers
an impetus that *soi-disant* kings of Tara could only envy.

(ii) Implications of "Englishness"

The attitude of their programmatic chroniclers was in fact cause as
much as effect of the divergent histories of early medieval France,
Germany and England. A community of English saints was an
obvious by-product of an Ecclesiastical History. The most firmly
established cults in pre-conquest England were those of Bedan
heroes. But beyond that, the dynasty of Alfred could cast its wars
with the Vikings in the same sort of ideological mould as Carolingians and Ottonians, with the additional advantage that their role
made sense of the whole historical scheme that Bede had laid
down. They had been provided by Bede with a ready-made "ideological artefact"; one which, unlike those of Frankish or Saxon
hegemonies, squared up with the shape of their political ambitions.
They made idea into fact, not *vice versa*.

It is no surprise, then, that Bede's *History* was among the works
translated into the vernacular at King Alfred's court (Whitelock
1962). (This translation survives in five-pre-conquest manuscripts
plus one fragment, which, alongside up to nine copies of the Latin
original, makes it the third most-widely distributed non-Biblical
book in England before 1100.) Alfred's own account, when introducing his new educational programme, of "happy times" when
"kings were obedient to God and his messengers, and upheld peace
and morals and authority at home, and also extended their territory
abroad, and prospered both in warfare and in wisdom", was obviously drawn from Bede's story of the English Church in its seventh-
century Golden Age. His stress on "what temporal punishments
came upon us when we possessed only the name of Christians, and
few possessed the virtues" pointed the moral (Alfred 1967: 4–7).
Further, his lawbook took the Old Testament model further than
Charlemagne. It begins with a translation of three whole chapters of
the Law of God as given to Moses in the Book of Exodus, before
going on to describe how this had been modified by the Christian
Church and transmitted "throughout the whole world, also to the
*Angelcynn*". On the one hand this showed Anglo-Saxons how like

their own law was to that given by God himself. On the other, it invited them to remodel themselves in Israel's image. This was to be a kingdom not just of bodies but of souls.

Old Testament logic was that the cause of political disaster was sin and crime. To obey God's law was a *sine qua non* of lasting worldly success. Anglo-Saxon experience, whether Northumbrian, Mercian. Kentishman or West Saxon, was that Bede's implied warning had almost come to pass when another pagan people crossed the North Sea and threatened to remove their own hard-won promised land as the punishment of their backslidings. By contrast, the kings "of the English" in the tenth century had flourished like the Green Bay-Tree, by ensuring that enemies of God's word were their own, and penalizing them accordingly. Any further lapse could well mean that the English would finally suffer what they had themselves inflicted on the Britons. What-ever the actual tergiversations of the ninth century, this was an unappealing prospect from the viewpoint of the tenth. Obedience to the new English government was the price of survival. Rough handling of selected ruling-class interests could still be squared with God's plan for the class as a whole. "England" was welded by the compound of force, cajolery and propaganda that is the stuff of statecraft in any age. But its craftsmen had a blueprint from which to work.

Nothing highlights this better than the shape which it eventually took. Though its emergence was obviously assisted by an amenable geography, to single out the kingdom's compact size and physical homogeneity as factors in its viability is to overlook the fact that this island does have two "natural frontiers", and one of them is on the Humber. The logic of geopolitics was that Northumbria *should* have gone its own way. But Lothian was the only slice of one-time Anglo-Saxon territory that southern kings were prepared to jetti-son. Close reading of Bede revealed that in 685 the bishopric of Abercorn on the Forth had been abandoned by the "*Angli*" as a matter of policy (*Hist. Eccl.*: 428–9). Otherwise, Bede's own Northumbrian origin meant that a Kingdom of the English neces-sarily enfolded the whole of the area otherwise likeliest to hive itself off. Left to themselves, the high-reeves of Bamburgh may well have opted for a Scottish identity. But Cuthberht's Lindisfarne lay off-shore. Once West Saxon kings had staked a claim, it was above all St Cuthberht's church, after 995 in its impregnable Durham bastion, that stood for "English" rule. Its support was vested in lavish gifts of land, privilege and treasure from southern kings (Bonner and others 1989: 367–446). It was underwritten too by the fact that Cuthberht's definitive biographer was Bede. Bede's relics were stolen from Jarrow *c.* 1030, to be interned in Cuthberht's church where they lie today. It is a nice vignette of their significance that the thief was the man whose "discovery" of King Oswine's relics set off the 1065 rebellion; but his namesake and great-grandson was Ailred of Rievaulx, a Yorkshire abbot who was as much at home at the Scottish as the English court in an age when kings of Scots still laid claim to the northern shires, yet whose sense of his Englishness seems never to have wavered (Walter Daniel 1950: xxxiii–xlviii; cf. Gransden 1974: 289; and Kapelle 1979: 98). Within the bounds of England itself, English dominion was "integrative" well before it was "bureaucratic" (cf. Davies 1993: 4).

## Conclusions

There was a historian in the times of the Britons named Gildas, who wrote about their misdeeds, how their sins angered God so excessively that finally He allowed the army of the English to conquer their land. Let us take warning: we know of worse deeds among the English than we have heard of among the Britons. Let us turn to the right and leave wrong-doing. Let us love God and follow Cod's laws' (*EHD*: vol. I, 933–4).

This is the "Sermon of the Wolf to the English" preached by Archbishop Wulfstan of York in 1014 when his fellow-countrymen were in fact about to be overrun by the Vikings once more. Wulfstan was echoing a letter by the Northumbrian, Alcuin, written in shock at the Viking sack of the Holy Island of Lindisfarne in 793 (Allott 1974: 62). Alcuin knew men who had known Bede. It can be assumed that he had taken the point of the *Ecclesiastical History*. And Wulfstan, more than any other spokesman of later Old English culture, stood for the implementation of the "Law of God" among all members of society, as the condition not only of their heavenly salvation but also of their earthly fortune. The several law-codes that he drafted to this end are actually quite difficult to distinguish from his sermons. But Wulfstan's importance extends further than this. His 1014 sermon was not so much a warning as an explanation of Englishmen's traumatic experience (Goddon 1994). Defeat made sense in terms of the failure of the English to meet the standards that their founders had expected of them. Wulfstan went on to be the main architect of Cnut's new regime. He founded it, logically enough, on restatement of the established principles of tenth-century English law in Cnut's great code. All of this was in the nature of a dress rehearsal for the far more acute crisis when the Vikings returned yet again, in 1066. From the dawn of their regime, Norman kings professed respect for "the Law of King Edward" (*EHD*: vol. II, 1012, 434). By early in the reign of Henry I. a French-speaker who was by no means *au fait* with the obscurities of Old English legal vocabulary, but who certainly considered himself an

Englishman, was assembling a large collection of Anglo-Saxon law in Latin translation, with Cnut's code as its centrepiece (Wormald 1994a).[17] At the same sort of date, two half-Englishmen were writing histories which rephrased Bede's message for their new world. William of Malmesbury's *Gesta Regum Anglorum* took Bede's story from its beginnings with Hengest and Horsa through to Henry I. Orderic Vitalis, who had made his own personal copy of Bede, wrote what has been called (though not by him) a *Historia Ecclesiastica Gentis Normannorum* (Davis 1989). For both these writers, it was the sins of the English which had brought their drastic punishment upon them, and the Normans who had been its instrument (Gransden 1974: 151–85). But the English were not thereby obliterated, only warned once and for all. Copies of Bede circulated even more widely than before. His model had proved its adaptability, hence its timeless relevance.

English identity was thus equipped by its historical ideology to leap the yawning fissure that the Conquest opened up in the continuity of the kingdom's ruling class. It gave a pattern of events for Norman and Englishman alike. Its protean durability was sufficient to absorb the Norman Myth, just as the English language outlasted the French (Davis 1976). By the late-twelfth century, a new historical ideology had began to match the appeal of Bede's. The medieval manuscripts of Geoffrey of Monmouth's *Historia Regum Britanniae* would be three times as numerous as those of the *Ecclesiastical History*. Its advantages included the requisite Trojan origin, a model of the whole British Isles (and more besides) ruled from London, slight interest in sin and its consequences, and perhaps not least that very little of it was true (Campbell 1984). Yet God's Englishmen did after all have a longer future than Arthur's Britons. That "God is English" was not an idea born in the sixteenth century (Corrigan and Sayer 1985: 57, 59; cf. J. Wormald 1994). The sixteenth century saw the rebirth of many of the circumstances of the tenth. In each era, English allegiance was fused by adherence to a special Church and soldered by fear of its godless enemy. Had Richard Hooker written, "There is not any man of the *ecclesia Anglorum* but the same man is also a member of the *regnum Anglorum*". Wulfstan could have endorsed his every word. To say this is of course to beg the question of the transmission of the notion of Englishness over the half-millenium from the Norman Conquest to the Reformation. Yet, given that it is *Englishness* that is at issue, it might reasonably be thought that the *onus probandi* lies on those who would deny that such a sense remained embedded in the bulk of the English population throughout this long period. Unless a sense of English identity had penetrated towards the roots of society, it is very difficult to understand how it survived at all. It had after all been the English elite, i.e. the upper foliage, that was lopped off in 1066. There is a tendency among scions of the intellectual left to explain features of popular consciousness that do not fit their model as elite impositions (Hilton 1989: cf. n. 13 above). But awareness of belonging to an extended community that transcends the bounds of family or contiguous settlement is not in fact a very complex concept. Even if it were, this need not mean that it was one to be grasped only by an educated or commercialized society. The political education of European peoples recommenced in the aftermath of Rome's fall with the simple but explosive idea that God might single out a distinct culture for His special favour in return for its enforced conformity with His Will as its authorities perceived it. That idea bore its first fruit in the concept of the English. The indestructability of their political *persona* is the proof of its power.

In an eleventh-century manuscript with Worcester connections is a fragment of what may be the sole surviving private letter from one relatively ordinary Anglo-Saxon to another. It survives only because its author urges his "brother Edward" to take action against the lavatorial orgies of country womenfolk in which food and drink were (literally) recycled, and was thus incorporated into a short tract on other unclean habits. But the letter's first complaint relates to Edward's hairstyle: "You do wrong in abandoning the English practices which your fathers followed, and in loving the practices of heathen men, and in so doing show by such evil habits that you despise your race (*cynn*) and your ancestors, since in insult to them you dress in Danish style with bared necks and blinded eyes". (Kluge 1885; *EHD*: vol. I. 895–6 (bowdlerized!): Brooks 1986). The style was presumably that of Cnut's court: it can be seen being sported by Normans on the Bayeux Tapestry. So "Little England" is finding its voice a millenium before Maastricht. Among all the factors that have made for the English state's eleven-hundred-year history, none counts for more than the instinctive prejudices on which it still complacently rests.

## Notes

* This paper was first presented to the seminar on "The Formation of the English State" under the general management of Gerald Aylmer. Philip Corrigan. Derek Sayer and Gavin Williams. I am grateful to members of the seminar for many insights, and to one of them, Dr Jenny Wormald, for subsequent encouragement and refinement of my views. Companion pieces, whose argument in part overlaps with this paper's, are Wormald 1992 and Wormald 1994b.

[1] The fist of these narratives is pieced together from *Sax. Chron.*: vol. I, 190–2; "Florence" of Worcester: vol. I, 222–3: and *The Life of King Edward*

*the Confessor*: I vii, 50–4; the best (though not flawless) modern account is Kapelle (1979): 94–100. The account of the German revolt is taken entirely from Lcyscr (1983).

   [2] A further paradox in this instance is that, as William of Malmesbury was well aware, the Irish at least had once played a major role in instilling Christianity into the English.

   [3] The seminal modern work is Wenskus (1961): see also Wolfram (1970); and, for a typically Intelligent "layman's catechism", James (1988): 5–10.

   [4] This story emerges mistily from the semi-legendary sources assembled at Durham in the twelfth century, "Historia de Sancto Cuthberto" (1882): 203, cf. *English Historical Documents [EHD] I*: 286–7, but is no less plausible for that; in particular, this source calls the Vikings "*Scaldingi*", an echo of the name of their heroic "*Scyldinga*' dynasty in *Beowulf* – and a reminder that the Characteristic literature of the Anglo-Saxon warrior class was no basis for a view of Vikings as "national enemies": see the lastingly valuable (and coincidentally Weberian?) account of warrior aristocrat political priorities by Chadwick (1912): especially 30–40, 329–37.

   [5] In two of his charters issued in that year: Birch (1885–99): vol. II, 663–4. But Alfred himself and his son, Edward the Elder, both used "*rex Anglorum Saxonum/Angulsaxonum*": Keynes and Lapidge (1983): 179, 227–8.

   [6] In his address to the Anglo-American Historical Conference of July 1991 (under the appropriate chairmanship of Sir Geoffrey Elton), the distinguished French medievalist Jean-Philippe Genet argued that much of what is considered characteristic of the early modern state – and which has provided the programme, partly drafted by Genet, for the international project on "*La Genèse de l'état moderne*" – was already in evidence in the France of Philip "the Fair" (1285–1314). Like Genet, Professor Strayer was fist and foremost a historian of France, and his "*Medieval Origins of the Modern State*" have a similar vintage. But it is hard to escape the suspicion that both of these scholars were indulging the French historian's usual habit of confusing the history of France with that of Europe. Englishmen familiar with the vigour of English government on either side of the Norman Conquest would be tempted to take their story at least three centuries furthcr back.

   [7] See Stafford (1989): 65–8; chapters 2–6 of this book are an admirable account of the "national"/"regional" politics of dynastic disputes, whose conclusions are all the more telling in that she is also the author of one of the few regional monographs of the Anglo-Saxon period (Stafford, 1985).

   [8] See now Fleming (1991), which is a case in point: Dr Fleming evidently aligns herself with those disinclined to credit the viability of the Confessor's regime; yet the great bulk of her argument is devoted to documenting the ascendancy of the house of Godwine; and only on her book's antepenultimate page does she concede the vital point that the accession of Godwine's son Harold restored the crown's fortunes ten months before the Battle of Hastings by pooling its resources with those of his own West Saxon earldom.

   [9] The early English oath is a central theme of Wormald (forthcoming), especially chapter 9. Anglo-Saxon laws bearing on its administration and implications are Alfred 1–1:8. II Edward 4–5:2, IV Æthelstan 3:2, V Æthelstan Pr:3 (*Laws*, 1922: 62–5, 120–1, 148–9, 152–3): III Edmund I, III Edgar

7:3, V Æthelred 22–31:1, II Cnut 20–20:1 (*Laws*, 1925: 12–13, 26–7, 84–9, 184–5). On "frankpledge", see Morris (1910), with the account of its Alfredian origin by William of Malmesbury (1887–9: vol. I, 129–30); and, for its later application, Crowley (1975), with a glance at Blackstone (1979): vol. I, pp. 354–6. On felony, cf. II Cnut 64 (*Laws*, 1925: 206–7): with "*Leges Henrici Primi*" 43:7 (Downer, 1972: 152–3); "Assize of Northampton" 3 (Stubbs 1924: 179); and Pollock and Maitland (1968): vols. I, 303–4, and 11, 464–6. For the Carolingian dimension, see *Capitularia* 23: 18, 25:4,33:2–9, 34:Add, 260:2–8 (+ Add.), 261:Add., 278: 1–3 (1882–97); vols. I, 63, 67, 92–3, 101, and II, 271–4, 278. 344–5): with Kienast (1952): 15–33; and Campbell (1975): 46–7.

   [10] For the officially-sponsored expansion of one family of West Saxon "new men", see Sawyer (1979): xli; for the lands of Earl Byrhtnoth, who, though quite possibly a descendant of the Mercian royal house, won renown as the loyal hero of the Battle of Maldon, see Hart (1987): 67–71; and for maps of the holdings of the Godwinesons and Leofricsons, see Hill (1981): 103–4.

   [11] The seminal assessment was Duby ( 1953); for excellent English-language accounts of what was happening, see Dunbabin (1985): 27–123, 133–245; with Wickham (1981): 169–93.

   [12] For Norman government before 1066, the indispensable guide is now Bates (1982). That Dr Bates can show that Normandy's comparative institutional vitality was a function of relatively well-preserved Carolingian organs (*not* "feudalism") bears in an important way on the diagnosis for preconquest English government, with its strikingly Carolingian physique.

   [13] Impatience with the nauseating political views of *some* who have cherished notions of "ongoing Englishness" deserves every sympathy (Anderson 1974: 159–60). But it should perhaps be remembered that those who seem to have been the first to claim an "English" political heritage against intrusive elites carried impeccably radical credentials (Hill 1958).

   [14] The significance of the generality "English" is of course enhanced rather than reduced by its use in distinction from such variant elements as could still be identified: see the admirable paper by Ann Williams (1986) on the "short-lived" impact of the settlement of Cnut's Scandinavian followers.

   [15] A celebrated *aperçu* of the politics of saints' cults in another context is Brown (1973).

   [16] For arguments that Bede did indeed have in mind something like what we mean by "English" rather than merely his Anglian fellow-Northumbrians, see Wormald (1992). My confidence in these arguments has been very materially advanced by the fact that many of them occurred simultaneously and coincidentally to Nicholas Howe (1989). I ought also to acknowledge, as I overlooked in 1983, that some of the same case is made by Cowdrey (1981).

   [17] Given the importance of concessionary royal charters in post-1066 England, it is of some interest that Cnut may have prefigured that pattern too: Stafford (1981); Kennedy (1982).

## Bibliography

Abrams, Philip (1988) "Notes on the Difficulty of Studying the State", *JHS* 1.
Ælfric (1881–5) *Lives of the Saints*, ed. Skeat W.W. O: Early English Texts Society, 2 vols.

Agobard (1889) *Epistolae*, ed. E. Dümmler. Mon. Germ. Hist. Epistolae Karolini Aevi III.

Alfred, King (1967) "On the State of Learning in England". *Sweet's Anglo-Saxon Reader in Prose and Verse*, rev. edn by Whitelock, D. OUP.

Airlie, Stuart (1985) "The political behaviour of the secular magnates in Francia, 828–79". (Unpubl. Oxford D. Phil. thesis).

Allott, S. (1974) *Alcuin of York*. York: William Sessions.

Anderson, Perry (1974) *Passages from Antiquity to Feudalism*. L: NLB.

Aylmer, G.E. (1990) "The Pecularities of the English State". *JHS* 3.

Barlow, Frank (1979) *The English Church 1000–1066*. L: Longman. 2nd edn.

Bartlett, Robert (1993) *The Making of Europe*. L: Allen Lane.

Bassett, Steven (1989) *The Origins of Anglo-Saxon Kingdoms*. Leicester UP (Studies in the early history of Britain).

Bates, David (1982) *Normandy before 1066*. L: Longman.

Birch, W. de Gray (1885–99) *Cartularium Saxonicum*. L: Whiting & Co., 4 vols.

Blackstone, William (1979) *Commentaries on the Laws of England*. Facsimile edn by S.N. Katz, Chicago. 4 vols.

Bonner, Gerald, Rollason, David, and Stancliffe, Clare, eds, *St Cuthbert, his Cult and Community*. Woodbridge: Boydell.

Brooks, Nicholas (1986) *History and Myth, Forgery and Truth. Univ. Birmingham inaugural lecture*.

Brown, Peter (1973) "Aspects of the Iconoclast Controversy". *English HR* LXXXVIII; repr. in Brown, Peter *Society and the Holy in Late Antiquity*. L: Faber (1982).

Byme, F.J. *Irish Kings and High Kings*. L: Batsford.

Campbell, James (1975) "Observations on English Government from the tenth to the twelfth century". *Trans. Roy. H. Soc.* 5th series 25; repr. in Campbell (1986).

Campbell, James (1979) *Bede's Reges and Principes*. Jarrow Lecture; repr. in Campbell (1986).

Campbell, James (1984) "Some Twelfth-Century Views of the Anglo-Saxon Past". *Peritia* 3: repr. in Campbell (1986).

Campbell, James (1986) *Essays in Anglo-Saxon Hisbry*. L: Hambledon. (1986).

Capitularia (1883–97) *Capitularia Regum Francorum*, ed. Boretius A. and Krause V. Mon. Germ. Hist., Legum Sectio II, 3 vols.

Chadwick, H.M. (1912) *The Heroic Age*. CUP.

Clarke, Peter (1994) *The English Nobility under Edward the Confessor*. OUP (Oxford historical monographs).

Corrigan, Philip, and Sayer, Derek (1985) *The Great Arch. English State Formation as Cultural Revolution*. O: Blackwell.

Cowdrey, H.E.J. (1981) "Bede and the 'English People' ". *JRel.H* XI.

Crowley, D.A. (1975) "The Later History of Frankpledge". *Bull. Inst. H. Res.* XLVIII.

Davies, Rees (1993) "The English State and the 'Celtic' Peoples 1100–1400". *JHS* 6.

Davis, R.H.C. (1976) *The Norman Myth*. L: Thames and Hudson.

Davis, R.H.C. (1989) "Bede after Bede". In Harper-Bill C., ed. *Studies in Medieval History presented to R. Allen Brown*. Woodbridge: Boydell.

Downer, L.J. (1972) *Leges Henrici Primi*. OUP.

Duby, Georges (1953) *La Société aux XI- et XII- siècles dans la région mâconnaise*. Paris (Bibliothèque générale de l'école pratique des hautes études).

Dumville, David (1993) *Liturgy and the Ecclesiastical History of late Anglo-Saxon England*. Woodbridge: Boydell.

Dunbabin, Jean (1985) *France in the Making, 843–1180*. OUP.

EHD (1979) *English Historical Documents Vol. I, c. 550–1042*, ed. Whitelock D. L: Eyre Methuen, 2nd edn. EHD (1980) *English Historical Documents Vol. II, 1042–1189*, ed. Douglas D.C. L: Eyre Methuen, 2nd edn.

Fleming, Robin (1991) *Kings & Lords in Conquest England*. Cambridge UP (Cambridge Studies in Medieval Life and Thought).

"Florence" of Worcester (1848–9) *Chronicon ex Chronicis*, ed. Thorpe B. L: S. & J. Bentley, 2 vols.

Gerberding, R.A. *The Rise of the Carolingians and the Liber Historiae Francorum*. OUP (Oxford historical monographs).

Gillingham, John (1971) *The Kingdom of Germany in the High Middle Ages*. L: Historical Association pamphlet series.

Gillingham, John (1992) "The Beginnings of English Imperialism". *JHS* 5.

Gluckman, Max (1973) *Custom and Conflict in Africa*. O: Blackwell repr.

Godden, Malcolm (1994) "Apocalypse and Invasion in late Anglo-Saxon England". In Godden, M. and others, eds, *From Anglo-Saxon to Middle English. Studies in Honour of E.G. Stanley*. OUP.

Gransden, Antonia (1974) *Historical Writing in England c. 550–c. 1307* (London, 1974).

Harmer, Florence (1914) *Select English Historical Documents of the Ninth and Tenth Centuries*. CUP.

Hart, C.R. (1987) "The Ealdordom of Essex". In K. Neale, ed., *An Essex Tribute. Essays presented to F.G. Emmison*. CUP.

Hill, Christopher (1958) "The Norman Yoke". In Hill, Christopher *Puritanism and Revolution*. L: Secker and Warburg.

Hill, David (1981) *An Atlas of Anglo-Saxon England*. O: Blackwell.

Hilton, Rodney (1989) "Were the English English?". In Samuels R, ed. *Patriotism: The Making and Unmaking of British National Identity*. L: Routledge, 3 vols.

"Historia de sancto Cuthberto" (1882), ed. Arnold T. *Symeonis Monachi Opera*. L: Rolls Series, 2 vols.

*Hist. Eccl.* (1969) *Bede's Ecclesiastical History of the English People*, ed. & trans. Colgrave B. and Mynors R.A.B. OUP.

Howe, Nicholas (1989) *Migration and Mythmaking in Anglo-Saxon England*. New Haven: Yale UP.

James, Edward (1982) *The Origins of France*. L: Macmillan.

James, Edward (1988) *The Franks*. O: Blackwell.

Kapelle, William (1979) *The Norman Conquest of the North*. L: Croom Helm.

Kennedy, Alan (1982) "Cnut's law code of 1018", *Anglo-Saxon England* 11.

Kienast, Walther (1952) *Untertaneneid und Treuvorbehalt in England und Frankreich*. Weimar: Böhlau.

Kirby, D.P. (1991) *The Earliest English Kings*. L: Unwin.

Kluge, F. (1885) "Fragment eines angelsächsischen Briefes". *Englische Studien* VIII.

*Laws* (1922) *The Laws of the Earliest English Kings*, ed. & trans. Attenborough F.L. CUP.

*Laws* (1925) *The Laws of the Kings of England from Edmund to Henry I*, ed. & trans. Robertson A.J. CUP.

Leyser, Karl (1968) "The German Aristocracy from the ninth to the early twelfth century. A historical and cultural sketch". *PP* 41.

Leyser, Karl (1979) *Rule and Conflict in an early medieval society. Ottonian Saxony*. L: Arnold.

Leyser, Karl (1983) "The Crisis of Medieval Germany". *Proc. Brit. Acad.* LXIX.

*Life of King Edward the Confessor* (1962), ed. & trans. Barlow F. L: Nelson's Medieval Texts.

Morris, W.A. (1910) *The Frankpledge System*. Harvard UP (Historical studies XIV).

Nelson, Janet (1991) *Annals of St-Bertin*. Manchester UP (Manchester medieval sources series).

O'Corráin, Donncha (1978) "Nationality and Kingship in pre-Norman Ireland". In Moody T., ed., *Historical Studies XI*. Belfast UP.

O'Rahilly, T.F. (1946) *Early Irish History and Mythology*. Dublin: Institute for Advanced Studies.

Pollock and Maitland (1968) *History of English Law to the accession of Edward I*. CUP, re-issue ed. Milsom S.F.C.

Regino of Prüm (1890) *Reginonis Prumensis Chronicon*, ed. F. Kurze. Mon. Germ. Hist., Scriptores rerum Germanicarum.

Robertson, A.J. (1956) *Anglo-Saxon Charters*. CUP, 2nd edn.

Rollason, David (1978) "Lists of Saints' Resting-Places in Anglo-Saxon England'. *Anglo-Saxon England* 7.

Rollason, David (1989) *Saints and Relics in Anglo-Saxon England*. O: Blackwell.

*Sax. Chron.* (1892–9) *Two of the Saxon Chronicles Parallel*, ed. Earle J. and Plummer C. OUP, 2 vols (translations of this text are supplied from *EHD*).

Sawyer, P.H. (1979) *Charters of Burton Abbey*. O: British Academy Anglo-Saxon Charters series, vol. II.

Sayer, Derek (1992) "A Notable Administration: English State Formation and the Rise of Capitalism". *AJS* 97.

Stafford, Pauline (1981) "The Laws of Cnut and the History of Anglo-Saxon royal promises", *Anglo-Saxon England* 10.

Stafford, Pauline (1985) *The East Midlands in the Early Middle Ages*. Leicester UP (Studies in the early history of Britain).

Stafford, Pauline (1989) *Unification and Conquest. A political and social history of England in the tenth and eleventh centuries*. L: Arnold.

Smyth, Alfred (1977) *Scandinavian Kings in the British Isles 850–80*. OUP (Oxford historical monographs).

Stenton, Sir F.M. (1971) *Anglo-Saxon England*. OUP, 3rd edn.

Strayer, J.R. (1970) *On the Medieval Origins of the Modern State*. Princeton UP.

Stubbs, William (1924) *Select Charters*. 9th edn, ed. H.W.C. Davis. OUP.

Tellenbach, G. (1957) *Studien und Vorarbeiten zur Geschichte des gross-fränkischen und frühdeutschen Adels*. Freiburg (Forschungen zur oberrheinischen Landesgeschichte 4).

Thorpe, Lewis (1975) *Gregoy of Tours. The History of the Franks*. Penguin Classics.

Wallace-Hadrill, J.M. (1962) "The Work of Gregory of Tours in the Light of Modem Research". In Wallace-Hadrill, J.M. *The Long-Haired Kings*. L: Methuen.

Wallace-Hadrill, J.M. (1971) *Early Germanic Kingship in England and on the Continent.* OUP.

Walter, Daniel (1950) *Life of Ailred of Rieuaulx,* ed. & trans. Powicke F.M. L: Nelson's Medieval Texts.

Wenskus, R. (1961) *Stammesbildung und Verfassung.* Köln-Graz: Böhlau.

Werner, K.-F. (1970) "Les nations et le sentiment national dans l'Europe médiévale". *Revue Historique* 244.

Wickham, Chris (1981) *Early Medieval Italy.* L: Macmillan.

William of Malmesbury (1887–9) *De Gestis Regum Anglorum,* ed. Stubbs, William. L: Rolls Series, 2 vols.

William of Malmesbury (1928) *Life of St Wulfstan,* ed. Darlington R.R. L: Camden Society 3rd series XL.

Williams, Ann (1986) "Cockles among the Wheat: Danes and English in the West Midlands in the first half of the eleventh century". *JMidlandH* 11.

Whitelock, D. "The Dealings of Kings of England with Northumbria in the Tenth and Eleventh Centuries". In Clemoes P., ed., *The Anglo-Saxons. Studies presented to Bruce Dickins.* CUP.

Whitelock, D. (1962) "The Old English Bede". *Proc. Brit. Acad.* XLVIII.

Wolfram, Herwig (1970) "The Shaping of the early medieval kingdom". *Viator* 1.

Wormald, Francis (1934) *English Kalendars before AD 1100.* L: Henry Bradshaw Society.

Wormald, Jenny (1994) "The Union of 1603". in Mason R., ed. *Scots and Britons: Scottish Political Thought and the Union of 1603.* CUP.

Wormald, Patrick (1983) "Bede, the *Bretwalda* and the Origins of the *Gens Anglorum*". In Wormald P., Bullough D. and Collins, R., eds. *Ideal and Reality in Frankish and Anglo-Saxon Society. Studies presented to J.M. Wallace-Hadrill.* O: Blackwell.

Wormald, Patrick (1992) "The Venerable Bede and the 'Church of the English' ". In Rowell G., ed., *The English Religious Tradition and the Genius of Anglicanism.* Wantage: Ikon.

Wormald, Patrick (1994a) " 'Quadripartitus' ". In Hudson J. and Garnett G. eds. *Law and Government in England and Normandy. Studies presented to Sir James Holt.* CUP.

Wormald, Patrick (1994b) "On Second Thoughts: the Making of England". *History Today* 44.

Wormald, Patrick (forthcoming) *The Making of English Law. King Alfred to the Noman Conquest.* O: Blackwell.

Yorke, Barbara (1990) *Kings and Kingdoms of Early Anglo-Saxon England.* L: Batsford.

# The Beginnings of English Imperialism

## JOHN GILLINGHAM

**Abstract** This article looks at a critical stage in the forcible anglicisation of Ireland, Scotland and Wales, and argues that the set of cultural images which provided the moral energy for English imperialism first emerged in the twelfth century, i.e. about four centuries earlier than is commonly supposed. By early twelfth century profound economic, social, military and cultural developments had so transformed England as to mean that the English and Celtic worlds were now sufficiently far apart for the differences between them to be visible to contemporaries, notably to William of Malmesbury, the first to articulate this "significant otherness" in terms of the classical contrast between civilisation and barbarism.

## I

As is well-known "a large part of medieval and modem 'British' history can be seen as a process of conquest and forcible anglicisation, extending of course to Ireland as well as to Wales and Scotland" (Aylmer 1990:94). Corrigan and Sayer suggest, surely rightly, that for the English to construe the brutality of conquest and/or the rapacity of commerce as a "civilizing mission", "took a national culture of extraordinary self-confidence and moral rectitude". (Corrigan and Sayer 1985: 193–4). From what date can an English national culture of this type be said to exist? In what social, economic and political context did the set of cultural images which "provided the moral energy for English imperialism" first emerge?

Imperialism as a subject has been very largely monopolized by modern historians and as a group they tend to think that there is a great divide, often labelled the Renaissance, between their world and that of the "Middle Ages".[1] Thus most modern historians have associated the emergence of this "national culture" with what they see as profound changes in government, religion and society in the sixteenth and seventeenth centuries. This consensus is reflected in, for example, Hugh Kearney's *The British Isles, A History of Four Nations* (1989), where Chapter Seven, entitled "The Making of an English Empire", begins: "In the early sixteenth century, a new period began in the history of the British isles. It was characterised by the emergence of an 'English empire' or, more precisely, an empire based on the wealth, population and resources of southern England over the rest of the British Isles". Naturally the historical sociologists who, with necessary optimism, rely on historians for the data from which they construct their theories, tend to accept this dating. Michael Hechter, for example, surveying the relation between core and periphery in the British Isles over a remarkably long period (from the Romans to the twentieth century), wrote that, "From the seventeenth century on, English military and political control in the peripheral regions was buttressed by a racist ideology which held that Norman Anglo-Saxon culture was inherently superior to Celtic culture" (Hechter 1975:342). Corrigan and Sayer (1985:194) trace the imperialist culture from the heroic myths of the 'elect nation' in the sixteenth and seventeenth centuries to the more philistine, secular and complacent but no less missionary motifs of the nineteenth".[2] Here I shall first argue that an imperialist English culture emerged in the twelfth century, then suggest reasons why it emerged some four hundred years earlier than is commonly supposed.

At first sight there is something of a paradox here since for most people the hundred years or so after the Norman Conquest was a time when Frenchmen ruled the roost, when the English were an oppressed people and their culture a necessarily subordinate one – hardly the most plausible soil for the growth of an imperialising English culture. Thus the momentous expansionist movement of soldiers, settlers and ruling elites from England into Wales, Scotland and Ireland which characterised the twelfth and thirteenth centuries, if interpreted in imperialist terms at all, is generally seen as Norman rather than English imperialism. Once again Kearney's chapter titles nicely reflect this widespread perception. Chapter five, beginning in 1066 and covering the twelfth and thirteenth centuries, is called "The Norman Ascendancy"; chapter six, dealing with the next two centuries, is called the "The Decline of the Norman French empire". One of the most striking symptoms of this view is the use of the nineteenth century term "the Norman Invasion" – now omnipresent in Ireland – to refer to the invasion of 1169–70, whence book titles such as *Ireland under the Normans* or *Ireland before the Normans* (Gillingham 1993b).

Since this perception is both widespread and seriously misleading, it is perhaps best to begin with a few observations on the subject. No one would deny that the Norman Conquest created a deeply divided society. But these divisions passed. In this context the question is, when? In my view it took a long time, i.e. two generations, perhaps seventy years, but by the 1130s and 1140s the French connexion was no longer a source of national or ethnic tension. In his entry for 1107 the author of the *Anglo-Saxon Chronicle* wrote "it was the forty-first year after the French had been in control of this country." The next time (1127) the Chronicle refers to "the French", it is not as those who are not us and rule over us, but as those who are not us because they are the subjects of the king of France. By this date French is no longer the language of foreign oppressors, it is already, as it was in the thirteenth century, the polite language of the English elite (whether perceived as oppressive or not).[3]

What are the implications of this for the sense of identity of the French speaking members of the landholding elite? In this context the views of one of the greatest English historians, William of Malmesbury, are particularly revealing. His main historical work, the *Deeds of the kings of the English*, completed by 1125, survives in a lot of manuscripts and was very widely known (Gransden 1974: 178–9; Guenée 1980: 250–1, 270). He wrote history, as he himself said, "out of love for my country", and by his *patria* he meant not some cross-Channel Anglo-Norman realm but England. Not surprisingly he has long been thought of as a very "English" historian. When Sir Richard Southern suggested that there was "a distinctive character to English historical writing" based upon "a tradition of research which had been started in the twelfth century and renewed in the sixteenth century", he identified William as "the most talented" of all the twelfth century researchers. The tradition which Southern had in mind was essentially an antiquarian one, one which, in his words, "had the great merit of beginning with the ordinary needs of life, and not with any intellectual programme whatsoever" (Southern 1973: 253, 263). I am not entirely convinced that this quite does justice to William. In his own view he was the most important English historian since Bede, i.e. for four hundred years, and he certainly saw a very clear pattern in the course of English history. As he makes explicit in his reflections on the significance of 1066, William looked upon English history as a progress from barbarism to civilisation – a smug assumption in which he was to be followed by many modern historians of England, from David Hume onwards.

In William's view the civilising process started at the sixth century court of King Ethelbert of Kent. Since Ethelbert was the first English king to be converted it is easy to assume (Jones 1971a; 391–2) that William equated civilisation with Christianity. In fact in William's eyes the process predated the king's conversion. The critical moment was his marriage to Bertha, the daughter of the *rex Francorum*, since it "was by this connexion with the French that a once barbarous people began to divest themselves of their wild frame of mind and incline towards a gentler way of life". Later William described how the ninth century King Egbert of Wessex, in exile in France, learned foreign ways "very different from his native barbarism", for the French, William observed, "are unrivalled among western nations in military skill and in polished manners". In this passage it is the present tense which is particularly striking.

In William's view then it was French culture, not Christianity alone, which made the English civilised (Gillingham 1991: 107–8). Naturally, William saw this as a process which was continuing in his own day. In political terms he perceived the battle of Hastings as "a day of disaster for our sweet country". He lamented that even now (c. 1120), no Englishman was able to hold high office in England – though he also believed that this state of affairs was about to end (William of Malmesbury 1887: i, 278; ii, 304, 495–6).

For William, Norman conquest and continuing domination was one thing, but the acquisition of French culture and customs quite another. In William's eyes the more "Frenchified" England and the English became, the better.

In this cultural context for a man to use the French language need not have been a denial of his English identity, of a sense of continuity with the Anglo-Saxon past – any more than the use of English by the Irish, Scots and Welsh of today necessarily separates them from a keen awareness of their own national pasts. It might be objected that a highly cultivated monk writing in Latin is no guide to the feelings of people outside monasteries, but William was a widely travelled man who had good connexions with the royal court, by no means a recluse.

Then there is the evidence of the *Estoire des Engleis* by Geoffrey Gaimar (c. 1140). Gaimar's milieu was secular, aristocratic Lincolnshire society. His English history goes from the Anglo-Saxon settlements to the court of Henry I. He is capable of admiring Hereward the Wake and of criticising William the Bastard. Since Gaimar's is the earliest history known to have been written in the French language, it is worth dwelling on the fact it was precisely a history of the English and not – as might have been expected – a history of the French (Short 1990). What it shows is that French-speakers living in England could see the Anglo-Saxon past as their past. The king and a tiny handful of the very greatest magnates, holding vast estates in Normandy as well as in England and Wales, may have thought of themselves primarily as Frenchmen, but the overwhelming majority of the landowners of England knew that they were English, French speaking, of mixed ancestry – as William of Malmesbury was – (usually French on their father's side and proud of their forefathers' achievements), but English even so.[4]

What the writings of Malmesbury and Gaimar suggest is that nineteenth and twentieth century scholars, when looking for evidence of a sense of English identity, have taken too Germanic a view. Here, it may be is a context in which seventeenth century developments in the history of ideas have been important: the notion that the qualities which made English institutions the best and the freest in the world were an inheritance from Germanic or Teutonic forefathers, i.e. the beginnings of the Stubbsian view that English history was "the pure development of Germanic principles" (MacDougall 1982). One result of this emphasis was – and still is – the assumption that the Englishman could not recover his true identity until he had shaken off the Norman Yoke, until after 1204 when John lost Anjou and Normandy and the French connexion was very largely broken. But to apply this much later definition of English identity to the Francophile and francophone twelfth century is to be anachronistic. In the twelfth century the French language was increasingly becoming the *lingua franca* of a cosmopolitan, Europe-wide community. To speak it, or write songs in it, was one way of showing that you were the sort of Englishman who counted, who shared the civilised values of western Europe. This was clearly not an insular sense of Englishness, but it was, for all that, a kind of Englishness.[5] And though the twelfth-century Englishman "failed" to feel a "healthy contempt" for continentals, he undoubtedly felt distinctly superior to his fellow-islanders, the Celts. If "a defining characteristic of imperial expansion is that the center must disparage the indigenous culture of peripheral groups" (Hechter 1975: 64), then this is of critical importance.

## II

Consider the assumptions of the unknown author of the *Gesta Stephani* writing in the 1140s. England he describes as the "seat of justice, the abode of peace, the apex of piety, the mirror of religion". Wales, by contrast, he saw as "a country of woodland and pasture- . . . abounding in deer and fish, milk and herds, but breeding a bestial type of man". Happily by 1135 the activities of Richard Fitz Gilbert and his fellows, imposing peace on the Welsh by castle-building and law-making, "had made the country so to abound in peace and productivity that it might easily have been thought a second England (*secunda Anglia*)" (*Gesta Stephani* 1976: 3, 15–17). Some years earlier William of Malmesbury had described King David I of Scotland as "made civilised by his upbringing amongst us. In consequence the rust of his native barbarism was polished away". Indeed William portrays David as a kind of missionary for civilisation among the Scots, promising exemption from the triennial tax to any of his subjects "who would live in a more civilised style, dress with more elegance and learn to eat with more refinement" (Anderson 1908: 157; cited in Davies 1990: 114). Later in the century Ralph Diceto, dean of St. Paul's London, visualised the Irish coming to Henry II and promising to embrace English customs (Ralph of Diceto 1876: vol. 1, 350–51). In these and similar passages there is a very strong sense that "we" in England are civilised; "they" in Wales, Scotland and Ireland are crude barbarians.

Amongst the clerical elite a prevailing perception of the otherness and inferiority of Celtic peoples is easy to document (Jones 1971b; Bartlett 1982; Davies 1984–5). John of Salisbury, writing in the 1150s, said that the Welsh "are rude and untamed; they live like beasts and though they nominally profess Christ, they deny him in their life and ways". "Who would deny that the Scots are barbarians?" wrote another mid twelfth century English author.[6] The north country William of Newburgh, often, in the light of his observations on Thomas Becket and King Arthur, regarded as the most judicious of twelfth-century historians, refers to a Scottish army as "a horde of barbarians". That this was more than a routine condemnation of an invader is made clear by his description of their behaviour. "Everything was being consumed by the Scots, to whom no food is too filthy to be devoured, even that which is fit only for dogs. It is a delight to that inhuman nation, more savage than wild beasts, to cut the throats of old men, to slaughter little children, to rip open the bowels of women" (Anderson 1908: 250–51). Then, of course, there is Gerald de Barr – usually but misleadingly known as Gerald of Wales (Gillingham 1993b) – on the Irish. "They are so barbarous that they cannot be said to have any culture . . . they are a wild people, living like beasts, who have not progressed at all from the primitive habits of pastoral farming" (Gerald of Wales 1982: 101).

In the last decade work done by historians like Robert Bartlett and R. R. Davies has shown that by the mid and late twelfth century such views were commonplace. But when did such attitudes first emerge? This question has not so far been explicitly addressed.[7] Medievalists who, as a group tend not to fall into "the early modern trap" sometimes write as though this set of attitudes has always existed, as though it was in the nature of the Anglo-Saxon to despise the Celt. Sir Maurice Powicke, for example, referred to "that age-long racial struggle of Celt and Teuton" (Powicke 1950:xlvii). But neither a traditional enmity between neighbours, nor the virtually universal feeling that "we" are "better" than "them", is the same thing as the imperialist view that certain people are so inferior as to belong to a distinctly lower order of society. The imperialist view is one which leads to a striking inversion of other otherwise deeply ingrained values so that, for example, a fourteenth-century Irish court historian could complain bitterly of a world turned upside down where the general rule was "that the Gael is ignoble though a landholder and the Saxon noble though he lack both breeding and wealth" (Davies 1990: 119; Frame 1981: 109).

Onc of William Malmcsbury's most creative and influential achievements was to introduce this imperialist perception of Celtic peoples into history. It is true, of course, that an imperial outlook had existed in earlier centuries. Some tenth century English kings had claimed to be overlords of Britain. King Edgar, for example, has been called "the most imperial of the late Anglo-Saxon rulers" (Campbell 1984: 139) – and so in a sense he was. He was buried at Glastonbury together with – or so it was believed – the great saints of the British Isles: Patrick, David, Gildas and Aidan. But as that grand assemblage of saints show, the culture of Celtic peoples was not disparaged in tenth-century Wessex. The West Saxon court was happy to see its great king associated in the grave with men from Ireland, Wales and Iona. In the tenth century Anglo-Saxons and Celts shared a common cultural world in which Ireland could still be regarded as a source of learning and virtue (Bethell 1971). Tenth-century English kings may have been imperial rulers in that they ruled, or claimed to rule, over a number of kingdoms; but they were not imperialists.

Reading works written within the Anglo-Saxon world during the ninth, tenth and eleventh centuries what strikes me is the absence of any clearly defined attitude towards the Welsh, the Scots and the Irish.[8] It is as though they were regarded as simply people like any other. In the case of the Welsh this is particularly striking since Bede had described the British king Cadwalla of Gwynedd as *barbarus* – and the Welsh were the successors of the Britons. Yet Bede's view of a fellow Christian seems to have found no echo until the twelfth century. During the previous three centuries Latin authors use the word *barbarus* as a synonym for pagan: the pagan Vikings are frequently referred to as barbarians. By contrast the various authors of the Anglo-Saxon Chronicle treat the Welsh and the Scots neutrally, occasionally even sympathetically. But William adopted a distinctly different tone (Gillingham 1990–91: 105–6). For him the Celts, Irish, Scots and Welsh, are "barbarians". In other words hc is discarding thc familiar concept of barbarian as equivalent to pagan and formulating a new one – one which allowed for the possibility of Christian barbarians. Indeed in William's eyes even people who were so Christian that they went on crusade could none the less be barbarians. Thus when recounting Pope Urban II's preaching of the crusade, he tells us that some of those who responded to Urban's call lived *in nationibus barbaris*: and he lists them, the Welsh, Scots, Danes and Norwegians. It looks as though William's extraordinary familiarity with classical literature and his admiration for the ancient world (Thomson 1987), has enabled him to "rediscover" the classical concept of the barbarian and "discover" that it applied to Celtic peoples in his own day. This is indeed antiquarian research, but hardly "programme-free".

## III

Why did William's perception of Celtic peoples as barbarians become commonplace? To answer this question, it is first necessary to sketch in the perceived characteristics of the barbarous Celt. I do this under three heads: the barbarian at work, the barbarian at war and the barbarian in bed.

1. *The barbarian at work.* This is, of course, a misnomer since it was widely believed that the barbarian was thoroughly indolent – "given only to leisure and devoted only to laziness", as Gerald described the Irish (Gerald of Wales 1982: 102). By the later twelfth century it was conventional to see the Celtic regions as fundamentally pastoral economies and to comment on the absence of towns, commerce and agriculture. The earliest author to make this explicit was William of Malmesbury, when drawing a striking contrast between England (seen as belonging to a more advanced European order) and Ireland. "Whereas the English and the French live in market-oriented towns enjoying a more cultivated style of life, the Irish live in rustic squalor, for owing to the ignorance of the farmers their land is inadequately cultivated". William evidently accepted the ancient notion that pastoral economies were unlikely to be able to sustain civilised life; and the comment of the author of the *Gesta Stephani* that Wales bred a bestial kind of people, suggests that he shared similar assumptions.

2. *The barbarian at war.* I turn to a mid twelfth century anonymous Hexham author's description of a Scottish attack on Northumbria (Anderson 1908: 91–3)

Gazing upon the church of St. Peter, blazing with the flames kindled by his men . . . King Malcolm commanded them no longer to spare any of the English nation, but either to slay them all or drive them away under the yoke of perpetual slavery. When his men received their king's licence, it was pitiable to see what they did to the English: old men and women were either beheaded by swords or stuck with spears like pigs destined for the table. Torn from their mothers' breasts, babes were tossed high in the air, and caught on the spikes of spears fixed close together in the ground. The Scots, crueller than beasts, delighted in this cruelty as in the sight of games . . . Young men and women, all who seemed fit for work, were bound and driven away into slavery. When some of the girls dropped to the ground exhausted by the pace of the slave-drivers, they were left to die where they fell. Malcolm saw all these things without pity: merely ordering his slave-drivers to make haste.[9]

What struck this author was the savagery of a war targeted against non-combatants. But for combatants too the risks of engaging in Celtic warfare were observably high. Gerald de Barri, for example, contrasts French warfare with Irish and Welsh warfare: "The French ransom soldiers: the Irish and Welsh butcher them and decapitate them" (Gerald of Wales 1978: 269).

3. *The barbarian in bed.* It was generally agreed that Celtic sexual and marital customs were animal-like. According to Richard of Hexham (c.1140), the Scots were "those bestial men who think nothing of committing incest, adultery and other abominations". Gerald writes of the Irish in similar tones. According to John of Salisbury (cited Bartlett 1982: 40), "the Welsh live like beasts . . . despising the law of marriage, they keep concubines as well as wives; whenever it suits them they get rid of them – for a price – to other men. They do not blush to indulge in incest. Their king Owain, for example, the prince of these barbarians, abuses the daughter of his uncle."

## IV

Such are the perceptions. The question is: are they based on reality? Essentially the answer is yes. Clearly in some respects these authors exaggerated – for example, the extent to which Celtic peoples relied upon pastoral farming. None the less there is plenty of evidence that in all of these spheres, economic, military and marital there were highly significant differences between twelfth-century England and contemporary Celtic realms.

### 1. Economy

A comparative chronology of economic development within the British Isles suggests that the fundamental differences between highland and lowland zones were being sharply accentuated during the course of the tenth and eleventh centuries. By the end of that period many English people no longer lived in isolated farmsteads or in hamlets, but in villages and market towns (Taylor 1983; Hinton 1990). In England there is clear evidence of the growth of a money economy. By the end of the tenth century moneyers were at work in some 70 English towns; "a very considerable intensification of minting" was taking place. Although a graph of the volume of coinage in circulation in England would certainly not show a constant upward trend from the tenth to the thirteenth century, the fact remains that by the 1220s – the date of the earliest extant figures for mint production – huge amounts of silver were being coined and pumped into the economic system, by the mid-thirteenth century in quantities which were not to be surpassed until the nineteenth century (Spufford 1988: 87–94, 202–05). By contrast, the highland zone and Ireland lagged some centuries behind. Put very roughly, the Celtic regions in the twelfth century looked rather like eighth-century England: a dispersed settlement pattern of farms and hamlets, not many coins, very few towns – and these situated on the coasts where they serviced international trade not, as in England, the needs of villagers going to their local market (Duncan 1975: 463; Barry 1987; Davies, W. 1982: 55–58).

One symptom of this fundamental transformation of England – urban growth and commercialisation of the countryside – was the appearance in England of settlements of Jews, seemingly moving across the Channel in the wake of the Norman Conquest – said William of Malmesbury. Jewish communities were established first in London and the south, then gradually spread west and north as far as Newcastle. Up to the time of their expulsion, by Edward I (1290), there were no Jewish settlements in Scotland, Wales or Ireland. In economic terms England can be put into the context of European development described as "the most profound and most permanent change that overtook Western Europe between the invention of agriculture and the industrial revolution", the growth of towns, markets and manufactures which together with government institutions of a new force, networks of officials "transformed Europe from a society of gift exchange into a money economy, with profound results for its entire structure of values and social custom" (Moore 1987: 102). These are the changes described by James Campbell as "the preliminary to the European conquest of the world" (Campbell 1989: 17).

We may if we like, from the vantage point of the twentieth century, look back at medieval England and see it as an overwhelmingly rural society, a primitive economy. But this is precisely the attitude adopted by twelfth century Englishmen when they looked towards their Celtic neighbours. "The Irish", in Gerald's words, "have not progressed at all from the primitive habits of pastoral farming. For while mankind usually progresses from the woods, and then from fields to settlements and communities of citizens, this Irish people scorns work on the land, has little use for the money making of towns and despises the rights and privileges of the civil life". Ireland, Wales and the highlands and islands of Scotland were perceived as poor and primitive societies – primitive in that they had failed to climb the ladder of evolution of human societies which twelfth century intellectuals like Gerald took for granted (Bartlett 1982: 176). By contrast the English saw themselves as prosperous, peaceful, lawabiding, urbanised and enterprising. As Richard of Devizes was to put it (in

1190s), "no one keen on making money need die poor here". For Richard FitzNigel (in the 1180s), England was a land characterised by its "untold riches" and by "the natural drunkeness of its inhabitants" (Richard of Devizes1963: 64; Richard FitzNigel 1983: 87). A land of yuppies and lager louts.

A further aspect of English economic development and social change was also important in helping to establish the set of imperialist images: the demise of slavery. Slavery, a significant feature of Anglo-Saxon society, was dead and gone by the early decades of the twelfth century. But not from contemporary Ireland, Wales and Scotland – though this is a history which still remains to be written. To William of Malmesbury slavery was a degrading and inhumane institution, and he condemned as "barbarians" those like the Irish who practised it. For John of Salisbury one of the indicators of Welsh barbarism was the fact that they engaged in the slave trade; and very obviously one of the things the Hexham Anonymous detested about the Scots was their involvement in slaving.

## 2. War and Chivalry

The socio-economic fact of slavery carried with it military implications (Patterson 1982: 113–21; Gillingham 1993). From the mid twelfth century onwards English observers found war as slave hunt utterly repellent, for it involved a form of total war, an attack not just on the property of non-combatants – as, in the form of ravaging, was the norm of warfare everywhere in Europe – but on their persons too. In order to capture potential slaves and drag them off into slavery it was in practice necessary to kill not only anyone who put up a fight, but also anyone who got in the way, elderly parents and young children for example – those categories of persons whom it was uneconomic to put to work but whose lamenting, clinging presence impeded the operation (Ade Ajayi 1967: 303). Thus the shocked language with which so many contemporary authors – Henry of Huntingdon, Orderic, Richard of Hexham – described the Scottish invasions of the North in 1137 and 1138, whereas in earlier centuries Scottish raids had been referred to in much more neutral terms by authors who, as members of slave-owning, slave-raiding societies themselves, presumably took for granted the basic characteristics of this form of war.

The new non-slave owning English culture explains why contemporaries of the Battle of the Standard (1138) portrayed it not just as a battle between Scots and English, but as a titanic and ferocious struggle between two different cultures, the civilised and the savage. Moreover accounts of the English victory at the Standard throw further light on the varying rates of economic development within Britain. The Scots lost because although they had an "innumerable army" they had only 200 mailed soldiers (Strickland 1989–90: 191–94). Thus they suffered terribly from the fire of the English archers to which they could make little response for although they possessed archers they were very short of arrows. These details explain why it was the English who were the expansionist power within the British Isles. We have here an unequal struggle between an industrially advanced power and a pastoral economy. A fully equipped man in mail armour would be carrying some 40 lb of iron, and iron was very expensive – relatively much more expensive then than it is now (Bartlett 1986). The English economy was able to cope with the mass-production of ammunition (i.e. arrowheads) and the English were able to mow down the inadequately armoured Irish, Welsh and native Scots. There is a lot of nonsense talked about the supposed military superiority of "feudal cavalry" and "Norman Knights". But it was not cavalry which dominated so many campaigns in Wales and Ireland in the twelfth century, it was armour and firepower. Also, of course, the capacity to build castles and to stock them. This too is a measure of the economic transformation which England had undergone – but which Wales and Ireland had not, and Scotland only to a very limited extent.

Throughout the British Isles succession disputes were one of the commonest causes of armed conflict. In the Celtic realms they were often fought out with great ferocity, losers being either killed or mutilated. Madog ap Meredith, for example, emerged as ruler of Powys in 1132 after two of his uncles and four cousins had met one or other of these fates (Davies 1987: 71–4). Welsh politics, like Irish and Scottish politics, was unquestionably a bloody business for the leading participants. To an observer like Gerald de Barri, who saw himself as a representative of English civilisation, all this was thoroughly reprehensible. When a prince died, he noted, "the most frightful disturbances occur . . . people being murdered, brothers killing each other and even putting each other's eyes out, for as everyone knows from experience, it is very difficult to settle disputes of this sort" (Gerald of Wales 1978: 261). And indeed this is not how succession disputes were handled in twelfth-century England. In earlier centuries power struggles within and between Anglo-Saxon royal dynasties seem to have provoked similar levels of violence, but by the twelfth century disputes about succession to high political office or succession to great estates, were handled, not without violence of course, but with violence which was controlled so as to spare the lives of the royals and aristocrats who engaged in it. Compared with Celtic politics the so-called "anarchy of Stephen's reign" was a very "gentlemanly" affair. This was a chivalrous society. In this sort of society, as Gerald observed, captured soldiers were ransomed, whereas in Wales and Ireland they were butchered and decapitated. Here too is another measure of English economic development, since the chivalrous custom of sparing the lives of highranking captives, either ransoming them for money or using them as bargaining counters in order to obtain possession of castles or towns were humane options which were not so readily available in societies which lacked castles and towns, and where coin was in relatively short supply.[10]


## 3. Sex and marriage

The outraged language used by English authors when referring to the "scandalous" sexual mores and marriage laws of the Celts reflects the way that in 12th Century England, as in the most of "civilised" Europe, men and women had come to accept that marriage was a matter of church law, not of secular law (Brooke 1989: 124–42). This increasingly meant that Christian ideas of marriage – that it should be monogamous, permanent and involve prohibitions against marrying cousins – came to be accepted as social norms, often breached, no doubt, but norms none the less. Celtic societies, however, continued to regulate these matters according to their ancient laws. In earlier centuries there had been a fundamental similarity between English and Celtic marriage customs – Edward the Elder (899–924), for example, married several women, one of them his second cousin, with different degrees of formality. An eleventh-century English law code still found it necessary to assert that no man should have more than one wife.

But developments from the late Saxon period onwards (Stafford 1989: 41–2, 163–68), meant that by the twelfth century customs had perceptibly diverged. Celtic marriage law was now regarded as thoroughly disreputable – especially, of course, by the most enthusiastic "reformers". Thus it is not surprising that it should be in the matter of sex and marriage and within the circle of ecclesiastical reformers that we can detect the earliest signs of the approach of a new and hostile attitude to Celtic peoples. In Lanfranc's eyes, Irish marriage law – a traditional law which made provision for divorce and re-marriage – was not a law of marriage but a law of fornication. A little later, Anselm of Canterbury was to accuse the Irish of wife-swopping "in the way that other men exchange horses" (Bartlett 1982: 43). For as long as Celtic societies remained true to their traditional family law – in Wales into the late middle ages, in Ireland into the seventeenth century – there were to be real differences here, and ones which did much to shape English hostility.

But Celtic family law did more than just upset a few puritanical ecclesiastics. At the level of high politics it also had significant consequences. By allowing Welsh or Irish kings to have a number of wives it made it more likely that they would have a number of sons and this increased the number of males with a claim to succeed, all the more so since Celtic custom posited no great gulf between "legitimate" and "illegitimate" sons. This had the effect of making succession disputes both more frequent and more complicated as different segments of the royal kindreds put in their bids for power (Smith 1986). Given the ferocity of these conflicts, the term used by anthropologically-minded historians – "segmentary strife" – is a faintly anodyne one.

In much of Europe by the twelfth century changes in the laws of marriage and in the customs of inheritance had led away from political conventions which simply took it for granted that successions would be fought over to conventions which were slightly more peaceful. This is a development which seems to go together with the recognition of the rights of daughters as heiresses – in England, but again not in the Celtic world. Thus "Welsh medieval history has none of those heiresses whose fortunes and fate are such a prominent feature of the territorial politics of medieval England" (Davies 1988: 101). Similarly in Ireland, both property and political office could be inherited only by males – at any rate in the centuries before the English invasion of Ireland, when it clearly suited the invading Strongbow, husband of Aoife, daughter of Dermot, king of Leinster, that his wife should be recognised as her father's heiress (Flanagan 1989: 95).

## V

The perception of Celtic societies as barbarous obviously functioned in part as an ideology of conquest. This is evident from the language of the *Gesta Stephani* on the benefits which the new rulers brought to Wales as also from the kinds of justification – like the papal bull *Laudabiliter* (forged or not) – which Gerald de Barri and others put forward in order to legitimise Henry II's conquest of an island to which he had no claim of the conventional type (i.e. based on some alleged hereditary right). But if I am right about the attitudes of authors in the ninth, tenth and eleventh centuries, then it is equally clear that the English had been invading Welsh – and Cornish – lands for centuries without needing an imperialist ideology. The greater significance of the imperialist outlook was the barrier it set up between conqueror and conquered – a barrier which inhibited assimilation. In Hechter's terms, "if the state conquers a peripheral territory without making the assertion of cultural superiority, assimilation is much easier to achieve" (Hechter 1975: 64). There are, it is true, a few signs that some late eleventh century French observers did regard the English as barbarians (Gillingham 1993a), but this perception soon passed, presumably because it had little basis in real differences between northern French and English society. By 1166 an "English" revolt against Norman rule is unimaginable. The descendants of William's followers had become English, speaking French, but living by English law, within a framework of English institutions, aware that they were the heirs of an English past. This is not how the newcomers lived in Wales and Ireland.[11]

For many centuries England and the Celtic world had been very similar societies (Wormald 1986). But in the course of the tenth, eleventh and early twelfth centuries profound European economic, social, military and cultural developments affected the south-east of Britain, a wealthy region close to centres of learning, much more rapidly and intensively than they did a remote upland fringe (Frame 1990: 72–3). By the twelfth century this development meant that they had grown sufficiently far apart for the differences between them to be visible to contemporaries. The author who first gave clear expression to this perception of "otherness" and who did so in terms of the classical contrast between civilisation and barbarism was William of Malmesbury. Some writers, Orderic Vitalis and Henry of Hungtingdon for example, were not immediately converted to seeing Britain and British history through William's eyes, but incidents in the late 1130s, when Scottish and Welsh troops "barbarously" invaded England, seem to have persuaded even them that William's terms of reference made good sense. As William's ideas were taken up, repeated and elaborated many times over in the next few decades, so a new, negative and condescending attitude to Celtic peoples was established, one which was to endure over many centuries. In the field of British history William was the most creative and influential of all English historians. That his ideas, themselves owing much to the depth and intensity of his own immersion in the literature of the ancient world, struck so many chords is doubtless due in part to the intellectual and cultural movement labelled the Twelfth Century Renaissance – here, as generally, a much more important movement than the later Renaissance of the fifteenth and sixteenth centuries. For all that he was a monk living in a formally – and in many respects self-consciously and radically reforming – Christian society, William's revival of Greco-Roman modes of perception resulted in the Christian view of the world, one which divided men and women into two basic groups – Christian and non-Christian – being decisively supplemented by a non-religious system of classification, one which divided men and women into the civilised and the barbarians. In the course of British history this was to be the great divide, the creation of an imperialist English culture.

*Writing this article was greatly facilitated by a generous research grant from the Leverhulme Trust.

## Notes

[1] Although ancient historians have attempted systematic comparisons with modern imperialism (Brunt 1965; Finley 1976), I know of no "medieval" equivalents.

[2] But as they make explicit (Corrigan and Sayer 1985: 11), their primary concern was "with English state formation in England" and here they take their analysis much further back in time.

[3] I should, however, make clear that most medievalists would regard this view as over-simplification, "obscuring crucial ambiguities" (Frame 1990: 52). The usage of R. R. Davies, "Norman" and "Anglo-Norman" before 1170–1200 and "English" thereafter, is much closer to current orthodoxy. This helps to sustain his argument that a crucial shift in attitude occurred in the 13th century, when the conquerors were no longer purveying law and order in general, "but *English* law and *English* governmental order in particular" (Davies 1990: x, 112–117).

[4] For other signs that this is the way things were going see Golding 1986; Ridyard 1986–87; Rollason 1989: 215–39; Green 1989.

[5] It has been suggested (Barrow 1980: 6–7) that, "from the 1070s to the 1170s the English were less confident about their own identity than in any period of their history before this present generation". This may be so, but however uncertain on this score the present generation may be, who would go so far as to deny their Englishness?

[6] When 12th century English authors referred to "Scots" and "Picts", they generally had the Irish-speaking inhabitants of the Highlands and Galloway in mind. In this period Lowland Scotland was being transformed by urbanisation and an influx of English settlers, the aristocrats among them French-speaking. This point in particular should be borne in mind whenever I over-simplify by lumping Ireland, Wales and Scotland together.

[7] However there may be an implicit answer to the question in such statements as "The Norman Conquest accentuated differences between the Celtic and English worlds by importing into England the Norman feudal regime, continental urban institutions, and the reformist ideals of Roman Christianity" and "From the time of the Norman Conquest forward these tribal, pastoral, politically decentralized, and economically marginal societies of oats-and-barley-growing, meat-eating and milk-drinking cattle raiders stood in marked contrast with the agrarian, feudalized, town- and village-dwelling, politically consolidated and more affluent society of wheat-growing and wine-drinking Englishmen" (Jones 1971b: 155–56). There are clearly important points made here, but also some highly questionable interpretations of the role of the Norman Conquest.

[8] As well, of course, as the problems created by the relative absence of sources and the possible silence of sources.

[9] Although ostensibly a description of an attack launched in 1070, there are grounds for regarding it as the work of a mid-twelfth century

author whose attitudes were coloured by his reaction to the Scottish raids of 1137 and 1138 (Gillingham 1993a).

[10] Thus when in Ireland the English tended to treat enemies in "Irish fashion" (Gillingham 1993b).

[11] Once again Lowland Scotland is different. See n.6.

## Bibliography

Ade Ajayi, J.F. (1967) "Samuel Ajayi Crowther of Oyo". In Curtin P.D. ed. *Africa Remembered.* Madison: U of Wisconsin P.

Anderson, Alan O. (1908) *Scottish Annals from English Chroniclers* L: David Nutt.

Aylmer, G.E. (1990) The Peculiarities of the English State. *JHS* 3.

Barrow, G.W.S. (1980) *The Anglo-Norman Era in Scottish History.* OUP.

Barry, T.B. (1987) *The Archaelogy of Medieval Ireland.* L: Methuen.

Bartlett, Robert (1982) *Gerald of Wales.* OUP.

Bartlett, Robert (1986) "Technique Militaire et Pouvoir Politique, 900–1300". *Annales, Economies, Sociétés, Civilisations* 41.

Bethell, Denis (1971) "English monks and Irish reform in the eleventh and twelfth centuries". *Historical Studies* 8.

Brooke, Christopher (1989) *The Medieval Idea of Marriage.* OUP.

Brunt, P.A. (1965) "Reflections on British and Roman Imperialism". *Comparative Studies in Society and History* 7.

Campbell, James (1984) "Some Twelfth-Century Views of the Anglo-Saxon Past". *Peritia* 3.

Campbell, James (1989) "Was it infancy in England? Some Questions of Comparison". In Jones M. and Vale M., eds., *England and her Neighbours 1066–1453. Essays in Honour of Pierre Chaplais.* L: Hambledon Press.

Corrigan, P., and Sayer, D. (1985) *The Great Arch: English State Formation as Cultural Revolution.* O: Blackwell.

Davies, R.R. (1984–85) "Buchedd a moes y Cymry. The manners and morals of the Welsh". *Welsh H.R.* 12.

Davies, R.R. (1987) *Conquest, Co-existence and Change. Wales 1063–1415.* OUP.

Davies, R.R. (1988) "The status of women and the practice of marriage in late-medieval Wales". In Jenkins D. and Owen M., eds. *The Welsh Law of Women.* Cardiff: U. of Wales P.

Davies R.R. (1990) *Domination and Conquest. The Experience of Ireland, Scotland and Wales.* CUP.

Davies, Wendy (1982) *Wales in the Early Middle Ages.* Leicester UP.

Duncan, A.A.M. (1975) *Scotland. The Making of the Kingdom.* Edinburgh: Oliver and Boyd.

Finley, M. I. (1976) "Colonies – an Attempt at a Typology." *Transactions of the Royal Historical Society* 26.

Flanagan, Marie Therese (1989) *Irish Society, Anglo-Norman Settlers, Angevin Kingship* O: Clarendon Press.

Frame, Robin (1981) *Colonial Ireland 1169–1369.* Dublin: Helicon.

Frame, Robin (1990) *The Political Development of the British Isles 1100–1400.* OUP.

Gerald of Wales (1978) *The Journey through Wales and the Description of Wales.* Penguin Classic.

Gerald of Wales (1982) *The Topography of Ireland.* Penguin Classic.

Gesta Stephani (1976) ed. and trans. K.R. Potter and R.H.C. Davis. OUP.

Gillingham, John (1990–91) "The Context and Purposes of Geoffrey of Monmouth's *History of the Kings of Britain.*" *Anglo-Norman Studies* 13.

Gillingham, John (1993a) "Conquering the Barbarians: War and Chivalry in Twelfth-Century Britain." *Haskins Society Journal* 4.

Gillingham, John (1993b) "The English Invasion of Ireland." In Bradshaw B. and others, eds. Representing Ireland. CUP.

Golding, Brian (1986) "Anglo-Norman Knightly Burials." In Harper-Bill C. and Harvey R., eds., *The Ideals and Practice of Medieval Knighthood*. Woodbridge Boydell Press.

Gransden, Antonia (1974) *Historical Writing in England c.550 to c. 1307* L: Routledge.

Green, Judith (1989) "Unity and Disunity in the Anglo-Norman State". *Historical Research* 62.

Guenée, Bernard (1980) *Histoire et Culture historique dans l'Occident médiéval.* P: Aubier.

Hechter, Michael (1975) *Internal Colonialism. The Celtic fringe in British national development.* L: Routledge and Kegan Paul.

Hinton, David A. (1990) *Archaeology, Economy and Society. England from the fifth to the fifteenth century.* L: Seaby.

Jones, W.R. (1971a) "The Image of the Barbarian in Medieval Europe". *Comparative Studies in Society and History* 13.

Jones, W.R. (1971b) "England against the Celtic Fringe: a Study in Cultural Stereotypes". *Journal of World History* 13.

Kearney, Hugh (1989) *The British Isles. A History of Four Nations*. CUP.

MacDougall, Hugh A. (1982) *Racial Myth in English History*. Montreal: Harvest House.

Moore, R.I. (1987) *The Formation of a Persecuting Society*. OUP.

Patterson, Orlando (1982) *Slavery and Social Death*. Cambridge, Ma: Harvard UP.

Powicke, F.M. (1950) *Walter Daniel's Life of Ailred, Abbot of Rievaulx*. L: Nelson.

Ralph of Diceto (1986) *Historical Works*, ed. W. Stubbs, L: Rolls Series.

Richard of Devizes (1963) *Chronicle*, ed. J.T. Appleby, L: Nelson.

Richard FitzNigel (1983) *Dialogus de Scaccario*, ed. and trans. C. Johnson and others. O: Clarendon.

Ridyard, S.J. (1986–87) "*Condigna Veneratio* Post-Conquest Attitudes to the Saints of the Anglo-Saxons", *Anglo-Norman Studies* 9.

Rollason, David (1989) *Saints and Relics in Anglo-Saxon England*. O: Blackwell.

Short, Ian (1990) "Gaimar et les debuts de l'historiographie en langue française". In *Chroniques Nationales et Chroniques Universelles*, Göppinger Arbeiten zur Germanistik 508. Göppingen: Kummerle Verlag.

Smith, J.B. (1986) "Dynastic Succession in medieval Wales", *Bulletin of the Board of Celtic Studies* 33.

Southern, R.W. (1973) "Aspects of the European Tradition of Historical Writing: 4. The Sense of the Past", *Transactions of the Royal Historical Society* 23.

Spufford, Peter (1988) *Money and its use in medieval Europe*. CUP.

Stafford, Pauline (1989) *Unification and Conquest. A Political and Social History of England in the Tenth and Eleventh Centuries*. L: Arnold.

Strickland, Matthew (1989–90) "Securing the North: Invasion and the Strategy of Defence in twelfth Century Anglo-Scottish Warfare". *Anglo-Norman Studies* 12.

Taylor, Christopher (1983) *Village and Farmstead.* L: George Philip.

Thomson, Rodney M. (1987) *William of Malrnesbury.* Woodbridge: Boydell Press.

William of Malmesbury (1887) *De Gestis Requm,* ed. W. Stubbs. L: Rolls Series.

Wormald, Patrick (1986) "Celtic and Anglo-Saxon Kingship: some further thoughts". In Szarmach P.E., ed. *Sources of Anglo-Saxon Culture.* Kalamazoo: Western Michigan U.

# Issues and Agendas

# The English State and the "Celtic" Peoples 1100–1400

REES DAVIES

**Abstract** The Medieval English state had been studied by historians largely on its own terms and from its own records, enriched by an occasional reference to continental comparisons and contrasts. This will no doubt remain the primary approach; but it can be usefully supplemented by also looking at the English state through its impact on other "Celtic" countries in the rest of Britain and Ireland which it brought, either permanently or temporarily, within the ambit of its power. English rule in Wales, Ireland and, briefly, Scotland can thereby serve as a mirror in which one may see refracted some of the essential qualities and *mentalités* of the English state itself – notably its increasingly self-consiously English character in terms of its own identity and institutions and the growing assumption that there should be a good measure of governmental uniformity and bureaucratic answerability in the lands which it had annexed. English rule in the "Celtic" countries also brings into sharp focus how dependent the medieval English state was for its operation on an effective relationship between state and society; the failure to replicate that relationship substantially in Wales and Ireland showed that there was more to successful political integration than military might and governmental uniformity.

Historians of the medieval English state do not, for the most part, give much attention in their studies to Ireland, Scotland and Wales, the "Celtic" countries (to use a convenient, if very misleading, shorthand phrase) which bordered on the English state and which occasionally formed satellites or annexes of it. It is not difficult to understand why. The early English state seems to be an essentially home-grown institution (however much recent scholarship has drawn attention to Carolingian parallels in its early history); two of its most noticeable features – its remarkably early institutional maturity and its equally remarkable continuity – appear to be already well-established long before its activities impinge in a sustained fashion on the "Celtic" countries. The history of that state has essentially to be written from its own records; the supcrabundance of those records, especially from c. 1200, hardly encourages the historian to look beyond the state's own archives for sources. Furthermore, one of the monumental achievements of medieval academic historiography in Britain, from the days of Stubbs and Tout onwards, has been to trace the organic growth of the English state in constitutional, institutional and political terms and in doing so to stress its quintessential Englishness. Historians of medieval Ireland, Scotland and Wales have, by and large, returned the compliment, cultivating the histories of their respective countries along the trajectories of their own perceived identities and construing the impact of the English state upon them in an essentially external fashion.

Historiographical habits are deeply embedded in intellectual attitudes and assumptions and in archival arrangements and opportunities. No one would deny that it is from within England itself that the nature, claims and assumptions of the medieval English state should primarily be studied. But one may occasionally wonder whether some of the distinctive features of that state and its mythology of legitimacy could not be even better appreciated if it were studied from its peripheries and satellites as well as from its metropolitan base and through county studies in England. Thus the studies of H.G. Richardson, Jocelyn Otway-Ruthven and others of the way in which the offices and personnel of English administration were transplanted and in some measure replicated in Ireland in the century or so after 1180 (to give one obvious example) might well help to bring some of the key features of the medieval English state at a particularly crucial stage in its development into clearer perspective. To overlook such studies on the grounds that they are part of "Irish history" would certainly be an act of intellectual impoverishment. Nor need students of the medieval English state restrict their gaze to those areas of Britain and Ireland to which the forms and personnel of English government were exported. It would also surely be rewarding to compare the English state with its only truly British comparator in medieval times, the Scottish kingdom. Here again the illuminating comparative exercises of historians such as Geoffrey Barrow, Alexander Grant and Robin Frame should help to alert students of the English state to attend to what is truly distinctive about it.

Comparative exercises which brought the Celtic countries and their peoples within the ambit of their consideration could enrich the study of the medieval English state in another direction. One of the key questions in the analysis of that state is the relationship between social and economic development on the one hand and state formation and power on the other. That such a link exists hardly admits of doubt; but the nature, centrality and chronology of that link still remain to be fully explored. English historians seem to be moving ever more closely to acknowledging the symbiosis between the early institutional maturity of the English state and what some of them now daringly refer to as "The First English Industrial Revolution". It is within the English evidence –

archaeological and numismatic as well as written – that the answer will have to be looked for; but comparisons with the contiguous "Celtic" countries could also surely be illuminating. Was the absence of towns (other than Viking ports), coinage and a well-developed network of markets a fatal drawback to political coalescence and state formation in Wales and Ireland and to the rapid circulation of surplus cash necessary both for commercial buoyancy and political consolidation? And if this were so, why do historians of Scotland – where towns and coinage were likewise notable by their absence before the twelfth century – make claims for "the precocity of a single kingdom of Scotia or Alba in the mid-ninth century" and refer to its "well-formed and independent political institutions"? In other words the issues raised by the precociousness of the early English state might well be brought into sharper focus by considering the contrasting experiences of the societies and polities which bordered on it. In this respect modern historians would only be pursuing a line of investigation that contemporary observers hinted at: they commented on the economic backwardness of the "Celtic" countries (especially Brittany, Ireland and Wales) and linked it with their political disorder; they even gave a chronological dimension to their comparisons, suggesting (as did William of Newburgh) that the Irish in the twelfth century were still politically at the same stage as the Anglo-Saxons under the Heptarchy.

The illumination that comparisons and contrasts often provide might, therefore, persuade the student of the medieval English state to pay more attention to the character of contemporary "Celtic" countries. But there is, of course, a more direct way in which the history of those countries casts light on the nature of the English state, namely through the impact of that expansionist state and its peoples on neighbouring "Celtic" societies and polities. The nature of that impact changed during the course of the medieval centuries, thereby reflecting the changing character, potential and power of the English state. English pretensions to the domination of the British Isles and to be rightful heirs to the province of Britannia were very old. Already in the eighth century, and more commonly by the tenth century, various English kings had arrogated titles – such as "ruler of the English and governor of other adjoining nations round about" or "king of the English and governor of the whole of Britain" – which proclaimed to the world their imperial pretensions to the hegemony of the whole island. But imperial pretensions were one thing, effective and sustained "state" control quite another. It is here that the experience of the changing character of English domination over the "Celtic" countries between, say, 1050 and 1300 helps to pinpoint changes in the

English state itself. To put it much too simply, in 1050 (or even in 1150) English domination appears essentially patriarchal and tributary in character – ceremonially manifested in the rituals of submission (be they rowing the king of England on the Dee or accompanying him on an expedition to Toulouse), economically underwritten by periodic or even regular tributes (such as the 4,000 oxen and 300 horses proffered by Lord Rhys of Deheubarth, southwest Wales, to Henry II in 1170), and eventually guaranteed by the threat of a punitive raid. By 1300 that domination was becoming more bureaucratic and integrative; it involved a measure of administrative, financial and judicial control of the areas annexed to the English state (by that date most of north and west Wales, south and east Ireland and lowland Scotland): it also involved the political submission of the subject "Celtic" peoples and the replacement of the overlordship of native provincial rulers (e.g. king of Scotland, prince of Wales) by a strict hierarchy of authority which tolerated eventually only one sovereign source of secular power, the king of England, who had also arrogated the title "lord of Ireland" and suppressed, at least temporarily, those of "king of Scotland" (1296) and "prince of Wales" (1282). This transformation in the pretensions, reach and character of English domination clearly had profound implications for "Celtic" peoples and their polities; but, more immediately relevant to the present argument, it surely signifies and serves to highlight a major transformation in, indeed arguably the emergence of, the English state.

## The Englishness of the Medieval English State
## c. 1170–c. 1300

It can, I believe, be plausibly argued that it was in the "long" thirteenth century – between c. 1170 and 1300 – that a truly *English* state emerged, or re-emerged. To claim as much is not to deny for one moment the remarkable achievements of the tenth-century kings or to doubt that pre-conquest England was, in James Campbell's words, a "formidably organised state"; equally it is not to deny what Jolliffe so aptly called "the unconvenanted strength" of the kingship of the Norman and Angevin kings. But there is, nevertheless, a case to be made that it was in the century or so before c. 1300 that this essentially patrimonial and feudal polity became a state whose powers impinged regularly and individually on its citizens, and also a distinctly and indeed aggressively English state. The loss of the monarchy's northern French lands (eventually formally accepted in 1259), the continuous residence of the king and his court in England (his last protracted non-campaigning period in his French lands was in 1286–9), the emergence of

Westminster as the religious and governmental headquarters of his lands, the marked growth of xenophobia in English domestic and ecclesiastical politics, and the exportability of what were now regarded as distinctively English laws and institutions are among the best-known causes and manifestations of the growing English-ness of the English state.

Perhaps not surprisingly the Englishness of the English state appears particularly conspicuous from the perspective of the Celtic lands. Take the Church for instance. It had once, in early Norman days, loudly paraded Canterbury's claim to the primacy of the whole of Britain, including Ireland and the Isles, and had done so, interestingly and precociously, in the name of the "union and solidarity of the kingdom". By the later twelfth century it was proclaiming the English Church as the one whose norms should be followed by Celtic peoples. "In all parts of the Irish church", so it was to be reported of the synod of Cashel in 1172 "all matters . . . are to be conducted hereafter . . . in line with the observance of the *English* church". Two years later one of the conditions of the so-called Treaty of Falaise imposed on the king of Scotland was that "the church of Scotland shall henceforward owe such subjection to the church of *England* as it ought to". I wouldn't want to claim too much for these phrases; but they do seem to suggest that English political superiority now entailed, at least in ecclesiastical matters, open acknowledgement of dependence on *England* and acceptance of its ecclesiastical norms as the touchstone of proper practice.

During the next century or so the growing Englishness and statecentred character of the advancing English domination of the Celtic countries become increasingly clear, all the more so as the impetus of Anglo-Norman aristocratic expansion and peasant colo-nisation in both Wales and Ireland seemed to be faltering badly by c. 1240. Conquest, submission and tributes were no longer adequate; governmental control from, and answerability to, West-minster became increasingly necessary and involved transplanting the assumptions, language and institutions of the English state to the Celtic lands. Thirteenth-century Ireland is the obvious example: in 1210 according to the chronicler the king "caused *English* laws and customs to be instituted in Ireland": over the next decades much of the country was shired, and a pattern of governmental institutions, practices and personnel was evolved on the English model. The story was different in Wales; but there likewise the *Englishness* and governmental masterfulness of *royal* domination became dominant themes in the thirteenth century: it is reflected in the conviction of contemporary English chroniclers (whether they were right or not) that it was the imposition of English laws and customs which drove the Welsh to revolt; it was manifested likewise in the great statute of 1284 which, by and large, imposed the norms and practices of English governance and criminal law on north-west Wales. The English state was now both the master and the norm: in 1296, after the defeat of the Scots at Dunbar, the exchequer established at Berwick was specifically to be modelled on that of Westminster; and when administrative ordinances were issued for Wales or Ireland they echoed to the refrain "come est fait en Angleterre", "come en Engleterre" ("as is done in England", "as in England"). The best guarantee of administrative conformity (and of political loyalty) was to reserve the key offices in these dependent areas for those well-versed in the habits and methods of the English state: so it was that either immigrant settlers or seconded personnel from England monopolised almost all the key offices of English rule in Ireland or Wales and, briefly, Scotland. Even immigrant settlers might come under suspicion of going native; therefore, as a command of 1342 put it, the king would "be better served (in Ireland) by English ministers having incomes and properties in *England*".

The command pinpoints an issue which came into clearer focus as the thirteenth century progressed. By 1300 the medieval English state and its aristocracy had extended their control over the whole of Wales, much of Ireland and (temporarily and, as it turned out, briefly) over parts of southern Scotland. How were these conquered and annexed lands to be governed? Were they to be integrated administratively, fiscally, judicially and even politically, in greater or lesser degree, into the fabric of the English state? The answer to that question depended in part on the date and the character of English domination. So it was that extensive parts of southern and eastern Wales retained their character as great aristocratic lordships for the rest of the middle ages because they had been largely conquered by "private" seignorial enterprise in the eleventh and twelfth centuries. In Ireland, on the other hand, the forms and to some degree the substance of the English state's institutions were much more evident because the conquest of Ireland coincided with the period of the rapid definition of the powers and machinery of the English medieval state. But the nature of the English state's governance of its subject "Celtic" peoples was also coloured, consciously or otherwise, by its perception of the status of those peoples. To put it crudely, were they sufficiently politically reliable and legally and governmentally mature to be admitted into full membership of the English state? The answer was in part surely shaped by the anxieties and aspirations of the very substantial communities of English settlers who had established themselves in the lowlands of southern and eastern Ireland and Wales. Groups such as "the English people of the county of Pembroke", "the

English liege people of Ireland" or "the English burgesses of the English boroughs in Wales" (to quote a few contemporary phrases) learnt to play the card of their Englishness to defend their privileges and to promote their cause.

The other side of the coin to an acceptance of the exclusiveness of the English settlers (however their Englishness was defined) was an acceptance that the native inhabitants were at best different, at worst inferior. Consciously or otherwise, the English state and its ruling elite defined their attitude towards the Celtic peoples whom they ruled during the course of the thirteenth and fourteenth centuries. We see the shaping of that attitude in tell-tale phrases such as "nothwithstanding that she is Welsh" or "although they are Irish", the emergence of the plea of "exception of Irishry" among the legal ploys of the English settler communities in Ireland, the exclusion of the native Irish from the benefits of English law and the failure of the campaign to reverse that exclusion, the institutionalisation of divisions between Welshries and Englishries in Wales, the legislation (starting in 1297 and culminating in the Statutes of Kilkenny of 1366) aimed at preventing English settlers from adopting Irish customs (degeneracy), the fiercely discriminatory national and local legislation against Welshmen prompted by the revolt of Owain Glyn Dŵr, and the appearance of letters of denizenship for those Welsh and Irish who wished to become fully-fledged English citizens. In the shaping of the psychology of English statehood and citizenship (and by implication the exclusion from, or at best the reluctant admission of others to, the benefits of membership of that state) the entrenching of such attitudes and categories are surely not without significance. The powers of the English state grew by leaps and bounds in the thirteenth and fourteenth centuries; but in its dealings with the "Celtic" peoples and provinces now under its control, the limitations of that state also stand out. They are partly limitations of military reach and governmental manageability at a distance (of which more later); but they are also limitations which arise out of perceptions and attitudes. To hold up the mirror to the nature of English rule in Wales and Ireland is to see refracted in it some of the essential qualities and *mentalités* of the English state.

## The Changing Character of English Domination of the "Celtic" Countries

The nature of the power claimed by this English state over 'dependent "Celtic" rulers changed perceptibly between the early twelfth and the late thirteenth centuries, thereby indicating that the state's external control of its client dependencies matched the state's growing internal control of its own citizens. The contrast can be highlighted by a pair of examples of ceremonies of submission. Take, first, two ceremonies separated by almost exactly a century: the first took place at Abernethy on the Firth of Tay in 1072 when, in the words of the Anglo-Saxon chronicle, Malcolm Canmore, king of Scots, "came and made peace with King William and gave hostages and became his man"; the second took place in 1171 on the banks of the river Suir in Ireland when the king of Limerick and all the princes of southern Ireland were admitted into Henry II's peace, submitted to him, agreed to pay him tribute from their kingdoms and then returned home, weighed down with the gifts he had bestowed upon them. On both occasions there could be no doubt that the king of the English had exacted submission, reinforced by the handing over of hostages and the acknowledgement of the need to pay tribute. But the overlordship claimed and acknowledged could hardly be regarded as intrusive or bureaucratic and in both cases it proved fragile and temporary, no more than one episode in an ever-fluctuating relationship between would-be clients and would-be overlord. Move on a century and one is in an apparently different world. In July 1283, within six months of the death of the last native prince, of Wales, assemblies were convoked in every district of north Wales in which the local communities and named individuals bound themselves over in large sums for their good behaviour to the king of England in future; in 1296 oaths of fealty to King Edward of England were likewise exacted from all substantial free holders in southern Scotland. What had happened? It is not merely that submissions hitherto exacted from kings and princelings were now demanded of freeholders and communities; it was also surely that an unitary state's demand for a consuming political loyalty was being ceremonially extended to new subjects brought within its ambit.

We can witness the same consuming exclusiveness of the English state in other directions. Take the question of titles. There was no suggestion at Abernethy in 1072 or on the river Suir in 1171 that the kings of Scotland and Ireland should surrender their titles. By the thirteenth century, however, matters were beginning to look different. It was, it is true, in part a gradual acceptance by petty native rulers that their pretensions to titles such as "prince" or "king" looked somewhat ridiculous on an European stage. But there was also deliberate slighting and downgrading by the chancery of the English state: thus in the 1240s Henry III never deigned to call the ruler of Gwynedd other than "David, the son of Llywelyn sometime prince of north Wales"; even when David's nephew, Llywelyn, extracted from Henry III the formal concession of the title of "prince of Wales" in 1267, the English king in his diplomatic correspondence quickly cut him down to size, referring to him as "one of the greater among the other magnates of our kingdom". After the conquests of the 1280s and 1290s the matter could be resolved in a fashion which gave the ruler of the English state (and subsequently, his eldest son) the monopoly of kingly and princely titles in the British Isles and Ireland. John had already appropriated the title "dominus Hibernie" so that no one else could claim to be high king of Ireland; after 1282 and 1296 respectively the titles of prince of Wales and king of Scotland were, at least temporarily, suppressed.

A sovereign state cannot tolerate another fully-fledged state within the ambit of its power. So it was that Wales, which had been formally, if reluctantly, acknowledged as a principality since 1267, was peremptorily relegated to the status of a land (*terra*) in 1282. Henry II had used precisely the same term to describe Scotland after its humiliation in 1174; so again did Edward I, most formally and menacingly in his Ordinance for the Governance of the land of Scotland in 1305. And in both countries the emblems of separate identity or statehood were removed to England and lodged at Westminster. What would have happened to Scotland had Edward's victory not been reversed is a matter for speculation, but that it should have been allowed to survive as an independent kingdom seems altogether unlikely. The pretensions of the unitary state would hardly have tolerated that.

For the language of the unitary state is, by definition, ultimately integrationist and uniformist; and language is, as always, a reflection of the way the world is, or should be, ordered. Contemporary language speaks of the crown and its inalienable rights, but in the sense that the crown increasingly stands for the common weal, for the state. In 1254 when the heir apparent was given, *inter alia*, the royal territories in Wales and the lordship of Ireland it was declared that they should "never be separated from the Crown, but should remain entirely to the kings of *England* for ever". Arguably even more indicative of the growing integrationist ideology than such solemn declarations' are the occasional giveaway phrases of royal clerks – referring for example to the need "for the unity of the king's lands" (in the context of saying that English laws should be observed in Ireland) or the need "to improve the state of our entire dominion" which on being glossed referred to England, Ireland, Wales and Scotland, or alluding to the prince of Wales or the king of Scotland as "our subjects, like others of our realm". One is tempted to paraphrase: "our realm" is an "entire dominion" is the English state.

The pretensions and the capaciousness of the English state are indeed vividly revealed in its control over the "Celtic" regions by the late thirteenth century. We can see its power in the creation of dependent, delegated provincial administrations at Caernarfon, Carmarthen, Dublin and, briefly, Berwick which were modelled on, and answerable to, Westminster; in the command of 1293 that the accounts of Ireland should be audited at the English exchequer; in the number of cases from Ireland that appear on the rolls of the English King's Bench; in the flood of petitions from Wales, Scotland and Ireland on the parliament rolls of 1305; in the insistence that the weights and measures of London were to be used uniformly throughout the lordship of Ireland; or in the brisk reminder that mandates under the great seal of England were perfectly valid in Scotland or Ireland. There were even hints that a single political forum for the expanded English state might be in the making; in 1277 one of the conditions imposed during diplomatic negotiations with the Welsh was that two of their princes should "come to our parliaments in *England* as our other earls and barons come"; after 1292 King John of Scotland was expected by Edward I "to come to our parliaments at our command . . . as our subject, like others of *our realm*". It is little wonder that Geoffrey Barrow, contemplating Edward I's measures for the government of Scotland in 1296, should admire "the calm ambitiousness and extraordinary thoroughness of the thirteenth-century English monarchy".

The medieval English state had achieved much in its relations with the Celtic countries in the century and a half since 1170. It explained its domination over those countries in a variety of ways. The easiest defence technically, but the most shallow one substantively, was to claim that the rulers of those lands had defaulted on their feudal obligations to the king of England and thereby paid the price of forfeiture to their superior lord. More interesting, if more sanctimonious, were arguments cast in terms of the English state's moral responsibilities, a medieval version, as it were, of the White Man's Burden. Such arguments might refer (as in Ireland) to the need to extend the boundaries and promote the values of an international church; they might also be mounted in the name of the scrutiny of native law and the extirpation of bad laws and customs (as happened successively in Ireland, Wales and Scotland); they might refer to the blessings of sound government and order which came in the wake of English domination; they might even, as Gerald of Wales put it disarmingly in explaining the English intervention in Ireland, refer to the need and opportunity to introduce Celts to "a better way of life". Arguments from moral legitimacy were supplemented by those from historical mythology, most notably in the pursuit of England's claim to the overlordship of Scotland. Such arguments reached their logical conclusion in the statements of English apologists and negotiators that Scotland and Wales were parts of Britain; Britain belonged, as all knew, to the king of England: *ergo* the English nation was the British nation, *inclyta natio Angticana alias Brytannica*. The English state was being converted into a British state; over the next few centuries political realities and institutional forms caught up, or tried to catch up, with mythological claim.

## The Limits of the English State's Power and Achievement

Yet one must enter a word of caution. The power of the English kings over their "Celtic" neighbours had increased dramatically in the century or so after 1170, reaching its apogee in the reign of Edward I. Such a dramatic accession of power was a striking testimony to the strength of the English state; but it was a strength not without its limitations. In military terms English control faltered as one entered what was increasingly called "the land of war" in Ireland, proved short-lived in Scotland and was even periodically challenged in Wales. The legal traditions and social structures of much of the "Celtic" countries made the wholesale transfer of the institutions of the English state thither unlikely, in spite of the uniformist rhetoric of the English royal chancery. Indeed one can argue that the problems of communication and technology in the medieval world inhibited the English state from being even able to contemplate bringing large swathes of the "Celtic" regions within its effective control.

Even in those parts of the "Celtic" regions where English control was fm and where it was underpinned by a considerable English settler presence, domination did not for the most part lead to the integration of these annexed districts fully into the political and institutional framework of the English state. In Wales the royal lands in the north and west, though ultimately controlled from Westminster, were organized as largely self-contained annexes under the justiciars of Caernarfon and Carmarthen; there was no Welsh representation in parliament (other than on two anomalous occasions); royal Wales, the Principality proper, let alone the Marcher lordships, was not part of the kingdom of England fiscally or, for most purposes, judicially. English achievement in Ireland, or rather in that half of Ireland which was under more or less effective English control, was in many respects much more impressive, largely because the conquest of Ireland took place in the very century when the institutions and capacities of the English medieval state were expanding rapidly. English Ireland shared the same law as England; its institutions of central and local government were regional variants of the English models; its judicial and financial affairs were closely scrutinized by, and ultimately controlled from, Westminster. Yet English Ireland, let along the Gaelic-controlled districts, was at a remove from the English state. It had its own governmental system, its own parliament, its own taxation, central and local; the configuration of its distribution of effective political and institutional power was very different from that of England; and by the fourteenth century its political community was developing and asserting its own identity. As for Scotland, both the institutional and political cohesion of the Scottish kingdom before 1290 and the brevity of the periods of English control of the southern lowlands suggest that beyond the temporary civilian arm of a military occupation (as in 1296 and 1303–6) any prospect of the sustained political or institutional integration of Scotland or part of it into the English state seemed unlikely.

All in all, the relationship between the English state and its Celtic neighbours in the period 1100–1400 is, I would argue, full of significance for an understanding of the nature of that state. Nowhere was the power of the English state more awesomely demonstrated militarily than in the deployment of men and resources assembled by Edward I to subjugate Wales and Scotland and to impose his authority on those countries. Similarly the self-confidence of the English state by the thirteenth century in its governmental institutions and legal practices is vividly manifested in the way that English law and institutions were transplanted to Ireland (from John's reign, in particular), in the magisterial definitiveness of the Statute of Wales 1284 which laid down the institutional and legal arrangements for the governance of conquered Wales, and in the Ordinance for the Government of the land of Scotland of 1305 which sketched the future guidelines for the English control of that country. The sheer range and minuteness of control that the English state could bring to bear on its subjects is likewise illustrated clearly in the extensive documentation in the English royal chancery, exchequer and judicial offices which deals with the affairs of Ireland and Wales, and to a much lesser degree Scotland. Finally if one looks for evidence of the way the English state explained the legitimacy of its power and the rationale of its activities, its relationship with the societies and polities of the "Celtic" countries, both before and after conquest, provides illuminating material.

But from that same material and from the same perspective one can also identify other features of the medieval English state in that very period (c. 1200–1350) when, in Gerald Harriss's words, "most of the institutions of early modern England took recognizable form". One was its confident Englishness. It defined the norms of justice, law and good governance by the yardstick of current English practice; it also accepted, and to some degree fostered, the notion of

Englishness as a qualification for membership of the English state, thereby confirming the status of the native Irish and Welsh and the Scots as separate peoples. Another feature of the English state which came into clear focus during this period was the dependence of that state for its effective operation on an effective relationship between state and society, more especially between king, aristocracy and gentry. Where that relationship could not be, or was not, effectively replicated – as was to an extent true of Wales and Ireland – there was a fragility about the legitimacy and effectiveness of that state. Such fragility was all the greater where the English state was seen as, and often acted as if it was, dominating a more or less alienated native society rather than working with the grain of it and where there was, thereby, a disjunction between state power and indigenous "political" society and aspiration. This was transparently true in Scotland from the 1290s, recurrently true of much of Gaelic Ireland, and to a degree still true of much of Wales in the fourteenth century. The failure of the English state – for all its strength, indeed because of it – to introduce measures for the effective integration of the parts of Ireland, Scotland and Wales that it controlled into its political community and patterns of patronage and loyalties as well as into its military and governmental control posed tensions which would be central to the relationship of the English state and the Celtic countries for generations to come. In terms of power the English state by c. 1300 might well claim that it was well on the way to establishing a British state; in terms of political texture and loyalties that was far from being so.

*** 

Earlier versions of this paper were presented to the History Workshop Conference at Oxford, November 1991 and to the Discussion Group on the Formation of the English State at St. Peter's College, Oxford, April 1992. It is published at the request of Gavin Williams. Since it deals with issues which I have considered elsewhere in print, I append a short note on bibliographic orientation rather a panoply of footnotes with which the essay could be provided.

## 1. The British Isles and Ireland: Overviews

G.W.S. Barrow, *Feudal Britain, 1066–1314*, L: Edward Arnold, 1956.

"Das Mittelalterlich Englische und Schottische Konigtum: Ein Vergleich", *Historisches Jahrbuch* 102, 1982.

R.R. Davies, *Domination and Conquest: The Experience of Ireland, Scotland and Wales 1100–1300*, CUP, 1990.

———— ed., *The British Isles 1100–1500. Comparisons, Contrasts and Connections*, Edinburgh: John Donald, 1988.

R. Frame, *The Political Development of the British Isles 1100–1400*, OUP, 1990.

M.T. Flanagan, *Irish Society, Anglo-Norman Settlers, Angevin Kingship. Interactions in Ireland in the Late Twelfth Century*, OUP, 1990.

A. Grant, "Crown and Nobility in Late Medieval Britain", *Scotland and England 1286–1815*, ed. R.A. Mason, Edinburgh: John Donald, 1987.

J. Le Patourel, *The Norman Empire*, OUP, 1976.

P. Wormald, "Celtic and Anglo-Saxon Kingship: Some Further Thoughts", in P.E. Szarmach ed, *Sources of Anglo-Saxon Culture*, Kalamazoo: UP Western Michigan, 1986.

## 2. England

J. Campbell, *Essays in Anglo-Saxon Histoy*, L: Hambledon, 1986.

M.T. Clanchy, *England and its Rulers 1066–1272. Foreign Lordship and National Identity*, L: Fontana, 1983.

R.A. Griffiths, "The English Realm and Dominions and the King's Subjects in the Later Middle Ages", *Aspects of Government and Society in Later Medieual England: Essays in honour of J.R. Lander*, ed J.G. Rowe, Toronto UP, 1986.

G.L. Harriss, *King, Parliament and Public FInance In Medieval England to 1369*, OUP, 1975.

J.E.A. Jolliffe, *Angeuin Kingship*, L: Black, 2nd edn. 1963.

M. Prestwich, *English Politics in the Thirteenth Century*, L: Macmillan, 1990.

W.L. Warren, *The Governance of Norman and Angevin England, 1086–1272*, L: Edward Arnold, 1987.

## 3. Ireland

A. Cosgrove, ed., *Medieval Ireland 1169–1534. A New History of Ireland*, vol. 2, OUP, 1987.

R. Frame, *Colonial Ireland 1169–1369*, Dublin: Helicon, 1981.

*English Lordship in Ireland 1318–61*, OUP, 1982.

"England and Ireland, 1171–1399", in M. Jones and M. Vale ed, *England and her Neighbours 1066–1483 Essays in Honour of Pierre Chaplais*, L: Hambledon, 1988.

A.J. Otway-Ruthven, *A History of Medieval Ireland*, L: Benn, 2nd edn. 1980.

H.G. Richardson and G.O. Sayles. *The Administration of Ireland 1172–1377*, Dublin: Irish Manuscripts Commission, 1963.

G.O. Sayles, *Documents on the Affairs of Ireland before the King's Council*, Dublin: Irish Historical Manuscripts Commission, 1979.

K. Simms, *From Kings to Warlords. The Changing Political Structure of Gaelic Ireland in the Late Middle Ages*, Woodbridge: Boydell and Brewer, 1987.

## 4. Scotland

G.W.S. Barrow, *Kingship and Unity. Scotland 1000–1306*, L: Edward Arnold, 1981.

*Robert Bruce and the Community of the Realm of Scotland*, Edinburgh UP, 3rd edn. 1988.

A.A.M. Duncan, *Scotland: The Making of a Kingdom*, Edinburgh: Oliver and Boyd, 1975.

A. Grant, *Independence and Nationhood. Scotland 1306–1469*, L: Edward Arnold, 1986.

E.L.G. Stones, *Anglo-Scottish Relations 1174–1328: Some selected documents*, OUP, 1970.

R. Nicholson, *Scotland. The Later Middle Ages*, Edinburgh: Oliver and Boyd, 1974.

M. Prestwich, "Colonial Scotland. The English in Scotland under Edward I", in R.A. Mason, ed, *Scotland and England 1286–1815*, Edinburgh: John Donald, 1987.

## 5. Wales

R.R. Davies, *Conquest, Coexistence and Change. Wales 1063–1415*, OUP, 1987.

J. Given, *State and Society in Medieval Europe. Gwynedd and Languedoc under Outside Rule*, NY: Cornell UP, 1990.

R.A. Griffiths, *The principality of Wales in the Later Middle Ages. I. South Wales 1277–1536*, Cardiff: UP Wales, 1972.

Ll.B. Smith, "The Statute of Wales, 1284", *Welsh History Review* 10, 1980–81.

W.H. Waters, *The Edwardian Settlement of Wales in its administrative and legal aspects*, Cardiff: UP Wales, 1935.

# Hand and Mouth: Information Gathering and Use in England in the Later Middle Ages

## COLIN RICHMOND

Because of the corporate, cooperative nature of the government of the England of the later Middle Ages, it is quite proper to consider "the government" as the governing class – all those from gentleman to duke who were "members of parliament". Beneath them (and the "them" in the towns of England were those merchants and businessmen who ran those towns and represented them in parliament), and bearing in mind those yeoman *alias* gentlemen of the fifteenth century who were unsure of their social identity but who undoubtedly were more governed than governors, were the governed proper: the more than ninety per cent of Englishmen and women. Some information about them was collected by their governors, in the main regarding their taxable capacity and their violent habits, for they had to be "exploited" at the same time as they were "controlled". That, however, is the story of government narrowly defined: it has been told many times. On the other hand, what news of great events was gathered by the governed, what their perceptions of such events were, and how they informed one another of them is another story altogether: it has not been told, perhaps because it cannot. All that remains of the story are tantalizing glimpses, particularly of the transmission of sedition – for example, by the lollards in 1431. The government on 13 May of that year ordered sheriff to proclaim that all who found defamatory or seditious bills should tear them into little pieces or bum them: if this was not done the finders or readers would be taken as the authors of the bills: for catching the writer of such a bill, a bill-poster or distributer there was a reward of £20 (*CCR 1429–35*: 123). These subversive networks need exploration: that, for example, which brought Sir John Oldcastle's lollard followers from the provinces to London for his reckless attempt at a *coup d'étatin* January 1414. The routes between Lollard cells, along which Lollards themselves, their books, sermons, and ideas travelled could be and ought to be studied. But not here.[1]

It is true that after 1300 (if not before) the government did give thought to communicating news of great events to the governed.

The people – undefined – were the audience for the proclamation of royal claims and titles, of victories won in France, of impending invasions, of truces and their duration, of general pardons, of the deaths of kings. Such news was to be "cried in the markets, fairs and other public places", as well as at the country courts (Maddicott 1978: 33–7). At London St Paul's cross was the place where such public announcements were made, the Chancellor himself in April 1461 coming to share the good news of Edward IV's victory at Towton (Hinds 1912: 66). Eighteen months previously the news for some had been bad: "A lewd doctowr of Ludgate prechid on soneday fowrtenyte at Powlys, chargyng the peple that no man schuld preyen for these lordys traytowyrs, &, and he had lytyl thank" (Davis II: 184). When were royal proclamations first printed and nailed up on the doors of market halls? What happened to those in the market place at Coventry in 1535 Professor Elton has unforgettably described (Elton 1972: 134–5):

In the morning of 25 November 1535. Coventry was humming with the shocking news that overnight someone had tom down the proclamations and statutes posted up in the market place, a manifest act of sedition at the very least. John Robbins, a tailor of the town, came to his friend George Wakefield and told him in horror that he had been "in company the last night" with those who had done the deed. What was he to do to clear himself? Wakefield replied that, now he had been told of it, it was his duty to inform the mayor: he would advise his friend thereafter: but the result of the information was that four men – Robbins, William Apreston of Windsor, Henry Heynes of Allesby (Warw.), and Robert Knottesford of Luttenvorth (all yeomen) – were called to be examined before the mayor, the recorder and eight aldermen. This solemn assembly heard the following tale. On the night of the 24th the four of them (presumably stimulated by the rare chance of all meeting together) went out drinking. About ten at night, being by this time "overseen with drink", they wandered from Rogers's tavern to "the inn at the sign of the pannier". After a further spell of drinking, they staggered forth from there to the cross in the market place where fate overtook them: "they all untrussed them and did their easement at the cross". One of them – probably Apreston – seeing the proclamations and so forth nailed to "tables" (noticeboards) in the market place, pulled some off "and cast the same to the said Heynes and bid him wipe his tail with them". In their drunken state, "they tore down part of the tables and tore in effect all the papers, but what further they did with the tables or with the rest of the said proclamations and acts" Robbins, at least, could not tell. The others were even vaguer; quite clearly, memories of the night before were extremely hazy, and while they admitted that the treasonable offence had been committed for the hygienic reason stated they could not exactly recall who had done what. They only remembered staggering around for a while before returning to the Pannier to sleep it off.
No more is known. It is not likely that these defilers of the King's legislative instruments got off without penalty, but one trusts (with some confidence) that their punishment was light. The authorities will hardly have wished to give wide publicity to this story. It is to be hoped that the ten worshipful men to whom it was revealed by the bedraggled crew before them had a sense of humour. What shines most clearly through the depositions is that fourfold monumental hangover.

Matters other than the extraordinary were also proclaimed; this was the only way the government could communicate its decisions which touched many or all: economic rules and regulations, outlawries, the crying of musters. Much of this by the later Middle Ages may have been conventional: the people who principally (and perhaps urgently) needed to know (corn dealers, innkeepers, the outlawed, soldiers and sailors) had already been notified through other, sometimes unofficial channels. Nonetheless, there was the general public, who in some cases certainly had to be advertised, for instance, about economic rates and regulations. Yet, many proclamations (and sermons and processions[2]) were not always, perhaps not often, explanatory. When "policy is made intelligible", it is "to those who must execute it", to adapt a phrase of Dr H.J. Hewitt (1966: 158); those authorities who are to make the proclamation or carry out a royal command are sometimes, perhaps usually, told the reasons why. The explanation might on occasion be elaborate. In February 1341 the mayors and bailiffs of selected coastal towns were required to arm ships of sixty tons and over to compose a fleet to defend the realm. They were told why:

If our fleet be prepared and armed in good time according to our commands it will have the start of the enemy fleet and we believe that in this way burnings, atrocities and other evils will be prevented.

Consultation was also part of the process: two townsmen from each port were to go to Westminster not only to report on what had been done but also to learn from the government what other measures were planned (Rymer V: 231–2). What we might call the commercial lobby had, a century later, become used to such meetings; at one in January 1454 its delegation became heated (Gairdner II: 299):

The meire and merchauntz of London, and the mair and the merchanntz of the staple of Caleys, were with the Chaunceller on Monday last passed at Lamhithe [Lambeth], and compleyned on the Lord Bonvile for takyng of the shippes and godes of the Flemmynges and other of the Duke of Burgoynes [Burgundy's] Lordships, and the Chaunceller yeve theym none answere to their plesyng: wherefore the substaunce of theym with one voys cryed alowed. "Justice. justice, justice!" wherof the Chaunceller was so dismayed that he coude ne myght no more sey to theym for fere.

Parliament was the occasion for consultation and explanation. As the "house of Commons" comprised the representatives of the Commons – a rural electorate finally defined in 1429 as consisting of forty-shilling freeholders and above, and an urban one almost invariably far more narrowly restricted by urban oligarchs – king and councillors had no obligation to explain themselves outside that assembly. This was certainly the case where taxation was concerned; the grant of a subsidy was in the form of a statute binding all; the issue of "no taxation without representation" did not arise, save in 1381 when the third poll tax was the final straw for the less than forty-shilling freeholders who duly demonstrated along the lines of that principle.

Men from the parliamentary, that is the governing, class were particularly interested in what went on in parliament, as the report of the Colchester burgesses on the 1485 parliament drawn up for and delivered to their fellow citizens famously illustrates (Benham 1902: 60–4). After all, what had "gone on" in parliament was that cooperative government which renders late medieval England such an interesting object of study. War against France had made that cooperation necessary: the king could not fight it otherwise, as Edward III reluctantly had conceded. In February 1341 we have glimpsed that coordinated war effort in action. It was a war which for well over a hundred years governing Englishmen were closely interested in and fully committed to: because they had an interest in it it was their war. Thus, Edward III, the Black Prince, and Henry of Lancaster wrote despatches to the Council at Westminster of the progress of their campaigns (Hewitt 1966: 155). So did Henry V and his brother Thomas, duke of Clarence to the city of London (Sharpe 1899: 183, 185, 199, 200, 224, 255). Henry (that most painstaking of kings) having in 1415 spoken himself to the mayor and aldermen of "his intention to cross the sea to reconquer the possessions of the crown and of his need of money" (Sharpe 1899: 135). Henry liked to be informed as well as inform. How good his intelligence gathering service was is shown by his nipping in the bud the two major plots laid against him, Oldcastle's rising of January 1414 and the Southampton plot of July 1415. There have been very few, if any, heads of state so skilful at such seemingly opposed aspects of their role as public order and public relations. Henry also won the battle of Agincourt – the finest piece of public relations and public order-keeping that there could ever have been. Agincourt, Henry, and the other Englishmen who won it display the cooperative government of late medieval England at its best, and, because here it was at its most harmonious, in its most perfect form.[3] he eleven parliaments of Henry's nine-year reign – parliament being, as we have observed, where most inter-communing was done – and the flow of information to and from the king in other ways on other occasions as between *confidants*, which is what Henry and his "people" may fairly be called, evidence the rapport of ruler and ruling class, essential to "good government" but so often lacking in other reigns. A breakdown in confidence between the Ruler (and rulers at Westminster) on the one hand, and on the other provincial governors – knights and esquires as well as barons and earls – was both cause and consequence of the non-communication between them. To such a dislocated time, the 1450s, I wish to turn for an examination of the unofficial means of getting information out of a government reluctant to give it. Good news is readily released, of bad news no one desires to be the bringer.

By 1450 the war was as good as lost. There had been only a handful of parliaments in the previous twenty years; if that had meant little taxation it also indicated the disassociation of government and taxpayers and their parliamentary representatives. In the decade which followed, civil war (chiefly cold) began: the disassociation became disengagement. How, in these circumstances, did men who wanted to know get the political information they sought? What kind of information was it? What did they want it for? Possibly tentative answers to these questions from the Paston Letters will lead to a final one: what perception of politics did these politicians have?

That men (and women) were interested in politics is evident from the number of news-bills and news-letters which have survived. I include women because of Agnes Paston's closing request in a letter of February 1445 to her son in London: "and I praye yow to send me tydynggis from beyond see, for here thei am aferde to telle soche as be reportid" (Davis I: 28). It was not the king's marriage to Margaret of Anjou Agnes was anxious to know about, but the possibility of an English withdrawal from the county of Maine. This Henry VI agreed to at the end of the year. It was a blow to all those, and they were many, who believed English territory in France had to be vigorously defended not surrendered on some half-baked notion of "peace in our time" (Griffiths 1981: 487–95; Richmond 1983: 52). It was Mr C.A.J. Armstrong many years ago in a classic paper who made the distinction between news-bills and news-letters (1983: 100–1). The news-bill was an official or officially sanctioned report, the news-letter part of private correspondence. News-bills (or copies of them) are hard to find.[4] Handbills, schedules of articles, and antigovernment verse, either passed around or nailed on doors, had by the fifteenth century become a feature of the politics of opposition.[5] As early as 1424 (Davis I: 8–9) the gentleman and soldier Walter Azlak had to William Paston

swiche [such] and so many manaces of deth and disrnembryng maden and puttyn by certeyns Englishe billes rymed in partye. and upon the yates of the priorie of the Trinite chirche of Norwiche and on the yates of the chyrche of the Freres Menures [minor] of Norwiche and the yates of the same cite called Nedeham yates and Westewyk yates, and in othre places wyth-inne the seyd cite, by the seyd Walter and Richard sette, makying mension and berying this undyrstondyng that the seyd William and hese clerkes and servantes schuld be slayn and mordered in lyke fourme as the seyd John Grys in the seyd fourme was slayn and rnordered;

conteynying also these too wordes in Latyn, "et cetera", by whiche wordes com-
munely it was undyrstandyn that the forgers and makers of the seyd billes jmagyned
to the seyd William, hese clerkes, and servantz more malice and harm than in the
seyd billes was expressed.

Still, the indignation of the government's opponents (and the less
than subtle use of latin by an aggrieved Norfolk landowner) are one
thing, government apologia are another. We can point to the justification for the attainders of the Yorkists in the parliament of 1459,[6]
the *Chronicle of the Rebellion in Lincolnshire* in 1470, and the
*Historie of the Arrivall of Edward IV in 1471*, but to little else. The
events of 1470–1 are a special case: as C.L. Kingsford pointed out
many years ago, for them "we obtain a fairly consecutive and full
account in a series of narratives and documents of a more or less
official character".[7] Government and opposition changed places
twice over, and each appealed, self-justified and propagandized on
a scale not seen before in broadsheets, proclamations, and what in
the case of *the Arriuall* we might call a lengthy press release for
foreign correspondents. It is, therefore, the newsletter on which we
should concentrate.

In another, equally canonical, article Mr Armstrong showed one
man's passion for political information (1983: 1–72). This was Sir
John Fastolf, retired soldier and patron of the Pastons. It is fair to
say that he was a committed opponent of the government from
the mid-1440s; the surrender of Maine was for him, a point of no
return. On one level. On another he was not only being twisted out
of East Anglian property by the thoroughly bent politician who was
running the government by that time, William, duke of Suffolk, but
also being excluded by the duke from exercising the local power he
had a right to exercise on his own and others' behalf. Entirely
justified personal animosity on the one hand, and righteous indignation over foreign policy on the other, made Sir John Fastolf eager
to discover what changes there might be in a government he
detested. It is from newsletters to Sir John's kinsman and coun-
cillor, John Paston, that we know the details of the murder in
mid-Channel of the duke of Suffolk in May 1450.[8] Fastolf was in
London and would have been told the news: Paston was in Norwich
and had to be written to: "Right worshupfull sir. 1 recommaunde
me untoyow in the most goodly wyse that y can. And forasmuche as
ye desired of me to send yow worde of dyvers matires here whiche
been opened in the parliament openly, y sende yow of theyme suche
as I can" (Davis II: 37). It is from reports sent to Fastolf, by then
living in his country house at Caister near Yarmouth, that we learn
so much about a battle whose outcome was vital for Fastolf's
interests and (as he conceived them) for England's, the first battle
of St Albans in 1455. One of these reports, the "Fastolf Relation",

was written by someone in Fastolfs service, probably his officer of arms, Fastolf Poursuivant, who also sent him from Paris a report on the trial for treason of Jean, duke of Alencon in October 1458 (Cutler 1981: 808–17). We should note Fastolfs "abiding interest in French affairs": he was aged seventy-eight: the Hundred Years War had ended five years previously.

It was through his servants, who knew the information he wanted, that Fastolf was kept in touch with political events, if he himself was not on the spot – as he was, for instance, in July 1455 when he went to London after the battle of St Albans to be on hand during its political repercussions and consequences (Davis II: 123). Fastolfs secretary, William Worcester, whom Mr K.B. McFarlane immortalized for his dogged accumulation of every sort of information, especially historical (McFarlane 1981: 199–224), sent his master the London political "nouveltees" and "tydyng of beyond see" as well as the metropolitan price of figs and raisins (Davis II: 531–4 cf Davis II: 92). Another Fastolf servant, William Barker, wrote newsletters to William Worcester for him to read to Fastolf,[9] while another, John Bocking, after Fastolfs death sent a report of the Coventry parliament of 1459 to Worcester – "a grete bille of tidinges" – together with a list of the Yorkists attainted in that parliament enclosed in another letter to John Paston, William Yelverton and Henry Filongley, which mainly concerned the business of Fastolfs will, the business on which they had sent him to Coventry (Davis II: 187–8). William Worcester probably kept Bocking's newsletter – his son, or "the pseudo-William Worcester", making use of it later in the "Annals" he compiled (Armstrong 1983: 101: McFarlane 1981: 209) – just as Fastolf kept the articles of the Jack Cade rebels he sent another of his servants, John Payn, to Blackheath in June 1450 to fetch, a dangerous mission successfully accomplished (Davis II: 313–4); the articles (the collecting of which almost lost John Payn his head) survive among the Fastolf papers at Magdalen College, Oxford, testimony to Fastolfs desire for hard news and first-hand information even at the risk of his servants' lives.[10] Did Fastolf also possess – even have a hand in composing – the second set of articles of accusation against William, duke of Suffolk of a month or so previously?[11] I raise the question to emphasize that it was primary evidence which Fastolf sought as well as reportage. As he kept all his documents so carefully (McFarlane 1981: 212–6), we certainly may say he constructed a contemporary history archive. How else are certain items in the Paston Letters to be accounted for? For example, how did Fastolf or Paston get hold of (in order to copy) the duke of Suffolks moving letter to his son, which turned out to be his last letter to anyone?[12] Or Robert Winnington's jingoistic letter to Thomas Daniel of his exploits on the high seas, which they kept: it is the original.[13] As is the letter of Richard, earl of Warwick to Sir Thomas Tuddenham asking "that ye wyll lend us xli., or twenty, or what the seyd Maister Robert wants of hys payment".[14] Thomas Daniel and Thomas Tuddenham were no friends of Fastolf and Paston. How did they come by the letters of their enemies?[15] Or is this a non-question, which may be asked also of the five letters addressed to John, viscount Beaumont[16] and the four Howard documents[17] to be found in the Paston collection? By non-question I mean: might not these documents have become "Paston Letters" only in the eighteenth century, that is, have attached themselves to the *ur* Paston papers as those passed through the hands of the Norfolk antiquaries and collectors, Peter Le Neve, Francis Blomefield and Thomas Martin, before they reached John Fenn and publication?[18] Even if that is the case, there are more than enough examples of the concern of John Fastolf and the Pastons to have copies of current political material[19] to show that it was not only estate documents and legal records which the landed class kept. Moreover, property documents accumulated of their own accord, political "evidence" had deliberately to be collected.

The manner in which some of the collecting was done is apparent from other items in the Paston Letters. These are copies of documents sent as enclosures within letters or separately to accompany them. "Item, I send unto you a copy of a letter that was taken uppon the see, made by the Lord Hungerford and Whityngham", wrote Henry Windsor to John Paston; the Hungerford letter (in Windsor's hand on paper with the same watermark as his own letter) from "the state of the dorse [Professor Norman Davis tells us] must have been carried separately" (Davis II: 252). Windsor gives no reason for sending the Hungerford letter: there was no functional one. There was with another enclosure. In October 1450 William Wayte, clerk to William Yelverton, enclosed a copy of a letter from Richard, duke of York to the government of Henry VI. It told that government to get off its backside and do more than it was doing to prevent the country – reeling from the murder of the duke of Suffolk, the keeper of the privy Seal, and the royal confessor, from a major popular demonstration (rebels in occupation of London for a week, murdering any other members of the government they could lay their hands on), and from the loss of the French provinces – from falling apart. William Wayte wrote. "Syr, I sende yow a copy of the bylle that my Lord of Yorke putte unto the Kynge, and, syr, late [let] copyes go abowte the cetye j-now [city enough], for the love of God" (Davis II: 49). In other, modem words: plaster this anti-government piece all over Norwich. Here we encounter history being made, not simply recorded.

Who did the collecting? John Stodeley's remarkable newsletter of January 1454 – or rather the copy of it which survives, and remarkable because it contains nothing but political news (and remarkable political news at that) – ends in this fashion:

Thise thinges aforseid ben espied and gadred by my Lord Chaun[cellor], John Leventhorpe. Laurence Leventhorpe. Maister Adam, Wlliam Medwe, Hobert Alman. John Colvyle, Richard of Warderobe. and me. John Stodeley. And as sone as we kun knowe any more in substance we shull send home word.

Home was East Anglia, probably Framlingham, and the addressee a servant (like Stodeley) of the Duke of Norfolk. Even if "my lord Chaun" is not the Chancellor, cardinal John Kemp (and I do not see who else could be referred to in this way), the Leventhorpes were men of the royal court, John an esquire of the king's and Laurence (though much later) a "king's alms knight" at Windsor, while Richard of Warderobe is more likely to be a servant of the king's than of the duke of Norfolk's household (Wedgwood 1936: 537–8). The point I am making is that these were "insiders". Mr Armstrong judged: "Most people were largely dependent on picking up hearsay."[21] I question that "largely". The information-gatherers John Stodeley names were first-hand witnesses of what he related. This was not hearsay. Not most of it. A little of it was:

And as for suche tydynges as ben contened in the lettre sent home by John Sumpterman, I can nat hiderto here [hear] the contrarie of any of theym, but that every man that is of th'opynion of the Duke of Somerset makethe hym redy to be as stronge as he kan make hym.

Even then it had been double-checked. Let me take three other examples.

In October 1455 James Gresham sent John Paston an account of the atrocious murder of Nicolas Radford in Devon; he included reported speech, the exchange between the earl of Devon's son and Nicholas before Nicholas was set upon and his throat cut. "This was told to my lord Chaunceler this fornoon [by] massengeres as come of purpos owt of the same cuntre", wrote Gresham (Davis II: 127). How had he heard so quickly? That afternoon he had been in Westminster Hall, is my guess. Perhaps the Chancellor himself announced such scandalous news, reading out the letters he had so speedily been sent (Armstrong 1983: 114). Here is the second example. William Paston tells his brother John how he learned of Edward IVs decisive victory at Towton (Davis I: 165):

Please you to knowe and wete of suche tydyngys as my lady of York hath by a lettre of credens under the signe manuel of oure soverayn lord Kyng Edward, whiche lettre cam unto oure sayd lady this same day, Esteme Evyn, at xj clok, and was sene and red be me, William Paston.

Cecily, duchess of York was almost certainly living at Sir John Fastolf's former house in Southwark, claimed by the Pastons to have been left to them (Davis II: 216; Carlin 1985: 44–7): William had reason for being there. He did not write his letter: Thomas Playter, once the foremost legal adviser of Sir John Fastolf and now of the Pastons, did that. Nor did William copy out the casualty list which, on a separate slip, accompanied the letter, nor did Thomas Playter; someone else did that. All William did was to sign the letter.[22] But it was he who at first-hand had observed the arrival of the momentous news of Towton and he who had read for himself the king's letter to his mother. Was that the king's only letter? I doubt it, for that very afternoon (as we have seen) the Chancellor, after a Te &urn at St Pauls, proclaimed the victory at St Paul's cross. Also the king had written to the Treasurer.[23] The third example is a letter to John Paston from another of his brothers, Clement: it is of 11 October 1461 (Davis I: 201–2):

Brother, I recommende me to you, after all dewe recommendacions, &c. Sir, it was told me by rythe a worshipfull man that loveth you rythe well, and ye him, and ye xall [shall] know his name here-after, but put all things out of doubt he is such a man as will not lye. On the xj th day of October the Kinge seid, "We have sent two privy sealys to Paston by two yeomen of our chamber, and he disobeyeth them; but we will send him a-noder to-morrowe, and by Gods mercye and if he come not then he xall dye for it. We will make all oder men beware by him how they xall disobey our writinge. A servant of our hath made a complainte of him. I cannot thinke that he hath informed us all truly, yet not for that we will not suffer him to disobey our writinge; but sithen he disobeyeth our writinge we may beleve the better his gydinge is as we be informed." And therwith he made a great a-vowe that if ye come not at the third commandement ye xulde [should] dye therefore.

This man that tolde me this is as well learned a man as any is in England . . . This letter was written the same day that the Kinge said these words, and the same day that it was told me, and that day was the xj[th] day of October as abovesaid; and on the next morning send I forth a man to yow with this letter, and on the same day send the Kinge the third privye seale to you.

It is clear that John Paston had rapid and accurate access to government information. It is also clear how and why. He, or members of his family, or those lawyers and attornies whom he employed, or their friends, may not have been the shapers of great events, but they were intimate with those who were.

It is this intimacy of the governing class, its limited size, its interconnectedness (by kinship and through the ties binding patron and client), and its openness, which make the circulation of information within it easy. Did everyone who was anyone know everyone else who was? To me it looks like it. The image of the nineteen-year old Edward IV stamping his foot because John Paston had not responded to his letters is indelible. And revealing: of the personal nature of medieval kingship and government. Such government was effective. When John did appear he was arrested and imprisoned in the Fleet. Not for long. He was out by the end of October, being replaced by his opponent Sir John Howard. Howard, as sheriff of Norfolkand Suffolk, was attempting to overturn Paston's election the previous summer as knight of the shire for Norfolk. The young king, endeavouring to keep a precarious general peace, was evidently being bombarded by a variety of versions of what had happened at the election in the county court at Norwich on 15 June 1461 and at its re-run on 11 August. Ultimately he opted for the Paston version and in January 1462 a third meeting of the county court confirmed John Paston's election.[24] In this political set-to John Paston was a participant. As such he was a provider of information, not only a receiver – as were all the members of the ruling elite, being sometimes one, sometimes another, sometimes both, so enmeshed were they in the business of governing the country. Nor, of course, were they doing so only in the regions. A distinction between central and local governors is not valid for later medieval England. Not only are "central" and "local" meaningless terms within so small a country, which by the fifteenth century had been much and closely governed for five hundred years, the personnel at Westminster and in the localities over-lapped, intermingled, interconnected. That is why and how infor-mation was conveyed to and fro so freely, so casually. Everyone, or almost everyone who was anyone, was in the know. This was open government.

Let me try to illustrate what I mean. About the personnel first. John Paston's legal advisor Thomas Playter was (or had been) "of the Chancery". In 1466 on John Paston's death an inquisition into his landed property was required and its result sent to the Chan-cery; this is what happened (Richmond 1981b: 42): Thomas Playter

was present at the funeral, and successfully manipulated the subsequent inquisi-tion post *morfem*; the jury's return was a mere recital of the Paston case concerning Fastolfs will, both official copies being in the hand of John Pampyng, a Paston servant. Presumably Playter himself had composed it. Certainly he delivered the Chancery copy there on 8 November, something readily done as he had been appointed escheator of Norfolk and Suffolk (for the only time in his life) three days previously. So much for the impartiality of government.

Playter's *entrée* at Chancery was undoubtedly one of his principal qualifications for those who retained him. Not only did he learn there information regarding them – in June 1461, for example, he wrote to John Paston "ye arn jnbylled to be made knygth at this coronacion"[25] – he was also involved in the manufacture of what that information actually and officially consisted of, so that it favoured you or did you least damage. The same was true of

Edmund Bowen [or Bohun] "of the Exchequer", retained by William Hopton and a "specyal frend" of John Paston's second son, John Paston, in the 1470s. In 1475 John had indented to serve in the king's army bound for France; he wrote to his mother:

Ryght worchepfull modyr, after all humbyll recommendacyons as lowley as I can I beseche yow of your biyssyng. Pleasyt yow to wet that late yesternyght I cam to Norwyche purposeing to have been as thys day wyth yow at Mawtby, but is so that I may not hold my purpose, for he that shall pay me my quarter wagys for me and my retenew is in Norwyche and waytyth ourly when hys money shall com to hym. It is oon Edmund Bowen of the Cheker [Exchequer], a specyall frend of myn, and he avysyth me to tery tyll the money be com lest that I be unpayed: for who comyth fyrst to the mylle fyrst must grynd.

At the very least knowing such an "insider" was handy (Davis I: 593 cf Richmond 1981a: 196–7).

Where John Throckmorton was concerned it was far more than that. He too was of the Exchequer but no mere auditor as was Edmund Bowen; John Throckmorton was a chamberlain of the Exchequer and under-treasurer of England. He was a knight of the shire and sheriff of Worcestershire; he was a justice of the peace in that county (and of the *quorum*) for thirty years. A life long member of the council of the great Richard Beauchamp, earl of Warwick. with the unusually high fee of twenty marks a year, he was one of the earl's executors at his death in 1439. Ms Carole Rawcliffe comments, "we cannot tell how useful he proved to be in securing preference for him [the earl] at the Exchequer" (Rawcliffe 1979: 96); no, but we can have a good guess. In November 1440, one of John Paston's young colleagues at the Inns of Court, Robert Repps, wrote to him in Norfolk – John had gone home to get married – of the news current in London (Davis II: 22). One of the items was the following:

Ferthermore, ye be remernbryd that an esquyer of Suffolk called John Lyston recoveryd in assisa nove disseisine [an assize of novel disseisin] vij c. marc in damna [damages] ayenst Ser Robert Wyngfeld &c. In avoydyng of the payement of the seid vij c. marc. the seide Ser Robert Wyngfeld sotylly hath outlawed the seide John Lyston in Notynghamshire be the vertue of qwych outlagare [outlawry] all maner of chatell to the seide John Lyston apparteynyng am acruyd on-to the Kyng, &c. And anon as the seide vtlagare was certyfyed my lord Tresorer grauntyd the seide vij. c. marc to my lord of Norffolk for the arrerage of hys sowde [soldiers] qwyl he was in Scotlond, and acordyng to this assignement forseide taylles [tallies] delyuered. &c. And my lord of Norffolk hath relesyd the same vij. c. marc to Ser Robert Wyngfeld. And here is greet hevyng an shovyng be my lord of Suffolk and all his counsell for to aspye hough this mater kam aboute, &c.

That is a perfect illustration of the utility of an "insider" to his friends (and their friends), in this case *the* "insider", for it was Ralph, lord Cromwell, the Treasurer of England, who was "securing preference" for a friend. Mr Simon Payling is revealing for us just how crooked Ralph, lord Cromwell could be – on his own behalf (Payling 1986). Was John Throckmorton like that? Perhaps not. There was another side to him. In his will of 1445 he states, "I have been all the days of my life in my country's service in the world as the world asketh", and he left six shillings and eightpence to every prison in London. This corroborative evidence is sufficient, I believe, to identify him as the Throckmorton for whom an exceptionally rigorous daily programme of devotion was drawn up (Pantin 1976). It is a side to John which otherwise we would not suspect: it is ignored by those who have used him as an exemplar of what colonel Wedgwood called the "fifteenth century combination of county, parliament and executive".[25] There is no need to decide where John Throckmorton's duty mainly lay, merely to observe that it lay in many places: God, the king, the Treasurer, the earl of Warwick (and at least four other lords with whom John was connected), the county community, his clients (for he was, of course, a lawyer), his family (in a broader definition than one comprising only his wife, two sons and six daughters), his tenants at Coughton and Fladbury. These allegiances were not irreconcilable. That is my point. As it was, I suppose, Colonel Wedgwood's.[27]

Only two further observations ought to be made. The first is: imagine the quality as well as the quantity of information John Throckmorton supplied to the government. Such a man, and all those gentlemen bureaucrats like him, stood pivotally – as, for that matter, did the royal household knights, esquires and gentlemen -between capital and county, Westminster and the provinces, government and governing elite.[28] Through such men information passed both ways, moved all ways within the governing class. It was not simply government itself which hinged on them, it was everyone else whose life depended upon current, accurate news of the political situation and upon informed assessment of that situation, that is everyone in the English governing class. Which is the second observation. Politics in late medieval England was the sum of those individual lives. A study – such as Dr Anthony Smith's of Sir John Fastolf in the crisis year of 1450 (Smith 1982) – shows how men have to act in their own and the national interest when that sum is not being correctly balanced by central government. Good government, it does not require an Aquinas to tell us, is government in the interest of each and all. Achieving it is the difficult part. It could be done in England in the later Middle Ages. Henry VI failed to do it because he took the wrong advice, received faulty information and could not be bothered to check it. Sir John Fastolf and his friends became justly aggravated because their information was not getting through. Was not being received. The skilled juggling of individual, as well as the aggregate, self-interest of a few thousand men – soldiers, mechants, bureaucrats, and country gentlemen – was what "government" was, was what policy of state amounted to. The intricate mesh of patronage which linked king, lords and gentlemen was also an information network, highly personal and highly charged. We might say the state depended on it: certainly welfare of state depended upon how carefully, how sensitively the king tuned in on it. Only Henry V got perfect reception. I labour the obvious.

I end with what I regard as an engaging illustration of the smallness of that circle within which information was exchanged. John Gyn, a Paston employee at Snailwell in Cambridgeshire writes to John Paston, an undergraduate at Trinity Hall, Cambridge (Davis II: 21):

Right worthy and worshlpfull ser and my good maister, I cornaund me to yow. Like it yow to witte that on the Soneday next after the Ascencion of Oure Lord in the high weye betwex Cambrigg and the Bekyntre toward Newmarket I fonde a purs with money ther-jnne. Th'entent of this my symple lettre is this: that it please to your good malstership by weye of charlte and of your gentilnesse to witte If ony of youre knowleche or ony other. swich as yow semeth best in your discrecion, have lost swich a purs: and the toknes ther-of told he shal have it a-geyn, what that ever he be, by the grace of Oure Lord, who ever have yow in his blissed kepyng.

The fifteenth-century English political community was a small world.

## Notes

[1] A reading of McFarlane (1952: ch. 6), of Thomson (1965: *passim*), of Aston (1984: ch. 3), and of Anne Hudson's magisterial work on Lollard sermon cycles, their composition and transmission, is a starting point. It must be, and for obvious reasons, a "Lollard scholar" who tackles the matter of the sect's communication network; this reached, after all, as far as Prague and Cracow.

[2] For war publicity see most recently Jones 1979 and McHardy 1982. In 1346 Edward III employed the Dominicans "to explain his reasons for going to war" in public and private sermons (Jones 1979: 27). McHardy (1982: 224) concludes that the clergy "were regularly asked to make . . . religious ceremonies in support of the English war effort. To do this they used liturgical forms already available . . . but sometimes supplemented them with patriotic speeches designed to be intelligible to all."

[3] As Dr Gerald Harriss has definitively shown (1985: chs. 1, 11, VII, VIII, X). Skilled as Henry was at "controlling" and "exploiting" the Commons, did he not take seriously the poet's advice, "The leste lygeman, with body and rent/He is a parcel of the crowne"? See "God Save King Henry V" (Robbins: 1959: 45, lines 15–16); I owe this reference to Miss Deborah Fossey.

[4] Mr Armstrong commented: the "Brief Notes" (in Gairdner 1880) are "largely composed of these". This is his only example, and I cannot readily

think of others. The "Brief Notes" (Lambeth Palace Library, London, MS 448), composed at Ely after 1462, deserve, after a hundred years, another look.

[5] Wilson 1952: 197–206; Robbins 1959: 63–4, 207–10; Davies 1856: 80ff. With regard to the ballad set on the gates of Canterbury in 1460, Robbins 1959: 369 makes an important point: "the presence of numerous biblical quotations in Latin raises a question of the poem's effectiveness as a popular handbill." The same question may be asked of the scattering by the Emperor Sigismund's entourage of numerous broadsides ["cedulas plures"] in the streets of Canterbury on the Emperor's departure from England in August 1416 (Taylor and Roskell 1975: 156). I also owe this reference to Deborah Fossey. The question should certainly be asked of certain of those "tables" placed in churches, those, that is, written in Latin, like the Glastonbury "Magna Tabula": four boards [each 3′6″ by 1′6″] covered in parchment on six sides with the "history" of the abbey, the names of the saints and kings buried there, the stories of Joseph of Arimathea, Arthur, and St Patrick, and lists of relics and indulgences thereon (Bodleian Library, Oxford, MS lat.hist.a 2, a remarkable survival and extraordinary sight, described by Hall (1965: 63–4) and, when it was still at Naworth Castle, by the Rev. Bennett (1888: 117–22 and frontispiece)). Dated 1400, the Glastonbury "MagnaTabula" was clearly intended for pilgrim visitors: how many of them would have read Latin? For other, similar "tables", apparently in Latin, see Gerould 1926: 439–40, viz. at Stone priory, St George's chapel, Windsor, and Worksop priory: and Gerould 1933: 326, footnote, viz. at St Paul's, Lincoln, and Lichfield cathedrals. These information boards were, I suspect, commonplace by 1500. William Worcester (Harvey 1969: 105, 113, 313) describes the tables at the Temple church, Bristol, in Tavistock church, and at the college in Penryn near Falmouth. In the Charterhouse at Sheen "on the walls on each side of the nave of the church hang many devotions and good reminders to devotion and the arousing of all Christian souls to God, both smaller and larger tables . . . to the number of about 34, nor have I seen in any other monastic church even the twentieth part of these tables so fully written" (Harvey 1969: 271). Were these devotional boards an innovation of continental reformers? Both Jean Gerson and Nicholas of Cusa had them made (Connolly 1928: 131 and fn2). At Penryn (Harvey 1969: 105) the board began: "Me liketh to tell, or in fuced situation/Set down what I've heard for the next generation". The late medieval historical tables of York minster are still in existence (Aylmer and Cant 1979: 108 and fn). Those once at Bawburgh in Norfolk over the Shrine of St Walstan told his life metrically in English: understandably so, for those who came to the shrine were farmers and farm-workers, St Walstan being the patron of rural labourers. This popular East Anglian cult of a prince who gave up all to follow the gospel is itself astonishing: it warrants further study. Meanwhile, see Farmer 1978: 397–8, in error where it says the Latin life was written on the wooden triptych (James 1917: 238–67. with a diagram of the long-missing triptych at 249). In the case of Latin tables it is almost as if the posting of the notice ended the authorities' responsibility: whether folk did or could read it, let alone understand it, was none of their business. This appears to me to be an aspect of government publicity and publication of any peacetime age in England before 1939 and after 1979.

[6] For which see most recently Kekewich 1982: 27–34. It is to be noted (p. 28) that "no attempt was made to appeal to the people, a normal

device of Yorkist propaganda, indeed, they were dismissed as foolish and unreliable . . . so it is unlikely that the tract was intended for a wide circulation".

[7] 1913: 173. To the accounts cited must be added the proclamations of a nervous government and the opposition's explanatory pamphlet, "The Manner and Guiding of the Earl of Warwick at Angiers" (*ChWR* 1845: 225–41).

[8] Davis II: 35–6. William Lomnor (for all the detestation) opens his letter: "Ryght worchipfulle ser, 1 recomaunde me to yow, and am right sory of that I shalle sey, and have . . . wesshe [washed] this litel bille with sorwfulle terys". This is a figure of speech: the actual letter (British Library [henceforth BL] Add MS 43488, f.13) shows no signs of having been wet.

[9] Gairdner III: 32. This is BL Add Ms 43488, f.28. A few words at the end and a short non-political postscript are omitted by Gairdner (following Fenn). The letter is addressed on the dorse, and there are marks of folding and of a seal.

[10] Griffiths 1981: 635–6. The articles (Magdalen College, Oxford, Cartae Misc 306) are printed in *HMC*, Eighth Report: 266–7, which says "the handwriting is like the composition", that is "rugged". I disagree. The hand is bold and open, not wild, but legible and practised. It is not a clerical hand; it is a lay one. Dare one suggest it is yeomanly? Face to face with such a document – orderly, in numbered paragraphs, a clean, fair copy – one is unavoidably confronted by the question of its genesis. I am grateful to Dr Gerald Harriss, the librarian, and Mrs Brenda Parry-Jones, the archivist, for making Cartae Misc. 306 available to me. 1 am pleased to see that Isobel Harvey in her outstanding thesis arrives at a similar understanding of this document as a yeomanly manifestation of a yeomanly demonstration (1988: 153–4).

[11] These are now Bodleian Library, MS Eng.hist.b. 119. They were in the Nevill of Holt collection and are printed in *HMC*, Third Report: 279–80. See Griffiths 1981: 682–3. The Norfolk references in these articles, especially that to the executors of Sir John Clifton. are suggestive of a Fastolf involvement. Fastolf was a feoffee of Sir John Clifton, as was the duke of Suffolk (*CPR 1446–52*: 111–2; *CCR 1447–54*: 120). Sir John Clifton of Buckenham Castle, Norfolk, who died in 1447, had made the duke of Suffolk one of the three supervisors of his will: the others were his son-in-law Sir Andrew Ogard. Fastolfs friend, and Sir Thomas Tuddenham, one of Suffolk's creatures and Fastolfs enemy: an executor, John Heydon, was another of Fastolfs principal antagonists. The will is at the Norfolk Record Omce, NCC, Register Wylbey, f.103. There had already been trouble at the inquisition post mortem (*CPR 1446–52*: 421–3). The articles themselves are written in a secretary hand on the recto side of three sheets, only the final clause being written on the dorse of the last sheet. About a third of the first sheet has been tom away. The document is a fair copy or final draft: it is unamended. I fancy (though it may only be fancy) the hand is a Fastolf-associated one: Professor Norman Davis might recognize it. The style, especially the references to Judas Iscariot and particularly the contrapuntual sentences, is of a master. Is it also fanciful to think the superior composer William Worcester? Fastolf certainly possessed a copy of the Commons' impeachment articles (Gairdner II: 120). This (it seems to me) is a fair copy. It (BL Add MS 34888. fs. 36–9) consists of two sheets formerly stitched together head to foot in the middle of what is, though there is no numbering, the

fourth item. In the middle of the sixth item a second hand (it appears to me) takes over: it is this writer who endorses the first sheet "Compleyntys ayens the Dewke of Suffolk". The second hand I think I recognise as that of a Fastolf servant.

¹² Gairdner II: 142. This (BL Add MS 43488. f.12) is a contemporary copy with an endorsement, which, as Gairdner wisely reckoned (without having seen it), "is probably not quite contemporaneous". It is of the sixteenth century. The writer of it endorsed other, more strictly Paston documents, most notably Richard Calle's letter to Margery Paston (Davis II: no. 861). On that letter, which ought to have been burnt not kept (Richmond 1985: 32), he wrote in Latin "a letter of Richard Calle to Margery Paston, daughter of John Paston esquire, whom afterwards he married". Professor Davis describes and discusses this knowledgeable and busy annotator, apparently at work after 1570, in his introduction: Davis I: xxxi–xxxiii. For other such endorsements see note 19 below. It should be pointed out that the duke of Suffolk's letter is *not* paragraphed (as it is in Gairdner II: 142–3) and its last line is written continuously, "Wreten of myn hand the day of my departyng from this land".

¹³ Gairdner II: 103. This is BL Add Ms 43491, f.7. It is one sheet with marks of folding and of a seal.

¹⁴ Gairdner II: 117, which is BL Add Ms 43588, f.22. Is it significant (for his greatness) that the great earl did not trouble to sign this letter himself, even though he dictated "For there is nonne in your cuntre that we myght wryght to for trust so well as unto you; for, as we be enformed, ye be owr well wyller, and so we pray you of goud contynuaunce"? How curious is that "for, as we be enformyd, ye be owr well wyller".

¹⁵ Remarkably, for example, of a letter of 10 October 1468 to Thomas Bourgchier, archbishop of Canterbury, from that Judas in the Paston case concerning Fastolfs will, Thomas Howes (Gairdner IV: no. 688). This is BL Add Ms 34889, f.66, which is the letter itself. In this instance, could Howes' letter have come to Sir John Paston in 1470 as a result of his agreement with William Wainfleet over the Fastolf estate? Wainfleet undertook to hand over his Caister archive (Davis I: 425) among which the letter appropriately may have fetched up, the archbishop, who was the foremost supervisor of Fastolfs will, having handed it on to Wainfleet, the principal executor.

¹⁶ These are Gairdner II: no. 65 (BL Add MS 43488. f.8); Gairdner II: no. 78 (BL Add Ms 43488, f. 7); Gairdner II: no. 100 (BL Add MS 34888, f.35); Gairdner III: no. 361 (BL Add Ms 43488. f.39: the concluding phrase, "Your trew brodir wich prayth you herttely to excuse me to the Kinges heghnesse" and the signature are in the earl of Salisbury's own hand): and Gairdner III: no. 382 (BL Add MS 43488. f.53: in a secretary's hand throughout, including the duchess's signature).

¹⁷ These entirely misplaced strays all in the same hand are Gairdner III: no. 622 (BL Add MS 34889, f.38): Gairdner III: no. 658 (BL Add MS 34889. f.51): Gairdner III: no. 668 (BL Add MS 34889. f.59): Gairdner III: no. 669 (BL Add MS 34889. f.61). The two last certainly, all four most probably, relate to "The Howard Household Books" – for Gairdner III: nos. 668 and 669 see Botfield 1841: 170. For a likely explanation of their displacement see the text and following note.

¹⁸ For the itinerary of the Paston Letters see Gairdner I: 3–6; Davis I: xxv–xxvii. The likelihood that the Beaumont letters and other non-Paston items were gathered in by one or other of these collectors is strengthened

by the fact that "The Howard Household Books" were in the possession of Peter Le Neve and Thomas Martin (Botfield 1841: xciv, cf Collier 1844: i), just as that fact is a convincing indication of the Howard documents slippage from a "Howard Collection" to the Paston one.

[19] Both Gairdner II: no. 210 (BL Add MS 34888. f. 82) and III: no. 410 (BL Add MS 34888, f.149) are such contemporary copies. Both were endorsed by the sixteenth-century "commentator" (see note 12 above) – in English on these two occasions; no. 210 bears the comment, "A Copie of the duke of N. Letter wch shewith that notable Iniuries were commytted by the L. Scales and his adherentes", and no. 410, "The Copie of Thearles of Warr" and Salisbur' letter whereby appear the suspected life of Tudenham Heydon and others'.

[20] Gairdner II: 295. This is BL Egerton MS 914 and not now in the Paston collection. It is a single sheet [about fifteen inches by eight inches] cleanly written in paragraphs. It is unaddressed but has been folded.

[21] 1983: 101. Surely most people were kept well informed by relatives and friends, as old Sir John Pelham was of Henry V's war: see the sequence of letters in Lyell 1934: 268–76.

[22] Davis I: 165. In an earlier letter (Davis I: 162) written by Playter and signed by William, who added on this occasion a short postscript, is the graphic account of the reception at Calais of the earl Rivers after his taking off from Sandwich by the rebel Yorkist lords in January 1460. Who had described this scene to William Paston?

[23] Hinds 1912: 66. This "authentic letter" of the Treasurer's was wrong (we should note) as Henry VI had not been captured. For another Towton casualty list, see Richmond 1977: 86.

[24] McFarlane 1981: 7–9. Thus, we should not be surprised that Edward IV knew John Paston. Besides, John's eldest son was at this time in, or on the fringes of. Edward's household and Edward's memory for "the names and circumstances of almost all men, scattered over the counties of the kingdom" was exceptional enough to be remarked upon by the Crowland Chronicler (Pronay and Cox 1986: 153).

[25] Davis II: 236. He continued, "Wheder ye have understandying before hand I wot not; but and it lyke you to take the worship uppon you, consyderying the comfortable tytynges a-fore sayd, and for the gladnesse and plesour of al your welwyllers and to the pyne and dyscomfort of all your jllewyllers, it were tyme your gere necessarye on that by-halfe were purveyed fore. And also ye had nede higth you to London, for as I conceyve the knygthes schuln be made upon the Saterday by-for the coronacion." John did not become a knight: either Playter's information was wrong or John did not "lyke to take the worship".

[26] 1936: 852. From where I have also taken the details of John's will. For a discussion of John and his like, see Criffiths: 109–130; John figures: 113–4. As he served with the earl of Warwick in Normandy in 1417–8 (Roskell 1954: 124). should not soldiering be included as yet another dimension of his many-dimensioned life?

[27] A point he made more directly in his brief "Parliamentary Prologue" in Carter 1936, with reference to Richard Quartremain of London and Rycote, Oxfordshire (d. 1477). He concluded: "The history of the Quartremains family history is as perfect as any county history can be. But no family history can be more than woof till the warp is woven to make clear the pattern. That warp is the History of the personnel of Parliament, of the governing class at large".

[28] For gentlemen bureaucrats, see Storey 1982: 90–129 and Storey 1984: 196–204. For royal household knights, esquires and gentlemen, see Morgan 1986: 15–35.

## Bibliography

Armstrong, C.A.J. 1983: *England, France, and Burgundy in the Fifteenth Century* (London, 1983)

Aston, Margaret 1984: *Lollards and Reformers* (London, 1984)

Aylmer, C.E. and Cant, Reginald 1979: eds., *A History of York Minster* (Oxford, 1979)

Benham, W.G. 1902: (ed) *The Red Paper Book of Colchester* (Colchester, 1902)

Bennett, Rev. J.A. 1888: "A Clastonbury Relic", *Proceedings of the Somersetshire Archaeological and Natural History Society*, XXXIV (1888), pp. 117–22 and frontispiece.

Botfield, Beriah 1841: (ed) *Manners and Household Expenses of England in the Thirteenth and Fifteenth Centuries* (Roxburghe Club, 1841)

*CCR: Calendar of Close Rolls* (HMSO, London, various dates)

*CPR: Calendar of Patent Rolls* (HMSO, London, various dates)

ChWR 1845: *Chronicles of the White Rose* (London, 1845)

Carlin, Martha 1985: "Fastolf Place, Southwark", in *Richard III: Crown and People*, ed. J. Petre (Cloucester, 1985), pp. 44–7.

Carter, W.F. 1936: *The Quartremains of Oxfordshire* (Oxford, 1936)

Collier, J.P. 1844: (ed) *Household Books of John Duke of Norfolk* (Roxburghe Club, 1844)

Connolly, James L. 1928: *John Gerson* (Louvain, 1928)

Cuttler, S.H. 1981: "A report to Sir John Fastolf on the trial of Jean, duke of Alençon". *English Historical Review*, XCVI (1981), pp. 808–17.

Davies, J.S. 1856: (ed) *An English Chronicle of the reigns of Richard II, Henry IV, Henry V, and Henry VI*, Camden Society, LXIV (1856)

Davis I and Davis II: Norman Davis, ed., *The Paston Letters and Papers of the Fifteenth Century*, volume I, (Oxford, 1971): volume II (Oxford, 1976)

Elton, G.R. 1972: *Policy and Police* (Cambridge, 1972)

Farmer, D.H. 1978: *The Oxford Dictionary of Saints* (Oxford, 1978)

Gairdner I–VI: James Gairdner (ed) *The Paston Letters*, volumes I–VI (Library edition, London, 1904)

Gairdner, J. 1880: (ed) *Three Fifteenth Century Chronicles*, Camden Society, New Series, XXVIII (1880)

Gerould, G.H. 1926: " 'Tables' in Medieval Churches". *Speculum, I* (1926), pp. 439–40.

Gerould, G.H. 1933: *The Bodleian Quarterly Record VII* (1933), p. 326, footnote.

Griffiths, R.A. 1980: "Public and Private Bureaucracies in England and Wales in the Fifteenth Century", *Transactions of the Royal Historical Society*. Fifth Series, XXX (1980), pp. 109–130.

Griffiths, R.A. 1981: *The Reign of Henry VI* (London, 1981)

Hall, D.H. 1965: *English Medieval Pilgrirnage* (London, 1965)

Harriss, G.L. 1985: (ed) *Henry V. The Practice of Kingship* (Oxford, 1985)

Harvey, John 1969: (ed) *William Worcestre. Itineraries* (Oxford, 1969)

Harvey, Isobel 1988: "Popular Revolt and Unrest in England during the second half of the reign of Henry VI", unpublished Ph.D. thesis, University of Wales, Aberystwyih, 1988.

Hewitt, H.J. 1966: *The Organization of War under Edward III* (Manchester, 1966)

Hinds, A.B. 1912: (ed) *Calendar of State Papers relating to Milan* (HMSO, London, 1912)

HMC: *Historical Manuscripts Commission* (HMSO, London, many reports of various dates)

James, M.E. 1917: "Lives of St Walstan", *Norfolk Archaeology*, XIX (1917), pp. 238–67.

Jones, W.R. 1979: "The English Church and Royal Propaganda during the Hundred Years War", *Journal of British Studies*, XIX (1979), pp. 18–30.

Kekewich, Margaret 1982: "The Attainder of the Yorkists in 1459: Two Contemporary Accounts", *Bulletin of the Institute of Historical Research*, LV (1982), pp. 27–34.

Kingsford, C.L. 1913: *English Historical Literature in the fifteenth Century* (Oxford, 1913)

Lyell, Laetitia 1934: *A Medieval Post Bag* (London, 1934)

McFarlane, K.B. 1952: *John Wycliffe and the Beginnings of English Non-conformity* (London, 1952)

McFarlane, K.B. 1981: *England in the Fifteenth Century* (London, 1981)

McHardy, A.K. 1982: "Liturgy and propaganda in the diocese of Lincoln during the Hundred Years War", *Studies in Church History*, 18, ed. Stuart Mews (Oxford, 1982), pp. 215–27.

Maddicott, J.R. 1978: "The County Community and the making of public opinion in fourteenth-century England", *Transactions of the Royal Historical Society*, Fifth Series, XXVIII (1978), pp. 27–43.

Morgan, D.A.L. 1973: "The King's Amnity in the Policy of Yorkist England", *Transactions of the Royal Historical Society*, Fifth Series, XXIII (1973), pp. 1–25.

Morgan, D.A.L. 1986: "The Individual Style of the English Gentleman", *Gentry and Lesser Nobility in Late Medieval Europe*, ed. Michael Jones (Gloucester, 1986), pp. 15–35.

Pantin, W.A. 1976: "Instructions for a Devout and Literate Layman", *Medieval learning and Literature: Essays presented to R.W. Hunt*, eds. J.J.G. Alexander and M.T. Gibson (Oxford, 1976), pp. 398–422.

Payling, S.J. 1986: "Inheritance and Local Politics in the Later Middle Ages: the Case of Ralph, Lord Cromwell, and the Heriz Inheritance". *Nottingharn Medieval Studies*. XXX (1986), pp. 67–95.

Pronay, Nicholas and Cox, John 1986: (eds) *The Crowland Chronicle Continuations* (London, 1986)

Rawcliffe, Carole 1979: "Baronial Councils in the Later Middle Ages". *Patronage, Pedigree and Power*, ed. Charles Ross (Gloucester, 1979), pp. 87–108.

Richmond, Colin 1977: "The Nobility and the Wars of the Roses, 1459–61", *Nottingham Medieval Studies*, XXI (1977), pp. 71–86.

Richmond, Colin 1981a: *John Hopton: a fifteenth-century Suffolk gentleman* (Cambridge, 1981)

Richmond, Colin 1981b: "The Expenses of Thomas Playter of Sotterley, 1459–60", *Proceedings of the Suffolk Institute of Archaeology and History*, XXXV (1981), pp. 41–52.

Richmond, Colin 1983: "After McFarlane", *History*, 68 (1983), pp. 46–60.

Richmond, Colin 1985: "The Pastons Revisited: Marriage and the Family in Fifteenth-Century England", *Bulletin of the Institute of Historical Research*, LVIII (1985), pp. 25–36.

Robbins, Rossell Hope 1959: *Historical Poems of the XIVth and XVth Centuries* (New York, 1959)

Roskcll, J.S. 1954: *The Commons in the Parliament of 1422* (Manchester, 1954)

Rymer, Thomas (ed) *Foedera* (twenty volumes, London, 1727–35)

Sharpe, R.R. 1899: (ed) *Calendar of Letter Books of the City of London, Letter Book I* (London, 1899)

Smith, Anthony 1982: "Aspects of the Career of Sir John Fastolf, 1380–1459", unpublished Oxford D. Phil. thesis, 1982.

Storey, R.L. 1982: "Gentlemen-bureaucrats", *Profession, Vocation and Culture in Later Medieval England: essays dedicated to the memory of A.R. Myers,* ed. C.H. Clough (Liverpool, 1982), pp. 90–129.

Storey, R.L. 1984: "England: Amterhandel im 15. und 16. Jahrhundert", *Amterhandel im Spatmittelalter und irn 16. Jahrhundert* ed. Ilja Mieck (Berlin, 1984), pp. 196–204.

Taylor, Frank and Roskell, John 1975: (eds) *Gesta Henrici Quinti* (Oxford, 1975)

Thomson, John A.F. 1965: *The Later Lollards 1414–1520* (Oxford, 1965)

Wedgwood, J.C. 1936: *History of Parliament 1439–1509, Biographies* (HMSO, London, 1936)

Wilson, R.M. 1952: *The Lost Literature of Medieval England* (London, 1952)

# Civilizing Northumberland: Representations of Englishness in the Tudor State[1]

## STEVEN G. ELLIS

**Abstract** Taking Northumberland as a case study, this paper explores the wider implications of the Tudor strategy of reform by centralization, uniformity, and cultural imperialism. It reappraises the notion that the growth of centralized government at the expense of regional magnates was unambiguously a form of modernization; and argues that the essential character of the Tudor state and the radical nature of Tudor reform have been obscured by the historians' practice of viewing developments in terms of the rise of the nation.

*****

"The southern part, which is also the more civilized, obeys the English king," wrote John Major of Ireland in 1521. "The more northern part is under no king, but remains subject to chiefs of its own."[2] Sixty years later, Richard Stanyhurst remarked more particularly of southern Ireland that the countess of Ormond was "the only meane . . . whereby hir husband's country was reclaymed from the sluttish and unclean Irish custome to English habits, bedding, house-keeping, and civilitie."[3] Thus, two sixteenth-century writers from very different backgrounds – a Scot, and one of the Old English of Ireland – endorsed this characteristically English identification of Englishness and civility, Irishness and savagery. Of course, there was nothing very new about these ideas in Tudor times. The English had traditionally described developments in later medieval Ireland and Wales in these terms; and, as Professor John Gillingham has recently argued, this juxtaposition of Englishness and civility can be traced back to William of Malmesbury in the early twelfth century.[4] Yet what was perhaps much less traditional was the way in which the Tudors exploited these ideas in the context of state formation. Taking Tudor Northumberland as a case study, this paper argues that these concepts were redefined in the sixteenth century and used by the Tudors in support of a strategy of state formation which effected a radical restructuring of the English state.

It is itself a measure of the state's success in moulding a concept of Englishness that this theory has occasioned scarcely any debate among English historians. English history is allegedly about England, the English nation, and the English state; and the Tudor period, we are told, witnessed the emergence of an English nation-state. Yet these statements raise some basic questions about

English history which are largely ignored in traditional Tudor historiography. In the first place, the concept of Englishness encapsulated three different sets of ideas with overlapping definitions regarding people, country, and culture. First, Englishness referred to a people or nation, the English, distinguishable from other peoples by customs and culture. Second, it had a geographical aspect, with reference to that part of Britain settled by the English before 1066, the kingdom of England. Finally, Englishness had a pronounced cultural dimension, denoting such things as the English language, English law, and government. It is significant, for instance, that the Gaelic language employs no less than three separate sets of terms (*Saxain* country; *Gaill* people, culture; *Béarla* language) to describe these different aspects of Englishness. In addition, England and the English state were not synonymous. The kingdom of England did not exist in isolation: the emerging nation-state of which it was the dominant part included Wales and parts of Ireland; and the king's subjects included Welsh, Irish, Scots, and even French, as well as the English. The English state which the Tudors inherited was, like most so-called nation-states, actually multi-national; and ideas of Englishness were quite widely drawn, to include, for instance, the kin-based societies and marcher lordships of the English borderlands.

During the sixteenth century, however, perceptions of English identity changed quite significantly, and Englishness was more narrowly defined. In particular, the cultural norms of English identity were further sharpened through the parallel advance of concepts of "English civility." In 1500, for instance, the English nation comprised all those of free birth, English blood and condition, born within the territories under the allegiance of the king of England. It included the English of Calais, Ireland, and Wales – not just those born in England. By 1600, however, English identity was more closely tied to the national territory and, as is well known, it had acquired a pronounced religious character – the product of Protestant perceptions of England as God's elect nation.[5] Of course, Englishness and civility had long gone hand in hand: since God was an Englishman, "civility," as the manifestation of English culture, had to be closest to godliness. To the extent that other peoples departed from English norms, they were less civil. As Professor Rees Davies has recently argued, even the English could degenerate through contact with less civilized nations, such as the mere Irish and Welsh;[6] nonetheless, the English were *ipso facto* a civil people. This assumption underpinned the decision to transplant to Co. Roscommon in 1608 one of the most disruptive of the border "surnames,"[7] the Graham clan: although "a naughty and factious people" at home, they were "a witty and understanding people, and withal very civil" who, allegedly, would soon reduce the wild Irish to tillage and English civility. Unfortunately, things turned out very differently![8] Yet the evidence suggests that, in practice, these elastic concepts of Englishness and civility were increasingly redefined under the Tudors to mean lowland England and its cultural norms. As such they supplied the ideological weapons for a radical programme of cultural imperialism, administrative centralization, and uniformity.

If we survey the inherited patterns of geography, society, and culture throughout the British Isles at the start of the Tudor period, it quickly becomes apparent that the south-east was unlike any other region within these islands. In most areas, pastoral uplands with their more dispersed settlement patterns and lineage-based societies were interspersed with lowland regions of nucleated villages and predominantly arable farming: very often this upland-lowland divide was reinforced by its coincidence with linguistic and cultural boundaries between Celtic- and English-speaking peoples. By contrast, society in the south-east was more homogeneous. Even if we exclude Scotland and Gaelic Ireland, which only later became part of the same state, the overall pattern remains the same. Despite the precociously centralized and uniform administrative structures of lowland England, the Tudor state as a whole was a comparatively fragmented polity, a land of many marches, in which peace was precarious and central authority weak. In this highly regional land, with its turbulent marcher society, ties of kinship remained strong, and real power rested with a powerful territorial nobility who organized the rule and defence of their compact lordships through a numerous and warlike tenantry.[9] No doubt there were, in other respects, fundamental differences between the English north, Wales, and Ireland. Yet, particularly when viewed from London, and in an administrative context, they also had much in common, and the problems they presented were a good deal more typical of the wider Tudor state than the supposedly normative south-east.

The response of the Tudors to this inherited range of problems was at once both predictable and highly individualistic – predictable in the attempt to weld these disparate territories together into an English nation-state, individualistic in the methods chosen to achieve this. The preferred Tudor method of state formation was by centralization and uniformity. Briefly, the Tudors tried to turn the borderlands into little Englands by imposing on them the cultural and administrative norms of lowland England. Administratively, these territories were turned into royal shires through the abolition of feudal liberties, and they were governed through the same combination of local officials headed by sheriffs and justices of the peace, all directed from the centre. Culturally, the campaign was characterized by the attempt to foster concepts of "English civility" among the predominantly upland, marcher societies of the border-lands. Thus, the administrative reorganization of the mid-1530s in Wales, Ireland, and the far north, and then the imposition in these regions of the Bible and Book of Common Prayer in southern English, were major steps in a fundamental restructuring within the Tudor state of relations between core and periphery.

Tudor historiography naturally reflects in many ways the beliefs and concerns of contemporary Tudor officials. Yet these ideas need to be critically assessed. In this context, the traditional assumption underpinning analyses by English historians of socio-political change in the Tudor provinces is that the Tudor pursuit of an ordered, civil society was a realisable goal throughout the Tudor state, to be achieved by the establishment of peace and good government, coupled with firm, impartial justice. Bastard feudal-ism and over-mighty subjects needed to be curbed, private fran-chises abolished, and the local gentry weened from dependence on the great provincial magnates and encouraged to look toward the court for advancement. In effect, the extension of royal government and kingly power have been invested with a strongly progressive quality, as offering the best prospects for good rule. Good govern-ment was allegedly synonymous with royal control and adminis-trative uniformity: it led automatically to the achievement of the central goal of "English civility." By contrast, feudal particularism and entrenched magnate power are identified as essentially reac-tionary forces which impeded progress towards "English civility." Yet, if conditions in lowland England were normative, one question which needs far more consideration than it usually receives is whether Tudor policy was not in fact vitiated from the outset by the allegedly exceptional problems encountered in the borderlands – problems of defence and communication, combined with differ-ences of geography and so of social structure. Was it possible, for instance, to govern a large, predominantly upland shire which lay 300 miles from London by the same centralized structures as were developed for a small, lowland county like Bedfordshire? And if marcher lordships were dismantled, how could the border be defended without a standing army? The central problem raised by Tudor policy is how effective it was in discharging the basic duties of monarchical government in providing justice, good rule, and defence for the king's subjects.

There is a substantial modern literature on Tudor Northumber-land, ranging from Tony Pollard's fine regional history of *North-eastern England During the Wars of the Roses*,[10] which analyses developments to 1500, to D.L.W. Tough's pioneering study of *The*

*Last Years of a Frontier*,[11] and S.J. Watts' stimulating analysis of the borders in transition, *From Border to Middle Shire: Northumberland, 1586–1625*.[12] Mervyn James's collected essays on the Tudor north also offer important insights into Northumbrian developments,[13] and there are numerous older works of a more antiquarian bent. Running through this literature is the assumption that the exclusion of successive Percy earls of Northumberland from power, the gradual undermining of Percy influence, and the break-up of Percy estates in the county were necessary steps in the creation of an ordered, civil society there. Even so, juxtaposing the work of medieval and Tudor historians is sufficient to raise serious doubts about the alleged efficacy of royal government and centralized control as a means of promoting good rule throughout Northumberland. "By no stretch of the imagination," concludes Pollard, "was northeastern England a remote, poor and backward corner of the land." Dismissing suggestions that the region was "an extended frontier zone," he argues that only "the border dales of Northumberland, which formed a distinctly different society created by the experience of endemic warfare, could possibly be described in these terms."[14] Accordingly, Henry Tudor's "refus[al] to allow a local magnate to exercise quasi-regal power" and his "clear-sighted determination . . . enabled him, in the face of several obstacles, to bring the north-east under his firm control."[15] And writing of the 1569 rising, Rachel Reid argues that "[t]he movement which culminated in the Rebellion of the Earls and their followers was essentially retrograde," since "[i]ts aim was the perpetuation of a system . . . which the mass of the nation had outgrown." "The extension of royal control over the outlying parts of the kingdom was essential to the growth of national unity."[16] Happily, by 1570 the crown had broken the influence of the Percies and banished the earl of Northumberland to Petworth in Sussex. As Watt explains, in their place power in Northumberland had been diffused among a new group of royal officials, and a crown interest had gradually been built up among the local gentry. Yet, despite the assumptions of English historiography and continuing Tudor efforts to tame the wild borderers and to promote "English civility," Elizabeth was now confronted with what her officials described as a "decay of the borders." Endemic unrest and chronic raiding disrupted an increasingly impoverished countryside which was further weakened by family feuds and rivalries among the gentry. The reality was that Tudor attempts to assimilate Northumberland administratively and socially into lowland England had little or no impact on levels of public order in the county.[17]

The far north was a region of compact lordships. Over half the land in the geographical area of the modern county of Northumberland was held in early Tudor times by four major tenants-in-chief. Administratively too, about half of it comprised feudal liberties which lay outside the medieval shire. Three of the leading landowners, who were also lords of liberties, were normally absentees. The bishop of Durham's palatinate included three detached members, collectively known as North Durham, which lay geographically in Northumberland. The most extensive of these, Norhamshire, separated the military outpost of Berwick-on-Tweed from the royal shire, while to the south-west, also on the border, lay the liberties of Tynedale and Redesdale. Tynedale had recently come into crown hands, but Redesdale was held by the absentee Tailboys of Kyme. South of Tynedale was another liberty, Hexhamshire, held by the archbishop of York, while the prior of Tynemouth had a small liberty east of Newcastle.[18] This fragmentation of authority complicated the administration of justice and the maintenance of order, since in each liberty the lord enjoyed regalian rights. The liberties provided a sanctuary for criminals fleeing from the sheriffs of surrounding counties. The proximity of the border also prompted the creation of other non-standard institutions, such as the warden courts and march law. Yet the basic aim of these administrative structures was to facilitate the region's defence. The grant of regalian rights enhanced the lord's *manraed*: it is unhelpful to castigate these structures for failing to maintain "good rule."

Politically, however, by far the most important landowner was the Percy earl of Northumberland who held the baronies of Alnwick, Beanley, Prudhoe, and Warkworth in the eastern lowlands and the barony of Langley in the central highlands. Altogether, the Percy estates in Northumberland were worth about £900 a year.[19] Yet since they were located in a turbulent marcher society and were all vulnerable to a Scottish invasion, the atmosphere of insecurity hampered the lord in his financial exploitation of these estates. They included many sprawling manors whose net yield was comparatively small. Two of the earl's manors were still waste in 1505, for instance, after three years of peace with Scotland.[20] In short, the Percy possessions in Northumberland needed a resident lord to defend them, but because they were so extensive, the earl dominated the shire when he was in residence. The influence of the march helped to shape the character of lordship. The earl of Westmorland, Lord Dacre, and Lord Roos also held some land in Northumberland, but in their cases these isolated and exposed marchlands were too marginal to their main interests to induce them to reside. Apart from the Percy earl, the only other peer who normally resided in the county was Lord Ogle, a border baron who held eighteen war-torn manors in Northumberland worth a little under £200 a year but, significantly, almost no land elsewhere.[21]

Patterns of landholding, together with the region's geography, in turn helped to shape the county's social structures. The economic base of the northern marches was much poorer than the southern lowlands. Newcastle was the only substantial town, and in the western half of Northumberland, which was predominantly upland over 500 feet, the nucleated settlements of the arable lowlands gave place to isolated farmsteads. An inquisition taken in 1428 into the number of knights' fees in Northumberland suggests that the crown had about forty knight-service tenants under baronial rank in the county. Only twenty-two held as much as half a knight's fee, however. Thus there was actually quite a small potential pool of substantial and independent county gentry to which the crown could turn to rule the shire in place of over-mighty subjects like the earl of Northumberland. Almost half of the leading crown tenants were also mesne tenants of the Percies, and altogether the numbers of Percy knight-service tenants were scarcely less impressive than those of the crown.[22] Moreover, very few substantial gentry families of any sort lived in the highland zone.[23] Ridley of Willimontswick in south Tynedale had estates worth 100 marks a year, as did a junior branch of the Heron family residing at Chipchase in north Tynedale. Further up the valley, there was only one tower house – the normal gentry residence in the marches – situated at Hesleyside, which belonged to the head of the Charlton surname.[24] And in Redesdale and Hexhamshire there were no important gentry families at all.

Structures of lordship also had an impact on the operation of government in Northumberland. The administration of the numerous liberties in the region was in the hands of the lords' officials. And in the central highlands at least, these were usually headed by outsiders, since there were very few gentry available to take charge of local government. As lord of Hexham, for instance, Wolsey assigned the government of the shire to Lord Dacre and his brother Sir Christopher; and in 1507, when the regality was in the king's hands, the commission of the peace for Hexhamshire had comprised three clerics and four neighbouring gentry with lands there, headed by Nicholas Ridley, then sheriff of Northumberland.[25] Within the royal county, the institutions of shire government can certainly be compared with those further south, as Pollard shows. Yet sheriffs did not operate in the normal manner. The 4th earl of Northumberland was appointed sheriff for life in 1474; by 1506 the shrievalty of Northumberland was farmed by the local gentry; from 1515 the warden-general nominated the sheriff; and in 1532 the 6th earl of Northumberland was granted the farm of the shrievalty for life.[26] Some years there was no sheriff at all, "wherby the kinges prosses and oder mennes cannot be serued nor sessions kepit as they shuld be."[27] The conditions under which sheriffs worked were also quite different. They were much more involved in organizing the defence of the county; they were excluded from many parts by the existence of honours and liberties, and elsewhere they frequently needed to raise a posse to serve writs; and they did not account at the exchequer in London. In the mid-1530s, the exchequer made process to account against a long list of sheriffs and escheators of Northumberland going back to 1515. A search of the records showed that amercements had frequently been inflicted on sheriffs for failing to make their proffers at Easter and Michaelmas, for not returning writs, and for not making their accounts; but since the sheriffs never appeared at the exchequer, these fines could not be collected. Subsequent inquiries revealed that no sheriff or escheator had accounted at the exchequer since 1461.[28] Sheriffs neither answered for issues and profits of land in the king's hand nor returned the king's process, and escheators failed to return inquests which they took. Thus the king "losyth the seruices of hys tenauntes and thaduauntage of yssues, ffynes & [a]merciamentes that shuld growe" and likewise "losyth the wardes, mariages & relieffes of hys tenauntes . . . & many other aduauntages & rightes."[29] In response, former sheriffs and escheators asserted that "a grete parte of the grounde whereof the proffitts and revenues of the said offices shulde be levied and gathered hath been oftentymes wast and unoccupied," and that they were at great costs in defending the county and executing process "agaynst the wylde and unruely persones dwelling and abiding nygh unto the said borders of Scotland."[30] Eventually, a statute of 1549 ordered that sheriffs of Northumberland should account for the profits of their bailiwick at the exchequer, like other sheriffs.[31]

Similar difficulties surrounded the work of the justices of the peace in their quarter sessions. Pollard has noted that the Northumberland bench was small and infrequently renewed, but the county had far fewer substantial gentry available to serve on the peace commissions than smaller southern shires. Under Henry VII, Northumberland peace commissions usually numbered between eleven and fourteen, including eight or nine local gentry.[32] They had tripled in size by the middle of Henry VIII's reign, but the number of local gentry on the commissions was still only around sixteen: the others were mainly regional magnates, lawyers, or members of the northern council not normally resident in the shire.[33] In 1526, when the government's attention turned to border administration, Cardinal Wolsey was told that there were so few J.P.s in Northumberland, particularly of the quorum, that quarter sessions had not been kept for a long time. An enlarged bench and three more justices of the quorum were requested.[34]

The basic problem was that comparatively few substantial gentry families lived in Northumberland, particularly in the western highlands. In 1528, when the 6th earl of Northumberland was appointed warden of the east and middle marches, the majority of the Northumberland gentry were retained by the king to assist the warden – Lord Ogle, plus five knights, thirteen squires, and thirty-one other gentry, plus nineteen gentry from Norhamshire which was administratively part of North Durham.[35] Another list was drawn up of those gentry who were not being retained: it numbered 55, although in the event twenty of them were included among the king's retainers. Thus, if we include the wardenry officials and the Norhamshire gentry, altogether 118 gentry lived in the area of the modern county in 1528.[36] By lowland English standards, this was a remarkably small number, but it was not untypical of pre-dominantly upland shires elsewhere in the Tudor state. Only about thirty of these gentry were knightly: that is, they were eligible for knighthood because they possessed net annual incomes from land of £40 or more. And only about thirty more had the £20 a year in land which was the statutory minimum for a J.P.: there were at least eleven gentlemen (especially younger sons and cadet branches of leading families) whose annual income of between £4 and 10 marks was well below the accepted threshold for an English gentleman at that time. Thus, comparatively few of the Northumbrian gentry had sufficient possessions to be included on the bench. Even fewer had much legal knowledge: in 1528 John Bedenell was described as "the chief lerned in the cuntre," but he was not, apparently, included on the bench.[37] By comparison, it has been calculated that in the North Riding of Yorkshire c.1500, the families of the manorial squirearchy (i.e. those gentry who held at least one manor) numbered around 130, of whom at least forty-five were knightly; and below them were the many families of mere gentry whose incomes were only a little more than that of a yeoman.[38]

For the purpose of feeing the gentry, however, what concerned the authorities was not so much landed income and legal educa-tion, as their military capacity – how many horsemen the gentry kept to serve the king on the borders, how far their chief residence lay from Scotland, as well as any other qualities which would enhance the value of their military service. For instance, Gilbert Swinhoe of Cornhill on Tweedbank, with twenty horsemen, was described in 1528 as "a sharpe trew gentilman and kepith a good house," while Gerard Selby of Pawston, two miles from Scotland, "haith buyldit a stoone howse now lately vpon the Bordours and plenished the ground which haith layd waist sith the Scottes feld [1513] and is a sharpe borderer."[39] By contrast, it was reported in 1537 of two of the county gentry, Sir Cuthbert Radcliffe and Sir

Roger Grey, both J.P.s, that Radcliffe kept a hundred horsemen and was "a wyes man, well learnyd and well myndyd to justice, very meet for counsell, but no adventurer to the ffeeld," and Grey with forty tenants and servants was "meanly scet to justice . . . and hath left hys pryncipall howse voyed whych stondyth very necessarye for the strength of the countie."[40]

One of the main methods by which the work in local government of the sheriff and justices of the peace was coordinated was through the justices of assize. But the justices of the northern circuit only visited the far north once a year, usually holding assizes at Newcastle, Carlisle, and Appleby during the summer. Their business did not detain them in the region beyond a week, even when the assizes were not curtailed because of war.[41] Reports of the Newcastle assizes in summer 1523 – when the government was keen to improve the enforcement of the law – give some indication of the perfunctory nature of their work in Northumberland at that time. Upon proclamation of the sessions by the king's lieutenant, the earl of Surrey, several thieves living in Northumberland who had committed felonies fled into Hexhamshire, and before the judges' arrival four more thieves had escaped from Alnwick castle and eight out of Newcastle. "[Y]et," as Surrey related, "we had at the bar xj others. And for nothing that I and the Iudges could spek or saye, there was not one man that wold gif any evidence againste any one of theym." Likewise, at the Durham assizes "right litle matier was founde by the Inqueste and but one hanged who was an Irisheman." Surrey attributed this unwillingness to convict to two causes: first, so few of the Northumbrian gentry were not harbourers of thieves that they were unwilling to give evidence against the tenants and servants of others; and more especially, that the whole shire was convinced that "all the brute of Iustice too bee mynystred in thics parties" was not serious but meant only to scare them "as it hathe bee in tymes past."[42]

Finally, if the king's subjects remained dissatisfied with the quality of justice available in the shire, they could travel up to London to plead their case in the central courts. The evidence suggests that very few chose to do so. A search of the De Banco rolls for cases relating to Northumberland has revealed that throughout the fourteenth century three or four cases per annum came before the justices of common pleas. Business then tailed off significantly, and during the reigns of the first two Tudors only 38 cases came before the justices, an average of less than one per annum.[43] This was not, apparently, because the king's council in the north offered a less remote forum for the settlement of disputes: common pleas was no more active in hearing Northumberland cases during those periods when the northern council was not sitting. In fact, almost all plaintiffs in proceedings before the justices were substantial landowning gentry or wealthy Newcastle merchants: no doubt few others could afford the costs of litigation in the central courts.

In sum, here was a county which was as English as Bedfordshire, governed by English law and local government, whose inhabitants were probably even more English than those of Cornwall or Cheshire. Yet its patterns of landholding and its political, social, and governmental structures, although unmistakeably English, exhibited marked differences from those in lowland England. The overriding concern of marcher society was security and defence, not peace and good government. Even in peacetime the marches remained disturbed and troubled by petty raiding: in wartime the border communities were threatened by wholesaledestruction. Large parts of Northumberland were vulnerable to Scottish raids. Accordingly, most of the gentry kept horsemen for defence. It was estimated, for instance, that the total *manræd* at the disposal of the 55 gentlemen who were not to be retained in 1528 amounted 976 horsemen.[44] This in turn represented a substantial charge on the land, further reducing their landed income. Inquisitions *post mortem* relating to lands of Northumberland gentry show that manors and tenements frequently lay waste in whole or in part owing to destruction wrought by the Scots.[45] All along the border, large tracts of land lay waste during "warre or a troublous peace"; conversely, as prospects of peace or a firm truce increased, "the pore subiettes of both the realmes ar drawne to the bordours."[46] In many parts close to the border, destruction by Scottish raids was so predictable in wartime that separate valuations could be given for peace and war. Learmouth township, just south of Wark, for instance, was destroyed by Scottish raids in 1521, 1523, and 1533: it was worth £35 6s. 4d. in peacetime and nothing in wartime.[47]

Most exposed of all was the extensive manor of Otterburn in the liberty of Redesdale, which lay within a region of constant war. After the death of its absentee lord, Sir Robert Tailboys, it was valued in 1494 at a mere twenty marks a year, and the lord's castle of Harbottle in nearby Coquetdale was worth nothing at all. Large parts of Otterburn were entirely waste because they lay "in the march of Scotland . . . and no profit can be taken therefrom on account of the Scots and others of Scotland dwelling near the said messuages and tofts in Scotland." The manor had several free tenants whose tenements lay "within the march in the kingdom of England near the Scots" and who anciently paid rent, but "in time of war between England and the Scots they pay no rent, nor anything else, but give their help together with their lord there to keep the vale, or valley, of Redesdale and those who dwell there from plunderers, enemies, and robbers."[48]

Raids and invasions by the Scots were not the only cause of instability, however. Over the previous two centuries, the endemic warfare and insecurity of the Anglo-Scottish marches had fostered the emergence of the border surnames – semi-autonomous, pastoral clans with elected captains, inhabiting the upland parts of the west and middle marches and living by reiving and robbery – who were inured to conditions of continuous warfare and raiding. Not only were they not amenable to law, but in other obvious ways they differed from the normal habits and lifestyle of Tudor Englishmen, practising transhumance, partible inheritance, and common ownership of land. Contemporary descriptions of the border surnames leave little doubt that Tudor officials regarded them as a species of *Homo silvestris*, a primitive pastoral people living in mud huts in woods or mountains. Properly handled, the English surnames could in wartime provide a welcome and very substantial addition to English military might. Yet Tynedale and Redesdale in particular were quite unable to support their accustomed levels of population, and during periods of peace or prolonged truce the border surnames tended to supplement their income by preying on the richer lowland communities of eastern Northumberland and Durham. In a bad year, such as 1525, bands of up to 400 thieves raided south into the Palatinate and to within eight miles of Newcastle, and the surnames had to be reduced by a military campaign.[49] As Tudor officials were aware, this was a considerable task since the border surnames were a substantial military force in their own right. The Northumbrian surnames alone numbered 403 in Tynedale and 445 in Redesdale when "booked" by the government in 1528.[50] And when mustered with the rest of the shire in 1538, all 391 of the Tynedale thieves were then equipped with horse and harness, as were 185 of the Redesdale thieves. Considering that the muster returns for the whole shire totalled 6,375 able men, of whom 2,913 were equipped with horse and harness, the surnames of Tynedale and Redesdale supplied about 13% of Northumberland's available manpower and almost 20% of the most highly prized troops in Anglo-Scottish warfare, the mounted spearmen.[51]

Thus, although Scottish armies had not penetrated south of the Tyne since 1388, border raiding was not just a case of localized disturbances along the border line, which could be quietened with the help of the Scottish warden.[52] In the marches, the normal tensions between upland and lowland communities were greatly exacerbated by the military exigencies of the frontier: all the gentry kept horsemen for the purpose of defence, and during extended periods of peace or truce, Northumberland's surplus military manpower turned its hand to other pursuits. The activities of English and Scottish surnames meant that under the early Tudors the far north remained an extended frontier. In these circumstances, the main priority of government was not firm, impartial control by king and council in London – the alleged ideal of Tudor government – but energetic local leadership in the marches, to repel raiders and repress thieves.

The obvious person to assume this role was the earl of Northumberland. The location of the earl's estates and the absence of other major landowners helps to explain the earl's traditional dominance in the county during the fifteenth century. Thus, when, after the murder of the 4th earl in 1489, Henry VII decided to exclude the family from its traditional role in the marches, some other system of rule and defence needed to be put in its place. Initially, the king had no other choice, because the 5th earl was barely eleven years old on his father's death. A complete outsider, the earl of Surrey, was appointed the king's lieutenant instead and took over the leading role in the rule of the marches; but gradually what had originally seemed like a stop-gap measure to deal with a particular emergency became deliberate policy. Power was diffused among a group of lesser lords and leading gentry, and after Surrey's departure in 1499, the office of lieutenant became an emergency appointment, filled only during periods of actual war with Scotland.[53] The king's council in the north which, in administrative terms, was Surrey's successor, itself disappeared in 1509; and in military terms, the crown drastically reduced its traditional provision for border defence in the form of inflated salaries for the wardens and ample garrisons for military outposts like Berwick-on-Tweed.[54] Thus, Northumberland's exclusion from the wardenship, at a time when absentee lordship was already a serious problem in the region, greatly weakened the defence of the marches. When, at the start of his fourteen-year stint as warden-general in 1511, Thomas Lord Dacre took charge of the traditional structures for border rule and defence, he assumed control of what was, in effect, an empty shell.

The drastic curtailment in the crown's provision for the marches extended far beyond the well-known reduction in the wardens' salaries. From 1515, Thomas Lord Dacre received £280 a year as warden of the east and middle marches, whereas the traditional salary had been £2,500 and double in wartime.[55] The real difference lay rather in the direction of Dacre's interests and ambitions as a regional magnate and the significantly smaller scale of his private resources. In this respect, Dacre was at least *comparable* with the Percy earl, which is more than could be said of some of Henry VII's later warden lieutenants – newly created peers like Lord Darcy or local gentry such as Edward Radcliffe.[56] By 1525, Dacre's landed income exceeded £1,500 a year, or about half that of the 5th earl of

Northumberland.[57] Yet Northumberland's extensive estates in the county provided him with an army of almost 2,000 tenants; and at the time of his death the 4th earl had also built up a powerful connexion for the defence of the marches by spending no less than 42% of his income on retaining eighty-four lords, knights, and esquires, beyond his immediate household and legal needs.[58] By contrast, Dacre had only recently acquired lands in the county. His barony of Morpeth, worth approximately £180 a year, provided him with a modest base in the middle marches, but he had no lands at all in the east marches. Moreover, although he served the king loyally as warden-general, Dacre's main interests lay in Cumberland and he showed no interest in challenging the earl's traditional dominance in Northumberland by building up a rival connexion there. He could, in a crisis, call upon his numerous tenantry in northern Cumberland for the defence of the middle marches. He also had some following among the upland squires there, and developed an understanding with the Northumbrian border surnames.[59] Overall, however, the east and middle marches were much weaker under Dacre because the king's decision to exclude the 5th earl from the wardenship meant that his private resources and his extensive connexion could not easily be deployed in the crown interest. The Northumberland gentry complained in 1525 that "for lak of doing iustice" many of the commons "ar becommen common robbours and theves," townships were deserted, and the country "like shortely to be most enhabited with thives Englisshe & Scottishe, and the kinges true subiectes ther either to be expelled or els to become subiectes to the said thives."[60]

For ten years from 1527, this "decay of the borders" was temporarily arrested by Henry VIII's reluctant appointment of the young 6th earl of Northumberland as warden of the east and middle marches when disorder threatened to get out of hand. Then, in 1537, much more fundamental changes became necessary. With the earl's surrender of the family estates to the crown shortly before his early death, the traditional arrangements for the rule of the marches became unusable for a generation. In place of the time-honoured strategy of harnessing the private resources of provincial magnates to buttress royal authority in the marches, the king was left with no option but to pursue a much more interventionist policy. Other recent developments had also underlined the need for a fundamental reorganization of northern government. The disgrace in 1534 of William Lord Dacre, warden of the west marches, had further discredited the region's traditional ruling magnates. Moreover, those now entrusted with the rule of the north – the earls of Cumberland and Northumberland, and the attenuated king's council there, revived in 1525 – had collectively failed to prevent the

Pilgrimage of Grace, the major rebellion which engulfed the whole region in 1536–7. Yet, if royal government and centralized control were the advance that they seemed in administrative terms, then the fall of the Percies represented a great opportunity.

Hitherto, the liberty of Tynedale and the small baronies of Bamburgh and Embleton (Dunstanburgh) had comprised the only substantial royal estates in the county,[61] but the acquisition of the Percy lands established the king for the first time as a major landowner there and brought many more of the local gentry into a direct relationship with the crown. The king's holdings were further strengthened by the lands of Hexham and Tynemouth priories, which came into crown hands following the dissolution of the monasteries, and through the acquisition by exchanges of Redesdale and Hexhamshire from the Tailboys heiress and the archbishop of York, respectively.[62] At the same time, the 1536 statute against the liberties had strengthened crown control over the extensive feudal franchises within Northumberland, providing that only the king could appoint judges and J.P.s in Hexhamshire, Redesdale, and North Durham, or pardon serious crimes. Redesdale, indeed, was soon incorporated into Northumberland, although Hexhamshire not until 1572.[63] Thus, within a few years, the traditional structures for the rule and defence of the marches had been thoroughly dismantled, and the whole region opened up to royal government.

What, then, was the impact of this major extension of royal power and government on the rule of the borders? At first sight, Henry VIII's new administrative arrangements looked quite substantial. In January 1537, the king appointed himself warden of the east and middle marches and commissioned two local gentry, Sir William Eure and Sir John Widdrington, as his deputies. He also appointed new keepers of Tynedale and Redesdale, and retained thirty-three of the leading borderers to assist the deputy-wardens.[64] At the same time, the king's council in the north was remodelled and its jurisdiction extended to the far north, so bringing the wardenries under its control.[65] Altogether, the new arrangements for the king's council and the rule of the marches cost the king £2,607 6s. 8d. a year in fees.[66]

Yet, perhaps because the peace brokered with Scotland in 1534 seemed to be holding, no enhanced military provision was made for border defence; and financially too, the new arrangements cost much less than the income from the new accessions of crown land in the far north. In other words, this apparent extension of royal power represented more a redistribution in the crown's favour of the region's existing financial and military resources, public and private, than the provision of additional resources. And so far as

Northumberland was concerned, this was true also of the arrangements for civil administration. At one level, the suppression of the remaining feudal franchises and their incorporation into Northumberland may have facilitated the administration of justice in the region, but this was offset by the overall reduction in the size of the bureaucracy charged with this task: in effect, the already inadequate administration for a large and turbulent county was simply burdened with additional duties.

What the government singularly failed to do was to address the wider implications of its decision to adapt the existing defensive system rather than to create a new one, for instance by the building up of standing border garrisons. Basically, the traditional system had relied on defence in depth. Despite suggestions to the contrary, the far north was, in fact, an extended march, with a militarized society, in which the more disturbed conditions accentuated the importance of strong resident lordship geared chiefly to defence, of a lord's *manraed* and his tenants' loyalty. It encouraged marcher lords to hold a battle-hardened tenantry ready to repel raiders and resist invasion. The thrust of early-Tudor policy, powerfully accentuated by the administrative reorganization of the mid-1530s, was to marginalize the fact of this long landed frontier and of other differences in land usage and settlement which reflected its predominantly upland character. Instead, the region was to be administered as if it were an extension of lowland England, in the hope that the standardization of government would rapidly promote peace, good rule, and "English civility" in the region.

This strategy may have had partial success in more sheltered parts like the Durham lowlands, but in Northumberland it proved disastrous. "The whole countrey" of Northumberland, reported Sir Robert Bowes in 1550, "is much given to wildnes." Already, the east and middle marches had been seriously weakened by the failure of major landowners to reside there. Since they were no longer entrusted with the wardenship, they had less need of border service from their tenants, and they raised their rents and entry-fines in response to inflation. It was thought, for instance, that the 4th earl of Northumberland had been able to raise 1,000 spearmen from his tenants in the county, but that the 6th earl could only raise a hundred. Other lord's tenants were similarly affected, so that by 1543 only 1,000 men were properly harnessed in Northumberland and the county could only raise 300 horsemen.[67] Thus, the most obvious result of the crown's emergence as the largest landowner there was the crisis of lordship which followed the replacement of resident lords by an absentee. And the situation was further exacerbated when, as in 1542, the crown had the wardship of a leading borderer, like Grey of Chillingham. By then, royal commissioners reporting on the state of the borders were alarmed by the failure of leading gentry in the east marches to ensure that their townships on the border line were properly tenanted and defended. A major cause of "the great decaye" of the borders, they reported, was that the owners of fortresses, "not regardinge their said uttermost fortresses or houses at the fyrste made for defence & strengthninge of the said borders . . . have suffered them by lyttle & lyttle to fall in extreme ruyne & decaye," and "for their more easye quyetness & savynge of expences did w^th draw themselfes in fermes or other smaller houses w^th in the cuntreye further distante from the sayd borders." Many towers and fortresses which had been destroyed in the Scottish war of the 1490s, or during the Flodden campaign, remained unrepaired.[68] In the west marches, by contrast, even though Lord Dacre remained in disgrace, conditions were less critical, because of the survival there of traditional power structures.[69]

The middle marches were scarcely better defended than the east marches. By 1550, Bowes asserted, there was a great conspiracy between "the wyld people of Tynedale and Redesdale and the Scots of Liddesdale": the inhabitants continually "commytted more heynous & detestable offences, declyninge ever from evell unto wourse." By contrast, "the common sorte of people" were "weake & tymorous of harte & courage & so evell prepared of horse harnes & other necessaries for defence." This was either, the commissioners supposed, because they were

not so well cheryshed by their lordes maysters and offycers as yt were convenynte they should have bene in suche a troublous quarter, or elles bene they abashed & oute of courage by the greatt & manyfolde losses hurtes & overthrowes w^ch they have of late susteyned & had by & of the said Tynedales Ryddesdales & Scottes of Lyddesdale.

And despite the growing pressure of population, the number of wastelands along the border seemed to increase. Thus, "excepte those wylde countries may be stablyshed in better order," the "waste & dyssolate countries be lyke to encrease & waxe greatter in those parties." Accordingly, the commissioners recommended that in order to restrain the passage of thieves from Tynedale, Liddesdale, Gilsland, and Bewcastledale, two old fortresses in North Tynedale – the one built by the prior of Hexham forty years before and now belonging to the crown, the other the inheritance of John Heron of Chipchase – should be rebuilt and "inhabyted & plenyshed w^th some trew & honest defenceble men."[70] A further report in 1550 noted that the king's own castles and fortresses in the middle marches, including Alnwick, Warkworth, Prudhoe, and Langley which had formerly belonged to the Percies, were likewise "much in decaye because theire is no yearely reparacions allowed to be done uppon them . . . to the ruine and destruction of the countrey."[71]

In the absence of acceptable local magnates to organize its defence, the crown was also obliged in wartime to appoint southern nobles to the office of warden of the marches.[72] It was reported in 1543 that "the strength of men" on the borders was "much decayed": malefactors "have goten the over hande of the goode men (if there be any)," so that "thole countrey . . . is sore robbed and spoyled, specially the husbandmen," for the gentry "practyse or be at kyndnes wth the thevis" in order to "have their goodes and catalles saved."[73] The county was no longer able to defend itself in wartime, and a large paid garrison of between 2,000 and 3,300 men had to be stationed there.[74] Likewise, the promotion of a new group of crown officials and pensioners and the disintegration of the old Percy connexion also gave a new edge to family feuds and rivalries among the gentry. Unrest and disorders escalated: in the middle marches, Lord Lisle reported that there was "such envy, hatred, disdain and malice" among the gentry that they refused to rise to assist each other, so further undermining the defence of the marches.[75] At every disturbance, those without pensions cry: "let the pensioners go." And the pensioners claimed that they were "not bound to go but at the days of trewe and at the wardens' calling."[76] By 1559, after another war with Scotland, the verdict of Sir Ralph Sadler on the state of the borders was utterly damning:

It is more than xx yeres ago syns I had som understanding of this frontier, and yet dyd I never know it in such disorder; for now the officer spoyleth the thefe, without bringing forth his person to tryall by the law; and the thefe robbeth the trew man, and the trew men take assuraunce of the theves that they shall not robbe them, and give them yerely rent and tribute for the same.

Things had reached such a pass in the last war "that English borderers were assured by the Scottes from burning and spoyle, and for the same in lyke wise payed the Scottes certen rent and tribute" – a development "which I never harde of before." Sadler placed the blame for this on "the lacke of stoute and wise officers," no doubt meaning Thomas Percy, 7th earl of Northumberland, warden of the east and middle marches, whom he mistrusted.[77] Yet Sir Thomas Percy had only regained the family estates and the earldom in 1557, and he had only had sole charge of the wardenry since January 1559.[78] Unwittingly, therefore, Sadler's verdict on the earl's wardenship in effect amounted to an indictment of Tudor rule in the far north. Under Elizabeth the situation went from bad to worse. As border defences collapsed, the English marches were increasingly destroyed by Scottish reivers. Dr. Philip Dixon's analysis of recorded complaints of livestock theft, 1510–1605, suggests that the English marchers increasingly lost out in cross-border reiving, most especially the inhabitants of North Tynedale, Redesdale, and Bewcastledale, whose growing poverty was reflected in the region's architecture – the building of poorer-quality pele-houses instead of the more expensive towerhouses preferred elsewhere in the Anglo-Scottish marches.[79] The growing incidence of blackmail levied by Scots on English borderers points in the same direction, as do the dwindling numbers of horsemen which the English surnames could muster – in the case of Redesdale, down from 300 in 1558 to 91 in 1580 and little more than twenty in 1586, and 134 from Tynedale in 1580, dwindling to only 21 in 1595.[80]

In short, Tudor officials cast the blame for the crown's manifest failure to discharge the most basic duties of monarchy in the region on anything from the moral decline of the commons, to the malice of the Scots and the decline of border service, but never on Tudor policy itself. Finally, as the Reformation took hold in lowland England, the conservatism of the north also appeared to undermine its civility. Already in 1560, Archbishop Parker could warn Secretary Cecil that if bishops were not quickly appointed to northern sees, the region would become "too much Irish and savage."[81] About 1580, however, only three Northumberland livings outside Newcastle were worth more than £30 a year, including Simonburn in north Tynedale. Allegedly, the inhabitants of Tynedale and Redesdale had so profited from annual visits by the famous Puritan preacher, Bernard Gilpin, that

at this present their former savage demeanour is very much abated, and their barbarous wildness and fierceness so much qualified that there is hope left of their reduction unto civility.

Despite this, a preacher who was subsequently offered the living claimed in 1596 that he was "unable to live in so troublesome a place and his nature not well brooking the perverse nature of so crooked a people." Likewise, William Camden dismissed the borderers as nomads.[82]

Overall, therefore, the government's efforts to promote peace, good rule, and "English civility" in the far north by reducing noble power, extending royal government, and building up crown lands and a crown interest among the border gentry proved spectacularly counterproductive. Tudor policy turned out to be a *pis aller* between medieval English methods of border defence and the mercenary forces built up by contemporary French and Spanish kings. Traditionally, the responsibilities associated with the wardenries had encouraged border magnates to tailor their estate management policies to defence needs and to keep a warlike tenantry ready with horse and harness. The office's customary fees and perquisites had also allowed the wardens to reward border service. Yet, with the exclusion of the magnatesfrom offices whichwere traditionally theirs, they were less interested in their tenants' military service – hence, the allegedly modernizing tendencies of the estate management policies of Northumbrian landowners under the later Tudors.[83]

In sum, the Tudors had simply exchanged one problem for another: having ensured that great lords with their numerous tenantry were unable to exploit the wardenships to challenge the crown, they now found themselves unable to discharge the basic duties of monarchical government in maintaining defence and good rule for the king's subjects. The pursuit of an ordered, civil society, and the maintenance of traditional methods of frontier defence proved mutually contradictory goals. Indeed, under the impact of these policies, the realm experienced a more general decline in military preparedness, so that by the mid-1540s foreign mercenaries (including Irish kerne) had to be employed to defend the borders.[84] After Henry VIII's death, Protector Somerset tried a different solution to the problem of the far north, establishing garrisons in southern Scotland in a futile bid to protect the region by advancing the border into enemy territory. In the longer term, however, the government was saved by the advent of better relations between the English and Scottish courts. The policing and defence of the border became less of a problem until finally, in 1603, England's northern frontier disappeared. The Union of the Crowns with Scotland and the simultaneous completion of the Tudor conquest of Ireland rendered superfluous these military frontiers and eliminated the need for the kind of territorial marcher lordship by which the Tudors' northern and western frontiers had traditionally been defended.

An analysis of Tudor reform in Northumberland places a well-known aspect of English state formation in an unfamiliar light, at the same time highlighting a weakness of Tudor historiography. Technically, the English marches toward Scotland constituted England's only landed frontier, since the marches of Calais, Ireland, and Wales lay outside the realm. If by English history is meant the history of England, narrowly conceived, then Tudor Northumberland was a highly exceptional region ruled and defended in a very unusual manner. But of course, under the impact of Tudor reform, major landowners throughout the English far north, the Welsh marches, and Tudor Ireland all faced the same problem in organizing the defence of their estates. The difference is that, outside England, Tudor reform could plausibly be presented by Tudor officials as the promotion of English civility through the imposition of English law and government on the mere Irish and Welsh; leaving modern historians to debate the wider implications of this subtle piece of Tudor propaganda. In the case of Tudor Northumberland, however, this approach is less persuasive, if only because its population was manifestly English and the shire had long been part of England. Essentially, Tudor officials were driven to suggest that its inhabitants were not really civil Englishmen at all, and modern historians have either argued that the reduction of feudal particularism and over-mighty subjects were essential to the growth of the nation or tried to explain away the problem altogether.[85] Yet, if civility was a central characteristic of Englishness, how could an English county lose its identity?

Unfortunately, because of the nation-based character of modern historiography, what was actually a very comparable response by these remote marcher communities to Tudor reform has been divided up into separate English, Irish, and Welsh experiences, and historiographically transformed into the growth of national unity out of feudal particularism. Yet, it is important also to view the English borderlands the way contemporaries saw them, as a problem of government. The reality of the much vaunted Tudor achievement in curbing over-mighty subjects and yet ruling England without a standing army was that the traditional burden of defence was simply shifted to the frontier regions rather than shared evenly among all the king's subjects. In short, the Tudors failed in their basic duties toward their subjects – the provision of good rule and defence. Lowland England became more peaceful and civilized because the far north and English Ireland became wilder and more disordered. And these changes also destroyed the traditional balance within the English state between the political influence of the richer, more urbanized English lowlands and the military and strategic value of the semi-autonomous borderlands. The borderlands were assimilated administratively and culturally to the centre, but politically they were marginalized.

**Notes**

[1] This paper was presented at the English State Conference, held at St Peter's College, Oxford, in March 1998. I am grateful in particular for the comments of Professor Philip Corrigan and Dr. John Walter who have kindly pointed out that the approach adopted here also has applications outside the far north of England (defined here as the four most northerly counties) in respect of other regions and periods of English history.

[2] D.B. Quinn, "Aristocratic autonomy, 1460–94" in Art Cosgrove (ed.), *A New History of Ireland II: Medieval Ireland, 1169–1534* (Oxford, 1987), p. 591.

[3] Stanyhurst's Chronicle, in R. Holinshed, *The . . . Chronicles of England, Scotlande and Irelande* (ed. H. Ellis, 6 vols., London, 1807–8), vi, 280.

[4] John Gillingham, "Foundations of a Disunited Kingdom" in Alexander Grant and Keith Stringer (ed.), *Uniting the Kingdom? The Making of British History* (London, 1995), pp. 48–64; idem, "The Beginnings of English Imperialism" in *Journal of Historical Sociology*, v (1992).

[5] This topic may be approachedthrough R.A. Griffiths,"The English Realm and Dominions and the King's Subjects in the Later Middle Ages," in John Rowe (ed.), *Aspects of Government and Society in Later Medieval England: Essays in Honour of J.R. Lander* (Toronto, 1986), pp. 83–105; S.G. Ellis, "Crown, Community and Governmentin the English Territories, 1450–1575" in *History*, lxxi (1986), pp. 187–204; S.G. Ellis, "Writing Irish History: Revisionism, Colonialism, and the British Isles" in *The Irish Review*, no. 19 (spring/summer 1996), pp. 1–21.

[6] R.R. Davies,"The Peoplesof Britain and Ireland, 1100–1400 III. Laws and customs" in *Transactions of the Royal Historical Society*, 6th ser. vi (1996), pp. 11–13.

[7] The "surnames" inhabited parts of the frontier districts of the Anglo-Scottish borders, particularly the west and middle marches. They were clan or kinship groups who acted together in all things, collectively sought vengeance when one of their surname was harmed, and often accepted joint responsibility when an individual got into trouble. See also below, pp. 142–3.

[8] S.G. Ellis, *The Pale and the Far North: Government and Society in Two Early Tudor Borderlands* (Galway, 1988), pp. 27–8.

[9] For an elaborationof this perspectivein relationto the English lordship of Ireland, see Robin Frame's seminal article, "Power and Society in the Lordship of Ireland, 1272–1377" in *Past and Present*, no. 76 (Aug. 1977), pp. 3–33. For a general survey of Tudor problems of state formation, see S.G. Ellis, "Tudor state formation and the shaping of the British Isles" in idem et Barber (ed.), *Conquest and Union*, pp. 40–63, on which this and the next three paragraphs are based. Specific aspects are also treated in my *Tudor Frontiers and Noble Power: The Making of the British State* (Oxford, 1995).

[10] (Oxford, 1990).

[11] *The Last Years of a Frontier: A History of the Borders during the Reign of Elizabeth* (Oxford 1928).

[12] (Leicester, 1975).

[13] *Society, Politics and Culture: Studies in Early modern England* (Cambridge, 1986).

[14] Pollard, *North-eastern England*, p. 397 (which offers a differentdefinition of "the far north" as "the border dales" in "the immediate vicinity of the Scottish border").

[15] Pollard, *North–eastern England*, pp. 172, 392 (quotation).

[16] R.R. Reid, "The Rebellionof the Earls, 1569" in *Transactions of the Royal Historical Society*, 2nd ser. xx (1906), pp. 171–203 (quotations at pp. 176, 201).

[17] Watts, *Border to Middle shire*. See also Robert Newton, "The Decay of the Borders: Tudor Northumberland in Transition" in C.W. Chalklin and M.A. Havinden (ed.), *Rural Change and Urban Growth 1500–1800: Essays in English Medieval History in Honour of W.G. Hoskins* (London, 1974), pp. 2–31.

[18] Pollard, *North-eastern England*, pp. 90, 99–101.

[19] J.M.W. Bean, *The Estates of the Percy Family 1416–1537* (Oxford, 1958).

[20] *Cal. inq. p.m. Hen. VII*, iii, no. 7; Bean, *Estates of the Percy Family*, esp. pp. 14–15, 23, 30–35, 45–6; Pollard, *North–eastern England*, maps 4, 5.

[21] P.R.O., C 142/27, no. 126; C 142/75, no. 16; *Cal. inq. p.m., Hen. VII*, i, no. 157, iii, no. 14.

[22] *Inquisitions and Assessments Relating to Feudal Aids . . . 1284–1431* (4 vols., London, 1899–1906), iv, 76–90. See also James, *Society, Politics and Culture*, pp. 68–70.

[23] See Pollard, *North–eastern England*, maps 1–2; Watt, *Border to Middle shire*, maps 1, 3.

[24] P.R.O., SP 1/45, f. 106 (*L. & P. Hen. VIII*, iv, no. 3639 (4)); John Hodgson, *A History of Northumberland* (3 parts in 7 vols., Newcastle, 1820–25)), III, ii, 204, 231–3 (Bowes and Ellerker's survey, 1542).

[25] *A History of Northumberland: Vol. III Hexhamshire*. Ed. A.B. Hinds (London, 1896), pp. 46–9, 81–3; *Cal. pat. rolls, 1494–1509*, pp. 652–3; Ellis, *Tudor Frontiers and Noble Power*, pp. 53–4, 161.

[26] *Cal. close rolls, 1500–09*, no. 657; P.R.O., E 36/214, pp. 397, 403; Pollard, *North-eastern England*, pp. 159–160; Ellis, *Tudor Frontiers and Noble Power*, pp. 54–5, 151.

[27] B.L., Calig. B II, f. 262 (*L. & P. Hen. VIII*, iii, no. 1225), f. 346v (*L. & P. Hen. VIII*, iii, no. 1883).

[28] P.R.O., SP 1/11, f. 5v (*L. & P. Hen. VIII*, ii, no. 596), SP 1/75, ff 222–4 (*L. & P. Hen. VIII*, vi, no. 410); Hodgson, *Northumberland*, I, i, pp. 363–6.

[29] P.R.O., SP 1/75, f. 222v (*L. & P. Hen. VIII*, vi, no. 420).

[30] Hodgson, *Northumberland*, I, i, 365.

[31] Statute roll, 2 & 3 Edward VI, c. 34 (*Statutes of the Realm* (ed. 1819), iv, 74); Hodgson, *Northumberland*, I, i, 363.

[32] *Cal. pat. rolls, 1485–1494*, pp. 495–6; *1494–1509*, pp. 652–3; Pollard, *North-eastern England*, p. 163.

[33] E.g., *L. & P. Hen. VIII*, iv, no. 1610 (11), v, no. 119 (53), 909 (23), Add., i, no. 828. Cf. S.J. Gunn, *Early Tudor Government, 1485–1558* (London, 1995), pp. 28–9, 67.

[34] *L. & P. Hen. VIII*, iv, no. 2435.

[35] *L. & P. Hen. VIII*, iv, no. 5085, Add. i, no. 618; Edward Barrington de Fonblanque (ed.), *Annals of the House of Percy* (2 vols., London, 1887), i, app. XLVII (printed from B.L., Cotton, Caligula, B. III, 65).

[36] Calculatedfrom *L. & P. Hen. VIII*, iv, no. 5085, Add., i, no. 618; P.R.O., SP 1/45, ff 104–7 (*L. & P. Hen. VIII*, iv, no. 3629 (4)). Cf. Hodgson, *Northumberland*, I, i, 346–8, II, i, 67–8; *L. & P. Hen. VIII*, xii (ii), nos. 249–50 (lists of gentry retained, c. 1537); *L. & P. Hen. VIII*, ix, no. 1078 (shorter list of gentry).

[37] P.R.O., SP 1/45, f. 105 (*L. & P. Hen. VIII*, iv, no. 3629 (4)).

[38] Pollard, *North-eastern England*, pp. 86–90. Cf. Carol Arnold, "The Commissionof the Peace for the West Riding of Yorkshire, 1437–1509" in A.J. Pollard (ed.), *Property and Politics: Essays in Later Medieval English History* (Gloucester, 1984), pp. 116–38.

[39] P.R.O., SP 1/45, f. 104 (*L. & P. Hen. VIII*, iv, no. 3629 (4)).

[40] Printed, Hodgson, *Northumberland*, II, i, 68.

[41] J.S. Cockburn, *A History of English Assizes 1558–1714* (Cambridge, 1972), pp. 19, 25, 45; C.J. Neville, "Gaol Delivery in the Border Counties,

1439–1459: Some Preliminary Observations" in *Northern History*, xix (1983), pp. 45–60.

[42] P.R.O., SP 49/2, f. 18 (*L. & P. Hen. VIII*, iii, no. 3240); Hodgson, *Northumberland*, III, i, 36.

[43] F.W. Dendy, "Extracts from the De Banco Rolls Relating to Northumberland, 1308 to 1558" in *Archaeologia Aeliana*, 3rd ser., vi (1910), pp. 41–88.

[44] P.R.O., SP 1/45, ff 104–7 (*L. & P. Hen. VIII*, iv, no. 3629 (4)).

[45] E.g. *Cal. inq. p.m. Hen. VII*, i, nos. 565, 638, 671, iii, nos. 8, 13, 16.

[46] Hodgson, *Northumberland*, III, ii (Bowes's survey, 1550), 184, 222, 225, 229; P.R.O., SP 49/1, f. 155v (*L. & P. Hen. VIII*, iii, no. 2612).

[47] *A History of Northumberland: XI Carham, Branxton, Kirknewton, Wooler, Ford*. By K. H. Vickers (Newcastle-upon-Tyne, 1922), p. 74. See also Pollard, *North-eastern England*, pp. 44–6.

[48] P.R.O., C 142/10, no. 6 (*Cal. inq. p.m. Hen. VII*, i, no. 971).

[49] Ellis, *Tudor Frontiers and Noble Power*, pp. 61–71, 165–7.

[50] P.R.O., SP 1/48, ff 117–34v (*L. & P. Hen. VIII*, iv (ii), no. 4336 (2)).

[51] The 1538 musters for Northumberland are printed from the originals now in the P.R.O. by John Hodgson in *Archaeologia Aeliana*, 1st ser., iv (1855), pp. 157–206. In addition, the returns for Newcastle-upon-Tyne which was mustered separately totaled 1,097: printed in ibid., 1st ser., iv (1855), pp. 124–35.

[52] Pollard, *North-eastern England*, pp. 14, 171–2.

[53] Margaret Condon, "Ruling Elites in the Reign of Henry VII" in Charles Ross (ed.), *Patronage, Pedigree and Power in Later Medieval England* (Gloucester, 1979), pp. 116–18; Ellis, *Tudor Frontiers and Noble Power*, pp. 148–9.

[54] Ellis, *Tudor Frontiers and Noble Power*, pp. 34, 49, 148–9, 152; Condon, "Ruling Elites," pp. 116–18.

[55] Ellis, *Tudor Frontiers and Noble Power*, pp. 49, 151–2.

[56] For Henry VII's later lieutenants, see P.R.O., E 403/2558, ff 116, 127v, 142; E 405, ff 79, 150; SP 1/12, f 49 (*L. & P. Hen. VIII*, ii, no. 1365).

[57] J.M.W. Bean, *The Estates of the Percy Family, 1416–1537* (Oxford, 1958), p. 139; Ellis, *Tudor Frontiers and Noble Power*, p. 106.

[58] Pollard, *North-eastern England*, pp. 125–6; James, *Society, Politics and Culture*, pp. 60, 76; Bean, *Estates of the Percy Family*, pp. 128–32.

[59] Ellis, *Tudor Frontiers and Noble Power*, chaps. 3, 5.

[60] Hodgson, *Northumberland*, III, i, 35–6.

[61] Pollard, *North-eastern England*, pp. 100, 145.

[62] Hodgson, *Northumberland*, I, i, 371, II, i, 6–7. And see Watts, *Border to Middle shire*, map 2.

[63] Hodgson, *Northumberland*, I, i, 371; Ellis, *Tudor Frontiers and Noble Power*, p. 35; John Guy, *Tudor England* (Oxford, 1988), p. 176.

[64] *L. & P. Hen. VIII*, xii (i), nos. 225, 291, 636, xii (ii), no. 249. The impact of the governmental reorganization in the far north has also been discussed, with differing conclusions, in James, *Society, Politics and Culture*, ch. 3; M.L. Bush, "The Problem of the Far North: A Study of the Crisis of 1537 and its Consequences" in *Northern History*, vi (1971), pp. 40–63.

[65] R.R. Reid, *The King's Council in the North* (London, 1921), pt. 2, ch. 1.

[66] *L. & P. Hen. VIII*, xii (ii), nos. 249, 914.

[67] Hodgson, *Northumberland*, III, ii, 244 (quotation); *L. & P. Hen. VIII*, xviii (i), no. 800.

[68] The border surveys of 1542 and 1550 are printed in Hodgson, *Northumberland*, III, ii, 171–248 (quotation, p. 193).

[69] *L. & P. Hen. VIII*, xviii (i), nos. 799–800; *S.P. Hen. VIII*, iv, 309–15; Ellis, *Tudor Frontiers and Noble Power*, ch. 8.

[70] Hodgson, *Northumberland*, III, ii, 229, 237–8.

[71] Hodgson, *Northumberland*, III, ii, 244–5.

[72] Bush, "Problem of the Far North," pp. 51–2.

[73] P.R.O., SP 1/179, f. 157 (*L. & P. Hen. VIII*, xviii (i), no. 800 (quotation)).

[74] P.R.O., SP 1/179, f. 157 (*L. & P. Hen. VIII*, xviii (i), no. 800); Bush, loc. cit., p. 60.

[75] *L. & P. Hen. VIII*, xviii (i), no. 141 (quotation).

[76] *L. & P. Hen. VIII*, xviii (i), no. 800 (quotation).

[77] Arthur Clifford (ed.), *The State Papers and Letters of Sir Ralph Sadler* (2 vols., Edinburgh, 1809), i, 444.

[78] James, *Society, Politics and Culture*, pp. 127, 135, 282.

[79] Philip Dixon, "Towerhouses, Pelehouses and Border Society" in *Archaeological Journal*, cxxxvi (1979), pp. 240–52.

[80] Watt, *Border to Middle shire*, pp. 26, 109; Ralph Robson, *The Rise and Fall of the English Highland Clans: Tudor Responses to a Mediaeval Problem* (Edinburgh, 1989), pp. 215–16.

[81] John Bruce and T.T. Perowne (ed.), *Correspondence of Matthew Parker, D.D. Archbishop of Canterbury* (Parker Soc., Cambridge, 1853), p. 123.

[82] Watts, *Border to Middle shire*, pp. 86–8; Ellis, *Tudor Frontiers and Noble Power*, p. 71.

[83] Newton, "Decay of the Borders," pp. 3–5.

[84] Bush, "Problem of the Far North," p. 61; D.G. White, "Henry VIII's Irish Kerne in France and Scotland" in *The Irish Sword*, iii (1957–8), pp. 213–25.

[85] B.W. Beckinsale, "The Character of the Tudor North" in *Northern History*, iv (1969); the references are in notes 14–15.

# Science, Power, Bodies: The Mobilization of Nature as State Formation

### PATRICK CARROLL

**Abstract** This paper brings together recently developed perspectives in science studies and the historical sociology of state formation. It focuses on how scientific and government practices together construct the relationalities. Identities, natures, and material environments of the bodies that constitute the modern state. The paper argues that the modern state is an effect of these practices, a techno-scientific political formation in which political government and scientific practice are woven together in a heterogeneous yet definitive network.

\*\*\*\*\*

If, then, the state wants to obtain from medical science all the advantages that it can yield, it must use the physician not only for curing but also for preventing the diseases which threaten the great mass. Among the causes of these diseases are many which neither the physician alone nor the individual citizen can prevent or cure; only a Medical Police, provided with the proper power and authority can implement the rescue plan which medicine has drawn up.

Johann Peter Frank, *A System of Complete Medical Police*, (1779–1819).

We are, I believe, at the beginning of a huge crisis of a wide-ranging reevaluation of the problem of "government".

Michel Foucault, *Remarks on Marx*, (1978).

The relationship between science, government, and the state has received ample attention for the twentieth century, not least because of the brutally obvious forms it assumed through the Manhattan Project and the Cold War. But the longevity and indeed profundity of that relationship is less well understood.[1] Science studies, particularly the sociology of scientific knowledge, cultural history of science, and feminist/cultural studies of science and technology, has revolutionized the analysis of science over the past quarter century. In place of the view of science as a domain set apart from (and indeed in opposition to) culture, "a culture of no culture" as Sharon Traweek aptly puts it,[2] science studies has historicized science, situating it in social and political context, and emphasizing the local and contingent character of its production. The old watch-words of "rationality", "objectivity", and "correspondence", have been displaced by those of "practice", "culture", and "power".[3]

Yet with few exceptions[4] science studies has been remarkably silent on the question of the state. Crucially important work has been conducted which unites political history with the history of science and philosophy,[5] but the nature of "the state" has generally been viewed unproblematically. Indeed the tendency to treat the state as a reality not itself requiring analysis, characterizes most literature on the relationship between science and the state.[6] The state is left untheorized, the story proceeding in terms of a contract-like relationship between what are taken as two completely separate and distinct forms. Challenging such a tendency, this paper presents an historical inquiry into the relationship between science and the modern state that draws on the insights of science studies, on approaches to state formation active in historical sociology, and on the work of Michel Foucault.[7] It focuses on the intersections of government and science in practices that construct subject-bodies, and on how the effects of such practices relate to modern state formation. The empirical case is Ireland from the mid-eighteenth to late nineteenth centuries, but before getting to the case some comments are necessary regarding the terms of the analysis, terms such as "science", "the body", "network(ing)", and "the state".

I want to suggest that the modern state,[8] in a crucial sense, is a configuration of subject-bodies and material spaces, realized within a network of heterogeneous practices, in which both government and science are integral. The state is the *effect* of these practices, subsisting in governed material, relational, representational, per-formative, and practiced (i.e., ongoing) forms. By relationality I mean the multiple "identities" organized around the categories of individuality, sexuality, gender, ethnicity. race, nation, class, and kinship. Such relationalities/identities, though not necessarily originating in the modern period, come to be secured in their modern form through material practices of objectification and sub-jectification which invest and seek to define/constitute subject/object bodies. But this conception incites, for me, a kind of (somatic) crisis of representation. Thus in an attempt to escape the contra/diction of either/or-ism inherent in the dichotomies[9] of body/consciousness, subject/object, and individual/society, I adopt and deploy the term "socio-corporeity". "Corporeity" refers specifically to the condition of *being* material substance. Thus it can affirm the materiality of the body without losing reference to the lived experience of self. In this sense it has certain advantages over the terms corporal, corporeal(ity), and "the body", all of which tend towards the object side of the equation. I add the prefix "socio" so as never to lose sight of the fact that material being is a profoundly social reality. Thus the practices with which I am con-cerned do not act wholly upon either "the body" or "the mind", the "population" or the "individual". Reference to socio-corporeity offers an alternative to the dichotomies of micro and macro, material and immaterial, emphazing the practical embeddedness, in the modern period, of action upon the body politic and the body natural. It is not meant to replace the latter entirely, which would be hasty if not practically impossible, but to release analysis from the straight-jacketing effects of a singularly dualistic frame.

The complexity of modern socio-corporeity is such that its regulation and constitution can only be realized through multiple and heterogeneous practices. These practices may be abstracted and purified under the heads, for instance, of police, health, morality, discipline, sanitation, engineering, architecture, and biology, but all become integrally involved, from the eighteenth century, with the productivity, reproduction, subordination, and relization of the forces of socio-corporeity. Such practices, furthermore, are always concerned with generating knowledge and securing truth, and are coterminous with the realization of power. It is always a question, to paraphrase Haraway, of what comes to count as nature, as human, sexual, racial, or class nature, and who comes to count as a body: how, when, and for whom.

Modern socio-corporeity subsists in a culturally constructed and socially integrated material space, what I call a "socio-material" space, consisting of a historically worked over "land", a built environment, and the "landscapes", both rural and urban, that are anchored to and grow from this material space. Modem socio-material space, furthermore, is inhabited, if not saturated, with material technological forms. Thus the practices of investment extend to the entire material environment in which socio-corporeity subsists. Through the sciences, for instance, of cartography and engineering, a socio-materiality of enclosed territorial and agricultural spaces is realized, as is an urban space, constituted of paved hygienic streets, public washrooms, sewage systems, and the supply of running water. It is in conjunction with such investment that a sanitized and subjected socio-corporeity is realized. Mukerji's work on the transformation of landmasses into territories through scientific practices, the realization of a new socio-material political culture of land, is illustrative in this respect in that it demonstrates how modern state formation "was as much an engineering fcat as a political one."[10] The state, then, subsists in material forms as much as moral regulations, enforced building codes as much as systems of naming, in the socio-materiality that is the effect of government practices as much as in the "language" of law. It is the entire configuration, of bodies, spaces, practices, relationalities, and identities, that together explains its durability. Even as mundane a thing as the plumbing siphon found under every sink, designed to prevent "noxious gases" from entering buildings, is a governed and scientifically realized material form.[11] As Corrigan, Sayer, and Denis suggest (if in different ways than I), the modern state is not in or above society, it is a society, a socio-material space ubiquitously colonized by governed and governing forms.

So the state, I suggest, is realized not by a power that is located in a centre and spreads out in concentric circles, but in multiple locales in which socio-corporeity and socio-materiality are invested, and through the networking of all of these by a government which claims a unitary and univocal voice over "life". And it is this latter clause that in part distinguishes *the* government from government generally, the government, for instance, of school and work. "Network(ing)" is used here in the plain sense of the term, to designate that through which otherwise separate phenomena, spaces, or practices, are connected together. The network subsists in heterogeneous forms: social, material, discursive, natural, and cultural forms; in nodes and linkages that are both "human" and "nonhuman"; in roads, vehicles, reports, statistics, books, and pamphlets, modes of dress and address, and persons and objects that move in socio-material space, as well as in meta-discourses on rationality, sexuality, morality and economy, which subsist with and through these persons, books, objects etc. My usage of the term "network", then, is similar both to that associated with "actor-network theory" in science studies[12] and to the way Foucault speaks of a "dispositif": "a thoroughly heterogeneous ensemble consisting of discourse, institutions, architectural forms, regulatory decisions, laws, administrative measures, scientific statements, philosophical, moral and philanthropic propositions". The major question, which I do not claim for a moment to answer adequately here, is "the nature of the connection that can exist between these heterogeneous elements."[13] Since I suspect that the elements are connected in definitive (if at present unclear) ways, I use the term "network" which, as distinct say from "web" or "rhizome", connotes this definitiveness. The network is thus the means of realizing, from a multitude of localized practices, a supra-local social formation, a formation subsisting in and of relations of power and knowledge, associated material practices, and material hybridizations of nature and culture. The story of state formation I want to pursue, then, is the story of bodies, their landscapes, and natures in the making, a making in which metaphor, metonym, language, discourse, and social grammar play a crucial role, but also, and no less importantly, a material making, the material hybridization of nature and culture, in the land, the built environment, and the body.

It is in the linking together of the knowledges that are always generated locally that I find the analytic of discourse at its most powerful. This is not to imply that discourse is simply a kind of social glue, for local material practices are themselves discursive practices, but that material and discursive practices, though inseparable, are irreducible one to the other. For though socio-corporeity, and hence practice, is always localized, rooted in socio-material space-time, discourse, itself always generated by situated bodies, exhibits the special power of being able to escape locality and network within itself with other locally generated discourse. The words of the physician and the administrator, the biologist and the moralist, the living and the dead, are brought together through signifcatory linkages in articles, pamphlets and books, statistical forms and official reports, architectural plans and technological instruments, and the material semiotic generative nodes, as Haraway defines bodies,[14] who move between and within the local socio-material spaces in which specialized practices occur. Discourse here is in no way free-floating, but bound to the material practices which both generate and support it, to the immutable mobiles[15] through which it travels, and to the socio-material arrangements in which it is realized. Networking facilitates trans-local epistemic and ideological formation, what Foucault might call regimes of truth, which rather than demanding a practice of puri-fication that attempts to detach the epistemic from the ideological, to realize puntfied domains of "truth" set in opposition to other domains, requires attention to how knowledge, power, and politics are woven together in specific historical periods, and how con-sideration of such can yield a better understanding of the way particular social and natural forms are realized. Abstraction and purification separate domains which in practice and effect are inextricably mixed together.[16] And a social realism which reduces natural forms to social forms is not a valid alternative to the naturalism which views "nature" as the "real" basis upon which social forms are constructed. Both these reductionist moves only make sense in contra/diction to the other, and rely on an opposi-tion between nature and culture which itself requires explanation. Thus I do not, at the outset, make essential distinctions between social and natural forms, or social and natural science, for the processes and practices through which such positivities emerge, the purifications and boundary work that effect and maintain them, require explanation in terms of, and not before, the machinations that are at work in the business of mobilizing and subordinating "nature". Instead I attend to any practices that locate around the objectification of socio-corporeity, whether defined in terms of morality, biology, health, chemistry, or discipline.

I adopt the term "mobilization of nature" precisely because it refers to the on-going and dynamic hybridization of nature and culture. Here "nature", by virtue of its mobilization, is always inside (though never coterminous with) culture. In this sense, the subject-bodies that constitute the modern state are neither wholly socially constructed, nor wholly natural. The particular form of socio-corporeity that I wish to represent is a material hybrid form, the product of specific historical practices. "The body", *par excellence*, is nature mobilkzed in and by culture. Subject-bodies are the socio-material intersection of a historically specific natural and social order. Finally, it should be noted that the isolation of any single group of practices whose object is socio-corporeity runs counter to my argument that it is the entire ensemble of such practices that together bring the profundity of the science-state relation into view, and reveal the modern state as a techno-scientific political formation. This paper, therefore, is just a beginning, a presentation of some broad coordinates for the purpose of figuring and debate.[17]

Ireland provides a particularly illustrative case for putting such an analysis to work, because the lines of the state network of government and scientiflc practices are so clearly visible. As England's door-step colony, the country became a "field" where experiments were conducted through the national systems of education, health, penal correctionalism, police and poor law. As Nassau William Senior put it in conversation with Alexis de Tocqueville, "Experiments are made in that country on so large a scale. and pushed to their extreme consequences . . . that they give us results as precious as those of Majendie".[18] Now I should perhaps note immediately that those who most supported experimental government would gladly have carried out similar experiments in England had conditions permitted, Indeed many experiments were conducted, if of a more localized and limited nature.[19] It is important in this regard to realize that the experimental philosophy of a small group of men in the seventeenth century had developed, by the nineteenth, into a fairly diffuse experimental culture, particularly among the bourgeoisie. William Petty, a founding member of the Royal Society, is an early example of one who wanted to bring the "experimental way" to bear upon the "body politic". In his *Political Anatomy of Ireland* he emphasized the parallels between "the Body Natural, and Body Politic, and between the arts of preserving both in health and strength", and presented Ireland as a "Political Animal" which, being analogous to the "cheap and common" animals upon which students of anatomy practiced, was ideal for conducting experiments.[20] Petty's views were unusual (though not unique) in the late seventeenth century, but over a century and a half later the experimental attitude toward government and the body politic commanded significant assent, as is exemplified, for instance, in the discourses of the National Association for the Promotion of Social Science.

One early advocate of experimental government, which I suggest is by definition interventionist, is Johann Peter Frank, author of *A System of Complete Medical* Police. "Police", as Frank used the term, was much broader in reference than our usage of the word today. General police science concerned itself with all matters relating to the "internal security of the state". The word police derives from the Latin for "policy", which in turn derives from the Greek "polis". In seventeenth century Europe "police" could mean "policy". Though in the second half of the eighteenth century policy and police became more differentiated, it is unclear exactly how Frank used the term. The discursive connections between polis, citizenship, government, "reason of state", policy, and police, seem fairly intimate such that police as originally used referred to government interventions to secure the "population", a designation which itself emerged through the "statistical" objectification of the body politic.[21] Frank explained that a considerable part of medical police was "to apply certain principles for the health care of people living in society . . . Medical Police, like all police science, is an art of defense, a model of protection of people and their animal helpers . . . promoting their physical well-being . . ."[22] He included the following under the rubric of medical police:

Human Procreation and Marriage Institutions; Preservation and Care of Pregnant Women, their Fetuses, and of Lying-in Women; Food, Drink and Vessels; Laws of Moderation, Unhealthy Clothing, [and] Popular Amusements; Layout. Construction, and Necessary Cleanliness of Human Dwellings; Public Safety Measures as Far as they Concern Public Health; Interment of the Dead; Medical Science and Medical Educational Institutions; and the Examination and Confirmation of Medical practitioners.[23]

Frank's concern is with both "moral and physical" conditions, and with the relation between them. Thus he does not confine himself to the question of healthy bodies set apart from their social conditions. His concern is with bodies as "citizens", a concern he extends into women's wombs. In two of six volumes, he "treated everything that was said about human procreation, and endeavoured to put all subjects of Medical police up to the instant of the birth of a new citizen into a bright light".[24] He complains about "lechery", "debauchery", "fornification", and "venereal poison", which he holds is "all the more deleterious to public health, the more it escapes the supervision of the police". If such matters are not made concerns of the government, he continues, "all the good predispositions for future procreation of a durable species are destroyed, and the best forces of the citizens are wasted to the greatest disadvantage of a state."[25] The object of medical police, then, is socio-corporeity, the body as physical and moral citizen, as an element of the body politic and in part the basis of the state's power and wealth. As Erna Lesky put it, "Frank taught the monarchs that the greatest wealth of a state lies in its subjects, who should be as numerous, healthy, and productive as possible".[26] As Foucault suggests, the aim of the new art of government is to develop individual lives in such a way as to strengthen the state.[27]

It is not my intention here to suggest that developments in the "United Kingdom of Great Britain and [or] Ireland" in the nineteenth century can be directly connected to Frank's work, but the connection can be made in terms of the substance of the science of medical police and the practices through which it was constituted. The specific designation of "medical police" did, nonetheless, make its way to the English speaking world. In 1798 Andrew Duncan, professor of the institutes of medicine at the University of Edinburgh, introduced the concept of medical police into the curriculum, defining it as consisting of "the medical precepts which may be of use to the legislature or to the magistracy, relating not only to the welfare of individuals but the property and security of nations, being perhaps the most important branch of general police, since its influence is not confined to those whom accidental circumstances bring within its sphere, but extends over the whole population of the State."[28] Duncan listed the following topics for the curriculum: "hygiene of procreation, personal and environmental sanitation, control of communicable diseases, accident prevention, occupational hygiene, and administration of hospitals and other public institutions concerned with health problems".[29] In 1807 a professorship of medical jurisprudence and medical police was created in the Faculty of Law at Edinburgh. The course was still offered in 1863, as was a similar one in Glasgow. A student's *Handbook on Forensic Medicine and Medical Police* reached a third edition in 1879, mutating into a handbook on "public health" around the turn of the century, and reaching a tenth edition in 1940.[30] Apart from "public health", the practices of medical police were variously named throughout the nineteenth century as "state medicine", "sanitary science", "political medicine", the "science of hygiene", and "preventative medicine".[31]

Though no agency under the name of "medical police" was created in either Ireland or Britain, all the activities identified by Frank were brought within the scope of the London government. The process on the island of Ireland was facilitated by the institution, in 1801, of direct rule. London responded to the 1798 rebellion of the "United Irishmen" with the creation of the "United Kingdom of Great Britain and Ireland". At the head of the new government of Ireland, aside from the London parliament, was the chief secretary, who resided in London and answered directly to the prime minister.

His immediate subordinate was the under secretary, who ran the administration directly from Dublin Castle. The administrative arrangement was not itself particularly new, but the Union created the conditions through which the London government extended its reach throughout the first half of the century, particularly in the form of the national police force, the national boards of health, public works, convict prisons, and education, the national inspectorate of engineers, the ordnance survey, census commissioners, and poor law commissioners. By 1850, for instance, the London/ Dublin government had 14,000 police under its authority, and by 1870 the country was twice as heavily policed as England, with a ratio of one to 425.[32] The conception of "police" as nothing other than a repressive state apparatus, however, does not stand up when confronted with the heterogeneity of early police activities. W.E. Vaughan, for instance, whose style is as understated as one is likely to encounter, refers to the scope of their activities as "most remarkable" on more than one occasion. Such activities included, for example, reporting on the wages of agricultural laborers, on the number of constabulary who left to join the papal army, and enforcing the Dogs Regulation Act, the Chimney Sweepers Regulation Act, and the Nuisances Act. The police collected the annual agricultural statistics and the decennial censuses, reported on evictions and loan funds, and inspected weights and measures. They were instructed to identify prostitutes and other "immoral", "loose", and "disorderly persons", and to collate lists of inhabitants, public houses, and forges, with special attention being given to the formation of a knowledge of "individual characters" within districts. Little wonder that Sir Duncan McGregor, in testimony to a select committee of the House of Lords investigating illicit distillation, could report that the police knew "every man who raises an acre or half an acre of oats or barley."[33]

Some of these activities, such as the regulation of prostitutes, fall directly within the definition of medical police as laid out by Frank, as do others, like the enforcement of regulations concerning accidents and nuisances, "the art of defense". Among the latter one might mention those which came under the Summary Jurisdiction Act of 1851, which made it "an offence to leave a cart unharnessed on a public road, to leave stones, dung, timber, or turf 'so as to cause danger", to have dogs unmuzzled or unlogged within fifty yards of a public road, to carry loads that projected more than two feet beyond the wheels of a cart, to allow swine to wander on the roads, to sell livestock on the roads, and to fly a kite from the road."[34] Police activities as they related to public health increased in the second half of the century, culminating in the Public Health Act of 1878, which made it illegal to keep pigs in a house or to have a wake for a person who had died of a dangerous disease. Convictions could also be secured against those who failed to remove manure when instructed to do so by a justice, or who did not disinfect houses whose inhabitants had died of infectious diseases, or who failed to vaccinate their children. And there were significant numbers of convictions, particularly when compared with the rates in England and Wales for similar offenses.[35] Vaughan suggests, however, that the "police's great administrative achievement of the 1860s . . . was the prevention of foot-and-mouth disease",[36] not insignificant when one considers that the new chair of "State Medicine" in Vienna in 1804 was filled by a man who had published a book on the prevention "of cattle plague and other serious diseases" and the eradication of "those which had already broke out."[37]

While all this may not appear to be concerned with bodies, with socio-corporeity, it was centrally so, for in the end it was the condition of the living that was at issue. It was always a question of how a kite, or a lump of dung, or a particular activity, could lead to injury, disease, immorality or morbidity. Police, as practiced in the eighteenth and nineteenth centuries, was a science in itself, and though we might not want to consider it such today, it was certainly considered so by its early advocates, and not without good reason. It was a practice networked and informed by other sciences, and did itself constitute a network of heterogeneous practices with an object, a method, tools, a set of techniques, and a general "theoretical" schema that informed and gave it coherency.

Health and social order were bound together in practice, a fact equally evident in those other practices prescribed by Frank which came to be substantively embodied not in the "police", but in the "health system" itself. To follow the links from police to health is not to move from a purely repressive apparatus to a domain of pure science, still less to an ideological apparatus. The notions and practices signified by "health police"[38], "sanitary police"[39], and medical police, may appear by twentieth century lights (or shades) to be peculiar or even oxymoronic, but if we historicize such terms and cease to view "health" and "police" teleologically, and in terms of some imagined and imputed essences, the apparent confusion dissipates. If one abandons the boundaries established through practices of analytic purification and abstraction, and instead follows on the ground the network of knowledge-power, one cannot help but find that the connections between police and health, the state and science, are so effectively stitched up that the entire fabric appears almost seamless.

In the eighteenth century Ireland was an active site for the establishment of hospitals and, as Foucault has insisted, such initiatives did not simply occur at the direction of the government, "but rather with the emergence at a multitude of sites in the social body of health and disease as problems requiring some form or other of collective control measures."[40] In Ireland, however, the hospitals received central government grants. No other "private" hospitals in the United Kingdom of Great Britain and Ireland received such government support. Six Dublin doctors opened the first voluntary hospital in the "British Isles" in 1718, which was no more than a house with accommodation for four patients. The establishment grew, moving to bigger premises in 1745 with capacity for 183 patients, and moving again, in 1786, to its present location at Jervis Street, the number of patients increasing to 620. A Charitable Infirmary was also opened in 1718. Steven's Hospital was opened in 1733, Mercer's in 1734, and St. Patrick's in 1757. The first maternity hospital in the "British Isles" was opened in Dublin in 1745, moving in 1757 to a lavish building and becoming the Rotunda Maternity Hospital.[41] Foucault situates the founding of such institutions in the emergent politics of health in the eighteenth century. As well as providing socio-material spaces in which disease could be isolated in the body and subjected to the clinical gaze,[42] the clinical hospitals appear at "the point of intersection of a new 'analytical' economy of assistance with the emergence of a general 'police' of health."[43] Charity, in this context, unites with police. Thus *The Philanthropic Society*, established in Dublin in 1788, was "founded for purposes of efficient good, and its promoters were persuaded of the truth and importance of . . . charity and police."[44]

The central government involved itself institutionally in health in Ireland as early as the eighteenth century. Every "county, and every county of a city or town, inherited from the eighteenth century at least one infirmary and one fever hospital maintained largely by public funds: and by the 1830s all appointments to these seventy-four institutions were being made by public authorities."[45] Almost immediately after the Act of Union, a provision in 1805 established public dispensaries for which government supplied half of the funding. By the 1840s over 650 dispensaries had been established.[46] Crop failures, malnutrition, disease, social discontent, and political agitation, clustered around the notion of a "healthy state". An investigation into the condition of the laboring poor in the 1830s, for instance, reported that "the signs of growing prosperity are unhappily, not so discernible in the condition of the labouring people, as in the amount of the produce of their labour. The proportion of the latter reserved for their use is too small to be consistent with a healthy state of society."[47] Though Malthusian arguments abounded and *laissez faire* as a "doctrine" was in the ascendancy, the reality was a steady increase in the amount of government intervention.[48] In 1838 an extensive work-house system was established, modeled to some extent on the English Poor Law, but with the important difference that a much greater emphasis was put on medical practice. Irish workhouses were built with infirmaries for males and females attached, and medical officers were appointed to supervise their operation.[49] When the Great Famine occurred in 1845, an act was passed empowering the Viceroy to appoint a "central board of national health" (1846), the directors of which were, as with the other national boards, answerable to the under secretary. In response to a previous famine (1816–17), "local boards" of health had been established, as were special fever hospitals. "General" boards of health were also created in 1820 and 1832, so the response in 1846 was not without precedent. Yet while each of these responses might be incited by a specific emergency or exigency, they together constituted part of a developing pattern of scientifically informed government of sociocorporeity.[50] Legislation was passed dealing with sewage (1865), poisons (1870), lodging houses (1853/60), housing (1866/67/68), nuisances (1855/60/63), sanitation (1866/68/70), water (1870), disease prevention (1855/60), and "public health" (1848/74/78), all of which can be understood as an extension of medical police. While some of the legislation created special "inspectors" and "officers", the regular police were also empowered to enforce the various health codes.[51]

The 1846 board immediately attended to the question of nutrition, drawing on the work of chemists seeking to identify the nutritive elements of various foods. Indeed government became a regular employer of chemists, in addition to establishing its own "analytic laboratories", in its attempts to know and regulate the contents of food, drink, and drugs. Legislation was passed in order to prevent adulteration, i.e., "the wilful and fraudulent addition of substances to, or subtraction of substances from, articles of food, drink, or medicine, so as to lessen the commercial, nutritive, or medicinal value and suitability for consumption."[52] In 1847 the new board informed the Relief Commissioners that:

a form of disease now very prevalent among the people, resembling in many particulars sea scurvy, is connected with or dependent on a defective nutrition, arising, *not from a deficiency of quantity, but from a deficiency of quality or variety* in the food. The potato, although not containing a large proportion of nutriment, is remarkable as containing within itself all the varied elements necessary for forming healthy blood; no one of the substitutes for it, with the exception of oatmeal, possesses this remarkable property; and hence the use of more than one article of food is necessary in order to secure a sufficient supply of the varied elements of nutrition, and thus to obviate the form of disease referred to.[53]

With the potato crop largely destroyed by the blight the board "strongly recommended the admixture of onions, leeks, scallions, or shallots, in cooked meal rations, or stirabout, which will both act as condiments, and will also furnish some of the elements of nutrition essential for forming healthy blood".[54]

This question of the variety and quality of food was also related to the "nature" and morality of the people. In the crudest sense this was an expression of the much adhered to notion that "one is what one eats". An article appearing in the *Journal of Social Progress* proposed "to trace the influence exerted over Industry by Domestic Economy in the article of Food," and argued that domestic economy "teaches the Mother of the Family to prepare its food in a varied and agreeable manner . . . In fine, she becomes a source of profit to the community, in that she rears up habits of order, the first element of moral and social organization".[55] The lack of variety in the peasants" food, the authors argued, led them to "vegetate, but not to live." The "exclusive use of Bread would end in effecting a fatal influence on the life of man, both physically and morally", causing a "demoralization", and "driving him to seek in factitious stimulants, such as tabacco and whiskey, the satisfaction which he cannot find in his food . . . Order and cleanliness disappear . . . self-respect is lost . . . [and] the people degenerate."[56]

In the "Irish Convict System" (1854),[57] "nutrition" was a crucial locus of practice. Experiments with rations and vegetarian diets sought to ascertain the quantity and quality of food necessary to maintain a body for a specific measure of labor. The chairman of the board "called upon the medical officer to try an experiment for two months with an absence of meat from the dietary; he tried that experiment; and then I had another experiment tried for three months: and at last we obtained four months".[58] Having only just taken office the directors suspended transportation to Australia, justifying their actions by quoting colonial authorities who complained that the convicts" "prostrate condition, physically and morally", rendered them weak, rebellious, and unmanageable, and thus useless to the colony.[59]

Throughout the discourses on penal correctionalism the condition of the body of the person was seen as bound to their "natures" and moral state. This was particularly so in representations of differences held to exist between men and women. Mary Carpenter, one of the most "enlightened" reformers of the mid-nineteenth century, spoke of "the organization of women, both mental and physical", being such that "when morally diseased and in an abnormal state, their reformation, and restoration to a healthy condition, is far more difficult than that of the other sex."[60] Women were held to have "delicate", "sensitive", "passionate", and "excitable" natures which when exposed to "evil" influences reduced them to a "torpid" and "morbid" state. Moral "depravity" was read directly off the body: "vice dreadfully disfigures the features of a women".[61] The cure for such women was "employment of a kind which will exercise their muscles and fully occupy their minds."[62] School instruction was reported as making them "more docile, more easily brought to see the value of cleanliness and order."[63] The head schoolmaster at Spike Island prison explained that the work of reformatory teachers was "like the prescriptions of physicians for chronic diseases". His job was to "cleanse them from the moral leprosy with which they had been tainted."[64] Successful reformation was likewise to be seen in the outward appearance, the "reclaimed" exhibiting "a great softening of expression, . . . in none did we observe that sullen, dogged, and rebellious look, which indicates that the governed and the governing party are not working harmoniously."[65] The success of the system rested "on a deep knowledge of human nature."[66]

The linking together of cleanliness and order, sanitation and morality, nature and the body, in the discourses on the art of governing socio-corporeity, meant that the governors continuously looked to "science" to make sense of such relations. Doctors, as in the workhouse and dispensary systems, naturally received a special status within the correctional penal institutions. Within the Irish Convict System each prison had its own resident medical officer who studied the bodies of the convicts. Statistics were gathered on the average number of prisoners in hospital on any given day, on the illnesses from which they suffered, and on the causes of death. In each annual report the resident physician gave a statistical breakdown of diseases, including, for instance, fever, measles, cholera, diarrhoea, catarrh, bronchitis, epilepsy, dysentery, rheumatism, and heart disease. As David Arnold has demonstrated with regard to India, one "of the few areas where the colonial state had relatively unobstructed access to the body of its subjects, the prison occupied a critical place in the development of Western medical knowledge and practice":

In accepting a responsibility for health inside the jails, the colonial state [I would say "government" rather than "state" – PCL] helped establish them as privileged sites of medical observation and experimentation. The importance of the colonial connection between medicine and penology was reflected in the voluminous medical literature which used prisoners as a source of statistical data and clinical observations or as a standard by which to calculate and evaluate the health of the population as a whole.[67]

A relationship between discipline, morality and health was forged in this socio-material site of practice as in others. Diseases of the heart and phthisis were said to develop "from the influence of the same physical and moral circumstances".[68] Apart from cases of "acute maniacal excitement" the directors complained of prisoners who, "for want of appropriate treatment in an early stage of the disease, ultimately, in some cases, become confirmed lunatics":

> One of our Board, conversant with medical subjects, is of the opinion, that these cases are referable to a disordered state of the body acting on an ill-regulated mind, untrained to moral restraint over thoughts and actions, and incapable of self-government, hence yielding to impulses and impressions, generated by the morbid condition of the brain, and gradually acquiring an ascendancy which the mind will not control. They are generally attributable, when not consequent on derangement of the abdominal viscera, or the circulation, to a peculiar type of scrofula, the prevailing disease of convicts and great cause of mortality amongst them, which appears to develop itself not alone in the form of phthisis and disease of the glands and joints, but also, it would seem, in many instances by a peculiar tendency to attack the cerebral organs, and influence their functions, leading to a perversion of the moral sentiments, the constant obtruding of false ideas and perceptions on the mind, and exciting to irregular and criminal impulses and the commission of crime.[69]

The member of the board conversant with medical subjects is as good an example as one is likely to find of a material semiotic generative node who moved between and within the local socio-material spaces in which specialized practices occurred. John Lentaigne, a medical doctor, had been a poor law "guardian", "magistrate", and "commissioner" of national education, before becoming a "director" of convict prisons. From there he became an "inspector general" of prisons and finally, in 1869, an "inspector" of industry and reformatory schools. He was also a long-time vice-president of the Dublin Statistical Society, as was his boss in Dublin Castle, undersecretary Larcom.

Prisons from the beginning were privileged locales of noso-politics. Sir Jeremiah Fitzpatrick, who in 1787 became the first inspector general of prisons in the "British Isles", instituted major reforms in Irish prison practices at the end of the eighteenth century, work inspired by the writings of John Howard. Howard had lamented the "gaol distemper" as a "national concern of no small importance", leading as it did to the simultaneous spread beyond the prison of both "wickedness" and "disease".[70] Fitzpatrick wrote two pamphlets which provide an early indication of the shift in statecraft that was at hand. The first dealt with "disease",[71] the second with "morality".[72] In the first he focused on the "pestilential fevers, fluxes, putrid sore throats &c., and the melancholy and irrecoverable state" of the prisoners, calling for a rearrangement of "physical appliances", and the imposition of a greater and stricter "regulation", so as to effect a state of "health", "order", and "ratio-nality". In the second, he called for the establishment of penitentiaries "for preserving the morals as yet untainted of the giddy and unthinking: for implanting a detestation to vice, and respectful submission to the laws, and for establishing in them principles of industry and regularity". Both pamphlets shared a common discourse of information gathering, materialized through statistical charts, and a discourse of isolation as both disease and immorality were held to be communicable. The solution for sick bodies and sick minds, often held to be one and the same when it came to the prison, was in both cases likewise the same: isolation, observation, and information gathering. Through legislation at least, late eighteenth century Ireland became, under Fitzpatrick's guidance, the site of what an Irish historian has rightly described as "a colorful configuration of early Victorian government in the social fields."[73] It was a beginning that was built upon, and half a century later doctors were established as central figures in the new system of punishment/treatment. As Foucault has suggested, this indicates a reconfiguration in which the state shifts from a formation in which the monarch exercised a right over death, to one in which the administration exercises a power over life.[74]

Regulation of sexual and gender relationalities and identities was central to the formation of the modem state. Though surgical intervention in bodies to secure a purified opposition of male and female in a deployment of compulsory heterosexuality is unique to the twentieth century, it was nonetheless prefigured in an interventionist activity that sought to inspect bodies so that they might be "correctly" situated in the socio-material spaces and the discursive material practices that constitute gendered and sexualized bodies. In the 1850s an article appeared in an Irish medical journal entitled "Observations on Hermaphroditism, illustrated by a remarkable Case". The author, Dr. Banon, was a fellow of the Royal College of Physicians, Edinburgh, and of the Royal College of Surgeons, Dublin, and was Surgeon to Jervis Street hospital in Dublin. The body to which his article referred, whose organs he placed in jars at the Royal College of Surgeons inviting readers to inspect them for themselves, came into his possession through another affiliation, that of Physician to the Richmond and Grangegorman Prisons, and acting Physician to the City of Dublin Prisons. Banon introduced his article in terms of the need to study "departures from a normal development of the generative organs" and to accurately determine "correct" sex so as to save the individuals in question from being "doomed through life to submit to the education and habits of the sex not truly their own."[75] After providing an overview of some famous historical cases and a detailed account of the autopsy, Banon reflected on the old "one sex" inversion model of human sexuality which, as Laqueur has demonstrated, held sway until the late eighteenth century when it was displaced by the "two sex" oppositional model:[76]

Long ago it was supposed that the generative organs of one sex were typical of those of the other, and that the female was nothing more than an inverted male; but, without going to that extent, there is reason for supposing that a strong analogy exists between them. Thus the ovary represents the male testis, the uterus the prostate gland, or, according to others, the vesiculae seminales.[77]

Clearly, as has been demonstrated repeatedly by feminist studies of science,[78] the patterns of patriarchal social forms extend unhindered into biomedical discourses, the female regularly represented as an inverted or analogous secondary form in relation to the primary form of the heterosexual male. Banon also situated oppositional heterosexual types into a hierarchical scale that encompassed all life forms,[79] the implication being that all "departures" from heterosexual "normality" were indicative of either a failure to evolve to a higher form, or a degeneration to a lower. Not surprisingly, as in the case of the "incorrigibles" who degenerated into "irrecoverable lunatics", the physiological source of regression was sought in the brain. Banon explained how the cranium of females has a greater "fineness of outline" than that of males, which he claimed to be the case with "Andrew R.", and that the left side of his brain, which "regulates" the development of the "generative organs", was more "prominent" than the right. Thus, he concluded, "we have here a direct physiological reason why the reproductive organs should have been developed with a tendency to the right side of the body."[80]

It is perhaps not insignificant that Andrew while alive, and his friends after he had died, were very reluctant to answer Banon's questions regarding his sex or sexual inclinations. Banon thought that "an account of his tastes, dispositions, and habits" would have added much interest to the question of his sexual anatomy. The implication throughout his discourse is that sexual orientation is bound to anatomy. Thus he correlated Andrew's lack of sexual desire for men, as Andrew had apparently told him that he preferred women, to a series of claimed male characteristics such as "deep-toned" voice, and the fact that he had "excelled in several of the manly exercises". Other features, "a feminine expression in the features of the upper part of the face" and a "plumpness natural to that sex", suggested a female anatomy. Unable to conceive of sexuality except in terms of heterosexual penetration, however, led Banon to conclude that Andrew could never have had an "*effectual* connexion with either male or female."[81]

Biology and medicine provided a crucial locus for the mobilization of nature in the service of securing patriarchal and heterosexual relationalities/identities. The knowledge of sex and sexuality constructed in the localized practices of the biosciences networked with government moral regulations and served to naturalize the range of laws and practices through which the government involved itself in sexual relations.[82] Yet while representations in biomedical science facilitated the naturalization and discursive purification of sexuality, the primary means of realizing patriarchal and heterosexual forms was the location of bodies in disciplinary spaces which were simultaneously architectural, analytical, functional, and hierarchical."[83] "Discipline" subsisted in practices that seized upon socio-corporeity, individualizing and totalizing it through literary and information technologies, situating it in socio-material and temporal space and subjecting it to meticulous regulation in terms of diet, sanitation, hygiene, movement, posture, and dress.

Before moving on to the technologies of discipline, however, I want to suggest that such not be seen in *opposition* to practices that have "population" and "nation" as their referent. Foucault's presentation of discipline as one side of a "bipolar" technology is unfortunate, because it has tended to be taken and integrated into the dichotomous diction of "individual" and "society". As a result, his insistence that the "two techniques", discipline and biopolitics, "were not to be joined together at the level of a speculative discourse, but in the form of concrete arrangements", has generally been obscured.[84] While there certainly develops a bipolar "discourse" upon socio-corporeity, one speaking to life and its processes, the other to the body and its mechanics, the practice of biopolitics, with its referents of "population" and the "health of the nation", is not detached from the practices of "discipline". "Institutions", I suggest, are no less instruments of biopolitics than of discipline. The school report, no less than the national census, is an instrument of information technology, a case of "political arithmetic", to redeploy the language of Petty. Indeed it is precisely the material integration of action upon the "body politic" with that upon the "body natural" that constitutes, to a large extent, the science/government network. Reference to "socio-corporeity", again, offers a means to speak of discipline and biopolitics which is not bound by the dichotomies and contra/dictions of the micro/macro frame.

Discipline is explicitly deployed as an "experiment" in the constitution of a "healthy", "useful", and "docile" state of socio-corporeity.[85] Schools form the front-line in this activity and in Ireland again we find, with the creation in 1831 of the National Board of Education and the rapid establishment of government funded schools, an intervention by government far in excess of what one generally finds in the rest of Europe at this time. A succinct example of the new government sponsored and regulated discipline is found in 1854 in a Dublin National School. Edward M"Gauran, later to become the head schoolmaster at Mountjoy model prison, made his report thus:

DISCIPLINE: No boy is allowed to speak unless on business and then he holds out his hand as a sign that he wishes permission. Orders, general and particular, are not only obeyed promptly but without the least sign of reluctance. In passing to and from, and also in moving through the school the children march in a single file keeping the step and with their hands behind. The great rule for order and regularity "a time and a place for everything and everything in its proper time and place" is constantly inculcated and rigidly adhered to. In fact, everything is ready five minutes before the period specified in the "Table", in order that there should not be a moment lost when the proper time has arrived for commencing the next subject . . . All confusion is avoided; the children have their books, or writing materials at their hands, classes supplied with instructors, and the whole machinery moves, as it were of itself – no noise – no bustle – no disorder of any kind.[86]

It was this meticulous organization of bodies that formed the material basis of discipline and of sanitized and clinical socio-material space. And since moral and physical conditions were seen as bound together, "moral contamination" was viewed as no less unhealthy than "physical" contamination. "Communication" control was necessary if a morally sanitized socio-corporeity was to be realized. Thus the doctrine of silence facilitated the constitution of a fragmented state of socio-corporeity, a situation, to use the words of Tocqueville, where "they are really isolated, though no wall separates them".[87] Consider, for instance, the following statements:

1. No communication *is* permitted . . . Absolute silence is maintained 2. . . . the haunting fear of breaking rules, especially of breaking silence . . . 3. Strict silence must at all times be observed; under no circumstances must one . . . speak to another.[88]

One of these quotes is from a student of a Catholic convent school, one is from a prisoner of a penitentiary, and another is from a professor at Maynooth seminary. Without previous knowledge as to their source it would be impossible to decide which is which. This is no coincidence. Controlling communication within or between ranks was a central feature of disciplinary pedagogy. The first quote is from Maynooth seminary, where fear of "improper" communication was such that socio-material barriers were constructed to separate discursive "classes", "divisions", and "ranks": "Each of the two houses into which the college was divided hitherto, was subdivided into two divisions; with barriers between them; stone walls on the grounds and wooden partitions in the refectories, . . . a wall was built . . . between the Rhetoric and Logic Houses . . . outward separation of the divisions of the same house was completed by another wall. . . . In the senior house a strong wooden door was thrown across . . . to debar access to and outlet from St. Mary's Division".[89] The second quote comes from a Catholic convent school. Sissy O"Brien was confident that she and her fellow students would "have been lively and joyous, but for incessant repression and the haunting fear of breaking rules, especially of breaking silence". Instead they suffered "perpetual anxiety lest one should break rules, or having broken them, that one might forget to confess the sin."[90] The last of the three quotes is from Thomas Clark, a signatory to the Irish Proclamation of Independence (1916), who described the regimen of silence as "a scientific system of perpetual and persistent harassing."[91] While the technology of communication control was not bound to any particular institution, it did rely upon specific investments in, and construction of, socio-material space.

A temporal technology was likewise central to the disciplinary investment of socio-corporeity. The example of the mid-nineteenth century convent school, precisely because it is an experiential memoir rather than a clinical analysis, provides a living expression of the tyranny of the clock. The old woman remembered how she "pitied them [the nuns] for having to be obedient to the clock, praying, watching, teaching by the clock, on and on, all their lives."[92] She remembered watching them walking in the garden and how at the "first tinkle [of the bell] they turned like one nun to go in".[93] "Time penetrates the body and with it all the meticulous controls of power."[94]

A third aspect of disciplinary action, as Foucault has famously demonstrated, is optical architecture. The president's rooms at Maynooth seminary were strategically placed allowing panoptic vision of the squares on either side. When the bell rang indicating the end of recreation, the briskness of response, its uniformity or deviation, was instantly observable and measurable. This concept, total surveillance through architectural design, is often credited to Jeremy Bentham. He did, in 1791, publish its clearest expression in his *Panopticon-or the inspection house, containing the idea of a new principle of construction applicable to any sort of establishment in which persons of any description are to be kept under inspection.*[95] Six years earlier, however, the principle was incorporated by James Wyatt into his plans for one of the first penitentiaries in the "British Isles". The prison was later described by John Howard: "the prisoners cannot see one another, though they are all within the view of the chaplain."[96] Colonel Joshua Jebb, who designed Pentonville in London (1842) and Mountjoy in Dublin (1850), assured the secretary of state of the home department, in relation to Mountjoy, that "every move-

ment in the prison, whether of an officer or a prisoner, would be
under constant observation and control".

Discipline differentiated treatment so as to constitute differential
relationalities and identities, a fact given less attention by Foucault.
Our record of the middle class convent school for girls indicates
that inculcating "habits of self-reliance" was given little weight:
"Little was done by our teachers to encourage self-reliance and
independence. Rather the reverse. Those of us who were like
myself, nervous and fearful, were confirmed in our fear of life, our
suspicion and dread of people."[97] A statistician, writing in 1856,
emphasized that by "education" he did not simply refer to "school
knowledge", but to "a practical knowledge of the arts of life,
whereby men obtain their living; and of domestic economy, which
teaches women how to make house attractive": which, he held, "to
be essential for the promotion of virtue and happiness, and are
therefore necessary elements of education suited for the prevention
of crime, and the protection of life, property and social order."[98] In
the middle class convent school the girls were specifically educated
in "deportment and etiquette". In the prison, women's education
was "adapted to the wants of that class" by training them in
"cooking, laundry, sewing, knitting etc."[99] Male prisoners, on the
other hand, were principally trained in tailoring, shoemaking,
weaving, and stone-cutting, with the majority prepared for laboring
on public works.[100] Expected to become workers in employment on
their release, male convicts were given special instruction on "social
subjects, such as strikes, taxes, and the labour market at home
and abroad."[101] Four Wakefield justices, who visited the Irish
convict system in 1861, reported that the "lecturer, acting as mod-
erator, has an opportunity of pointing out mistakes, of combating in
a conversational way, the errors and prejudices of illinformed
minds, e.g., on such subjects as secret societies, strikes, etc."[102]
The lecturer reported how the male convict at Lusk, as a result of
this instruction, left the prison "a man of some common sense, and
of rather clear ideas for this class."[103]

A fundamental element of information technology is the tabular
form. The school-master at Philipstown prison explained how
"almost every particular which it may be requisite for the Chaplain
or Schoolmaster to know regarding the prison" was contained in the
tables in accessible form. The tables provided an "index to the
previous character and habits of the prisoners". The "Report Book",
a slightly altered version of that used in national schools, formed
"the best means of instituting comparisons, and tabulating
details".[104] It was through such technologies that the subject of
action was simultaneously made the object of scientific knowledge.
Through clinical observation, recording, classifying and experi-

menting, by tabulating results, and comparing divisions, a whole range of clinically derived norms were established. As Foucault succinctly put it, the "art of punishing, in the regime of disciplinary power, is aimed neither at expiation, nor even precisely at repression . . . The perpetual penalty that traverses all points and supervises every instant in the disciplinary institutions compares, differentiates, hierarchizes, homogenizes, excludes. In short, it *normalizes.*"[105]

Individualization, finally, was the "invaluable means by which we learn the natures and the dispositions of criminals. . . . No feature of our system is more important, none more pregnant with greater or more valuable results. If you desire to study character, you must individualize. . . . I cannot speak too highly of the importance of possessing a knowledge of the character, nature, dispositions, etc." of the convicts.[106] Thus in a crucial sense "discipline makes individuals", it serves to produce an "identity" which is official and is bound to the body. As with the instruments of biopolitics, the censuses and the registers of births, deaths, and marriages, the in/form/ation technology active in the practices of discipline constitute a documentation that marks and tracks socio-corporeity, individualizing and totalizing it. "Discipline" is one of the names given to an entire array of heterogeneous practices through which relationalities and identities are structured in ways that are aimed at developing "individual" lives so as to enhance the power of the state. And just as socio-corporeity is the object of these practices, so the technologies that constitute disciplinary practice organize around sight, speech, space, movement, and time, to produce optical, auditive, architectural, and temporal technologies, which in their distinctiveness and synthesis, constitute analytic forms of power and knowledge. These technologies occupy a crucial space in the general business of the government of life, and of biopower. And to link up with my earlier discussion of medical police, I would say that "national health" is realized here just as it is on the streets, in the houses, and through the engineered water and waste systems that constitute a sanitized socio-material space.

All these "matters", disciplinary and biopolitical, are brought together in the discourse of "Social Science", a discourse modeled on the natural sciences and fully networked with the latter through the practices of engineering, hygiene, medicine, biology, and chemistry. The professionalization, specialization, and epistemic purifications that separate each should not be seen as sufficient to occlude the connections that run through them, and which serve to network the general government of the body politic with the local and detailed government of the body natural. Theories and experiments in "social improvement" were vigorously expounded and debated by the Statistical and Social Inquiry Society of Ireland, the Dublin Sanitary Association, and the National Association for the Promotion of Social Science (NAPSS), all of which were intimately networked with government. The extent of this connectivity can easily be deduced through a consideration of the material semiotic generative nodes that constituted the congress of the NAPSS assembled in Dublin in 1861. Walter Crofton, chairman of the board of directors of convict prisons in Ireland, was a council member and chair of the Dublin chapters" executive committee. The president for 1861 was Lord Brougham. Six of seven vice-presidencies were held, respectively, by the Lord Mayor of Dublin, the Lord Chancellor, the Chief Secretary, the Attorney General, the Lord Chief Justice of Appeal, and the Lord Chief Baron. Each of the seven departments also had its own president, one of which was held in 1861 by an ex-Attorney General, one by an ex-Chancellor, one by the Attorney General, and another by a judge. The national council of the association had sixty members, seventeen of whom were members of parliament. Twelve of the latter were liberals, and at least six bourgeois. By the less precise category of "middle class", which includes professionals, small gentry (baronets), and low to middle ranking officials of state, more than two-thirds of the seventeen are thus definable.[107]

The Four Courts in Dublin "were placed entirely at the disposal of the Association",[108] and the *Freemans Journal* congratulated the Viceroy, Lord Mayor, Royal Dublin Society. Royal Irish Academy, Zoological Society, and Statistical Society. for making the event possible, describing it as an "assemblage of the elite of our metro-polis". Papers, it reported, had been read by "our ablest lawyers and our most distinguished judges".[109] The NAPSS and similar groups constructed discourses around a wide range of subjects, from morality, discipline, training, reformation, and police, to hygiene, sanitation, nutrition. and public health, bringing the analytics of government and science, "natural" and "social", into a direct and integrated relation. In every case there was "a practical as well as a scientific side", a "rational" as well as an "economic" consideration, and a concern to determine the proper "connexion of voluntary effort with government aid."[110]

Police, health, biomedicine, discipline, and practices of govern-ment, have their most material meeting ground in "the body". Ireland, it might be said, was a successful experiment from the point of view of all these domains. Between the mid-eighteenth and late nineteenth centuries, the socio-material state of the country, the state of socio-corporeity, was entirely worked over. While the effects of the science/government network should not be over-stated, and the impact of the famine, removing from the country through death and emigration, and in the space of a decade, about two million of the poorest people, should not be underestimated, the general trend, and its effects, were real enough.[111] The alteration of socio-material space was intimately related to the revolution of "respectability" that Ireland, like England, underwent in the mid-Victorian period. Not only had the country been dotted by newly built Catholic churches, but the parishioners who attended then were "clean and well dressed", the women's heads covered with shawls, the men in suit, tight-collar shirt, and tie. "Cleanliness and Godliness" were finally brought into a practised relation, the "moral" stitched into the "physical", and government of the body natural and the body politic bound together. Dr. Frank would have surely been impressed. Many of the measures of an effective medical police, as he understood them, had been "improved". Epidemics were relatively rare, livestock disease largely contained, famine a thing of the past, life expectancy extended, public wash-houses established, and hygiene and sanitation transformed. Streets were widened and sanitized – the thoroughfares of O'Connell Street and College Green a lasting memorial – and cleared of hawkers, "loiterers", and other "nuisances" (legislation used to this day to "move-on" the buskers of Grafton street in Dublin). Water and sewage systems were engineered, and extensive public health, police, and education systems had been created.

Government, by networking with science, secured a nation of subject-bodies whose "natures" were defined and material conditions enhanced. Socio-corporeity was both more effectively subjected, and made more productive. Ireland was without doubt a more "powerful" "state" in the early twentieth century than it had been in the late eighteenth. That state was the *effect* of heterogeneous practices that objectified and invested socio-corporeity and socio-material space. And as an effect of practices deployed over a long period of time, and in conditions not chosen, it could never be coterminous with a particular regime or government. Ireland enters the twentieth century as a cultural hybrid, subsisting in Irish, English, and European forms (at least). The rebellions which finally lead to the Irish Republic institute a new regime in an already constituted state, a state which today, in its education, health, police, and welfare, in its socio-materiality, and in its forms of identity/relationality, bears all the marks of that long nineteenth century work-over. It was through the networking of scientific and government practices that the specific form of modern Irish socio-corporeity was realized. This realization, I would say with little doubt, was central to the formation of the modern Irish state. The modern state can justifiably be defined as a techno-scientific political formation in which state power and scientific practices/

knowledge are woven together in a complex yet definitive network. It is at once a governed material state, and a state of material being.

## Notes

Special thanks to Chandra Mukerji and Philip Corrigan for advice, encouragement, and inspiration. Thanks also to Steven Epstein, Chloe Burke, and the *JHS* reviews for constructive criticisim on an earlier draft. I remain, of course, responsible etc.

[1] Chandra Mukerji, "Visualizations of Military Engineering in 17th Century France" (unpublished), 1.

[2] Sharon Traweek, *Beamtimes & Lifietimes: The World of High-Energy Physics* (Cambridge MA: Harvard University Press, 1988).

[3] For instance, Bruno Latour & Steve Woolgar, *Laboratory Life: The Construction of Scientific Facts* (Princeton: Princeton University Press, 1986); Chandra Mukerji, *A Fragile Power: Scientists and the State* (Princeton: Princeton University Press, 1989): Andrew Pickering (ed.), *Science as Practice and Culture* (Cambridge: Cambridge University Press, 1992); *The Mangle of Practice: Time, Agency, and Science* (Cambridge: Cambridge University Press, 1095); Donna Haraway. *Simians, Cyborgs, and Women: The Reinvention of Nature* (New York: Routledge, 1991); Steven Shapin, "History of Science and its Sociological Reconstructions", In *History of Science* 20: 157–211; David C. Lindberg & Robert S. Westman (eds.), *Reappraisals of the Scientific Revolution* (Cambridge: Cambridge University Press, 1990).

[4] Chandra Mukerji. "The Political Mobilization of Nature in Seventeenth Century French Formal Gardens", *Theory and Society* 23: 651–677 (1994); *A Fragile Power* (1989).

[5] Steven Shapin & Simon Schaffer, *Leviathan and the Air-Pump: Hobbes, Boyle, and the Experimental Life* (Princeton: Princeton University Press, 1985).

[6] See Peter Alter, *The Reluctant Patron: Science and the State in Britain 1850–1920* (Oxford: Berg, 1987); Philip Gummett. *Scientists in Whitehall* (Manchester: Manchester University Press, 1980); A. Hunter Depree, *Science in the Federal Government: A History of Policies and Activities to 1940* (Cambridge, MA: Harvard University Press, 1957); Ruth Barrington, *Health, Medicine & Politics in Ireland 1900–1970* (Dublin, 1987): Peter Kneen. *Soviet Scientists and the State* (Albany: State University of New York Press, 1984); Arleen Marcia Tuchman, *Science, Medicine, and the State in Germany: The Case of Baden 1815–1871* (New York: Oxford University Press, 1993); William McGucken, *Scientists, Society, and State: The Social Relations of Science Movement in Great Britain 1931–1947* (Columbus: Ohio State University Press, 1984).

[7] For instance, Philip Corrigan and Derek Sayer, *The Great Arch: English State Formation as Cultural Revolution* (Oxford: Blackwell, 1991 [1985]); Claude Denis, "The Genesis of American Capitalism: an Historical Inquiry into State Theory", In *Journal of Historical Sociology* 2:4 (1989); Derek Sayer, *The Violence of Abstraction* (Oxford: Basil Blackwell. 1987); Colin Gordon (ed.) *Power/Knowledge: Selected Interviews & Other Writings, 1972–1977* (New York Pantheon, 1980); L.D. Kritzman (ed.), *Michel Foucault: Politics, Philosophy, Culture – Interviews and Other Writings 1977–1984* (New York: Routledge, 1988); Paul Rabinow (ed.), *The Foucault Reader* (New York: Pantheon, 1984); Michel Foucault, *The History of Sexuality*

*Vol. 1: An Introduction* (NY: Vintage, 1990); *Discipline and Punish: The Birth of the Prison* (Middlesex: Peregrine, 1979).

[8] I should note that I am speaking only to the notion of "modern western states". Theorists and historians disagree on the periodization of the formation of such states. I tend to locate their emergence in the fifteenth to seventeenth centuries, but see them only being fully formed in the late nineteenth to early twentieth centuries.

[9] Philip Corrigan, *Social Forms/Human Capacities: Essays in Authority and Difference* (London: Routledge, 1990). I am particularly grateful for conversations with Professor Corrigan on the problems of contra/diction and dichotomy, and on the difficulties of finding a way beyond dualism.

[10] Mukerji, "Political Mobilization of Nature" (1994), 656.

[11] See Charles Cameron, *A Manual of Hygiene, Public and Private* (Dublin, 1874), 228.

[12] See John Law, *Modernity, Myth and Materialism* (Oxford: Blackwell, 1993); Bruno Latour, *Science in Action: How to Follow Scientists and Engineers through Society* (Cambridge: Harvard University Press, 1987); Michel Callon. John Law, & Arie Rip (eds.). *Mapping the Dynamics of Science and Technology: Sociology of Science in the Real World* (London: Macmillan, 1986).

[13] Michel Foucault, "The Confession of the Flesh", in Gordon, *Power/Knowledge* (1980), 194.

[14] Haraway, *Simians, Cyborgs, and Women* (1991), 200. Haraway uses this phrase to describe bodies as objects of knowledge. I extend it to describe mobile actors who generate such knowledge.

[15] Bruno Latour, "Drawing Things Together", In Michael Lynch and Steve Woolgar (eds), *Representation in Scientific Practice* (Cambridge, MA: Massachusetts Institute of Technology Press, 1990).

[16] See Haraway, *Simians, Cyborgs, and Women* (1991). Bruno Latour, *We Have Never Been Modern* (Cambridge, MA: Harvard University Press, 1993).

[17] Only so much is possible in a single paper, and there are many limitations to this one. Major forces, for instance, "capitalism" and "resistance", are not addressed at all. Rather than treating such issues in a cursory and therefore unsatisfactory manner, I leave them out of the present narrative entirely. No complete account of modern state formation would be adequate, however, without references to such forces. But I believe the approach I am proposing is such that these forces can be fully integrated into the analysis. Working out how precisely to do this is central to my current research.

[18] Quoted in Oliver MacDonagh, *A New History of Ireland* v. 5 (Oxford: Clarenton Press, 1989), 206.

[19] *See Transactions of the National Association for the Promotion of Social Science* (London, 1857–1875).

[20] William Petty, *The Political Anatomy of Ireland* (London, 1691 [1672]), 7–8.

[21] For an early example see William Petty. *Several Essays in Political Arithmetick* (London, 1699); *An Essay Concerning the Multiplication of Mankind etc.* (London, 1686); John Graunt [& William Petty], *Natural and Political Observations upon the Bills of Mortality etc.* (London, 1662).

[22] J.P. Frank, *A System of Complete Medical Police* 6 vols. Edited with an Introduction by Erna Lesky (Baltimore: Johns Hopkins University Press, [1779–1819] 1976), 12.

[23] Frank, *Medical Police* (19761, v.

[24] Frank, *Medical Police* (1976), 8.

[25] Frank, *Medical Police* (1976), 100.

[26] Frank, *Medical Police* (1976), ix.

[27] Michel Foucault, "Ornnes et Singulatim: Towards a Criticism of Political Reason", In Kritzman, *Michel Foucault: Politics, Philosophy, Culture* (1988).

[28] Quoted in George Rosen, "The Fate of the Concept of Medical Police 1780–1890", in *Centaurus* 5–2: 97–113, (1957), 107. See also John Roberton, *Medical Police: or, the Causes of Disease, with the Means of Protection: and Rules for Diet, Regimen, etc.* (Edinburgh, 1809); James Black, "Lectures on Public Hygiene and Medical Police", in *Provincial Medical and Surgical Journal* (1844); W. Strange, "On the Formation of a System of National Medical Police and Public Hygiene etc.", in *London Medical Gazette* n.s. II: 452–57 (1846); W. Strange, *The Health and Sickness of Town Populations, considered with reference to proposed Sanitary Legislation, and to the Establishment of a Comprehensive System of Medical Police and District Dispensaries etc.* (London, 1846); Louis Elsberg, The Domain of Medical Police", in *American Medical Monthly* (1862); David Hosack, *Observations on the Means of Improving the Medical Police of the City of New York* (1820).

[29] Rosen, "The Fate of the Concept of Medical Police" (1957), 107.

[30] H. Aubrey Husband, *The Student's Hand-Book of Forensic Medicine and Medical Police* (1879).

[31] See, "Essays in State Medicine", in *The Dublin Quarterly Journal of Medical Science* XXII: 146–50 (1856); "Public Health in Ireland" in *Dublin Quarterly Journal of Medical Science* 119–37 (1874); *The Quarterly Journal of Public Health and Record of Medicine* I (1855); Cameron, *A Manual of Hygiene* (1874).

[32] R.V. Comerford, "Ireland 1850–70, Post-famine and Mid-Victorian", in *A New History of Ireland* v.5 (1989), 390. See also Kevin Boyle, "Police in Ireland before the Union", in *Irish Jurist* (1972–73): Brian Griffin, "The Irish Police 1836–1914: A Social History" (Ph.D: Loyola University, Chicago, 1990); Stanley Palmer, *Police & Protest in England and Ireland 1770–1850* (Cambridge: Cambridge University Press, 1988).

[33] Quoted in W.E. Vaughan, "Ireland *c.* 1870", In *A New History of Ireland* v.5 (1989), I rely on Vaughan for this list of police activities.

[34] Vaughan, "Ireland c. 1870" (1989), 767.

[35] Vaughan, "Ireland c. 1870" (1989), 768.

[36] Vaughan, "Ireland c. 1870" (1989), 767.

[37] Erna Lesky, *The Vienna Medical School of the 19th Century* (Baltimore: Johns Hopkins University Press, 1976), 87.

[38] John H. Griscom, *Anniversary Discourse before the New York Academy of Medicine* (New York, 1855), 54.

[39] Henry G. Clark, *Superiority of Sanitary Measures over Quarantines* (Boston, 1852), 8.

[40] Michel Foucault, "The Politics of Health in the Eighteenth Century", in Rabinow, *Foucault Reader* (1984), 275.

[41] J.L. McCracken, "The Social Structure and Social Life, 1714–60," in *A New History of Ireland* v.4 (Oxford: Clarendon Press, 1986), 50.

[42] Michel Foucault, *The Birth of the Clinic, An Archaeology of Medical Perception* (New York: Vintage, 1994).

[43] Foucault, "The Politics of Health" (1984), 278.

[44] *First Report of the Philanthropic Society* (London, 1788).

[45] Oliver MacDonagh, "Ideas and Institutions, 1830–45", In *A New History of Ireland* v.5 (1989), 209.

[46] MacDonagh, "Ideas and Institutions; (1989), 209.

[47] Quoted in L.M. Cullen, *An Economic History of Ireland since 1660* (1972), 109–10.

[48] See, on this apparent contradiction, Corrigan and Sayer, *The Great Arch* (1991).

[49] Barrington, *Health, Medicine & Politics* (1987).

[50] I am not suggesting that relief measures during the famine were adequate: they clearly were not. It is not possible to go into that issue here. I will simply add that the interventions which I refer to were motivated not by a concern for the "welfare" of "the people", but by a concern to "secure" the "population". For some of the more dogmatic adherents of *laissez faire* the latter was to be achieved by *not* deploying wholesale economic assistance in times of distress.

[51] E.g., 37 & 38 Vict., Cap. 93: An Act to amend the Law relating to Public Health in Ireland (1874).

[52] *Irish University Press Series of British Parliamentary Papers (IUP)* Health, Food & Drugs, v. 3.

[53] *IUP* Famine, Ireland, v.8, 51. Italics in original.

[54] *IUP* Famine, Ireland, v. 8, 51–2.

[55] Anon., "On Domestic Economy", In *Journal of Social Progress* (Dublin, 1864), 26.

[56] "On Domestic Economy" (1854), 28–31.

[57] On the history and specificity of the "Irish Convict System" see Patrick Carroll, "Reform and Rehabilitation: The Origins of Corrective Incarceration in Ireland 1763–1870" (Masters: St. Patrick's College Maynooth, 1991).

[58] Quoted in May Carpenter, *Reformatory Prison Discipline as Developed by the Rt. Hon. Sir Walter Croflon in theIrish Convict Prisons* (London, 1872), 15.

[59] Quoted in, *First Report of the Directors of Convict Prisons in Ireland* (1855), 3.

[60] Carpenter, *Reformatory Prison Discipline* (1872), 67.

[61] Carpenter, *Reformatory Prison Discipline* (1872), 80.

[62] Carpenter, *Reformatory Prison Discipline* (1872), 69.

[63] Carpenter, *Reformatory Prison Discipline* (1872), 74.

[64] Head Schoolmaster's Report, Spike Island, In *Second Report of Directors of Convict Prisons in Ireland*, (1856), 40–1.

[65] Carpenter, *Reformatory Prison Discipline* (1872), 86.

[66] Carpenter, *Reformatory Prison Discipline* (1872), 23.

[67] David Arnold, "The Colonial Prison: Power, Knowledge, and Penology in Nineteenth Century India", in *Subaltern Studies VIII: Essays in Honour of Ranajit Guha* (Delhi: Oxford University Press, 1994), 179. I would like to thank Jill Didur for bringing this work to my attention.

[68] *First Report of the Directors* (1855), 57.

[69] *Third Report of the Directors of Convict Prisons in Ireland*, (1857), 11–12. See also John Blake, *Defects in the Moral "keatment of Insanity in the Public Lunatic Asylums of Ireland* (Dublin: John Fowler, 1862).

[70] John Howard, *The State of the Prisons* (1784 [1777]), 8.

[71] Jeremiah Fitzpatrick, *An Essay on Gaol-abuses etc.* (Dublin, 1784).

[72] Jeremiah Fitzpatrick, *Thoughts on Penitentiaries* (Dublin, 1790).

[73] Oliver MacDonagh, *The Inspector-General: Sir Jeremiah Fitzpatrick and the Politics of social Reform* (London. 1981). 81.

[74] Foucault, *History of Sexuality Vol. 1* (1990), 135–9.

[75] Awly P. Banon, "Observations of Hermaphroditism. Illustrated by a Remarkable Case", in *Dublin Quarterly Journal of Medical Science* XIV: 66–87 (1852), 67.

[76] Thomas Laqueur, *Makug Sex: The Body and Gender* from the Greeks to Freud (Cambridge, MA: Harvard University Press, 1990).

[77] Banon, "Hermaphroditism" (1852), 79–80.

[78] For instance, Haraway, *Simians, Cyborgs. and Women* (1991); Ludmilla Jordanova, *Sexual Visions: Images of Gender in Science and Medicine between the Eighteenth and Twentieth Centuries* (Madison, WI: University of Wisconsin Press, 1989); Emily Martin, *The Woman in the Body: A Cultural Analysis of Reproduction* (Boston: Beacon Press, 1989).

[79] Banon. "Hermaphroditism" (1852), 82.

[80] Banon, "Hermaphroditism" (1852), 84.

[81] Banon, "Hermaphroditism" (1852), 78. Italics in original.

[82] See, for instance, Rachel Harrison and Frank Mort, "Patriarchal Aspects of Nineteenth Century State Formation: Property Relations, Marriage and Divorce, and Sexuality", in Philip Corrigan (ed.). *Capitalism, State Formation and Marxist Theory: Historicallnuestigations* (London: Quartet Books, 1980).

[83] Foucault, *Discipline and Punish* (1979).

[84] Foucault, *The History of Sexuality* (1990), 140.

[85] For instance, Anon., "Educational Experiments in Ireland", in *Dublin University Magazine* (March, 1857); Anon., "National, Factory, and Refoxmatory Schools", in *Irish Quarterly Review* (Dec. 1854; March 1855).

[86] Anon., "Our Juvenile Criminals: the Schoolmaster and the Gaoler", in the *Irish Quarterly Review* (1854), 27.

[87] Gustave Beaumont and Alexis de Tocqueville, *On the Penitentiary System in the Unites States and its Application to France* (Southern Illinois University Press, 1964), 81.

[88] Mary Carbery, *The Farm by Lough Cur*, (Cork, 1937). 10. *Maynooth Commission*, (1855); T.J. Clarke, *Glimpses of an Irish Felons Prison Life*, (Dublin, 1922). 3.

[89] Walter MacDonald, *Reminiscences of a Magnooth Professor*, (1925), 37.

[90] Carbery, *TheFarm by Lough Gur* (1937), 99–100.

[91] Clark, *Glimpses of an Irish Felon's Life* (1922), 6.

[92] Carbery, *The Farm by Lough Gur*, (1937), 100.

[93] Carbery, *The Farm by Lough Cur*, (1937), 104.

[94] Foucault, *Discipline and Punish* (1979), 151.

[95] Jeremy Bentham, *Panopticon, or Inspection House etc.* (Dublin, 1791).

[96] Anon., "Prisons and Prisoners", in the *Dublin University Magazine*, (July, 1856), 50.

[97] Carbery, *The Farm by Lough Gur* (1937), 136.

[98] James Haughton, "Education, the Surest Preventative of Crime", in the *Journal of the Dublin Statistical Society* (July 1856), 325.

[99] *First Report Directors of Convict prisons* (1855), 16.

[100] "Governor's Report, Spike Island", in *First Report Directors of Convict Prisons* (1855), 23.

[101] Lecturer's Report, Intermediate Prisons, in *Ninth Report Directors of Convict Prisons* (1863), 55.

[102] E.B. Whately *et al, Observations on the Treatment of Convicts in Ireland* (1861), 38.

[103] Lecturer's Report (1863), 55.

[104] Head School-master's Report, Philipstown. in *Second Report of Directors of Convict Prisons in Ireland* (1856), 125.

[105] Foucault, *Discipline and Punish* (1979), 182–3.

[106] Lecturer's Report, in *Fifth Report of Directors of Convict Prisons in Ireland* (1859), 131.

[107] G.W. Hastings, (ed.), *Transactions of the National Association for the Promotion of Social Science 1861* (London, 1862); Michael Stenson, *Who's Who of Britfsh Members of Parliament*, 2 vols. (Sussex, 1976).

[108] Hastings, "Aims of the Association", in *Transactions* (1862), xlix.

[109] *Freemans Journal* (August 21, 1861).

[110] Mary Carpenter, "On the Connexion of voluntary Effort with Government Aid", in *Transactions* (1862), 440.

[111] Jonathan Pim, *An Address Delivered at the Opening of the Thirtieth Session of the Statistical Society of Ireland, being a Review of the Economic and Social Progress of Ireland since the Famine* (Dublin, 1876).

# The Rise of the Information State: the Development of Central State Surveillance of the Citizen in England, 1500–2000

## EDWARD HIGGS

**Abstract** This essay examines existing sociological explanations of the development of the central surveillance of citizens in the light of the English experience, and finds them wanting. Sociologists see the state using surveillance for the benefit of capitalist elites, to reimpose social control over the "society of strangers" created by industrialisation. But surveillance pre-dated industrialisation, and the development of information gathering by state elites had more to do with their own need to preserve their position both within the English polity, and international geo-politics.

*****

## Introduction

If one were asked to create a list of the features of the modern Western state which sets it apart from previous political formations, the central collection and analysis of information, especially that on individuals, would be a strong contender for inclusion. This, it is argued, has given the state immense administrative power to direct the lives of its subjects. Sociologists who have examined this phenomenon have tended to see this as a reaction to the decay of older, "traditional", and "communal" forms of social control during the Industrial Revolution of the late eighteenth and nineteenth centuries. This, in turn, created, or so it is claimed, a "society of strangers", and of antagonistic classes. At this point the state stepped in to collect information on individuals to protect capitalism against the discontented, via the detection of deviancy and the planning of the physical environment. Collecting information on populations from the Enlightenment onwards, and the generation of statistics based upon it, has also been seen as a means of giving power and legitimacy to political and technical elites. Space precludes a detailed exposition of this literature but the necessary initial references can be found below.[1] This rather simple model of surveillance as social control in the interests of elites will be interrogated here in terms of an examination of the development of state surveillance of individuals in England from the early modern period.

## Surveillance in Pre-Modern English Society

In general terms, the information held on citizens in Britain by the modern central state is used to carry out a fairly limited number of functions – the extraction of taxes; the provision of welfare; the prevention of crime; the general identification of citizens and state employees; and the protection of property rights. There are also a number of general surveys, such as the population census, which are used directly to inform state policy-making and planning (Committee on Data Protection 1978: Appendix 6). What is striking about this list is that few of these activities were in any sense unknown in pre-modern England. Nor were they activities which were carried on in complete isolation from the central state. English kings had always taxed their subjects to fight wars from at least the tenth century onwards (Stenton 1971: 644–8). Similarly, the Old Poor Law, which paid the indigent of the parish a dole levied out of a parish rate, was Tudor state policy enshrined in acts of Parliament (Slack 1988). Royal justices itinerant had been trying local criminal cases since the twelfth century (Crook 1982: 2), and supervising local justices of the peace and parish constables since the later Middle Ages (Eastwood 1997: 10; Harris 1993). The registration of baptisms, marriages and burials by the clergy of the Church of England had been introduced by Thomas Cromwell in the role of Henry VIII's vicar-general in 1538 (Elton 1972: 259–60). Royal courts had been underpinning property rights in land since the reign of Henry II in the twelfth century via collusive court cases producing fictitious "fines", which were enrolled in the records of the central courts (Public Record Office 1963: 135–6).

However, although the central state in England might initiate and monitor such activities in the pre-modern period, the main focus of surveillance lay elsewhere. As John Hall has argued, the pre-modern state in England, as in most of Europe, was a dispersed "organic" polity. Medieval and early-modern monarchs lacked the power and resources to rule their domains via a state bureaucracy as in the case of imperial China or Rome. Instead, they entered into symbiotic relationships with local power elites to undertake the governance of the realm (Hall 1985a; Hall 1985b: 137–9). In early-modern England the Crown agreed laws in Parliament with the representatives of the landed elite, who also voted taxes for central state purposes, usually military. But it was the aristocracy and county gentry, acting as lord lieutenants of the county and justices of the peace, who saw to the workings of the local police and the overseers of the poor, and dispensed justice locally (Braddick 1991; Hindle 2000; Sharpe 1984: 21–34). Below them the "middling sort" of farmers, craftsmen and superior villagers maintained order in the parish via church vestries, and local, manor, hundred and borough courts (McIntosh 1998). The monarch was the head of the Church of England from the 1530s, and, therefore, ultimately responsible for the activities of church courts which regulated marriage and local morals. However, the Church bureaucracy was also localised, and the central state seldom interfered in its activities, except in matters of religious conformity (Houlbrooke 1979; Ingram 1990). Serious cases of deviancy could be passed "up" these hierarchies, from the local to the central legal apparatus, with the central state acting as the ultimate guarantor of social cohesion and internal pacification.

Via this decentralised system, the Crown gained its taxes, and prevented the dislocation caused by poverty and attendant social disorder, whilst local elites gained power, prestige and authority from acting as the local agents of the Crown. The rest of "respectable" society were protected from the worst excesses of crime; had some guarantee against poverty; and took advantage of the regulation of family and community relations (Griffiths, Fox and Hindle 1996). Indeed, it has been argued that the activities of the Tudor state in providing means to prevent vagrancy and regulate the poor, were merely codifying and supporting pre-existing, communal forms of social control (McIntosh 1998: 194–5). This whole structure was an incipiently formal and bureaucratic legal network. Social control in the early-modern period was not simply a matter of face-to-face relationships within the family, workplace, or the nexus of neighbours and friends. England was a "much-governed" country as early as the sixteenth century (Sharpe 1984: 21).

Since what surveillance of the population took place, and there was a lot of it in early-modern England, took place at the level of the locality, it was here that records of that activity are to be found. Suspected criminals were interrogated by justices of the peace; vagrants without visible means of support were examined by overseers of the poor; and neighbours "presented" evidence of immorality to ecclesiastical courts. Records of these activities found their way into the parish chest, local diocesan record offices, and latterly local county record offices, rather than into the archives of the central courts and departments of state (Tate 1951). Moreover, such records were usually written minutes of oral proceedings in courts or quasi-judicial gatherings, rather than the structured, standardised nominal records found in modern computer databases. Extracting information about individuals from such unstructured material was, and is, a difficult business.

Similarly, the levying of taxation certainly led to the creation of lists of taxpayers and their contributions to the royal coffers, which have found their way into various central state bodies in the medieval and early-modern periods (Jurkowski, Smith and Crook 1998). However, this did not imply a regularised system of central surveillance because of the essentially local nature of the administration of the taxation in England in that period. As already noted, local elites agreed the taxes with the Crown in Parliament and then undertook the formal assessment and collection of taxes locally before passing the receipts on to the Crown (Braddick 1994; Braddick 1996; Ward 1953). Abstracts of the sums charged on the townships, parishes and, less frequently, individual taxpayers within each administrative division, were sent to the King's Remembrancer in the Exchequer. The purpose of the lists held in London, however, was not to enforce payment by individual taxpayers but to act as a means of auditing the work of the local taxing officers. If the collectors failed to produce the sums assessed, they could be proceeded against in the Court of Exchequer (Braddick 1996: 92–3; Hoyle 1994: 16–25).

When the central state attempted to record information on its subjects directly in the early-modern period it was mainly for political or military purposes. Here one might include the oaths of allegiance and test oaths sworn periodically by office holders in order to ensure allegiance to the monarch, or to exclude Nonconformists and Roman Catholics from positions of authority (Public Record Office 1963: 39). The systematic recording of the Crown's military personnel was also an early example of state information gathering. Musters and pay lists relating to ships' crews in the Royal Navy were regularly maintained in the Admiralty from the seventeenth century onwards, as were army musters in the War Office from at least the eighteenth. These ensured the proper payment of wages and an extensive system of pensions, which were meant to ensure the loyalty of soldiers and naval personnel (Fowler and Spencer 1998; Rodger 1988). In 1696 the early-modern state even attempted to set up a register of merchant seamen, to act as a naval reserve. (Parkhurst 1962: 173–6). This was not primarily the state acting as the means of maintaining an internal order of domination on behalf of social elites but the monarch ensuring his or her own position within the decentralised organic state, and his or her means of pursuing an external foreign policy.

In general terms, therefore, one cannot see the modern forms of state surveillance as being entirely new social functions. What is new, however, is that many of these functions are now carried out by the central state rather than being dispersed throughout the "organic state" in the localities. This raises the general questions of when and why this move to the centre took place.

## The Introduction of Census-Taking and Civil Registration in England

The taking of the first national census in 1801 and the establishment of civil registration in 1837 has been seen by Anthony
Giddens as components in the first stage in the development of the
Information State in England (Giddens 1987: 179–80). But can
these be seen as directed towards the control of deviancy and the
central planning of social settings as he argues?

It is actually rather difficult to see the early censuses in terms of
the overt social control of individuals. The first census of 1801, and
all subsequent decennial enumerations until that of 1841, were
merely headcounts carried out by the clerks of the parish (Higgs
1989: 5–7). Although names and addresses were introduced in
1841, there is very little evidence that the state used this information to keep track of its subjects in the Victorian period. Names
were first included in order to ensure that local census enumera-
tors did not simply make up the returns, for which they were paid
on piece rates (Public Record Office RG 27/1, p. 5). Given the speed
with which the Victorian working classes moved their place of
residence, a decennial census would hardly have been of much
use for this purpose. The English census was never converted in
peacetime into a constantly updated population register, unlike
the situation in some other European countries (Randeraad 1995).
Indeed, for much of the late nineteenth century the central state
could not even keep track of the early nominal census returns
themselves. These were effectively lost, only being rediscovered in
the roof of the Houses of Parliament in the early twentieth century
(Higgs 1989: 19–20).

The first census was taken during the Napoleonic Wars, and it is
possible that it was intended to reveal the size of the population
able to bear arms. The questions asked included one on the
numbers of men and women in the parish "exclusive of men actually serving in his majesty's regular forces or militia, or exclusive of
seamen either in his majesty's service or belonging to registered
vessels". However, it is unlikely that the results of the census could
have been used for direct military purposes since it failed to ask for
ages. The only pre-Victorian census to ask for such details was that
of 1821. A more likely reason for taking the census in 1801 may
have been a desire to calculate how many people remained on the
land producing food during a period of economic blockade and
mass military mobilisation (Glass 1978: 96–8). The requirements of
geo-politics were to the forefront here.

However, the titles for all the decennial census acts until that
of 1841 indicated that they were for "taking an account of the

population of Great Britain, *and the increase and diminution thereof*". They were also associated with questions to the local clergy on the levels of parish baptisms, marriages and burials reaching back into the eighteenth century (Higgs 1989: 5–7). These early enumerations may, therefore, have been intended to settle an earlier political debate about the "state of the nation" under the Whig ascendancy, as reflected in the growth or decay of population, rather than as a direct attempt at central state planning. Whigs naturally believed that the population was growing under their careful husbandry of the state, whilst Tories and Radicals claimed that political and moral corruption was sapping the vitality of the nation, and leading to population decline (Glass 1978: 11–89). Again, the legitimacy of a political elite, rather than class domination, appears to have been the issue at stake. Population pressure was, of course, a key political issue in the early nineteenth-century, especially after the publication of Malthus's *Essay on the principle of population*. But rising population in the nineteenth century was generally welcomed, and was, if anything, used as an excuse for *decreasing* state involvement in society under the New Poor Laws. This may have increased the social control powers of employers but hardly those of the state.

The early censuses were organised by a clerk of the House of Commons but the 1841 census, and those which followed in the Victorian period, were taken by the General Register Office (GRO). This had been set up in 1837 to administer the new system of civil registration of births, marriages and deaths (Higgs 1989: 7–10). The questions asked in the census expanded but remained fairly modest until towards the end of the nineteenth century – name, sex, age, relationship to head of household, marital status, occupation, birthplace, and medical disabilities (Higgs 1989: 114–26). This information was tabulated and published on a national and local basis. However, although this information was plainly of use for government policy-making, the GRO's interest in the data was mainly for medical scientific purposes, and much of the application of this data to official action was at the level of local government. This was perhaps inevitable given the generally decentralised nature of the British state throughout the Victorian period. To understand the GRO's activities here, one needs to look at the census in conjunction with its other main task, the administration of civil registration.

Civil registration, like the census, was hardly instituted for the purpose of controlling deviancy. Recording where people were born, married or died was, and is, hardly the best way of keeping track of them. Indeed, one of its main purposes was to free Nonconformists from the inconvenience of having to register their baptisms, marriages and burials with the clergy of the State Church. But the over-riding reason for the institution of the new system, which included the maintenance of a central registry of vital events by the GRO in London, was the need to improve the title to middle-class property in a period of rapid economic change by recording lines of descent. The older, parochial system was seen as inadequate for this purpose due to the reluctance of the growing numbers of Dissenters to use it, and the dispersed and inadequate nature of its recordkeeping (Higgs 1996a: 115–24). The new system had to be generalised to all social classes in order to make it comprehensive – as in so many other ways, middle-class property rights had to be portrayed as universal human rights in order to make them enforceable (see Habermas 1992). The early Victorian period saw a proliferation of institutions for the recording of such property rights, including the Land Registry, the Public Record Office, and the Probate, Patents and Designs Registries (Higgs 1997a). Rather than the middle classes using the state to control the working classes during industrialisation, this reflected their use of state organs to improve their own property rights, and those of other classes in the process. Such rights were, of course, part and parcel of a particular capitalist and gendered concept of property but the introduction of the registration system did not experience any widespread resistance as a result. This was despite the initial absence of any sanctions against non-compliance.

Civil registration also involved the recording of cause of death, and this became the basis of a wide-ranging programme of medical research within the GRO. Its officers combined census with civil registration data in order to create national and occupational life tables, and statistics of deaths per thousand by locality and disease. Life tables were intended to facilitate the work of insurance companies, and of the friendly societies used by the working classes for saving against unemployment, illness and death (Higgs 1996a: 124–8). Mortality statistics were to be distributed widely as a means of shaming local authorities into improving sanitation in order to remove the human effluent which was seen as causing the high mortality in the cities (Szreter 1991). Mortality and morbidity were conceptualised, in turn, as the main causes of working-class poverty (Hamlin 1998: 84–120). The emphasis in the early and mid-Victorian censuses on family structure, age, and migration can be seen in terms of a scientific investigation into the forces creating the concentrations of urban populations, which was perceived as causing insanitary conditions. Similarly, the asking of questions on occupations, and specifically the materials being worked on, was part of a wider investigation into occupational ill-health and mortality (Higgs 1991).

Rather than subjecting the population to central control, however, the aim was to free the working classes from disease and poverty, and thus from the local state in the form of the Poor Law. In general, individuals were being given information to enable them to make decisions about where to live, how to invest their money, and what occupations to join. To this end statistical data in parliamentary reports was disseminated widely to such bodies as mechanics institutes (Public Record Office RG 29/1, p. 551). Such dissemination was also to facilitate the bringing to bear of local "public opinion" on local political elites. This was, to some limited extent, the recognition of a right to health. The work of the GRO was also implicated in the maintenance of political rights since vital registration data was used locally to help maintain electoral registers, whilst population data from the census informed the process of maintaining equitable electoral boundaries (Higgs 1996b: 298–99).

Little of this was directly concerned with controlling deviancy via deployment of punishment, or the control of physical space. Rather it represented part of the construction of what T H Marshall termed civil, political and social citizenship (Marshall 1994). However, the constitution of the citizen in terms of the ownership of property; the maintenance of family independence via saving; casting the vote in elections; and the right to the protection of health via local administrative action, delimited what citizenship implied. It certainly did not imply a redistribution of wealth, except that minimum available under the humiliating and penal Victorian Poor Laws. Nor did it imply a right to health in terms of rights to decent housing and an adequate diet, or to what Marshall termed the right "to share to the full in the social heritage and to live the life of a civilised being according to the standards prevailing in the society" (Marshall 1994: 9). This was not so much social control, in the sense of the identification and control of deviancy from social norms, than the constitution, in Phillip Corrigan and Derek Sayer's terms, of the social norms of a liberal capitalist society, and the socialisation of citizens into them, within the framework of the local and nation state (Corrigan and Sayer 1991). However, it is debatable whether this liberal concept of the citizen – as property owner, thrifty, familial, and politically participant via the franchise – was entirely alien to working-class moral codes and aspirations (see, for example, Harrison 1982: 157–216; Joyce 1991; Kidd 1999: 109–59).

But what of that other signal innovation of early to mid-nineteenth century England, the introduction of the new uniformed police forces? Established first in London in 1829, and directly responsible to the Home Secretary, the new police were extended over the rest of the country in the following decades, and have been seen as a powerful means of surveillance and social control (e.g. Donajgrodzki 1977; Philips 1980). Certainly the new police acted as a means of physically countering Chartist "disturbances" and strikes, and imposed middle-class concepts of order and decorum on the streets (see, for example, Emsley 1991: 24–57; Philips 1977: 76–7). But this was hardly done via the systematic collection of information, rather it involved physically watching for crime and deviancy via "pounding the beat". Most police forces did not even have extensive detective branches until the 1870s (Baldwin and Kinsey 1982: 11; Critchley 1978: 160; Porter 1987: 5). Given the high turnover of men in the early forces, and their low levels of education, skill and professional status, this was understandable (Bailey 1981: 14–15; Taylor 1998: 88–109). As with the older parish constables and night watchmen they replaced, the local information available to the Victorian policeman was mostly what he carried in his head. In some ways what was crucial to the working of the new police was not their surveillance of the public but their surveillance *by* the public. Deviancy was to be deterred by publicly parading round the streets in conspicuous uniforms (Baldwin and Kinsey 1982: 9–10; Critchley 1978: 158–9; Philips 1980: 188).

In sum, the period of the classic Industrial Revolution in England, and its immediate aftermath, does not appear to show the development of central state information gathering on citizens for the purposes of social control in a narrow sense. Rather than technologies of direct domination, institutions such as the census and civil registration can be seen in terms of creating rights, if of a circumscribed variety. Nor did the collection of information on the population as a whole lead to state policies to manipulate it as an entity. Rather, the classic liberal strategy was to alter the behaviour of individuals by providing them with information and the creation of rights and obligations. Population "thinking" did not lead to population policies at this stage.

## The Rise of the Information State, Imperial Crisis and Social Amelioration

Rather than the early nineteenth century, it was the last thirty years of the reign of Victoria, and the first two decades of the twentieth century, which saw the real foundation of the modern Information State in England. This can be seen in changes to the role of existing institutions such as the census and civil registration, and the institution of new forms of record keeping to facilitate the transfer of incomes at the level of the nation state.

Increasing concern in the late nineteenth century over the loss of British world hegemony, and rivalry with the USA and Germany, gave greater salience to the discussion of demographic issues and the need for "national efficiency" (Searle 1971: 6–12). Fears regarding the relative numerical, and absolute physical, decline of imperial manpower, exacerbated by the debacle of the Boer Wars, were linked in the Edwardian period to the issue of infant mortality (Lewis 1980: 27–32). In Britain, the need to manipulate conciously the size and quality of the population was thus a feature of the early twentieth-century state, rather than that of the early nineteenth, a process which culminated in the establishment of a Royal Commission on Population in 1937 (Soloway 1995). It could be argued that England simply lacked the internal and external threats which propelled other European states to more direct policies on population in the course of the nineteenth century. Given the British economic and naval hegemony of the early to mid-nineteenth century, there was a limited need for means to ensure industrial or military mobilisation (Strachan 1983: 108–11). These exceptional circumstances ceased to apply in the late nineteenth and early twentieth centuries, and the English state developed population policies more typical of the Continental powers.

These concerns led to the statistical work of the GRO being integrated more fully into a central state increasingly willing to direct local government to achieve national ends. The orientation of the GRO towards underpinning local and personal rights and responsibilities began to shift in the last decade of the nineteenth century. Thus, in the early years of the twentieth century, the GRO was directed by the Local Government Board at this time to give special attention in its publications to mortality in the first year of life, data which underpinned the state sponsorship of infant welfare measures (General Register Office 1907: cxviii). Similarly, in 1890 a deputation of social scientists, including Charles Booth and Alfred Marshall, met the President of the Local Government Board, the GRO's parent department, and the Chancellor of the Exchequer, to complain about the lack of information suitable for economic and social analysis. A Treasury Committee on the Census was established which led to the introduction of new questions on employment status into the decennial enumeration. Other government departments, such as the Board of Trade and the Home Office, which were themselves beginning to intervene more openly in national economic and social life, came to have a greater say in the design of the census (Szreter 1996: 114–20).

The early decades of the twentieth century also saw a fundamental shift in the use of the nominal records collected by the

GRO. Rather than simply providing actors in civil society with proof of their own identity, or acting as the basis of statistical analysis, they now began, in addition, to underpin personal rights and obligations at the level of the nation state. Census and civil registration records began to be searched on a regular basis for proof of age of those claiming national pensions under the 1908 Old Age Pensions Act (General Register Office 1911: cxxviii). Similarly, during the First World War proof of marriage and paternity in civil registration records became the basis for claiming separation allowances by the families of military personnel, and of widows' pensions in its aftermath (General Register Office 1916: lv). The Great War also saw the GRO administering a true system of state surveillance – national registration – for the purposes of identifying and calling up individuals for military service and war work. Citizens had to register themselves, and report changes of address (Higgs 1996b: 299). Such procedures, which were reintroduced in the period 1939 to 1952, can be seen as reactions to external geo-political threats to the State, rather than internal mechanisms for handling economic and social relationships in their own right. Moreover, in the aftermath of both World Wars, the system of national registration was abandoned in Britain on the grounds of its potential threat to civil liberties (Higgs 1996b: 300; Public Record Office. RG 28/201).

In the early twentieth century the Liberal Party also introduced a number of key innovations in social and economic policy. Old Age Pensions have already been mentioned, and to this must be added the 1911 National Insurance Act, which gave a portion of the working classes limited unemployment benefits and access to health care. In return, employed men, their employers and the central state paid into privately run "approved societies", the payments being recorded by the placing of stamps in books held by employees (Gilbert 1966). This nascent Welfare State immediately spawned a vast system of central-state record keeping to test the eligibility of claims and prevent fraud. By 1922 the Ministry of Labour's Claims and Record Office at Kew employed a staff of 3,600, and dealt with the exchange of 15 million employees' books a year by 1939 (Public Record Office. LAB 12/53). Similarly, the Ministry of Pensions' records office at Blackpool was employing nearly 4,000 civil servants by 1946, and processing 40,000 pensions claims a month (Public Record Office. PIN 23/7). Such surveillance expanded still further with the advent of the classic Welfare State during and after the Second World War.

Again, much of this might be best seen in terms of broader theories of social amelioration rather than social control in terms of the identification of deviancy – the incorporation of the working classes into the political nation, if on limited terms, rather than direct domination (Mann 1993: 597–627). The Edwardian Liberal Party saw welfare measures as a means of maintaining the allegiance of the increasingly important numbers of working-class voters who might switch their support to the newly formed Labour Party (Thane 1978: 99; Thane 1999), or to a Conservative Party advocating the abandonment of free trade to protect British industry (Harris 1984: 213–15, 235, 270–1). The state was becoming a pluralist one rather than a simple mechanism for direct social control in the interests of administrative and economic elites. But this was a "bounded" pluralism in the sense that it was pluralism within a capitalist framework.

These welfare rights and obligations could also be conceptualised in the context of the need for "national efficiency" and social cohesion to meet the threat to the British Empire from emerging industrial rivals (Gladstone 1999: 16–17; Searle 1971: 6–12). This might be seen as reflecting the needs of capitalists, although this "new" Liberalism tended to result in a shift of the political allegiance of employers to the Conservative Party (Emy 1973; Clarke 1972). One might argue, moreover, that rather than these developments being driven by the *internal* threats presented to British capitalism by the Industrial Revolution of the late eighteenth century or late Victorian competition, they reflected once again the *external* threats to the English state presented by the "Second Industrial Revolution" of the late nineteenth century which undermined Britain's international geo-political pre-eminence.

This centralisation of state surveillance also seems to have reflected a decline in the dynamism of local government. The expanding size of commercial concerns, and the increasingly impersonal nature of ownership with the spread of limited liability, concentrated wealth in a new, cosmopolitan rentier class. This undermined the coherence of local ruling elites. The rise of national forms of culture, and of an homogenised public-school ethos, further undermined provincial allegiances. Local government in late Victorian and Edwardian Britain was also in financial turmoil as it struggled to deal with the social costs of increasingly national and international economic trends. National rather than local solutions to social problems came increasingly to "make sense" (Harris 1994: 20–1, 200–1). This coincided with, and was arguably part of, the increasing professionalisation and bureaucratization found within all facets of British life in this period, as new national professional elites in government, businesses and trade unions created a corporate state (Perkin 1989).

## The Rise of Centralised Information Systems in the Police and Security Services

A mixture of responses to external and internal processes can also be seen in the development of surveillance functions by the police and security forces in the same period.

The 1869 Habitual Criminals Act and the 1871 Prevention of Crime Act gave the police greater powers to apprehend those who had been released early from prison on license and were subsequently suspected of committing further crimes. This reflected a moral panic over rising national crime rates, in a society which had recently been forced to abandon the transportation of criminals to its overseas colonies (Bartrip 1981; Wiener 1990: 148–51). An "Habitual Criminals Register" was to be kept of all persons convicted of a crime and sent to prison for one month or more. Prison governors were to be responsible for notifying particulars and personal descriptions to a person appointed by the Commissioner of Police of the Metropolis. The system of convicts reporting was initially a dead letter, however, since it was difficult to identify who the "appointed person" was. The Register was subsequently transferred to the Home Office but was not very successful (Committee on identifying habitual criminals 1893–94: 214–6).

Under the 1879 Prevention of Crime Act, however, a formal Convict Supervision Office was established at Scotland Yard in order to supervise convicts within the Metropolis. Given the scale of the movement of people into and out of London, this Office soon took on the character of a national surveillance body (Committee on identifying habitual criminals 1893–94: 217–8). This coincided with an increasing professionalisation of the police, the national expansion of plain-clothes detective branches, and the introduction of scientific methods of identification, such as fingerprinting, in the 1890s (Manwaring-White 1983: 192–3; Taylor 1998: 88–105). This decade also saw the return of the Habitual Criminals Register to Scotland Yard, and its integration with the work of the Convict Supervision Office (Public Record Office. HO 144/566/A62042). Although the early convict surveillance systems struggled to provide supervision of thousands of criminals because of limited personnel, they were the beginnings of systematic central information keeping by the police. Such systems were plainly for the purposes of suppressing deviancy but can hardly be linked to changing social and economic relationships during the classic Industrial Revolution.

There is in the Edwardian period, however, one very clear example of the establishment of a system of general police surveillance for the purposes of control in a "society of strangers" – the licensing of motor cars and their drivers under the 1903 Motor Car Act. Cars were now to carry identifiable number plates which could be traced by the police in local county registries indicating the names and addresses of their owners. Motorists were singled out for special treatment because of the number of accidents caused by "furious driving", and the anonymity of men and women swathed in motoring gear and goggles, who could traverse several counties in a day. Their vehicles could easily outpace the police pounding the beat on foot, or even on bicycle (*Hansard* 1903b: columns 529–30, 977). However, it should be noted that these harbingers of industrial modernity were hardly members of the working classes. With the cheapest car costing £130 or £140, this was a hobby for the rich, and one of the few deviant motorists mentioned by name in the parliamentary debates on the Act was none other than the Prime Minister, Arthur Balfour (*Hansard* 1903a: column 1055). This form of surveillance was certainly a form of social control but at its inception it was hardly evidence of domination by elites. Again, the state was acting pluralistically rather than as an organ of class domination in any simplistic sense. Although locally based, the system's later centralisation was of signal importance.

The late Victorian and Edwardian periods also saw the origins of surveillance by the security services but, again, this does not appear to fit the model of internal social control. The enemy was initially not the lower orders but foreign agents opposed to the British state. The early 1880s saw the establishment of the Special Branch in the Metropolitan Police to gather information on Fenian terrorists, foreign anarchists, and later the suffragettes (Porter 1987: 86–125). Finally, in 1909, MI5 was set up to develop counter-intelligence work against suspected German spies, and to act behind enemy lines if an invasion of England was launched (Public Record Office. KV 1/1). During World War I the size of the counter-subversion forces increased markedly. MI5 grew from 14 officers and staff in July 1914 to 844 by the end of the war. Special Branch expanded from 114 in November 1914 to 700 (Porter 1987: 179–80). As before, what was important here was initially the threat to the British state, rather than any direct threat to the existence of the capitalist system in Britain.

### The Generalisation and Integration of Central-State Data Gathering in the Twentieth Century

In many ways the expansion of the Information State in Britain was a feature of the twentieth century, rather than of the preceding 100 years. It was certainly then that the citizen body and intellectuals began to grow uneasy at the nature of information gathering by central government, and its perceived threat to civil liberties. This reflected numerous factors but three perhaps need emphasising here – the sheer scale of the modern British citizen's interaction with the state; the intertwining of the external geo-political threat to the British state and the internal threat to British capitalism; and the impact of new technologies of information handling.

Whereas most English men and women in the Victorian period only came into the information net of the central state when they were born, married, or died, or on census night, this was not true of the following century. Nor did these earlier forms of surveillance usually entail any further interaction with the state as a result of the provision of the required information. The rise of the centralised Welfare State, however, meant that citizens increasingly had to go through a process of interaction with central government agents to claim benefits. Similarly, car ownership, originally the preserve of the rich, became a fact of life for most families, and the acquisition of a driving license one of the typical rites of passage of adolescence. Thus, when the 1903 Motor Car Act was passed there were 8,000 cars but by the 1970s there were 19 million cars on Britain's roads (Mitchel and Deane 1962: 230).

The expansion of the social service state also led to the elaboration of a state statistical service to facilitate the central planning of the provision of goods and services. The state had to become more active in information distribution, apprising citizens of the services available to them. The effective working of official publicity, in turn, necessitated that the state become even more active in information gathering. (Grant 1994; LeMahieu 1988) A Government Social Survey Department was established during World War II, and undertook surveys of patients in the wartime emergency hospitals, morale, public perceptions of shortages, and so on. This was later to combine with the GRO to form the Office of Population Censuses and Surveys in 1970, and then with other government statisticians in the Office for National Statistics in 1996. A number of major longitudinal surveys, such as the National Food Survey, the Family Expenditure Survey, the General Household Survey, and the Labour Force Survey, were added to the decennial census in the post-war period as means of gaining general social intelligence (Nissel 1987: 86–96).

At the same time, the taxation net widened inexorably, sweeping larger and larger numbers into ongoing contact with the Board Of Inland Revenue, and other taxing bodies (Middleton 1996: 512). This process was attended by increasing centralisation. The decentralised taxation system of the early-modern period had been carried over into the workings of the Victorian income tax. However, when Sir Robert Peel reintroduced the tax in 1842 he inserted a clause into the act authorising its collection by which taxpayers could elect to be assessed by special commissioners employed centrally by the Board of Inland Revenue. But this was not conceived in terms of the centralised control of taxpayers but as a means of liberating them from the scrutiny of local lay assessors, who might be their rivals in trade. It was not until the 1931 Finance Act that the appointment of all collectors of taxes in England and Wales was vested in the Inland Revenue, although the City of London was not assimilated in the same way until 1945. Even then, assessments were still in theory made locally by general commissioners until the passing of the Income Tax Management Act of 1964, which converted them into civil servants (Sabine 1966; 187). In other words, the creation of a centralised system of mass surveillance for taxation purposes was mainly a feature of the present century, despite the importance of such revenue collection for the pursuit of state policy.

Providing civil servants with personal details thus became ubiquitous, and one of the vexations of modern life. One needs to ask, therefore, whether the creation of central databases of information was necessitated by the rise of a "society of strangers", or whether the shift to central responsibility for performing these functions created that anonymity? When welfare provision, taxation, criminal detection, and so on, became centralised was it then that the flow of information simply became too great to be carried on in the informal settings of oral proceedings, as in the previous decentralised system? This might, in turn, be seen as leading to the creation of formal methods of information handling to simplify and depersonalize such transactions (Luhmann 1995). The "informatisation" of interactions in this manner also appears to have attended the increasing scale of commercial organisations in the same period, especially in the USA. In the larger corporation of the late nineteenth century, informal, oral relationships of the workshop were replaced by bureaucratic forms of reporting and information management (Yates 1989). It can be argued that it was the larger scale of interaction and communication which created anonymity, rather than anonymity which necessitated large scale organisation, whether at the level of the international corporation, or of the nation state.

It was also in the twentieth century that external threats to the British state became inexorably entwined with internal threats to capitalism. In the mid-Victorian period of imperial hegemony, British politicians could, on the whole, stand aloof from Continental entanglements, to concentrate on imperial aggrandisement. This was not a strategy which any twentieth-century British prime minister had the luxury of pursuing. With the establishment of foreign powers, especially the USSR and China, on the basis of communism, many of the international threats to the British state could be seen as meshing with internal opposition to capitalism. In the course of the twentieth century both the resources at the disposal of the security forces and Special Branch, and the range of internal targets to which they applied themselves, increased. During the inter-war period, and in the depths of the Cold War, fringe political parties, "fellow travellers", trade unionists, peace activists, and numerous other groups have become targets for surveillance (Deacon 1991). The distinction between geo-politics and internal class politics had been blurred. The other main focus of increased surveillance by the secret state, Northern Ireland, involved a threat to the integrity of the United Kingdom, rather than to capitalism.

Lastly, the development of information technologies, and the invention of the database, made access to personal information, and its integration, much easier. Anyone who has attempted historical record linkage will recognise the difficulties that the English state prior to the twentieth century had in maintaining comprehensive profiles of its citizens. The invention of machine tabulation by Herman Hollerith for the 1890 US censuses, a technology introduced into the British census in 1911, allowed census information to be pre-recorded on punched cards (Higgs 1996c). Reusing data for supplementary analysis became, therefore, a practical possibility, as the Jews in Nazi Germany found to their cost when the census was used to organise the Holocaust (Luebke and Milton 1994). This discovery of the database need not be seen as technological determinism, because the general take-up of Hollerith's invention in statistical bureaux across Europe appears to have been linked to the increase in information to be collected and analysed in censuses as a result of an international expansion in state intervention in society (Higgs 1997b: 171–4).

The development of electronic means of data storage and analysis after the Second World War, allowed these databases to be easily integrated. In 1969, for example, the responsibilities of the local vehicle licensing authorities were transferred to the Minister of Transport, and in 1973 work in connection with the licensing of drivers and motor vehicle registration and taxation, was centralised and computerised at the Driver and Vehicle Licensing Centre (DVLC) at Swansea (Public Record Office (no date): section 628/2/8). In 1969 the government had given the go-ahead to set up a Police National Computer (PNC), the computers purchased having the capacity to hold 40 million records, one for every adult in the country, and these were soon upgraded. By 1973 each of the 47 police forces in England and Wales had at least one terminal accessing the central database. The first information to be put on the PNC was the lists of the millions of cars and their owners held on computer at the DVLC. Other files included an index to all 3,250,000 finger prints kept by the National Fingerprint Unit; an index to all the criminal records held at the Central Criminal Records Office; a file of all those under suspended sentences; a list of disqualified drivers; a list of wanted and missing persons; and a stolen vehicle list (Manwaring-White 1983: 55–60). The British Information State had come of age.

## Conclusion

Thus, the emphasis placed by some sociologists on the period and processes of the Industrial Revolution in the formation of the Information State in England is misleading. The involvement of the central English state in the surveillance of the population pre-dated the modern period, if in a symbiotic relationship with local elites. The belief that early-modern communities in England were insulated from the state is erroneous. Similarly, most nineteenth-century state data collection in England prior to about the 1870s was not essentially for central purposes, or to facilitate the suppression of deviancy, but to facilitate individual self-help and ensure local political accountability. Population might be the unit of state analysis but individuals rather than the state were to make use of the knowledge gained. It was the period after about 1870 which saw the development of the use of central information gathering to facilitate the suppression of deviancy, but much of this effort was not directed to policing economic or social relationships but to deal with direct threats to the state. The central state's interest in using statistical data to manipulate populations as a whole also increased in this period but the application of statistics to policy was strictly limited.

The twentieth century emerges as the period of the true burgeoning of central state surveillance, linked to the provision of various forms of welfare benefits, taxation and technological change, and to increased interest in manipulating the characteristics of the population as a whole. In sum, it is difficult to argue that capitalist industrialisation led directly to increased central state surveillance, at least in the case of the "First Industrial Nation". The needs of the British state as state in a period of imperial crisis at the end of the nineteenth century, rather than as a bulwark of capitalism at the beginning of the century, appears more important in explaining the rise of the modern Information State. Rather than the direct control of deviancy, state surveillance can also be conceived as underpinning the creation of the civil, political and social rights envisaged by T H Marshall, although such rights, and related obligations, can plainly be seen as an indirect means of ensuring compliance with the norms implicit in the capitalist status quo via social amelioration and socialisation within a pluralist state. Such rights can thus be seen in terms of the construction of society and the citizen in a form suitable for the reproduction of capitalism as argued by Corrigan and Sayer. The question is, of course, whether the underlying norms of the liberal, capitalist society in England were not shared by the majority of the working classes. The rise of central state surveillance thus reveals a plurality of interlinking forces acting upon, through and from the state in a manner not unlike the broader overview of state activity provided recently by Michael Mann (1986; 1993).

Of course, none of this might necessarily invalidate the general applicability of a simple social control model of central state information gathering, as long as one sees England as an exception to the general Western rule. There is, perhaps, some truth in this, but if the First Industrial Nation is an exception to the industrialisation model of state surveillance, then it is not a model which can be applied without extensive caveats. Also, some of the factors which appear to make England an exception had very little to do with industrialisation and the functional needs of a capitalist society, and a great deal to do with geo-politics and the needs of the state *qua* state. It was not so much the nature of society which had changed but the nature of the state and the context, both internal and external, in which it operated.

## Note

[1] State information gathering as a means of mobilising power has been stressed by Anthony Giddens (Giddens 1987: 172–81), and Michael Mann (Mann 1993: 59–61). Both Giddens and Mann see such surveillance as a feature of the state from about the mid-eighteenth century (Giddens 1987: 179–80; Mann 1986: 527). Giddens has tended to see this activity in terms of social control to facilitate capitalist development (Giddens 1987: 181, 1995: 218). For central state surveillance as a means of replacing "traditional" forms of social control during industrialisation, see Christopher Dandeker 1990: 110–17; and James Rule 1973: 27–8. For the role of "population thinking" in extending the powers and claims of the state to direct society, see Foucault 1982, 1991; Kreager 1992; Patriarca 1996; Perrot and Woolf 1984.

## References

Bailey, Victor (1981). "Introduction", in Victor Bailey (ed.), *Policing and punishment in nineteenth century Britain*, London, Croom Helm.

Bartrip, Peter W.J. (1981). "Public opinion and law enforcement: the ticket-of-leave scares in mid-Victorian Britain", in Victor Bailey (ed.), *Policing and punishment in nineteenth century Britain*, London, Croom Helm.

Braddick, M. (1991), "State formation and social change in early modern England: a problem stated and approaches suggested", *Social History*, 16 pp. 1–17.

Braddick, M.J. (1994). *Parliamentary taxation in seventeenth-century England: local administration and response*, London, Boydell Press.

Braddick, M.J. (1996). *The nerves of state. Taxation and the financing of the English State 1558–1714*, Manchester, Manchester University Press.

Clarke, Peter (1972). "The end of laissez faire and the politics of cotton", *Historical Journal*, 15 pp. 493–512.

Committee on Data Protection (1978). *Report of the (Lindop) Committee on Data Protection*, British Parliamentary Papers Cmnd.7341.

Committee on identifying habitual criminals (1893–94). *Report of a committee appointed by the secretary of state to inquire into the best means available for identifying habitual criminals . . .* , British Parliamentary Papers 1893–94, LXXII, c.7263.

Corrigan, Philip and Derek Sayer (1991). *The Great Arch. English state formation as cultural revolution*, Oxford, Blackwell.

Critchley, T.A. (1978). *A history of police in England and Wales*, London, Constable.

Crook, David (1982). *Records of the general eyre*, London, HMSO.

Dandeker, Christopher (1990). *Surveillance, power and modernity. Bureaucracy and discipline from 1700 to the present day*, Cambridge, Polity Press.

Deacon, Richard (1991). *British Secret Service*, London, Grafton.

Donajgrodzki, A.P. (1977). "Social police' and the bureaucratic elite: a vision of order in the age of reform", in A.P. Donajgrodzki (ed.), *Social control in nineteenth century Britain*, London, Croom Helm, pp. 51–76.

Eastwood, David (1997). *Government and community in the English provinces, 1700–1870*, Basingstoke and London, Macmillan Press.

Elton, G.R. (1972). *Policy and police. The enforcement of the Reformation in the age of Thomas Cromwell*, Cambridge, Cambridge University Press.

Emsley, Clive (1991). *The English police. A political and social history*, Hemel Hempstead, Harvester Wheatsheaf.

Emy, H.V. (1973). *Liberals, radicals and social politics, 1892–1914*, Cambridge, Cambridge University Press.

Foucault, Michel (1982). "The subject and power", in Hubert L. Dreyfus and Paul Rabinow (eds), *Michel Foucault: beyond structuralism and hermeneutics, with an afterward by Michel Foucault*, Brighton, Harvester, pp. 208–26.

Foucault, Michel (1991). "Governmentality", in Graham Burchell, Colin Gordon and Peter Miller (eds), *The Foucault effect: studies in governmentality*, London, Harvester Wheatsheaf, pp. 87–104.

Fowler, Simon and William Spencer, *Army records for family historians*, London, PRO Publications.

General Register Office (1907). *68th annual report of the registrar general for 1905*, London, HMSO.

General Register Office (1911). *72nd annual report of the registrar general for 1909*, London, HMSO.

General Register Office (1916). *77th annual report of the registrar general for 1914*, London, HMSO.

Giddens, Anthony (1986). *The constitution of society. Outline of the theory of structuration*, Cambridge, Polity.

Giddens, Anthony (1987). *The nation-state and violence. Volume two of A contemporary critique of historical materialism,* Cambridge, Polity Press.

Giddens, Anthony (1995). *A contemporary critique of historical materialism,* Basingstoke and London, Macmillan Press.

Gilbert, Bentley B. (1966). *The evolution of national insurance in Great Britain,* London, Michael Joseph.

Gladstone, David (1999). *The twentieth-century Welfare State,* Basingstoke and London, Macmillan Press.

Grant, Mariel (1994). *Propogandaand the role of the state in inter-war Britain,* Oxford, Clarendon Press.

Griffiths, Paul, Adam Fox and Steve Hindle (1996). "Introduction", in Paul Griffiths, Adam Fox and Steve Hindle (eds), *The experience of authority in early modern England,* Basingstoke and London, Macmillan Press, pp. 1–9.

Glass, D.V. (1978). *Numbering the people. The eighteenth-century population controversy and the development of census and vital statistics in Britain,* London and New York, Gordon & Cremonesi.

Habermas, Jürgen (1992). *The structural transformation of the public sphere. An inquiry into a category of bourgeois society,* Cambridge, Polity Press.

Hall, J.A. (1985a). "Capstones and organisms: political forms and the triumph of capitalism", *Sociology,* 19(2) pp. 173–92.

Hall, J.A. (1985b). *Powers and liberties. The causes and consequences of the rise of the West,* Oxford, Basil Blackwell.

Hansard (1903a), *CXXII,* 7 May to 26 May 1903.

Hansard (1903b), *CXXV,* 8 July to 22 July 1903.

Harriss, Gerald (1993). "Political society and the growth of government in late medieval England", *Past and Present* 138 pp. 28–57.

Harris, José (1984). *Unemployment and politics. A study in English social policy 1886–1914,* Oxford, OUP.

Harris, José (1994). *Private lives, public spirit: Britain 1870–1914,* London, Penguin.

Harrison, Brian (1982). *Peaceable Kingdom. Stability and change in modern Britain,* Oxford, Oxford University Press.

Higgs, Edward (1989). *Making sense of the census. The manuscript returns for England and Wales, 1801–1901,* London, HMSO.

Higgs, Edward (1991). "Disease, febrile poisons, and statistics: the census as a medical survey, 1841–1911", *Social History of Medicine,* 4(3) pp. 465–78.

Higgs, Edward (1996a). "A cuckoo in the nest?: The origins of civil registration and state medical statistics in England and Wales", *Continuity and Change,* 11(1) pp. 115–34.

Higgs, Edward (1996b). "Citizen rights and nationhood: the genesis and functions of civil registration in 19th-century England and Wales as compared to France", *Jahrbuch Für Europäische Verwaltungsgeschichte,* 8 pp. 285–303.

Higgs, Edward (1996c). "The statistical Big Bang of 1911: ideology, technological innovation and the production of medical statistics", *Social History of Medicine,* 9(3) pp. 409–26.

Higgs, Edward (1997a). "From medieval erudition to information management: the evolution of the archival profession," *Archivum (Proceedings of the XIII International Congress on Archives, Beijing, 2–7 September 1996),* 43 pp. 136–44.

Higgs, Edward (1997b). "The determinants of technological innovation and dissemination: the case of machine computation and data processing in the General Register Office, 1837–1920", *Jahrbuch Für Europäische Verwaltungsgeschichte*, 9 pp. 161–77.

Hindle, Steve (2000). *The state and social change in early modern England, c.1550–1640*, London, Macmillan.

Houlbrooke, Ralph A. (1979). *Church courts and the people during the English reformation 1520–1570*, Oxford, Oxford University Press.

Hoyle, Richard (1994) *Tudor Taxation Records*, London, PRO Publications.

Ingram, Martin (1990). *Church courts, sex and marriages in England, 1570–1640*, Cambridge, Cambridge University Press.

Joyce, Patrick (1991). *Visions of the people. Industrial England and the question of class 1848–1914*, Cambridge, Cambridge University Press.

Jurkowski, M., C. Smith and D. Crook (1998). *Lay taxes in England and Wales 1188–1688*, London, PRO Publications.

Kidd, Alan (1999). *State, society and the poor in nineteenth-century England*. Basingstoke and London, Macmillan Press.

Kreager, Philip (1992). "Quand une population est-elleun nation? Quand une nation est-elle un état? La démographie et l'emergence d'un dilemme moderne, 1770–1870", *Population*, 6 pp. 1639–56.

LeMahieu, D.L. (1988). *A culture for democracy*, Oxford, Clarendon Press.

Lewis, Jane (1980). *The politics of motherhood. Child and maternal welfare in England, 1900–1939*, London, Croom Helm.

Luebke, David Martin and Sybil Milton (1994). "Locating the victim: an overview of census-taking, tabulation technology, and persecution in Nazi Germany", *IEEE Annals of the History of Computing*, 16(Fall) pp. 25–39.

Luhmann, Niklas (1995). *Social systems*, Stanford, Stanford University Press.

McIntosh, Marjorie Keniston (1998), *Controlling misbehaviour in England, 1370–1600*, Cambridge, Cambridge University Press.

Macfarlane, Alan (1978). *The origins of English individualism. The family, property and social transition*, Oxford, Blackwell Publishers.

Mann, Michael (1986). *The sources of social power. Volume I. A history of power from the beginning to A.D. 1760*, Cambridge, Cambridge University Press.

Mann, Michael (1993). *The sources of social power. Volume II. The rise of classes and nation-states, 1760–1914*, Cambridge, Cambridge University Press.

Manwaring-White, Sarah (1983). *The policing revolution*, Brighton, Harvester.

Marshall, T.H. (1994). "Citizenship and social class", in Bryan S. Turner and Peter Hamilton (eds), *Citizenship: critical concepts: Vol II*, London, Routledge, pp. 5–44.

Middleton, Roger (1996). *Government versus the Market*, Cambridge, Cambridge University Press.

Mitchel, B.R. and Phyllis Deane (1962). *Abstract of British Historical Statistics*, Cambridge, Cambridge University Press.

Nissel, Muriel (1987). *People count. A history of the General Register Office*. London, HMSO.

Parkhurst, P.G. (1962). *Ships of peace*, New Malden, P G Parkhurst.

Patriarca, Silvana (1996). *Numbers and nationhood. Writing statistics in nineteenth-century Italy*, Cambridge: Cambridge University Press.

Perkin, Harold (1989). *The rise of professional society. England since 1880*, London, Routledge.

Perrot, Jean-Claude and Stuart J. Woolf (1984). *State and statistics in France 1789–1815*, New York, Harwood Academic Publishers.

Philips, David (1977). *Crime and authority in Victorian England. The Black Country 1835–1860*, London, Croom Helm.

Philips, David (1980). "A new engine of power and authority': the institutionalisation of law-enforcing in England 1770–1830", in V. Gatrell, B. Lenman and G. Parker (eds), *Crime and the law: the social history of crime in Western Europe since 1500*, London, Europa Publications, pp. 155–89.

Porter, Bernard (1987). *The origins of the vigilant state. The London Metropolitan Police Special Branch before the First World War*, London, Weidenfeld and Nicolson.

Public Record Office. HO 144/566/A62042 Report of the Committee to Inquire into the Method of Identification of Criminals 1900.

Public Record Office. KV 1/1 Organisation of secret service: note prepared for the DMO.

Public Record Office. LAB 12/53 Committee appointed to consider sick leave at the Claims and Record Office, Kew.

Public Record Office. PIN 23/7 Organisation and initial complements outstational executive depts: Blackpool staff.

Public Record Office. RG 27/1 History of the Census of 1841.

Public Record Office. RG 28/201 Discontinuance of the National Registration Act, 1939: proceedings in Parliament.

Public Record Office. RG 29/1 Outward Treasury Letters.

Public Record Office (1963). *Guide to the contents of the Public Record Office. Volume I. Legal records, etc.*, London, HMSO.

Public Record Office (no date). *Current guide to the contents of the Public Record Office. Part I. Administrative Histories.*

Randeraad, Nico (1995). "Nineteenth-century population registers as statistical source and instrument of social control (Belgium, Italy and the Netherlands)", *Tijdschrift voor sociale geschiedenis*, 21 pp. 319–42.

Rodger, N.A.M. (1988). *Naval records for genealogists*, London, HMSO.

Rule, James B. (1973). *Private lives and public surveillance*, London, Allen Lane.

Sabine, B.E.V. (1966). *A history of the income tax*, London, Allen & Unwin.

Searle, G.R. (1971). *The quest for national efficiency. A study in British politics and political thought, 1899–1914*, Oxford, Basil Blackwell.

Sharpe, J.A. (1984). *Crime in early modern England 1550–1750*, London, Longman.

Slack, Paul (1988). *Poverty and policy in Tudor and Stuart England*, London, Longman.

Stenton, F.M. (1971). *Anglo Saxon England*, Oxford, Oxford University Press.

Strachan, Hew (1983). *European Armies and the conduct of war*, London, George Allen & Unwin.

Szreter, Simon (1991). "The GRO and the Public Health Movement in Britain, 1837–1914", *Social History of Medicine*, 4(3) pp. 435–63.

Szreter, Simon (1996). *Fertility, class and gender in Britain 1860–1940*, Cambridge, Cambridge University Press.

Tate, W.E. (1951). *The parish chest. A study of the records of parochial administration in England*, Cambridge, Cambridge University Press.

Taylor, David (1998). *Crime, policingand punishment in England, 1750–1914*. London, Macmillan Press.

Thane, Pat (1978). "Non-contributory versus insurance pensions 1878–1908", in Pat Thane (ed.), *The origins of British social policy*, London, Croom Helm, pp. 84–106.

Thane, Pat (1982). *The foundations of the Welfare State*, London, Longman.

Thane, Pat (1999). "The working class and state 'welfare' in Britain, 1880–1914", in David Gladstone (ed.), *Before Beveridge. Welfare before the Welfare State*, London, IEA Health and Welfare Unit, pp. 86–112.

Thompson. F.M.L. (1981). "Social control in Victorian Britain", *Economic History Review, Second Series*, 34(2) pp. 189–208.

Ward, W.R. (1953). *The English Land Tax in the Eighteenth Century*, Oxford, Oxford University Press.

Wiener, Martin J. (1990). *Reconstructing the criminal: culture, law and policy in England, 1830–1914*, Cambridge, Cambridge University Press.

Wrigley, E.A. and R.S. Schofield (1981). *The population history of England 1541–1871. A reconstruction*, London, Edward Arnold.

Yates, JoAnne (1989). *Control through communication: the rise of system in American management*, Baltimore, Johns Hopkins University Press.

**DGOS (Discussion Group On the State) 2001: "When and What Was the State?"**
**St Peter's, Oxford, 29–31 March 2001***

* The DGOS papers published here were put together, and edited by (in no particular order): Gavin Williams, St. Peter's Oxford and Steve Hindle. Warwick University, current Responsible Editors, Derek Sayer and York-Sum Wong, and the Editorial Assistant, Kimberly Mair.

# Gerald Aylmer and DGOS: In Memoriam

It was Philip Corrigan who first introduced me to Gerald Aylmer, sometime in the early 1980s. Gerald had not too long before moved from York University to St Peter's College, Oxford. He had sought out Philip, having read and been enormously excited by the latter's doctoral thesis on the nineteenth-century British civil service, which still sits in the stacks in Durham University Library. Philip and I were by then certainly talking about, but had probably not yet started writing, the book that became *The Great Arch.*

The wicker chair in the corner of the study, which had belonged to Napoleon in his exile on St Helena, lent an appropriate touch of surreality to the occasion. With characteristic grace, Gerald put me at my ease. Soon it seemed the most natural thing in the world that the Master of an Oxford College should be sitting down with two rebellious young men, who were not even proper historians, to plan a conference on the English state.

That conference was the first of what turned out to be twenty annual meetings of DGOS, as it became affectionately known – the Discussion Group on the State – held at St Peter's. Some things did change over the years. We gradually crept into the nineteenth and even the twentieth centuries, a move that Philip in particular had always resisted, fearing the tyranny of present-centeredness. We spread beyond the English state and the British Isles, entertaining papers not only on India and Singapore, places that plainly were constitutive of Englishness, but on Mexico, Hungary and Bohemia as well. At some point, too, it became unacceptable to smoke during our proceedings, and Patrick Wormald had to lay aside his pipe, I my cigarettes, and Gerald his tin of small cigars.

The essentials, however, always remained the same. The ground rules were those that the three of us – truth be told, most of them, and without our quite noticing it, were those that Gerald – had laid down for the first DGOS, way back when.

The conference would convene on a Thursday evening over drinks in Gerald's room, followed by dinner in hall, and an after dinner opening session. There were usually two morning sessions on the Friday, followed by lunch. The afternoon was free. Gerald was insistent on this. Those of us from the provinces usually hit the bookshops. There would be two evening sessions, finishing around 10.30, after which some combination of Philip, Gavin Williams and I, depending on who was there that year, would present a few bottles of wine on behalf of *The Journal of Historical Sociology.* After one or two sessions on the Saturday morning we would end, always, with a discussion as to whether we should convene the following year. Gerald was insistent on this too. A historian of institutions, he did not want DGOS to continue to meet, year after year, merely out of force of habit.

A number of oddities – each a small and unremarkable thing, in itself – made DGOS a rather unusual gathering in an increasingly professionalized academic world. To an outsider it might have appeared as quintessentially Oxford (the accents, the tweeds), and quaintly old-fashioned. Wreathed in tobacco smoke, out of place, out of time. To me, it was always quietly subversive. Not in any overtly political way, but upsetting of established forms and norms of doing things – not unlike Gerald himself.

The overall theme of all DGOS meetings was the English/British Sate from its earliest beginnings. What "the state" was and when "it" can be said to have come into existence were, of course, themselves topics of debate from first to last. Each conference would look at some particular facet of state (finance, foreign policy, centre and locality) or take as its topic "the state and . . ." (religion, identity, education). Unusually, DGOS transgressed the periodizations that scaffold not only historical narratives but also many of the routines of history as a discipline, cheerfully throwing together medievalists, early modernists, and modernists. The results were often entertaining – and always enlightening.

DGOS was a small, invited, and unadvertised conference, an informal discussion group. Most meetings involved between fifteen and twenty-five participants, around half of whom, in any given year, would have attended a DGOS meeting before – a judicious blend of continuity and novelty. Papers, which varied from little more than telegrammic lists of points for discussion to fully worked-up articles, were not formally presented, still less read out loud, and there were no pre-assigned discussants – and therefore little of the gladiatorial posturing – of the sort we are familiar with from North American professional meetings. Instead, the papers were circulated in advance, and authors contented themselves with talking, for no more than ten minutes in most cases, about what they had written. As often as not they would choose to address things they had thought of since.

The rest of each two-hour session would be taken up with round-table discussion. Most years, threads would emerge from one session and be taken up in others, so that by the end, instead of the usual series of discrete individual papers and responses, the conference had produced a collective and remarkably focused discussion of the theme for the year: a whole greater than the sum of its parts. Some years were better than other – which years were the best, of course, will vary, depending on who is doing the remembering – but when DGOS worked, which it usually did, you went away with far more than the packet of papers Gerald (or latterly Gavin) had mailed out from St Peter's a few weeks earlier.

Over the years, a long list of articles that began lift as papers for DGOS have been published in the *JHS*. Their authors include, among many others, Edmund Fryde, Patrick Wormald, Steven Ellis, Colin Richmond, Antoinette Burton – and of course Gerald Aylmer. Gerald also served from the beginning on our editorial board, where he was the most assiduous, generous, and sharp of reviewers. On a more personal level, DGOS has not only been – self-evidently – a crucible within which many of the ideas Philip Corrigan and I developed in *The Great Arch* were tempered, but equally a place where I have thought through the conundrums of nationality, identity, and historical memory which preoccupied me in *The Coasts of Bohemia*. Without Gerald Aylmer and DGOS I seriously doubt either book would have got written.

The papers presented here break one of Gerald's cardinal rules for DGOS, which was that the papers given at out meetings would never be published as a group. Initially, I did not understand why Gerald should be so adamant in this self-denying ordinance. DGOS, after all, typically brought together some of the most renowned authorities and some of the brightest younger scholars writing on English history. Any one of our meetings held out the promise of a very good book. But the reason, I soon learned, was that only this guarantte of non-publication, together with the rest of DGOS's non-public informalities, would ensure that participants would be prepared to speculate, to take risks, to venture out of their periods – would let their hair down. As usual, Gerald proved to be right.

Publishing the papers from what is likely the final DGOS in Gerald Aylmer's honour is the kind of backhanded compliment I think he would have appreciated. We thank all their authors for their willingness to participate in this tribute, which will, we hope, convey something of the flavour of a rather remarkable institution, in memory of a very remarkable man. Minor corrections aside, the papers are reproduced here exactly as they were circulated at the DGOS 2001 meeting, the twentieth, at St Peter's College, Oxford.

Derek Sayer
November 5, 2001

# "When/What was the English State: the Later Middle Ages?"

## COLIN RICHMOND

**i**

The paper comes in three unequal parts. First, I will offer a few remarks of an introductory kind occasioned by a reading of Rees Davies's Ford Lectures: *The First English Empire 1093–1343*, Michael Clanchy's circulated paper, and Steve Hindle's suggestion that I think about the state's relation to other forms of authority as well as about the history of governance without reference to the state. I should add that I am beginning to feel as John Berryman felt a short time before he jumped off that bridge: I know what I want to say but I am not sure I can be bothered to say it. Or rather because I still feel up to speaking I am not sure I want to write even though I know what I want to write. This is because as the mighty Auden once said with regard to poetry: history has not changed the world. And why, therefore, did I not become a postman or road-sweeper rather than historian? Or is it worthwhile historians still seeking the truth a world does not care about: and how many of them are continuing to do so rather than making money or careers? In other words, is history still a form of resistance to the world's lies, half-truths, and carelessness about getting the record right – as is poetry? What have these twenty sessions done to make a better world? Perhaps they have helped prevent it being worse. I comfort myself with that thought as I put before you a few ideas that might help us to ward off God's wrath for a little while longer.

Countries are not laid up in heaven says Rees, but peoples surely are: the Jews most obviously, yet does not every other people believe they are too – and notably the English, Chinese, and Americans. As regards the latter: are they not heard to speak of God's own country? States evidently are not laid up in heaven, for they come and go, as in the case of Wales and Vietnam, Poland and Israel, or come very late in the day, as in the case of the Ukraine and Slovakia, Italy and Germany, or they do not come at all for the Basques or Ruthenians, or come only just, as in the case of Belarus and the Baltic Republics, or arrive partially as in the case of Ireland, or arrive like Austria before a people does.

Are states a state of mind, as Rees quoting Katherine Simms asks us to believe? Countries he says are made in the hearts and minds of men and women. England was made in this manner so early and so well he maintains that its political culture could not be and perhaps never can be inclusive. I think we have to ask whose hearts and especially whose minds. Here Michael Clanchy's "Does Writing Constitute the State" becomes highly relevant. Michael is as usual undoubtedly right. Take German literature which all commentators agree became a national one in the forty odd years before 1800 and engendered, at any rate in the minds of intellectuals, the national consciousness which led to the resistance against Napoleon and the events of 1848, before Bismarck stepped in to create the wrong sort of German state. Croatia for instance was only made in the minds of a handful of intellectuals about 1900 and the same might be said of the Ukraine at about the same date, and of Palestine even later. England was in the mind of Bede before it was made and in Alfred's mind too while it was at the outset of its making. Whose mind was Scotland in before 1296? Ireland and Wales were in the minds and hearts of poets as Rees reminds us long before they featured in the minds of politicians-politicians not having hearts. A country may be in the hearts and minds of its people without being written down: see Hugh Brody's work on the hunter-gatherer Inuit or Carleton Coon's on the Pygmies.

Incidentally, as Brody demonstrates, it is the so-called settled farmers who are the unsettled and unsettling people always on the move to new lands. Hunters and gatherers stay put in their own country: the opposition of the English to the Welsh and Irish is to be noted in such a context. The restlessness of the farmer of fields is surely where we might look for the origins of capitalism – that scourge of the ecological balance of the world because it needs new fields and pastures green in order to strip them: capitalism's very existence being dependent on destroying one thing after another. The enemy of the land is the plough as Native Americans rightly maintained: ripping up the earth. Hunters and gatherers cannot strip their own country the way capitalists do. The state seems here to be the natural ally of farmers – allowing them to exploit the land. And of capitalism too as Rees points out: the developed state aids development and development is what wealth and capital accumu-lation is all about – progress is barely a concept to hunter-gatherers and not much more to pastoralists: more livestock is good one supposes but either cows and sheep arrive naturally or they are taken in warfare from others, which in the view of those who know about such societies is also a fairly natural state of affairs. There is an oddity here about the use of language because while Rees's sympathies are all with forests as against fields even he slips into capitalist linguistics, speaking of a jungle political culture in pre-English Ireland – is not the real political jungle where the fields not the forests are?

Development, progress, expansion, enterprise: dirty words in my vocabulary, an anti-capitalist, anti-Western World vocabulary. Think of new horizons as being a bad thing. All this shows how deep the problem is. The problem of the state goes back to the Neolithic Revolution. Or do you consider that far-fetched? It is surely easier to see in 2001 that we West Europeans took another wrong turning in the twelfth century (and another in the fourteenth-fifteenth centuries and yet another in the eighteenth) than it was even twenty or thirty years ago. We can all see now that the planet is being destroyed for profit. And surely we will get what we deserve. Why has the rest of the world fallen for it? Twenty or thirty years ago we were still being taught that the twelfth-century Renaissance, the Renaissance, the Enlightenment, the Industrial Revolution were all "good things". To get out of that way of thinking is not easy. To do an about-turn on the Whole of Our History requires an imaginative effort – to get out of a Humanistic Tradition which has dominated the modern discipline of History as it has dominated everything else – until the Holocaust has put beyond doubt the inadequacy of any humanistic interpretation of history. The Garden of Eden story now makes sense as Hugh Brody points out: that sweat of the brow business and all the digging and delving farmer Adam had to do was to say the least prophetic. The extinction of the Dodo follows from the Fall. Which means I suppose where and when farming began in the Middle East was the beginning of the end. I wish I knew something about China and India.

That was a longish meditation on Rees saying that we ought to have reservations about the state we all admire. Because we cannot seriously admire the English state any longer can we? Its precocity was fatal – not only to the Welsh and Irish (and by example to the Scots) but to the English themselves. That is a point I have been making for a little while now. Also it was fatal to the world. What was once proudly called the English Speaking World though only by the English Speaking World is now World Wide Business Inc. No need to spell all that out. The conquest of the world by a Business Management Ideology is as clear at Oxford University as it is in the Amazon Basin. In England it begins says Rees in tenth-century Wessex. Those vestiges of an earlier pastoral culture which once was the culture of all the British Isles were cleared away he says between the tenth and twelfth centuries. It surely began in that state which put itself on a war-footing in the ninth century to combat the Danes: Wessex. As it has often been said Wessex was the Prussia of England. Manorialization has to feature here. To support soldiers the free peasantry had to be exploited with new rigour. Document-keeping became secularised. Did not Eric John teach us all this? From Bookland to Domesday Book is no great step: it is in the logic of a conquering state which Wessex became in the tenth century. Hence the manorialization of the Free Peasantry of East Anglia, which Sir Frank Stenton set us onto, as well as of the Midlands, save that in the Midlands the oppression was so thorough-going we cannot observe what had happened there in Domesday as well as we can in Norfolk and Suffolk. No one doubts that the manor is an instrument of tyranny: the best evidence of which is the dovecot, perfect example of manorial, that is entrepreneurial exploitation. Anymore than anyone nowadays believes that agricultural improvement is anything other than the language of profiteering landowners: management-speak. We should have listened to John Clare rather than Eric Kerridge.

I suppose rich regions – rich farming regions that is – must have a good deal to do with the origins of states. Where does China begin? Marc Bloch taught us that France began in the Ile de France. On these grounds it is evident why Denmark dominated Scandinavia for so long. And why Wessex becomes England. Having the power to exploit the farmers who work the rich regions is critical, but that power is got because, according to Marc Bloch, big men will dominate the small, or as the Chinese proverb has it: the richer the land the stronger the power of the landlord. The big men of Wessex took over in the ninth century and having seen off the Danes stayed put when Wessex became England. So where are the heartlands of old England? Are they the same as they have ever been? Somewhere in the triangle between Bath, Winchester, and Kingston on Thames with London close at hand. Never beyond the Ribble. And not much or often beyond Mersey and Tees either. I was reminded of all this the other day when Alan Watkins in the *Independent* spoke of the demise of Welsh rugby being a consequence of the money being poured in to make the English game more professional. There was no hope for the Welsh because no money was going to South Wales. Period. Where the money is there the professionals, the entrepreneurs, will be: an obvious truth and not one to be neglected by historians. In the twelfth century it was the English who were professional, the Welsh and Irish, like the Cornish and Cumbrians before them, who were the amateurs. Not much money to be made in those hills, certainly not enough for tax inspectors to make a visit. There still is not: it is an example of the "advance" of the state, however, that the inspectors have visited the Davies farm in North Wales in the lifetime of its famous son. Is that not why the European Community is a rich man's racket: what will ever be done for outlying regions like Scotland and Sicily?

Which brings us back to English political and surely social inclusiveness. For all the much vaunted receptivity of the English to non-English persons, the Huguenot and Mazzini myth it might be called and the fixed idea that the English have of themselves as a liberal society, I am sure Rees is right. The English have never cared much for non-English folk and non-English ideas. Take Bede and the British. But what about the Danes you ask? I suppose that is the point: when did the English and the English state become exclusive? After the Danes and Normans had been incorporated? By the time of Geoffrey of Monmouth? After the loss of Normandy? Did the English Empire have to wait until the end of the Angevin one? Or was there an overlap? At any rate English chauvinism was well entrenched by 1300. Which is why the political elite thought the French could be taken on in the 1330s. Why bother with being King of Scotland when you were King of France.

Has there been too little When/What was the State in all this? If the English state of mind came first, then the English state itself (how does one describe it when all the terms one might use seem to apply to mentality as well as reality or actuality, including reality and actuality?), the English state as effective authority over those within its boundaries, grew steadily perhaps even quickly. Not gradually. By 1300 on any definition that state was in place. Try to think of anything which we consider contributes to a definition which is not present. As James Campbell demonstrated many years ago the late Anglo-Saxon state was more powerful, more coercively powerful than its Anglo-Norman and Angevin successors. Even law was present by 1066 though not I suppose in its mature (developed?) Common Law form: by the early thirteenth century that was certainly the case. And the Common Law was surely a powerful engine of the English state. Bureaucracy yes. An army no. Does a state have to have a standing army? I think no more than it has to have a standing navy – which England did not have until Samuel Pepys invented one. Perhaps this is where we come to Governance. When does the Gentry State come into being? Who with the king (under the king: does not seem quite the correct phrase) governed the late Anglo-Saxon state? Thegns and Earls? Thegns or Earls? Who governed the Anglo-Norman and Angevin states? King and barons or king, barons and knights? Magna Carta we were told at school could only have come about because of those knights from beyond the Trent. The Community of the Realm in the 1290s is already a parliamentary one, England a parliamentary state.

When precisely the state becomes all King and Gents is not, therefore, easy to determine, but let us settle for somewhere between the 1290s and the 1340s. Is it not war that cements the alliance between the king and the gentry, taxation and the need for soldiers being the key to an alliance which lasted until the king disappeared from the political scene? War against the Welsh and Scots, followed by war against France, followed by war against the international church (to which we will return), a war against Spain, wars against the Dutch, and a long-running war against the English peasantry from the fifteenth to the eighteenth century. In such a "scenario" the Wars of the Roses and the Civil War seem no more than "blips on the screen". There was no dismantlement of the state or anything close to it in either case: the so-called anarchy of the fifteenth century was a Tudor idea sufficiently utilitarian to have lasted until Bruce McFarlane dispatched it into eternal oblivion in the 1930s, which is why the Wars of the Roses are hardly mentioned in this paper. In the nineteenth century I suppose we might even say there was a war against the industrialized working class. And I have not even mentioned the Gentry's War on Women. Once we got into the Business State after 1979 we can call talk about Thatcher's Wars-one of which might be called the War of Billy Elliot's Feet: I mean the one against the Miners and other unionised workers. In 2001 the endeavour to create a Social State (between 1906 and 1979) also seems to have been a mere "blip".

## ii

Rees's book is subtitled *Power and Identities in the British Isles.* I am aware that it is an obvious point but the state is a great destroyer of identities while it seeks to create its own Identity. Take the United States and Native Americans or Russia and the Siberians or the USSR and the Islamic nations on its southern border. Take Wessex. It is not only the Welsh and Irish who suffered from the creation and expansion of Wessex. What about the Mercians, East Anglians, and Northumbrians? They had to go the way Elmet and Lindsey had gone before them. The pagans of the Isle of Wight had been entirely exterminated had they not? Where Wessex was concerned there had already been the kingdoms of Kent and Cornwall to eliminate. The price a conquering and developing state exacts on regional identities is horrific. Even our use of the word "region" is as a victor's euphemism to describe a vanished state. Every state is founded on genocide, for we need to recall that the definition of genocide includes cultural obliteration. Etruria where art thou? As for Troy: did it not go down like Jericho had? The Israelites destroyed the gods of how many peoples? Soviet Russia exterminated a peasant culture they called Kulak.

There may be more to an obvious point than meets the eye. Is ultimately all human "progress" regressive? Ecological disaster looms. It has been predictable (as has been said above) since Adam had to dig and delve. The infinite variety of Nature did not exclude Humankind. How infinitely varied were the tribes and peoples of the world at one time, that time being before the state, whether the state was Assyrian, Roman, Chinese, or Mayan. Prussian too: name the vanished peoples of the Baltic littoral. And the same goes for England. Perhaps not France: all those different pays and patois? Or Italy: all those ancient cities and stiff-necked countryfolk? Nor do regional identities go down without a fight (take the Lithuanians for example: a pagan peasantry sold down the river by their rulers for a mess of potage in Poland), nor do they do so overnight: is there a Breton as well as a Welshman in the audience? But regional identities and regional cultures do go down. Indeed even an English identity is disappearing under the onslaught of worldwide capitalism. Take Manchester United, once a football team from and of a particular part of one city in England, now a global enterprise for the sale of clothes and footwear. Take that old icon of decency, Sir Bobbie Charlton, and watch him sell his soul to the demon Profit. Faust where are you now? I have observed Poland do the same as Bobbie Charlton. In twelve years it has been ravished and is being ransacked by corporate business: almost better to have been partitioned or never to have been a state at all.

Are we witnessing the demise of states? They were not created in the mind of God, only in the minds of men and women. Good riddance some would say. Yet, it is not so simple. What appears to be happening is the craven submission of the state to supra-state businesses. The generation of wealth is at the heart of this. England is not what it was in that department and governments seem no longer willing to tax their wealthy citizens. (Have they ever been? All states follow the English model in one respect: they are or become Gentry States.) I suppose this means the end of the state as an end in itself. Good riddance all might say. Begone dear Hegel might be another phrase for it. As once the state replaced tribes and clans, families and peoples, now the state itself is being subsumed into a worldwide consortium of corporate businesses. Eat the same burger, wear the same trainers, and do not forget to wear your baseball hat back to front. And drink budweiser in Oxford. What happened to the sort of world Pierre-Jakez Helias described where villages had different identities at either end of a single street and not only were there different hats every five kilometres but hats for every occasion? The impoverishment of the world is to me an almost insupportable sadness.

Some of all this is to be discovered in Michael Clanchy's standardization as an aspect of the state: "the routinization of charisma" by means of writing. Think of form-filling: no novelty even to the clerks who compiled Domesday – how many pigs, chickens, and ducks. Clerks are of interest here but I think they are best dealt with when we come to look at the Church. Michael mentions the standardization of thinking. Which takes a long time. And one hopes is never complete. Nor is the state the only agency. The medieval church it seems to me was not very effective in standardizing belief. Yet conformity is a mark of the English mentality. The Lollards were few and among the influential were even fewer. The strength of the English state and conformism to the demands it made is always said to be one reason reformation never got anywhere in England once Henry V decided he needed the cooperation of the international church in his national enterprise in France and for his project of a United Europe. Is it the case that the "early-ness" of the English state accounts for the docility of the English? Perhaps, but what about 1381 and 1450 and the Pilgrimage of Grace? It seems to me, the English were in their most rebellious mode during the time when the Gentry State, in being since 1350, had not fully established itself, when husbandmen, yeomen, and those on the margins of gentility still were able to make their voices heard, their desires known. Come back Robin Hood: England's lost leader. After 1559 (or is it 1569?) the English Gentry have it absolutely all their own way.

Which is where the church comes in. The Anglican Church is notoriously the English Gentry at prayer. The gentry demolished the English branch of an international church in the course of the sixteenth century not quite in the teeth of popular opposition but almost. They used the apparatus of the state to achieve their purpose. And then they established a church after their own Little Englander hearts. Not without dispute among themselves, of course, although it was always a falling out among gentlemen, despite that stalwart son of a yeoman Oliver Cromwell. A pity he had no successor. After he had gone it was back to more of the same as before. Was the Commonwealth a lost opportunity? No more than the General Strike was. Or 1945 for that matter: oh why did they not nationalize the banks and shoot all the bank managers like my old Dad, voting Labour for the only time in his life in that year, suggested: he was a bank clerk. Back to 1536 and the Pilgrimage of Grace, another lost opportunity, arguably the last opportunity of getting rid of the bureaucrats at Westminster and the entrepreneurs of London, or at any rate of keeping at least England beyond Trent out of their Wessex-like clutches. I know I am old-fashioned but I continue to believe in the political, social, and above all cultural significance of the English Reformation. So far as When and What the State goes, surely the 1530s, however well prepared for over generations, saw such a gross augmentation of the power of those who ran the state that the state itself so to speak filled out into the spaces left vacant in men's minds. A magisterial state came into being. The magistrates became the unchallengeable cadre of the modern English state. Farewell to the clerks.

Those who have written on the secularisation of the English bureaucracy in the later Middle Ages (like Robin Storey and Ralph Griffiths) demonstrate that the game was already up by 1500 if not before. What Englishmen had any affection for Rome? Aside from John Fisher and a handful of Carthusians and Franciscan Obser-vants, hardly, as they say, a soul. Thomas More's family did not understand him and rightly so. If they did not, what chance have we? The magistracy rallied to the state and dumped the church. Richard Rich is a paradigm of the type. Still, you will ask, do we not find his type earlier, much earlier? What about Ranulph Flambard, bishop of Durham, and the mind behind Domesday Book? What about Roger bishop of Salisbury, and the brain behind the creation of the Exchequer? Above all there was Hubert Walter, innovative chancellor, and puppet archbishop of Canterbury. As Michael rightly reminds us the English church before and after Becket was an agency of the English state. Thomas More was no historian. If he had been he would have known not to sacrifice himself for a cause already lost in 1170. What happened in the 1530s was not that clerics changed but that the church did. The state no longer made use of churchmen, the church was no longer simply the church of England, it was a State Church, its clergy were state officials, civil servants we might call them, even if Gerald Aylmer did not. Or did he?

### iii

What about the promised later Middle Ages? What indeed. The Wars of the Roses, like the far more terrible years of political and economic dislocation in Edward II's reign, and those of not much less bitter political, economic, religious, and social disjunction between 1377 and 1413, did not endanger the security of the English state. They were, as I have suggested already, merely a "blip on the screen". The state had been in formation for too long by 1300 for them to be otherwise. The ease with which Edward III, Henry V, and even the tyro Henry VII dealt with the post-dislocation situation shows that "problems of state" were never the issue. Control of the state was.

Do we continue to subscribe to a view of an ever more sophisti-cated state, broadening its range, increasing its sweep? Hard to do so if the late Anglo-Saxon state was as James Campbell has described it. What happened after 1688? One feature of the English state has demanded recent attention. It was an Unexacting State. At any rate from the point of view of a gentleman. Was the English state's easy-going-ness, its artfulness, its artifices and devices for making the lives of the landed classes safe, especially its ability to get public service out of them on the cheap, was all that because it was so well formed at so early a stage in the history of European nation states? I recall that the phrase "self-government at the royal command" is relevant at this point. But there is more to it than that, for the question of obedience resurfaces at this point. Why are the English an obedient nation? Obedience is probably a better word than the one I have used above, docility. One can see how deeply that particularly English habit of mind dominates by taking suburban trains during the recent and continuing Railtrack Crisis. No one in my presence has echoed Dickens' Mr Lawrence Boythorn: "Twenty-five minutes late. Put the coachman to death". My furious comments about murderous managers and public lynchings are met with stony stares. What my fellow passengers have displayed is certainly docility (as well as stoicism). Is it not also obedience to the powers that be? Still, the English are not like the Germans of the *Kaiserreich*, too many of whom appear to have believed policemen ought to be highly thought of and that notices saying Keep Off The Grass were not there to be ignored. However: what of those those typically English notice-boards reading Keep Out? We do not tear them down. The sacredness of private property, not the sanctity of public spaces, is what the English have come to believe in. Back to Suburbia: it is the private lawn one must keep off. I have moved too far from a discussion of the state and arrived at identity. Or is that not far enough?

For: does a "national" identity precede the formation of the state, or does such an identity follow from the state's formation? The English came before England, the Germans before Germany, but modern Lithuania made the Lithuanians (I have seen it argued), and modern Israel has created Israelis. And what difference does it make to have had a state but to have lost it or to have had it taken from you? The Polish example is the best. Did the British have Britannia before it was taken from them? Did the Irish have Ireland? I am beginning to repeat myself I think. Time to stop: can this really be page eight? My point is that the early-ness of the English state, which we all agree comes after a sense of Englishness was in some educated minds and uneducated hearts, surely does lead to a particular sort of English identity. What the English state has contributed to English identity is it seems to me a belief in the efficacy of government, a feeling that government is good, and this almost emotional commitment to Westminster and Whitehall is what makes the English a peculiar as well as a patriotic people.

Their commitment is expressed in terms of place: 10 Downing Street as well as the White Cliffs of Dover. Or has been until very recently.

A coda on Jews and the English state. Medieval English Jews, being a people made to vanish from England by the servants of the "new" English state, are easily forgotten. Walking through "Old Jewry" the other day I found no trace of them apart from the name. Here in the twelfth century they were London's first financial experts, yet they get no mention in the most recent City of London guide to the famous square mile. No plaque marks where the great synagogue once stood. And there are no Jews in Rees's book. But the expulsion of the Jews in 1290 is certain proof of the existence of the English state. It is too late a date for some, nevertheless the 1290 expulsion was the first from any European "state" and that English "first" is surely all we need to demonstrate the "early-ness" of England. The persecution of the Jews, which preceded the Expulsion, is as much a clear indicator of English "political exclusiveness" as is their final banishment, clearer even than those wars against the Welsh, Irish, and Scots. The Scots, Irish, and Welsh contrived to keep their identity. The medieval English Jews were the first to have theirs stripped from them. The English state saw to that. As ethnic cleansings go it was thoroughly successful and fairly efficiently managed, if not quite as "humanely" achieved as not long ago an elderly English gentleman seated in Shakespeare's schoolroom at Stratford-on-Avon, where I happened to be lecturing on the Expulsion, declared to me it had been.

A final comment is about the withering away of the state. Look what happened when that was tried. Historians, as Rees says, have always been happiest with the idea of the state. Always? Can anyone remember their reading of Herodotus and Thucydides? Nonetheless, it is not easy to think of an alternative to the state. Not easy for historians to think of writing history without it. Not easy for an English historian, for whom the English state is synonymous with England. And all because of Alfred of Wessex: according to Michael Clanchy, in whom we undoubtedly trust. We are back with Wessex and When/What the State? For, if Wessex is England, and a Wessex mentality is at the core of English identity, as I believe they are, they have not entirely withered away, worldwide corporate business and its frightful mentality notwithstanding.

# "The State as Monarchical Commonwealth": "Tudor" England

## PATRICK COLLINSON

**A.** Straws in the wind of political discourse:
"The governement of the realme shall still contynew in all respects."
(William Cecil, Lord Burghley, January 1585): said in anticipation
of a temporarily vacant throne, in the event of Queen Elizabeth I
dying a sudden and violent death, the succession uncertain and
contested.

"I do not say the king shall send you an Empson and a Dudley,
but this I say, the King must not want". (Burghley's son, Robert
Cecil, Earl of Salisbury, in Parliament, 1610): meaning, the king in
the last resort may have to ride roughshod over the law to take what
he needs. Salus regis suprema lex?

But salus regis may be the same thing as salus populi. "The King
and his subjects are correlatives". "If I . . . make a separation
betwixt the King and the subject, I were unworthy to sit here".
(Salisbury again, in the 1610 Parliament.)

"This kingdom enjoyeth the blessings and benefits of an absolute
monarchy and of a free estate . . . Therefore let no man think liberty
and sovereignty incompatible . . . but rather like twins . . . the one
can hardly live without the other". (Thomas Hedley M.P. in the same
Parliament.)

**B.** Where in this sometimes cross-purposeful political discourse do
we find "the state"? In "the government of the realm", which must
continue, whatever happens? In the person of the King who must
not want? In the benign correlation of king and subject, the compatibility of liberty and sovereignty? Was this potential ideological
conflict bound to lead to an attempt (unsuccessful) at violent reso-
lution? Some historians suspect a paradox: it was the Hedley-like
determination to believe that there was no conflict, and certainly no
political/constitutional mechanism to deal with it if there was one,
the mechanism of adversarial politics, which led to civil war.

The ambition of generations of historians to understand this
"crisis of the constitution" (Juxon) and to explain the Civil War,
whether in political/constitutional or socio-economic terms, or as a
"war of religion", has meant that there has been, at least until
recently, very little discussion as to whether "the state" existed, or

was merely in gestation in the Tudor-Stuart period: although the "functional" explanation favoured by "revisionists" does raise the question. There has been little doubt that the post-1649 Commonwealth was a state, in a sense that the pre-1649 monarchy perhaps was not. Gerald Aylmer's study of the civil service between 1625 and 1642 was called "The King's Servants", its sequel, 1649–1660, "The State's Servants". Was it only between the decapitation of Charles I and the restoration of the monarchy in the person of his son that there was an English state?

Surely not: but the variety of terms used to define what prerevolutionary England was, politically and constitutionally, is suggestive of conceptual confusion, even evasion: "Tudor", can predicate "constitution" and "government" (especially Sir Geoffrey Elton), "regime" (see Penry Williams, but also American historians applying to 16th-century England a collectivist American model of the "making" of a presidential regime), "polity" (popular with recent historians), "commonwealth", as well, of course, as "realm" and "kingdom", but never, and certainly not in the title of any book I can think of, "state". One reason for that is certainly the near total absence of "state" in anything like our modern sense in the contemporary political lexicography. (Early modernists, perhaps in reaction against Marxism, may be unusually pernickety in disallowing a terminology – "class" the best-known example – which was foreign to their period. The counter-argument, of course, is that you don't have to know that you have a medical condition to have one.)

The Whiggishness which it is hard for early modernists to altogether eschew is challenged by the medievalists, as they read and rethink their Max Weber. Michael Clanchy tells us that a nation-state, like England, is structured (long before 1500 was, presumably, so structured) around a common ethnic identity and that its rulers/kings exercise authority (only?) "as embodiments of this identity". Rees Davies suggests that many of the powers we associate with the state were vested within society itself; and that there was not a state, distinct from society, but rather a king who was central within society. Sir Thomas Smith in the mid-16th century defined a commonwealth as "a society or common doing of a multitude of free men collected together and united by common accord and covenants among themselves, for the conservation of themselves as well in peace as in war." John Pocock thought that that was no more than an origins myth; and indeed Smith went on to insist on the absolute nature of the English monarchy and the impossibility of getting back to a time when it didn't exist. But the generous and as it were sociological approach to the state of Clanchy and Davies sets a question mark over Pocock's dismissiveness.

**C.** Clanchy and Davies both interpret German social theory in exploring the relation of something called "the state" to something else called "society", which was not perhaps something else at all. Early modern historians know about this possibly false dichotomy, and are themselves insisting on the social context of all politics, the politics inseparable from society itself. (See Steve Hindle, "The State and Social Change in Early Modern England".)

But historians of the politics of Tudor England, insofar as they are in search of the state, are equally concerned with another dichotomy: the "realm", or "commonwealth" as an entity to be imagined apart from the monarchy, in certain circumstances capable of expressing and exerting what were believed to be its own interests, exclusive of the monarchy, and even self-perpetuating. This was the extreme situation envisaged by Burghley in the first of our quotes. But in a less extreme, more "constitutional" sense self-perpetuating impersonality, opposed to the supposed vagaries of personal monarchy, Henry VII checking his own accounts, was at the heart of Geoffrey Elton's "Tudor Revolution in Government". (At this point one could wheel in Habermas but that would be an anachronistic irrelevance – but the currently popular notion of "civil society" may not be out of place.) It is open to Clanchy and Davies and perhaps others to tell us that we are grappling with a "question mal posée", even a non-question.

If state and monarch are seen as at least potentially separable, then the doctrine of "the king's two bodies" (not only a natural and mortal body but a body politic which never dies) is perhaps on its way to becoming the body politic in our modern sense. This is another way in which Weber's "routinization" of charisma may work. (See also Christopher Hill how "God's people" may be on its way to becoming "the people".)

In other words, a condition for the emergence of "the state" in early modern England may have been a degree of de-monarchisation, although not necessarily in the violent circumstances of the 1640s. Until this happened to any extent, could the state be said to have existed? The lack of any public accountability or scrutiny of the royal revenues may be the crux. When Charles I laid claim to Ship Money in the 1630s, and his subjects for the most part coughed up, they supposed that they were giving to the king, personally, what he claimed to be his: a simple case of "meum" and "tuum". As long as taxation was so understood, the level of taxation was likely, in the mutual interests of both government and governed, to be low. If the state was an impersonal, rather than personal, fiscal machine, can it be said to have arrived before the sequel to the Revolution of 1688–9, which was a series of wars financed in a different way from the past? Again, there was a precocious anticipation of this kind of fiscality in the conditions of the Civil War. But although lessons may have been taught, and learned – this, like the abolition of monarchy itself, was something which the Restoration put behind it.

**D.** We can make a list of the factors which in the 16th century reinforced (without of course inventing) the sense of the realm or commonwealth as a public thing (recalling the original, Old English meaning of "thing", preserved now only in Iceland):

1) The sheer growth of government itself (the ever swelling statute book; the numbers of J.P.s increasing fivefold in the course of the 16th century; the Privy Council emerging, post-1640, as effectively a corporate executive with its own records and secretariat, equivalent, really, to "the government"; the burgeoning business and competence of lesser (state?) functionaries – "men of business"): Elton's "Revolution in Government" best understood as not a revolution at all but a significant and incremental change happening not just in Thomas Cromwell's 1530s but for the remainder of the century.

2) The enhanced sense of nationhood, making 16th-century England an exceptionally good example of Anderson's "imagined communities"; the root-springs of which may be subdivided as:

i. Civic humanism, imbibed from pedagogical humanism: Cicero, above all, with his mantra ("De officiis") a man is not born for himself alone but for his parents, his children, "and for his country". Henry Peacham said that this text lay "tossed and torne in every Schoole".

ii. The "triumph of English": Richard Mulcaster (1582): "I honour the 'Latin', but I worship the 'English' ". Mulcaster's pupil Edmund Spenser asks: "Why a God's name may not we, as else the Greeks, have the kingdom of our own language?" Add here the standardisation of the language, not, of course, a total standardisation, but greatly enhanced by such texts as the Bible and the Book of Common Prayer.

iii. The Reformation: not so much as an "act of state" ("this realm of England is an empire") as an indigenisation of religious belief and sensibility, centred on the English Bible. Tyndale insists that God spoke to ancient Israel in their own language. Why not to us too? Ancient Israel becomes paradigmatic of English nationhood. Adrian Hastings suggests that the Bible provided "the original model of the nation". As we approach the 17th century, the Protestant, monarchical, English nation almost defines itself in terms of Anti-Catholicism (1588, 1605, 1623).

iv. A national enterprise, patriotically motivated, to rediscover England in time and space: the British History, critically reexamined and contested; "chorography", from Leland to Camden – and Michael Drayton's "Polyolbion" (celebrating "Albion's glorious Ile" – My England . . . for which I undertook this strange Herculean toyle); Saxton's "Atlas" (in which, according to Richard Helgerson, the English "for the first time took effective visual and conceptual possession of the physical kingdom in which they lived"); Hakluyt's "Principal Voyages of the English Nation", describing and celebrating an empire which did not yet exist.

v. The age-old fact (but in this period the conviction that it was age-old is also a kind of nation-defining myth) that England was a society defined by and living by its laws.

vi. The particular resonances of "commonwealth". "Commonwealth" may be a neutral term, as in Giles Fletcher's description of Muscovy, "Of the Russe common wealthe" (1591), or a piece of spin-doctoring, exposed by Thomas More when he wrote in "Utopia" that all commonwealths were conspiracies of the rich the better to enjoy their own private commodity. But it could also express a genuine and instrumental ideology of membership, participation, common interest. "Commonwealth" was interchangeable with "republic", at least in Latin: see Smith's "De Republica Anglorum". But there could be, and for the most part were, monarchical republics. Algernon Sidney wrote that "all monarchies in the world which are not purely barbarous and tyrannical, have ever been Commonwealths." His great uncle Philip Sidney (Arcadia) was not a republican in the modern sense. But he seems to have thought that monarchy was too important a matter to be left to monarchs.

3) The peculiar dynastic circumstances which hung over the English nation for two generations, much like the Cold War in our own time: the ever-threatening legacy of what Francis Bacon called "these barren princes", the longest-running succession crisis in history and also, from 1568 to 1587, an exclusion crisis. The role of gender too. For all the elaborate and colourful smoke-screen surrounding the Virgin Queen, her male servants said things they would not have said to or about a king, assumed her to be naturally lacking in some requisite skills or knowledge, and were conscious of pursuing life-long careers within an anomaly. All this, and above all the ever-present threat of a total vacuum of power, meant that under Elizabeth the nation-state could not in an unqualified way regard its monarch (in Michael Clanchy's words) as the embodiment of its identity. The identity might lack any obvious alternative embodiment, but the identity of the identity was all the

more selfconsciously felt and pronounced for that very reason. In a speech demanding the execution of Mary Queen of Scots, a Member of Parliament said: "Since the Queen in respect of her owne safety is not to bee induced hereunto, let us make petition shee will doe it in respect of our safety." A future archbishop of York thought "in conscience ought she to have a singuler care of her safetie, if not for her selfe sake yet at leaste for the furtherance of Gode's cause and stay of her countrye". ("Ought" was the operative word.)

Two important footnotes:

This was an extraordinary situation from which no "Whiggish" lessons need be drawn. But like those marooned schoolboys in *Lord of the Flies*, it was a situation which revealed what leading figures in the polity (indeed, the leading figure, Lord Burghley) were capable of: the citizens concealed within subjects.

What was a "question mal posée" (in the 1960s and 70s) was whether, when they spoke of their "country", early modern Englishmen meant England or their own county. Clearly they could mean either or both, not to speak of localities much smaller than the county. When William Camden in his "Britannia" passed on from London he took leave of his "dear native country".

**E.** Having got thus far, we face a serious discrepancy in recent understandings of the early modern English state, not so much of what it was as of its effectiveness.

To those who are fixated on "fiscal-military" definitions and understandings, for much of the 16th and 17th centuries the English state was either non-existent or singularly impotent. Jonathan Scott ("England's Troubles") has recently written of "the absence of effective state-building in the sixteenth century", and of "a weak post-medieval [rather than proto-modern] monarchy". This state was barely able to survive, and quite unable to exert itself effectively, in a century which knew only two or three years of peace. Only 1688 and what happened next made an imperial future possible. (But note, yet again, the exceptionality of the militarised and heavily taxed 1640s and 50s.)

But conversely what might be called a "little England" school of historians is deeply impressed by the effectiveness of the English state inside its own frontiers and limits (which of course were expanding within "these islands"). Michael Braddick ("State Formation in Early Modern England c.1550–1700") writes of "an active and increasingly intrusive state apparatus"; Keith Wrightson ("Earthly Necessities: Economic Lives in Early Modern Britain") (both books, like Scott, dated 2000, and add a third, Steve Hindle's

"State and Social Change") of "the exceptional capacity of English government when it chose to act decisively". Outstanding examples are the implementation of the Protestant Reformation (iconoclasm, uniformity) which met with a high level of compliance, and the introduction and development of the late Elizabethan Poor Law.

Braddick will not allow deliberate "state building", there were no blueprints, but he does permit "state formation". There was a state, but it consisted in a burgeoning network of offices exercising political power, related to the centre but not centrally located (or, we might add, financed). This is entirely consistent with Davies's view "from the medieval periphery": "many of the powers we associate with the state were vested within society itself and groups . . . within it." All we have to do is substitute church wardens for marcher lords and Irish chieftains.

So is "When/What was the State?" itself a badly put, unnecessary question?

# Issues and Agenda

## The Medieval State: The Tyranny of a Concept?*

### REES DAVIES

### The Case for "the Medieval State"

Medieval historians seem to be falling in love with the word "state", and with all that it implies. Such at least might be the conclusion to be drawn from the titles of some of the books they have published recently: such as James Given, *State and Society in Medieval Europe. Gwynedd and Languedoc under Outside Rule* (1990); James Campbell, *The Anglo-Saxon State* (2000), a collection of essays mainly of the 1990s on early England as "an elaborately organized state"; Matthew Innes's path-breaking *State and Society in the early middle ages: the middle Rhine valley 400–1000* (2000); and, most recently, a *festschrift*, edited by John Maddicott and David Palliser, presented to James Campbell under the title *The Medieval State* (2000). Given that the authors who have contributed to this latter volume classify Northumbria, Wessex, Brittany, and Scotland as states, it comes as no surprise that we now hear murmurs of the Pictish state. Where will it all end?

Or perhaps, more to the point, where and why has it all begun? To a certain extent it is no doubt a reaction against the infuriating condescension of historians of the modern period towards medieval polities and kingdoms. Such historians seem to subscribe to the view that since the word "state" did not acquire its "modern" connotations until the fifteenth or sixteenth centuries, then the state itself is a post-1500 phenomenon. This is, of course, to confuse words with concepts and phenomena. It parallels the attempt of modern historians (Ernest Gellner, Eric Hobsbawm and Benedict Anderson among them) to appropriate the word and concept of "nation" for their own exclusive use.

As with "nation", so with "state", its usage is to that extent a deliberate act of defiance by medieval historians (Reynolds, 1980, chap. I; Hastings, 1997; Davies, 1994). They are tired of the over-simplified, cut-out models of medieval society often presented as a backcloth to, and precursor of, the modern world. These models focus on images of "feudal anarchy" (the two words have become twinned), the apparent weakness of effective "public" power; the dominance of inter-personal bonds as the only meaningful "governmental" cement, the prominence of "universal" bodies, notably the empire and the papacy, and the absence of exclusive coercive power and modern notions of sovereignty which (so it is asserted) are of the essence of the modern state. There may be a measure of truth to these characteristics in certain parts of Europe at different periods in the middle ages; but overall they present a patronisingly over-simplified view of the character of medieval European social and political life and measure its nature by reference to modern criteria. Furthermore such notions are infected, consciously or otherwise, by a Whiggish and evolutionary assumption that the modern world saw the state- and nation-building which rescued Europe from the political fragmentation and economic backwardness of the middle ages. It is little wonder that medieval historians have now launched a counter-attack against such views, sometimes openly as in Patrick Wormald's splendid (but as yet unpublished) Denis Bethell Memorial Lecture, "Could there have been an early medieval 'State'?", more commonly by assuming, in their terminology and in the titles of their books, that there were indeed such states, as does Susan Reynolds in her powerful historiographical review of the issue (Reynolds, 1997).

But there is more to the prominence of the word "state" than the bruised susceptibilities of medieval historians. During the last twenty years the state has become the focus of historians in general. To cite the titles of a few recent monographs on the early modern period makes the point immediately: Thomas Ertman, *Birth of the Leviathan. Building States and Regimes in Medieval and Early Modern Europe* (1997); Steve Hindle, *The State and Social Change in Early Modern England 1550–1640* (2000); Michael Braddick, *State Formation in Early Modern England c.1550–1700* (2000). On the continent the multi-volumed co-operative enterprise organized by Jean-Philippe Genet and Wim Blockmans on *The Origins of the Modern State* bespeaks the same fascination. The "state" is clearly one of the favoured historiographical terms of the last decade or so.

Nor is this merely a matter of changing historiographical fashions. Historians are only following where political scientists and anthropologists have already led. Political scientists have shifted their attention increasingly from the study of political behaviour and the study of society as composed of fluid, overlapping, competing networks to a concern with the state itself as one of the key shapers of political discourse and social change. The dramatic events of 1989–90 served to accelerate this reorientation as questions about state, empires, nationalisms and ethnicities and the relationship between them began to dominate the international

political agenda. Nothing better proclaimed the new-found importance of the state than the title of a collection of essays published
in 1985, *Bringing the State Back In* (Evans, Ruescheymer, Skocpol
(1985). As for anthropologists, they – including Radcliffe Brown,
Meyer Fortes, Evans-Pritchard and Max Gluckman – had already
raised fundamental questions about the nature and structure of
political power on the basis of their field-work on African communities. They had talked of 'early' and 'proto' states, of stateless
societies, of segmentary states and so forth. And they had apparently no qualms about using the term 'state', however much they
encrusted it with qualifying adjectives.

Medieval historians were, on the whole, slow to follow suit.
England and France present an interesting contrast in this respect.
It is one of the touching features of English exceptionalism that
the unbroken existence of the English state, indeed of the English
nation-state, is regarded as so self-evidently the case and indeed
so much the most natural form of human political and social association that it requires no explanation or exposition, even when it
transmutes itself into the British state. It is a datum (Bentley,
1993). As Keith Robbins (1990, p. 375) has put it: 'British historians have rarely found it necessary to ask themselves questions
about the nature of the state whose history they were writing. . . .
Identity was rendered secure by insularity'. In France, the assault
of the *Annales* school on old-fashioned institutional and governmental history and its dismissal of political history as so much
transient froth – *histoire événementielle* in its dismissive phrase –
served a death-blow to those genres. In their place was created a
brave new world of *conjoncture, la longue durée* and a forbidding
battery of massive regional studies. The state and all its works were
deeply out of fashion. Political history has, it is true, begun to make
a come-back; but its focus is nowadays less on states and institutions, more on political culture, elite networks and the interplay
of political power and social influence in the localities. Bernard
Guenée has been particularly influential in this respect. It is
notable that his remarkable overview, originally published in
French in 1971 and translated into English in 1985 as *States and
Rulers in Later Medieval Europe*, is still far and away the best
introduction to the nature and practice of governance in western
Europe in the later middle ages.

So, we may confidently assert, the "state" is now, once again, a
fashionable term in the lexicon of medieval historians. And why
not? It is true that historians of different countries may differ as
to the appropriate chronology for the usage of the word. Some
historians of Anglo-Saxon England have become very assertive in
applying the word to the English kingdom from at least the tenth

century on what they concede is "a maximum view" of the evidence (Campbell, 2000). Historians of France offer a very different chronology: they refer to France up to 1200 as "a stateless society" (Geary, 1986), prefer the term "seignorial regime" to the term "state" (Barthélemy, 1993, pp. 390, 1020) and assert quite categorically that "the state was born 1280–1360" (Genet, 1990, p. 261). As to Germany or Italy, "state" would appear to be an inappropriate term for what Karl Leyser (1994, p. 141) has termed "a multi-centred and regional society". But these differences in time-scale are what we would expect in a continent as divers in its political forms as was medieval Europe. In any case the proponents of the medieval state brush aside such reservations: "A good deal of western Europe", so they assert, "was governed *throughout* [my italics] in polities that can *reasonably* [my italics] be called states" (Reynolds, 1997, p. 132).

It is, presumably, with that word "reasonably" that they would begin to defend the usage of the word "state". They would be in good company. A. P. d'Entreves, the historian of medieval political thought, took the view that "the common sense usage" of the term "state" covered a variety of governmental forms (1967, p. 24). Is it not obtuse academic pedantry to have reservations about the appropriateness of the term simply because its medieval equivalent, *status*, had a different set of connotations? And, in any case, well-established common usage makes a mockery of the verbal fastidiousness of some medieval historians. Don't we refer without qualms to the ancient or early state (Claessen and Skalnék, 1978), the Papal State, the Italian city-states and so forth? Do not several anthropologists give the "state" a life-span of at least 5,000 years in history as "the most inclusive organisation in the history of the species" (Skalnék, 1989, p. 2)? The argument has been put forcefully by H. J. M. Claessen: "There is no reason . . . to consider . . . the realm of the Aztecs, Manrya India, the Mongol Empire, . . . or the late Roman empire *qua* political structure as qualitatively different from, say, France, Spain or England in the fifteenth century. They were all states, varying from early to mature" (Skalnék, 1989, p. ix). Faced with such sweeping ecumenism of time and space, any reservations on the part of the medieval historian must appear petty-fogging and myopic.

But if we descend from such Olympian heights to more mundane issues (or should we call them "affairs of state"!) there are arguments enough to defend the use of the term "state" in a medieval context. We can start with some negative arguments. The first illusion we must dispel is that "only modern states are true states, or the only ones worth discussing" (Reynolds, 1997, p. 118). This whips the mat from under the certainties of modern historians and virtually entitles us to use the word "state" in any sense which we think consonant with medieval practice. It is surely a sensible approach historically, aligning words with contemporary social, political, economic etc. phenomena of the period in question. It bestows an almost endless elasticity on the word and concept and prevents us from comparing the medieval state with some ideal Weberian, modern, model of the phenomenon.

Furthermore such an approach allows us to exclude from our definition certain features which have come to be regarded as of the very essence of a modern state. Two examples may be cited. When modern historians talk of state-formation, two of the characteristics they often have in mind are the centralization of political and administrative power and the development of a sophisticated, differentiated and paid bureaucracy. Both features have indeed characterised earlier (e.g. the Roman) as well as modern states; but neither is a *sine qua non* for a state. The state's power can be expressed forcefully, if not perhaps with the same degree of routine penetration, in other ways. Secondly, from the days of Jean Bodin to those of John Austin, and indeed later, sovereignty has come to be seen as one of the hallmarks of the state. Medieval polities, so it was argued, could not qualify for this badge of honour since their control of their own powers was ultimately compromised by membership of universal entities, the papacy and the empire. Apart from the shoddy history involved in such claims, we are nowadays far less confident than we were in the heady days of national states of the meaningfulness of ideas of national sovereignty. In the days of multi-national corporations and the International Court of Justice claims to sovereignty seem increasingly doubtful, both practically and philosophically.

But the defence of the idea of the state and its moral authority in medieval times can be asserted in more positive terms. Beneath the reluctance to acknowledge the possibility of a medieval state often lay an unconscious and unspoken assumption: that medieval men and women were too intellectually immature to develop and articulate the "public" language of the state. It was, so it was argued, only with the recovery of Roman law in the twelfth century and the translation of Aristotle's *Politics* into Latin in the mid-thirteenth century that medieval society began to acquire the verbal and conceptual tools to develop a sophisticated understanding of the nature and responsibilities of political power and governance. This half-truth has long since been challenged by medieval historians. Thus Janet Nelson in a series of extraordinarily powerful studies has insisted, and demonstrated, what an advanced view of the responsibilities of rulers and of the moral standards of behaviour in public office is assumed in Carolingian capitularies and statements, such as the writings of Hincmar of Rheims and Nithard (Nelson, 1986, 1988). It is a point which, in a very different fashion, Maurice Powicke had made in a seminal article in 1936 entitled "Reflections on the Medieval State" (Powicke, 1936). In particular, Powicke – as in so many of his writings – wanted to bring the impact the medieval thought – what he called (p. 8) "the capacity for orderly and self-directed expression" . . . [and] to think and to think abstractly' – to bear on our study of medieval politics and power. In short, it was a plea for putting mind and thought back into the history of "that abstraction, the medieval state" (p. 4).

We may occasionally feel that Powicke strays into the realm of the ineffable and the mystical in his claims; but we have also begun to appreciate that the so-called "feudal world" – so often presented as ruthless and amoral in its codes of behaviour – was in fact governed by a values system other than that of force (*vis et voluntas*) and emotion (*ira et malevolentia*). It was underpinned by the concepts and practice of counsel and aid, honour and fidelity, consensual decision-making and ecclesiastically-proclaimed norms. Anyone who reads the *Song of Roland* or *Raoul of Cambrai* can see as much, just as the relationship between the community (Welsh *gwlad*) and lord or prince (Welsh *arglwydd*) was one of the abiding preoccupations of early Welsh medieval law (Smith, 1996). Just because the language of socio-political relations did not deploy the lexicon and concepts of public authority, we should not dismiss these societies as amoral in their political values and aspirations.

Indeed some of the statements which they made might prompt us to question our own assumptions about them. Thus when a mid-eleventh-century French chronicle deplored the decline of "public law" (van Caenegem, 1988, p. 180), he was at least acknowledging such a phenomenon. In Germany such terms were certainly alive and meaningful at the period: it was the declared aim "to consult the interests of the commonwealth and everyone within it" (Harding, 2002, p. 84). Such language became commonplace with the recovery of Latin learning and Roman law from the late eleventh century. It comes as no surprise to us that John of Salisbury, highly educated and well-read man that he was, should style the prince as a *persona publica* and refer to the *potestas publica* (Van Caenegem, 1988, p. 208); it is more revealing that an English chronicler, Ralph of Diss, could observe, *en passant* as it were, that there was "no public authority among the Irish" (Ralph de Diceto, 1876, p. 350). Both authors from very different vantage points clearly dwelt in a conceptual world where notions of "the public" and the transpersonal nature of authority were perfectly familiar. From that position it was indeed easy to escalate to a definition of a medieval polity which might even prove to be music to the ears of the theorist of the modern state;

Everything within the boundaries of his kingdom belongs to the king in respect both of protection (*protectio*) and jurisdiction and power (*jurisdictio et dominatio*), and in respect also of the fact that the king can give, receive and consume the property of all individual things, in the name of the public utility and the defence of his realm (*causa publicae utilitatis et defensionis regni sui*) (quoted in Dunbabin, 1988, p. 490)

It is in respect of assertions such as this one made in 1305 that French historians have located the birth of the modern state in the late thirteenth century. Edward I and his spokesmen were using very similar language in England – talking fulsomely of *necessitas* and *utilitas regni* and *dignitas coronae*. But English historians believe that the rhetoric of state power lagged several centuries behind the practice in England. It is *not* the historians of the twelfth and thirteenth centuries in England who have been the most vociferous defenders of the medieval state, but rather the historians of late Anglo-Saxon England. They have grounded their claims not in abstract theory or ideological claims, but in the remarkable powers of the late Old-English monarchy – in matters such as control of coinage and its regular reminting, the assessment and collection of a national land tax (the geld), the continued issuing of royal legislation (whereas elsewhere in Europe the practice had gone into decline), the use of the vernacular as an agency for the transmission of government command, the close symbiosis of locality and centre in the processes of government and jurisdiction, the exaction of an oath of allegiance from all free men and so forth. It is empirical claims such as these which have persuaded James Campbell to characterize England in the pre-Conquest period as "a formidably organised state" (Campbell, 2000). Patrick Wormald has gone a stage further, declaring England to be 'the oldest continuously functioning state in the world' (Wormald, 1999). But this claim is specific to England; it is the basis for asserting England's precociousness and individuality, *not* a formula to be applied to medieval Europe *tout court*.

There is a final point which needs to be made in this search for the applicability of the word "state" to medieval conditions: it is quite simply that we are in danger of employing the period-bound criteria of the later modern state inappropriately to earlier periods. That is why Michael Mann (1986–93) refers to a great diversity of state forms (*formes étatiques*) before 1800 or why Charles Tilly (1975) should identify several hundred *unités étatiques* in Europe of the *ancien regime*. Wim Blockmans in his general review likewise concluded that what we find in Europe up to the seventeenth century or later is "*une foule de petits états*" (Blockmans, 1993, p. 3). At one level one cannot but welcome the introduction of historical specificity to an issue so long dominated by theoretical model-building and extrapolations from the evidence of later modern state-forms (cf. "nation"). But there is, of course, a price to be paid. The word "state" becomes encrusted with modifications and qualifications, e.g. "statelike, proto- or near-states, unstable mini-states, miniature states, small, provincial states, regional states, city states, the extended state", to cite but a few examples from recent writing (Reynolds, 1997; van Caenegem, 1998; Genet, 1998). It is little wonder that Alan Harding has concluded that the state is "a permanently ambiguous concept" (Harding, 2002, p. 295).

## The Modern State and Misconstruing the Medieval Past

Historians are, of course, familiar with ambiguous terminology and with slippery concepts; it is part of the price they pay for employing everyday language rather than developing their own jargon. But the reservations which some medieval historians have periodically expressed about the use of the term "state" for the medieval world is not merely or even mainly a case of lexical fastidiousness; rather does it arise ultimately from a view of the dynamics of social and political authority, of power, in medieval society. The assault on "the concept of the state" has been multi-pronged. Perhaps the most comprehensive critique was that of Otto Brunner, though the impenetrability of his German and his Nazi associations greatly blunted the impact of his epoch-making *Land and Lordship* (1943, 1992). The State, so Brunner averred, "is a concept of the modern political world. But in the nineteenth century it became the universal normative concept for political forms of organization, for all peoples and periods" (Brunner, 1992, p. 95). American medievalists – far less fixated with the state than their English or even French counterparts – took up the cudgels. F. L. Cheyette in his provocatively entitled "The Invention of the State" asserted that Europe in the eleventh and twelfth centuries "lacked the realm of discourse, the set of distinctions that are the foundation of the modern state" (Cheyette, 1978, p. 156); Patrick Geary had no doubts about referring to pre-1200 France as "a stateless society" (Geary, 1986); and in a series of recent writings Tom Bisson has called in question the appropriateness for the early medieval period of notions such as "government", "politics" and "administration" preferring to concentrate on "lordship", "patrimonial domination", and "power" (Bisson, 1989, 1995).

Elsewhere the post-Weberian definition of the modern state seems increasingly ill at ease with the socio-political realities of the medieval world. Two contrasting experiences may serve to make the point. Timothy Reuter in an article of far-reaching importance has identified Germany as "a polycentric realm" and acknowledged that "the Crown was not seen as the sole source of legitimate authority" (Reuter, 1993, pp. 190, 210). If that was true of the *Reich*, it was *a fortiori* more so of central Europe. That is why Robert Evans has insisted that "before the notion of a 'State' existed there could be no writing about the State, historical or otherwise. . . . Only by the start of the *nineteenth century* [my italics] was the State come to be perceived in a modern sense in Central Europe' (Evans, 1993, p. 203). One could set beside this opinion the recent view of a historian of early Christian Ireland:

"In a bureaucratic polity, there is a state apparatus distinct from civil society; there are thus powers exercised upon society by the organs of the state. Early Irish kings, by contrast, worked with the powers available within society at large. There was not a state, distinct from society, but rather a king who was central within society, whose power was effective, partly because he deployed the same powers as did other lords, but to a higher degree" (Charles-Edwards, 2000, p. 523).

It is easy to dismiss such a comment as referring to an early and peripheral society. But as a working definition of the interplay of power and society it surely strikes a more credible note for much of the medieval world than do the king- or state-centred abstractions of modern political theory.

The same point was made recently in a historiographical review of recent writing on the French state: "The risk of such interpretations", so it contends, "is to give the impression of a past where the State has long since been everywhere" (A. Guery, 1997, p. 247). Exactly. Even in England where the effective power of the king was indeed remarkable and remarkably precocious, there is growing recognition that the character of the documentation and an over-concentration on the royal centre can unbalance our picture of the distribution of social and political power in the country and the relationship between them. Thus Timothy Reuter, while acknowledging that "by tenth-century standards England was a highly centralized state", criticizes (very much as did K. B. McFarlane in a different context) "our tendency to ruler-worship" and gently chides "English political medievalists" as "peculiarly state-fixated: the importance of the state in our history becomes self-reinforcing" (Reuter, 1993, p. 204; 1998, pp. 59, 62). These are charges which have also been made in important recent studies by Paul Hyams (2000) and Matthew Innes (2000, esp. pp. 6, 12, 41, 253). None of these historians denies the monumental achievement or reach of late Old-English kingship; but they do claim that "political power was claimed and negotiated through the collective action of a series of overlapping and interleaving groups on a hierarchy of public stages" (Innes, 2000, p. 140). In short, the nature and dynamics of the exercise of power needs to be located fully in its social and local contexts; abstracting that power from such contexts is in danger of distorting its character.

Such a critique can quickly escalate into a much more fundamental assault on the very notion of a state. No one conducted such an assault with such vigour as the late Philip Abrams in a coruscating article. For him the state, any state, was "an ideological project" which 'legitimated subjection and explains political and economic domination' (Abrams, 1988, pp. 75–76). The state was, and is, a construct, a rhetorical tool; in the famous words of Radcliffe-Brown, the anthropologist, it is "a source of mystification". Nor are these necessarily extreme positions: thus Michael Mann, one of the most influential of recent political sociologists, is convinced that "to monopolise norms is a route to power". The state for him is one of "the concepts and categories of meaning imposed upon sense perception" (Mann, 1986, I, p. 22). In short, we should beware of reifying the state, of accepting its own definition of, and apologia for, itself. We need to adopt a far more critical, and far less reverential, approach to it.

We can, and should, take the argument a step further. The state has been given far too privileged a rôle in the analyses of power in earlier societies. It is striking in this respect that French historians increasingly use the concept of social power (*puissance sociale*) in preference to a more one-dimensional "political" or "state power" in their analysis. This choice of vocabulary recognizes that many of the attributes and duties which characterize the activities of the modern state are widely diffused throughout society in the middle ages (Given, 1990, p. 6). Given the slowness and difficulty of communication, the absence of a large, differentiated civil service, and dependence on the gentry for the rule of the shires, "the pluralistic nature of power distribution" was inevitable (Lewis, 1996, at p. 51; cf. van Caenegem, 1988, p. 179; Harriss, 1993). Power, which in the modern world is claimed exclusively by the state, was shared by numerous corporations and individuals. This was true even in England: the governors of the shires were indeed agents of the king; but they were agents of the king precisely because they were the leaders of local society (cf. Braddick, 2001, pp. 15–16).

This is precisely where the documentation of the state can be misleading. Nowhere more so than in England, whose royal archives are unparalleled in their richness and continuity. We can thereby study "the English government at work" in remarkable detail and we cannot but be impressed by what we see. Impressed maybe; but misled also. We see society as it engaged with the power of kingship; what we do not see is the alternative nodal points of power – ideological, economic, social, and military-political (to adapt Michael Mann's taxonomy of the sources of social power) – which both bring into focus, and demonstrate the limits of, the nature of royal power. Robin Frame's pioneering studies of late medieval Ireland are singularly revealing in this respect (Frame, 1982, 1998). The full panoply of English central and local governmental institutions was introduced into English-controlled Ireland and, in spite of destruction in the events of 1922, has left a most impressive detritus of record evidence. So much so that F. W. Maitland could refer to Ireland as "little England beyond the sea". So it might have seemed through the eyes of the government records. In truth reality was otherwise, in English Ireland as well as in Ireland generally. Power, if it was to be effective, had to come to terms with the modalities of local power, with aristocratic regional power-bases, with the compromises of frontier societies, with the inevitable processes of acculturation, and so forth. It has been part of Frame's achievement to reveal the multiplex nature of power in English Ireland and in the process to shatter the monolithic presentation of the "state" world-picture as promoted by the administrations in Dublin and Westminster. "Unmasking the state" may, arguably, have been easier to achieve in Ireland because the ethnic fissure was so profoundly built into the personality of the country; but, ethnicity apart, the temptation of being seduced by the documentation of the "state" is a generally applicable message. History, it has often been observed, is the handmaid of authority; it serves no authority better than that of the state.

Beneath and beyond this unease with the usage of the word "state" lies a further concern, which may be described as both metaphysical and historical. The concern was clearly articulated by Marc Bloch in a short review in *Annales* in 1934. "I have difficulty in persuading myself that it is really legitimate to describe a State without having first tried to analyse the society on which it rested" (Bloch, 1934, p. 307). He was thereby broaching an issue which has recurrently vexed historians. Where Bloch was tentative about his doubts, Otto Brunner led a frontal assault on what he called "disjunctive political history" and on the practice of projecting nineteenth-century ideas – on state and society, legitimacy, public and private power – into a world to which they were not applicable (Brunner, 1992, pp. xxiii, xx, 95–99). This, so he claimed, was to create social abstractions and to analyse the power of medieval polities in the terminology of the modern state. The strength of the political and constitutional traditions in England has not in general been sympathetic to these reservations. But the tide of historiographical opinion is at least beginning to address the issue. Historians have begun to recognize – with Susan Reynolds taking a leading rôle in this re-orientation (Reynolds, 1984) – that the power of kings and lords was matched, or at least contained, by that of communities. Kings and lords had to operate with the grain of social and economic power; they did not have the will or the means to transform the social structure. It is not surprising that an early medieval historian should have concluded that 'our modern categories of "'state' and 'society' tend to collapse into each other" and that an early modern historian should concur, proclaiming that "society and the state are not separate; they interpenetrate with each other" (Innes, 2000, p. 12; Hindle, 2000, p. 19).

There is a retreat from "the state" in other directions also. Much has been made of Max Weber's famous definition of the state, especially of its control or monopoly of the legitimate use of physical force or violence. We might first notice that in the original Weber prefaces his statement with the word "Today"; he is not claiming universal validity for his definition. It is also, frankly, a claim which begs many questions for the medieval period. Most historic states have not possessed a monopoly of organized military force and many have not claimed it (Mann, 1986–93, I, p. 11). As to legitimacy, it is self-arrogated and self-proclaimed; it is, in Philip Abrams's phrase, "an ideological project". It calls upon divine providence and the specious formulae of feudal dependence to further its claims. In a world where the church was, in Richard Southern's phrase, "a compulsory society", the church was surely the best claimant to legitimacy and coercive control. It will simply not do to dismiss the power of the Pope as depending on moral authority and influence. After all, the fear of the hereafter is potentially the most potent form of coercive control! It is a very modern and secular argument to ask how many battalions the Pope has!

Nor is the monolithic, institutional self-image of "the state" any longer convincing; rather is it part of the mythology which it has created for itself. This is what Talcott Parsons meant when he referred to the state as "a practice not an apparatus, processes not institutions". It is a view which has been regularly echoed of late by sociologists, political scientists and historians. The state, comments Steven Hindle, is not a set of institutions, but a network of power relations which become institutionalized to a greater or lesser extent over time (Hindle, 2000, p. 19; cf. Braddick and Walter, 2000, p. 16). In such a context the concentration on the exclusive power of the state and its control of coercive processes is regularly in danger of underrating the plurality and overlapping context of sources of social power, of failing to recognize the interstitial and non-institutionalized forms of power, of overlooking the informal power structures of earlier times. We unwittingly smuggle into our assumptions the distinctions of modern discourse of the state, especially the separation of private and public, thereby forgetting Otto Gierke's famous dictum that "in their concept of *dominium*, rulership and ownership were blent" (Gierke, 1900, p. 88).

What this amounts to claiming is that the categories, assumptions and discourse of the post-1800 state, notably the nation-state, are not fully commensurate with the realities of the medieval world. The "state" was not the fully differentiated organisation which we take for granted today. Power was not necessarily delegated from some putative centre, as contemporary legal formulations (especially by royalist lawyers) and the habits of modern constitutional historians often suggest. Power in most pre-industrial societies was extensive and essentially federal, not unitary, hierarchical and centralist (Mann, 1986–93, I, p. 10). Charisma was not exclusively a royal prerogative. It could equally be claimed by an aristocracy which, as in Germany, defended and explained its power by reference to divine grace (Reuter, 1993, p. 97). It is the uniqueness of the English experience, not its normality, which stands out in this, as in so many other, respects.

So we return to the original question: is the word 'state' so infected with the connotations of its modern associations that its usage distorts our very understanding of medieval society and its power relationships? Otto Gierke's response to that question was categoric: "In order to understand an age whose way of thinking is different from our own, we must operate only with the concepts of that age" (quoted in Brunner, 1992, p. xlix, n. 23). It is certainly true that the Latin word *status* does not have the connotations of the modern term before the fifteenth century, that its advance thereafter is rather hesitant, and that it is not until the eighteenth century that it becomes "the master noun" of political argument (Skinner, 1989 (1), at p. 123). The truth was that there was "no satisfactory conceptual structure in which states could be discussed" in medieval thinking, no sustained exercise in conceptualising about government (Dunbabin, 1988, at pp. 478–9). This is not simply the absence of a word, but the lack of the very concept which the word might designate. In short, the universe of understanding would need to change to adopt such a word. As Quentin Skinner has noted: "The surest sign that a group or society has entered into the self-conscious possession of a new concept is that a corresponding vocabulary will be developed, a vocabulary which can then be used to pick out and discuss the concepts with consistency" (Skinner, 1989(2), at p. 8).

If we were to follow this course of action, we would certainly need to be very circumspect in our usage of the word "state". We surely need to analyse the contemporary language of political power and political action. After all, it is now much more fully recognized than it once was that language and concepts indicate one of the major constraints on conduct itself. That is of itself one very good reason for proceeding very cautiously indeed in our usage of the word "state", *tout court* as it were. Yet Gierke's purist position was ultimately untenable, as Otto Brunner himself recognized (Brunner, 1992, pp. 96–7). It is an example of the historian's recurrent dilemma: how can he write about a past society using its language and concepts without becoming incomprehensible to his current audience; but equally how can he employ current concepts and vocabulary, with all their attendant encrustations of meaning and their part in present-day conceptual schemes, without distorting and skewing the past?

## Is "Lordship" an Alternative?

There is, so it seems to me, ultimately no way in which this dilemma can be adequately resolved. It is part of the price we have to pay for wishing to study past societies in approachable, current terminology. But recognizing that there is indeed a problem might be the beginning of wisdom. Nor can we brush the problem under our conceptual mats by referring to "statelike", "near", or "proto-states", "unstable mini-states", etc. because all such qualifications assume some norm of a "state" against which they can be measured. The self-awareness that there is indeed an issue to be addressed might also make us aware of the conceptual booby-traps which the "state" sets for the unwary historian. It privileges one kind of authority – kingship or the state – at the expense of other sources of authority and power and thereby simplifies and distorts the past. It imposes images of hierarchy and delegated authority which are both much too clear-cut and construct the world on terms on which centralising power wished it to be understood. It often distorts and "tidies up" the past with its Whiggish, teleological concern with "state formation" as the master concept of historical narrative. As Timothy Reuter observes mordantly but accurately: "it is only because rulers . . . with hindsight seem to have been the drops around which the rain clouds of the modern states could form that they have been so readily invested with its qualities" (Reuter, 1993, p. 210).

Ideas such as 'state-formation' have their place; but too often they are allowed to dictate the terms of historical narrative, in particular by constraining and restricting our view of the complexity of power structures and divorcing the "state" artificially from the society in which it is located. The danger of a reified and undifferentiated abstraction such as "the state" is that it blunts our chronological and contextual sensitivities, and for the historian these must be primary. It is not whether we apply the label "state" or not which is important, but an awareness that the relationship of *a* state to what we call "civil society" is an ever-changing one from period to period; it is part of what W. G. Runciman called the process of "social selection", with all the notions of mutation implied in such a phrase (Runciman, 1993).

At the end of the day it is largely a matter of personal choice whether one chooses to deploy the word "state" in a medieval context. And the usage then may be restricted to time and place. Since it is, to some degree, a matter of choice, it may be appropriate to end this short paper on a personal note – or rather two personal notes. My original historical research was focussed on a large group of lordships which lay between the English kingdom on the one hand and native-ruled Wales on the other. They are known collectively as the March of Wales or as the Marcher lordships of Wales. They were seen from an early date as anomalous and cited as such by English lawyers. English royal writs were not served in these lordships; the king's justices did not visit them nor did English law extend to them; and – with one exception – royal taxes were not collected from them. They are often termed "private lordships" or "immunities"; but both those phrases posit – and privilege – a unitary, centralized power. Neither phrase is really applicable; rather do such phrases demonstrate an anxiety to read, and re-write, the past from the perspective of the modern state.

Indeed by almost any criteria we care to adopt the Marcher lordships were virtual "states". Their lords called themselves "lords royal"; they raised their own taxes and mustered their own armies; they exercised what they called "regal jurisdiction" and "with full liberty"; they referred to the inhabitants of their lordship as "their subjects"; they claimed and exercised the right to wage war, to issue letters of credence (letters of march, as they were called) and to arrange extradition treaties and associated matters with neighbouring lords. It is not surprising that a sixteenth-century commentator should characterize them as "the soveraigne governors of their tenants and peoples" (Davies, 1978, esp. chap. 10). It would surely be casuistical to exclude them from being at the very least considered for membership – honorary membership, maybe – of the roster of medieval states as often nowadays defined by historians. Instead they have been cast into the oubliette as anomalous appendages of the English state or as seignorial units caught in a time-warp and awaiting absorption into the English/British state.

This brings me to my second personal note. Part of the problem with the promiscuous use of the word "state", and the associations which have come to be encrusted around it, is that it imposes a particular interpretative scheme on the past. In particular it diverts attention from a much more central issue: that of the mode of the distribution of power and shifts within it across time. In short we need a tool of analysis which encompasses a unitary kingdom such as England or a polycentric realm such as the German *Reich*, the "city-states" of Italy and the Marcher lordships of Wales. The word that readily recommends itself and is contemporary in its usage is lordship, *dominium, seigneurie, Herrschaft*. If there is a 'master noun' in the medieval lexicon of power, it is surely this one.

It is a word which respects the continuum of power, rather than necessarily privileging one particular form of power, and seeing other manifestations of power as derogations from, or aspirations towards, this privileged power. It is a word which readily crossed the lips of medieval men and women, be it from the exalted levels of the lordship of God and the king through the whole gamut of relationships between "lord" and "man". It resonated conceptually with the essentially familial and personal view of authority (including the authority of the lord abbot over his *familia*) and with the image of a kingdom as ultimately a household or an honour.

"Lordship" is not a term which has found much favour in England, not least perhaps because of the strong constitutional, administrative and regnal nature of its historiography. Not surprisingly "lordship" has figured much more prominently in German historiography. Lordship is indeed seen as the essence of kingship. As Walter Schlesinger put it: "The king could not exercise immediate lordship over the men and subjects of the nobility. . . . The king, therefore, did not rule the entire territory in the same way a the modern state governs within is boundaries" (Schlesinger, 1968, p. 90). French historians have, likewise, to a considerable degree turned their backs on the grand histories of French "state" institutions. Some of their most formative studies have been great regional monographs in which social power (*puissance sociale*) occupies centre-stage. So it was that when Robert Boutruche launched his great two-volumed study of medieval society he pregnantly entitled in *Seigneurie et Feodalité*. "Lordship", he commented, "is the power to command, to compel and to exploit; it is also the right to exercise this power" (Boutruche, 1959–70, II, p. 80). It is a dictum that is analogous to Max Weber's famous comment on the modern state. Nor would it have surprised contemporaries. When the peasants of medieval Roussillon commented that "a lord can and should *compel his subjects*" (my italics), they were identifying the coercive power and the acknowledged legitimacy of that coercive power which modern political scientists assert is the essence of "the state" (Bloch, 1966, p. 79).

Lordship, it might be objected, is relative; so is kingliness, kingship and the state (hence the qualifying adjectives with which they are often encrusted). Royal lordship is one form of lordship and eventually in many western European countries *became* the dominant one, at an earlier or later date. It then constructed a theory that it was the only "public" lordship and that other lordships were somehow "private", and derivative of and dependent upon royal lordship/state power. Studying how, when, and to what extent this happened is certainly part of the historian's business; it is not necessarily helped by positing a state or the state as a universal datum. In a rather different context K. B. McFarlane commented acidly that English historians have been "King's Friends" (McFarlane, 1973, p. 2); by the same token I would be tempted to suggest that they have also been perhaps too uncritically friends of the state and of state-formation.

Part of the appeal of the concept of lordship, *dominium*, is its very elasticity. It does not necessarily privilege one expression or process of power as against all others. Since politics and governance were of necessity woven into the texture of local social relationship, it is crucial to locate power fully in its social and ideological context. Studies of the "state" often seem to give the "state", on the contrary, an autonomy and a directive role which abstract it from society; it becomes a free-floating superstructure of power.

This is not, at the end of the day, a plea to exorcise the word "state" from medieval history or to replace it by what many will see as the hopelessly flabby concept of lordship. There is at the end of the day no simple or unilateral solution, any more than the word "feudal" can be banished by an unlikely consensus among professional academic historians. But we do need to be alert to what social anthropologists call the 'prior category assumptions' which we smuggle into our thinking about the past. We should be alert to the possibility that these assumptions confine and even distort our understanding of past societies. Admirable as it is to counter the condescension of posterity towards the medieval world, it does no service to that world to forget that the past is indeed a foreign country and that its conceptual world is not necessarily commensurate with ours. That is, to coin a phrase, the state we are in.

## Notes

\* The title of this paper deliberately evokes the title of a paper long since familiar to medieval historians, E. A. R. Brown, "The Tyranny of a

Construct: Feudalism and Historians of Medieval Europe", *American Historical Review* 79 (1974), 1063–88 and frequently republished. But there is a crucial difference: I am posing a question (hence the question mark) rather than making an assertion or seeking to demolish a current historiographical concept. The present paper is a much revised version of one originally prepared for the annual workshop on the English State held at St Peter's College, Oxford in March 2001. A summary of the original paper was published in the *Journal of Historical Sociology* 15 (2002), pp. 71–74.

## References

Abrams, Philip (1988) "Notes on the Difficulty of Studying the State", in *Journal of Historical Sociology* 1 (1988), 58–90.

Anderson, Benedict (1983) *Imagined Communities. Reflections on the Origins and Spread of Nationalism.* Verso: London.

Barthélemy, Dominique (1993) *La société dans le comté de Vendôme de l'an mil au XVIᵉ siècle.* Fayard: Paris.

Bentley, Michael (1993) "The British State and its Historiography" in W. Blockmans and J. P. Genet (eds.) *Visions sur le développement des états européens. Théories et historiographies de l'état moderne.* Ecole française de Rome: Rome.

Bisson, T. M. (1989) review of Judith A. Green, "The Government of England under Henry I", *Speculum* 64 (1989), 436–38.

Bisson, T. M. (1995), "Medieval Lordship", *Speculum* 70 (1995), 743–59

Bloch, Marc (1934) 'La France au XIIIe siècle (review-note), *Annales d'histoire économique et sociale*, 6, 307.

Bloch, Marc (1966), *French Rural History. An Essay on its basic characteristics* Routledge: London.

Blockmans, Wim (1993) "Les origines des états modernes en Europe 13–18 siècles: état de la question et perspectives", in W. Blockmans and J. P. Genet (eds.), *Visions sur le développement de l'état moderne* Ecole française de Rome: Rome.

Boutruche, Robert (1959–70) *Seigneurie et féodalité.* 2 vols. Aubier: Paris

Braddick, Michael (2000) *State Formation in Early Modern England c.1550–1700* Cambridge University Press: Cambridge.

Braddick, M. J. and Walter J. (2001) (eds.) *Negotiating Power in Early Modern Society. Order, Hierarchy and Subordination in Britain and Ireland.* Cambridge University Press: Cambridge.

Brunner, Otto (1943, 1992) *Land and Lordship: structures of government in medieval Austria*, trans. Howard Kaminsky and James Meltor. U. of Pennsylvania Press: Philadelphia.

Campbell, James (2000) *The Anglo-Saxon State.* Hambledon Press: London.

Charles-Edwards, Thomas (2000) *Early Christian Ireland.* Cambridge University Press: Cambridge.

Cheyette, F. L. (1978) "The Invention of the State" in *Essays on Medieval Civilization. The Walter Prescott Webb Memorial Lectures*, ed. B. K. Lackner and K. R. Philip, pp. 143–78. University of Texas Press: Austin.

Claessen, Henri and Skalnék, Peter, eds. (1978) *The Early State.* Mouton: The Hague.

Davies, R. R. (1978) *Lordship and Society in the March of Wales 1282–1400.* Clarendon Press, Oxford.

Davies, R. R. (1994) "The Peoples of Britain and Ireland 1100–1400. 1. Identities", *Transactions of the Royal Historical Society*, 6th series, vol. 4 (1994), 1 20.

d'Entreves, A. P. (1967) *The Notion of the State: an introduction to political theory*. Clarendon Press: Oxford.

Dunbabin, Jean (1988) "Government (c.1150–1450)" in *Cambridge History of Medieval Political Though*, ed. J. H. Burns, pp. 477–519. Cambridge UP: Cambridge.

Diceto, Ralph of (1876) *Opera Historica* ed. W. Stubbs. 2 vols. Rolls Series: London.

Ertman, Thomas (1997) *Birth of the Leviathan. Building States and Regimes in Medieval and Early Modern Europe*. Cambridge UP: Cambridge.

Evans, P. B., Rusescheymer, D., and Skocpol, T. (eds.) (1985) *Bringing the State back in*. Cambridge UP: Cambridge.

Evans, R. J. W. (1993) "Historians and the State in the Habsburg Lands", in Blockmans, Wim and Genet, Jean-Philippe (eds.), *Visions sur le développement des états européens*. Rome.

Frame, Robin (1982) *English Lordship in Ireland 1318–61*. Oxford UP: Oxford.

Frame, Robin (1998) *Ireland and Britain 1170–1450*. Hambledon: London

Geary, Patrick (1986) "Vivre en conflit dans une France sans état, 1050–1200", *Annales ESC* 41, pp. 1107–33.

Gellner, Ernest (1983) *Nations and Nationalism*. Basil Blackwell, Oxford

Genet, Jean-Philippe (1990) "L'état moderne: un modèle opératoire", in J.-P. Genet (ed.), *L'état moderne. Genèse, bilans et perspectives*. CNRS: Paris.

Genet, Jean-Philippe (1998) "Politics: theory and practice", in *New Cambridge Medieval History*, vol. 7 (1415–1500), ed. Christopher Allmand. Cambridge UP: Cambridge.

Gierke, Otto (1900) *Political Theories of the Middle Ages*, trans. F. W. Maitland. Cambridge UP: Cambridge.

Given, James (1990) *State and Society in Medieval Europe. Gwynedd and Languedoc under Outside Rule* (1990). Cornell University Press: Ithaca.

Guenée, Bernard (1971, 1985), *L'Occident aux 14ᵉ et 15ᵉ siècles. Les états*, translated as *States and Rulers in Later Medieval Europe*. Blackwell: Oxford.

Guery, A. (1997) "L'historien, la crise et l'Etat", *Annales. Histoire, Sciences Sociales* 52, pp. 233–57.

Harding, Alan (2002), *Medieval Law and the foundations of the State*. Oxford UP: Oxford.

Harriss, Gerald (1993) "Political Society and the Growth of Government in Late Medieval England", *Past and Present*, 138, pp. 143–78.

Hastings, Adrian (1997) *The Construction of Nationhood. Ethnicity, Religion and Nationalism*. Cambridge UP: Cambridge.

Hindle, Steve (2000) *The State and Social Change in Early Modern England 1550–1640*. Palgrave: Basingstoke.

Hobsbawm, E. J. (1990) *Nations and Nationalism since 1780* (1990). Cambridge UP: Cambridge.

Hyams, Paul (2001) "Feud and the State in Late Anglo-Saxon England", *Journal of British Studies* 40 (2001), 1–44.

Innes, Matthew (2000) *State and Society in the early middle ages: the middle Rhine valley 400–1000*. Cambridge UP: Cambridge.

Leyser, Karl (1994) *Communication and Power in Medieval Europe*. Hambledon: London.

Lewis, P. S. (1996) "Reflections on the role of royal clientèles in the construction of the French monarchy (mid-14th–end 15th centuries)", in Neithard Bulst et al. (eds.), L'état ou le roi. Les fondations de la modernité monarchique en France Maison de sciences de l'homme: Paris.

McFarlane, K. B. (1973) The Nobility of Later Medieval England. Clarendon Press: Oxford.

Maddicott, J. R., and Palliser, D. (eds.) (2000) The Medieval State. Essays presented to James Campbell. Hambledon Press: London.

Mann, Michael (1986–93) The Sources of Social Power. 2 vols. Cambridge UP: Cambridge.

Nelson, Janet (1986) Politics and Ritual in Early Medieval Europe. Hambledon: London.

Nelson, Janet (1988) "Kingship and Empire", in Cambridge History of Medieval Political Thought, ed. J. H. Burns, pp. 211–51. Cambridge: Cambridge University Press.

Powicke, F. M. (1937) "Reflections on the Medieval State", in Transactions of the Royal Historical Society, 4th series, 19, pp. 1–18.

Reynolds, Susan (1984) Kingdoms and Communities in Western Europe 900–1300. Clarendon Press: Oxford.

Reynolds, Susan (1997) "The Historiography of the Medieval State", in M. Bentley (ed.), A Companion to Historiography. Routledge: London.

Reuter, Timothy (1993) "The Medieval German Sonderweg? The Empire and its Rulers in the High Middle Ages", in Kings and Kingship in Medieval Europe, ed. Anne J. Duggan, pp. 179–211. King's College, London: London.

Reuter, Timothy (1998) "The Making of England and Germany 850–1050: Points of Comparison and Difference", in Medieval Europeans: Studies in ethnic identity and national perspectives in medieval Europe, ed. Alfred Smyth, pp. 53–70. Macmillan: Basingstoke.

Robbins, Keith (190) "National Identity and History: Past, Present and Future", History 75, pp. 369–87.

Runciman, W. G. (1993) "Origins of the Modern State and the Theory of Social Selection", in Wim Blockmans and Jean-Philippe Genet (eds.), Visions sur le développement des états européens. Rome.

Schlesinger, Walter (1968) "Lord and Follower in Germanic Institutional History", in Lordship and Community in Medieval Europe. Selected Readings, ed. F. L. Cheyette. Holt, Rinehart and Winston: New York.

Skalnék, Peter (ed.) (1989) Outwitting the State. Transaction Publishers: New Brunswick.

Skinner, Quentin (1989a) "Language and Political Change", in Political Innovation and Conceptual Change, ed. Terence Ball et al., pp. 6–22. Cambridge University Press: Cambridge.

Skinner, Quentin (1989b) "The State", in ibid., pp. 90–131.

Smith, J. Beverley (1996) "Gwlad ac Arglwydd", in Beirdd a Thywysogion, ed. Morfydd E. Owen and Brynley F. Roberts, pp. 237–58. University of Wales Press: Cardiff.

Tilly, Charles (ed.) (1975) The Formation of National States in Western Europe Princeton UP: Princeton.

van Caenegem, R. C. (1988) "Government, law and society (c.750–c.1150)", in Cambridge History of Medieval Political Thought, ed. J. H. Burns, pp. 174–210. Cambridge University Press: Cambridge.

Weber, Max (1991) From Max Weber. Essays in Sociology, translated and edited by H. H. Gerth and C. Wright Mills. Routledge: London.

Wormald, Patrick "Could there have been an early medieval 'State'?" Unpublished Denis Bethell Memorial Lecture, Dublin.

Wormald, Patrick (1999) *The Making of English Law: King Alfred to the Twelfth Century. Vol. I. Legislation and its limits.* Blackwell: Oxford.

# Responses

# There were States in Medieval Europe: A Response to Rees Davies

## SUSAN REYNOLDS

Rees Davies's questioning of the current fashion for talking about medieval states (Davies, 2003) is characteristically stimulating and persuasive. Not surprisingly, in view of his references to my essay on the historiography of the medieval state (Reynolds, 1997), I nevertheless find it not persuasive enough.[1] I agree with a lot of what he says but the main thrust of his argument seems to me to perpetuate the tendency of medieval historians to isolate themselves from discussions from which they could profit and to which they could have much to contribute.

I quite agree in deploring the fashion for using the word state in discussions of medieval polities without any explanation of the category to which the supposed state belongs and why it belongs there. I also quite agree that we should not go back to the old political history and its concentration on high politics or join in the teleological search for the origins of modern states. But politics and power matter. Historians who live in societies in which power is exercised in part through states have reason to think about the characteristics of this kind of polity, whether states existed in the periods they study, and the difference between societies with and without states. In other words, we should neither blindly follow the fashion for using the word nor stubbornly avoid it, but, as Davies suggests, think about our "prior category assumptions" when we use it.

Some historians who specify what they see as the defining characteristics of states in their period seem to start from what they think was new or important in that period, as do the early modernists who focus on absolutism, standing armies, regular taxes, bureaucracies, or professional diplomacy, or the later modernists who emphasise communications, education systems, economic policies, and the general contrast with the "traditional" states of the Ancien Régime. All this is fair enough in describing the characteristics of particular sorts of states, though the novelty of the chosen characteristics sometimes suggests that ideas about earlier polities come from old textbooks. Even less adequate is the way that many European (and not just British) historians seem to think

particularly in terms of their own state, its history and characteristics. The last thing I want to do is extend this habit of fitting the
definition to particular periods or countries so as to use the word
state "in any sense consonant with medieval practice" (Davies, p.
284). Doing that virtually rules out the kind of serious comparisons of polities and periods that we need if we are to turn mere
assumptions about variants and changes into solid arguments
based on evidence about each of the phenomena that one is
comparing. It seems to me easier to compare if one uses a common
vocabulary with some definition or recognition of the accepted
sense of the key terms in it. The prevalent tendency to equate
"state" with "modern state" cannot be accepted or questioned
unless one says what one means by state and looks at earlier
polities.

It seemed to me when I wrote about the historiography of the
medieval state that I needed to start from a definition that would
make it possible to compare and contrast polities in any period or
continent according to characteristics that look significant whatever the context. I did this by amending Max Weber's definition of
the modern state. That seemed to me, as it has seemed to others,
to be useful in its focus on the control of the legitimate use of physical force, but it also seemed to need amendment, not so as to fit
medieval states, but so as to fit most states in any period, including the modern ones for which he intended it. It would perhaps do
better as an ideal type than a class or category into which some
empirical examples would fit and others would not. My amended
definition, which I adopted, not as the best or only possible one,
but simply to make clear how I would use the word, was that a
state is an organization of human society within a more or less
fixed area in which the ruler or governing body more or less successfully controls the legitimate use of physical force. This differed
from Weber's chiefly in the substitution of "control" for "monopoly"
and the double addition of "more or less".

There seems to be a significant difference between societies or
polities in which the control of the legitimate use of physical force
is formally located in specific persons or institutions and those in
which it is not. Those in which it is, and which by this measure
count as states, admittedly constitute a huge category, with many
variations of economy and of social and political structures and
ideologies. Even modern polities which seem to be generally
accepted as states vary widely in size, internal structures of power,
and much else: some are federal, which raises problems (which I
shall not discuss here) even about the amended definition. So does
the common reference to their impersonal and differentiated institutions: formally impersonal institutions were not invented, and

interpersonal relations among politicians do not seem to have become insignificant, either in 1500 or 1789, while differentiation has become less clear in the age of privatization, quangos, and "private-public partnerships". Medieval polities varied too, and much more widely than the traditional talk of feudalism and universal empire suggests. There are, of course, many other questions to consider about medieval government, as well as about medieval societies in general, but, I suggest, it is nevertheless worth considering whether any medieval polities fell within either my amended definition or a better one. If they did, in what specific ways, without relying on labels like feudalism or vassalage, did they differ from later states?

My conclusion was, and is, that a good many medieval polities, whether kingdoms, dukedoms, counties, other lordships, or city-states, could be classified as states – not because I want to bestow "an almost endless elasticity on the word and concept" (Davies 2003, pp. 283–4), but because the evidence I have looked at suggests that they exercised a more or less successful control of the legitimate use of physical force within their borders. That does not mean that they eliminated crimes or even armed revolts, or even punished all or most of them, or that all their subjects regarded all that their rulers did as legitimate: to demand that would disqualify many modern states. What I argue is that the kind of control they exercised, with varying degrees of success, puts them in the category I have defined. I even included a good deal of post-Carolingian France as an area of unstable mini-states: unstable and very small but still states. To call it a society *sans État* or "stateless" is to ignore academic discussions about the characteristics of stateless societies. In eleventh- and twelfth-century France a very large proportion of the population (maybe 90%?) lived under a coercive control which they are as likely to have accepted as more or less legitimate as their descendants did under larger and more stable units of jurisdiction and government. The impression of statelessness is created by concentrating exclusively on the relatively small number of people whose disputes are recorded in cartularies and chronicles and by assuming that the only possible state in France is one that covers the whole country.[2] The evidence about the way government worked in early medieval France is scarce. Much more is known about the fourteenth-century lordships of the Welsh March, partly because there are more records, but chiefly because of the illuminating way Davies himself has used them. I reckon that his Marcher lordships were states – and not just "virtual states" (Davies 2003, p. 294; Davies 1978, esp. pp. 149–75), and I should have said so in 1997. The fact that they were peripheral to the kingdom of England and to English historians or that they later lost the independence they had is irrelevant to their classification. Teleological concentration on the manifest destiny of the modern state is unhelpful to the analysis of medieval politics whether in France, the UK, or anywhere else. It is more significant that some of the French or Marcher lords were not completely independent, whether formally or in practice. That, however, calls for closer analysis, rather than rejection of the primary classification merely because the words and concepts strike the casual reader as anachronistic. It might even invite comparison of the phenomena with the actual workings of international politics in the age of supposedly sovereign modern states. One source of power in medieval Europe that I firmly excluded from my category of states was the church (Reynolds 1997, pp. 119–20). As Davies says, its claims were very high and fear of the hereafter formed in medieval circumstances a very potent form of control. I would maintain, however, that it was not the kind of control that would put it (as opposed to the Papal state or other areas ruled by bishops in much the same way as secular rulers) into the category covered by my definition.

Before considering, however briefly, how polities changed at whatever time they are thought to have given way to "modern states", it may be useful to emphasise the distinction Davies draws between words, concepts, and phenomena.[3] We are both, in this context, primarily concerned with phenomena, that is, the existence or non-existence of medieval polities that we would either of us call states. To object to the use of the word state for medieval polities because the Latin word *status* then had different connotations from the modern English "state" is worse than "obtuse academic pedantry" (Davies 2003, p. 283). It is an obtuse confusion of categories. The notions or concepts that words represent are more important in this context, and it is important to distinguish one's own notions from those of people in the past. I am not sure that the middle ages had none that corresponded to any of the various modern notions of the state. Though not all the medieval polities that I consider states were kingdoms, and not all kingdoms were states, some references to kingdoms or discussions of kingdoms seem to me to suggest something close to modern ideas of the "nation-state" (Reynolds 1998). Whether that is so or not, it remains a different issue from whether any medieval polities came within my – or any better – definition: political structures can, after all, exist quite well without academic discussion about them.

It is no part of my argument to say that the structures and workings of governments in the middle ages were the same as those that came later. They were different, and not just because they were more primitive (whatever that means) or contained the seeds (whatever that means) of later developments. It would obviously be pointless to try to summarize here how and when medieval polities were transformed into modern states, even if I had the knowledge to do it. Here, however, are a few suggestions of a wildly broad kind which pay a bit more attention to what is known about the middle ages than modernists generally pay and to academic discussions of states in other periods and continents than medievalists generally pay. Medieval government was both hierarchical and collective, relying heavily, in theory and practice, both on voluntary submission and active popular participation. Popular participation of course means, as it generally meant until the twentieth century, only the participation of respectable, adult, male householders. Hierarchy, I suggest, became stricter in the later middle ages and after as increasingly professional law and bureaucratic government defined, enforced, and recorded it. The same forces meanwhile weakened collective government, though maybe less than was suggested in the nineteenth century by those who looked back disapprovingly on the Ancien Régime. With the eighteenth century wholly new ideas of a different kind of popular or collective government appeared that would shape new structures of government. Many of all these various changes in ideas and structures were influenced, perhaps at least partly determined, by economic changes and new technologies of communication and war. It is all too complicated to fit the Rankean picture of "the first states in the world" appearing in fifteenth-century Italy (quoted in Reynolds 1997, p. 117).

Excluding medieval structures from the history of statehood, or allowing one or two in simply as the prehistory of particular modern states, impoverishes the discussion of both medieval and later history. Using a common vocabulary, with care and thought for the concepts and phenomena one is comparing, ought to enrich both. In this kind of comparative discussion "lordship", though absolutely suitable in other discussions about medieval polities, is no substitute. As a word applied peculiarly to the middle ages, it discourages comparisons. It is also ambiguous, being used both for what I would call government and for relations of patronage ("good lordship" etc), which are surely quite different. Whether, given the different national historiographical traditions, it conveys quite the same as *Herrschaft* or *seigneurie*, or they convey the same as each other, I doubt. The reason Davies found French and German scholarship so refreshing when he was studying the Marchers after a diet of English works focusing on royal administration and Strong Central Government was, I suspect, not the words but the phenomena that the French and Germans were studying. The conditions they described looked more like his.

Professor Davies and I agree in wanting more comparisons. The only thing, I suspect, that we really disagree about is the vocabulary. He is afraid, to quote from an email he sent me, that using "a common vocabulary can lead to an unthinking assumption about concepts and phenomena" so that historians "unthinkingly equate the state with the modern state." I share his fears but I would rather be more optimistic. I want to believe that medievalists may gradually come to pay more attention to what non-European historians and scholars in other disciplines have to say about states and learn to use the vocabulary more critically and analytically. I also cling to the hope that modernists may gradually learn to pay more attention to a great chunk of European history that has more in it than they learned at school or as undergraduates. Maybe the kind of discussion that Rees Davies has inaugurated will help.

## Notes

[1] I shall not repeat here what I said then beyond what is necessary to reply to particular points Davies makes, and shall not repeat the references I gave there to other works.

[2] Patrick Geary, "Vivre en conflit dans une France sans État, 1050–1200", *Annales ESC* 41 (1986), pp. 1107–33, to whom Davies refers, himself uses the expression *sans État* only in his title and acknowledges the coercive control over the lower classes, though he suggests that it covered only the unfree, which seems debatable.

[3] The difference between them (using different terminology) was discussed by C. K. Ogden and I. A. Richards, *The meaning of meaning* (K. Paul, Trench, Trubner: London, 1923), pp. 13–15; further discussions in e.g. J. Lyons, *Semantics* (University Press: Cambridge, 1977), vol. I, pp. 95–119, 175: R. Tallis, *Not Saussure* (Macmillan: Basingstoke, 1988), 114–16. As applied to medieval history: R. Schmidt-Wiegand, 'Historische Onomasiologie und Mittelalterforschung' *Frühmittelalterliche Studien* 9 (1982), 49–78; S. Reynolds, *Fiefs and vassals* (Clarendon Press: Oxford, 1994), pp. 12–14.

## References

Davies, R.R. (1978) *Lordship and Society in the march of Wales, 1282–1400*. Clarendon press: Oxford.

———. (2003) "The medieval State, the Tyranny of a concept?" in *Journal of Historical Sociology* 16 (2003), 280–300.

Reynolds, Susan (1997) "The Historiography of the Medieval State", in M. Bentley (ed.), *A Companion to Historiography*, pp. 117–38. Routledge: London.

———. (1998) "Our Forefathers? Tribes, peoples and nations in the age of migrations", in A.C. Murray (ed.), *After Rome's Fall: Narrators and Sources of Early Medieval Histsory. Essays presented to Walter Goffart* (University of Toronto Press: Toronto, 1998), pp. 17–36.

# Contentions of the Purse between England and its European Rivals from Henry V to George IV: a Conversation with Michael Mann[1]

## PATRICK KARL O'BRIEN

\*\*\*\*\*

*"Wars are but contentions of the purse" Henry Dundas (Secretary of War in Pitt the Younger's Second Administration) 1798*

Before the current renaissance in global history, historians (operating within a Rankean paradigm for advance in their discipline and bunkered in national archives) relied on historical sociologists to formulate concepts that might help them impose order, coherence and connexions upon the data, sources and evidence that represented the complexities of pasts that they had painfully recovered.

Since, moreover, a majority of historians have always worked on the formation of states and the exercise of power, they greeted the publication of metanarratives incorporating the bounded and circumscribed research of their core concern by Barrington Moore, Theda Skocpol, Charles Tilly, John Hall, Michael Mann, Perry Anderson, Robert Brenner, Immanuel Wallerstein and many others with intense and sometimes hostile attention, but generally with critical acclaim. Historians found sociological writings contained vocabularies and taxonomies that they could exploit or reject. They confronted syntheses (rooted in the writings of Marx, Weber, Durkheim and other canonical social scientists) but reconfigured by modern sociology in terms of new historical evidence and theories more relevant for the wider concerns of the late 20th century.

Michael Mann's two volumes on *The Sources of Social Power* (1986, 1993), written by an historian retrained as a sociologist, were recognised immediately as controversial but seminal. The author dealt with history's dominant concern was deeply versed in political and sociological theory and had read deeply into histories concerned with the emergence, formation, development and actions of states over millennia going back to the civilizations and empires of Mesopotamia, Egypt, China, the Indus Valley, Mesoamerica, Assyria and Persia as well as Greece and Rome. The ambition and erudition on display was awesome, but seventeen years after the publication of the first volume, what can be concluded about the architecture of Mann's general theory and the historical evidence and narratives that lend it credence?

Social theorists, who dominate this timely volume of appreciation, continue to present critiques of Mann's assumptions, methods, definitions and to disagree with the nuanced weights he accorded to ideological, military, economic, social and political sources, selected and emphasized in his insightful analyses of power. Nothing as tightly focussed on Mann's general theory could be offered by historians, attempting (as they will) to juxtapose specialized knowledge of particular periods and places, alongside his impressive array of evidence, covering chronologies and geographies far longer and wider than their discipline allows.

Nevertheless, they can (as this essay proposes) read volumes 1 and 2 as a grand narrative designed and structured to explain the emergence, evolution and consolidation of "Weberian states". Although Mann does not quite use that term he would recognize "Weberian State" as a handy label for an ideal type of state that developed historically to become more or less safe from external takeover and politically stable enough to command "sufficient" sovereignty, revenue, information, administrative capacity and sustained organizational efficiency to provide its subjects/citizens with protection against external aggression, internal order, personal safety, legal and judicial systems and other functional institutions, as well as an evolving array of public goods, deemed necessary for their welfare?

Yet Mann's perspective on the evolution of states (which commendably included Eastern and Mesoamerican empires) emerges from a narrative that could be somewhat teleological and exposes him, unfairly perhaps, to the charge of Eurocentrism. As he observed in volume 2, spatially confined chronologies tend to forego the illumination derived from synchronic comparisons and that has led to a virtual neglect of the forms, development and operations of medieval and early modern states in Russia, India, China, Japan, the Middle East and Africa. Mann admits that "if we compared the European and Chinese civilizations, we could conclude that the European was more powerful only at a relatively late date, perhaps around 1600." Recent research has shifted that date forward to the late 18th century, but on the final page of volume 1, there is a disarming disclaimer: "at the end of the day these are only generalizations about the development of one civilization". Nevertheless, the omission of the Orient from a study (of otherwise extraordinary range and depth) begins to look like a defect for any kind of "general" theory that aspires to explain the social origins of power. Perhaps the book could be retitled and will be considered here as the social origins of power in the occident? My focus in this essay will be on the rise of States in Europe from the Middle Ages up to the Congress of Vienna in 1815. That seems apposite because chapters 12–15 of volume 1 can be read as a well conceived and executed historical introduction to "The European Dynamic", moving over three cogently delineated stages: "The Intensive Phase 800–1155", "the rise of coordinating states, 1155–1477" and on to the emergence and consideration of "organic, national states, 1477–1760". While chapters 4–6 and 11–13 of volume 2 take the narrative through to a conjuncture in European history marked by that famous Congress. Alas what was specifically and peculiarly European about the dynamic has not been analysed which makes the explanations offered for "European" dynamism (Ch. 15) and the attempt to delineate "patterns of world-historical development" (Ch. 16) incomplete both as a general theory and as a metanarrative in global history.

Although volume 2 includes the United States, Mann's theory is virtually confined in its application as he put it to "a single broad socio-geographical area; that fusion of the Western Roman Empire and the lands of the German barbarians we know as Europe". Thus his conception of and explanations for a historical trajectory beginning in 800 and culminating, after the Revolutionary and Napoleonic Wars, in the reconfiguration of "Western European power networks' into major national states and their colonies and spheres of influence" still represents a powerful stimulus for conversation and research that remains truly seminal.

Mann's trajectory (bounded by Europe) "contains a single set of inter-related dynamics, economic, political, military and ideological relations – tending to move in a single general direction of development". Historians could take up any one of these four carefully conceptualised sources of social power and deal with their evolution and interconnexions over time. My intention is to concentrate, as Mann does, upon two of the four categories of power, namely political power, (proxied and measured as fiscal capacity) and armed force (virtually equated with armies rather than navies). I also intended restrict my conversation with him to British history – a case which we both know best. Britain, moreover, plays the leading role in his exposition throughout those chapters in volume 1 concerned with "The European Dynamic"; so much so that no historian of Britain, of Britain in Europe or Europe in a British Mirror could resist the temptation to dwell far more than any *general* theory of social power might safely do upon the peculiarities and particularities of the British case.

They were numerous and Anglo-American historians are overly fond of traducing recondite examples of British exceptionalism. As the second volume more clearly demonstrates, Mann is certainly not Anglo-centric in that sense. Nevertheless, the weight of evidence, data, examples and references related to Great Britain embedded in his narrative of a "European dynamic" leading into a long 19th century (1815–1914) does stand out and leads me to pose my major question of how far the British trajectory towards a Weberian state could somehow "represent" a dynamic which culminated in the reconfiguration of West European power networks into national states?

There is certainly a problem of when and how that occurred and whether the long span of history, eloquently elaborated in volume 1, can be *connected* with the rise of modern states in Britain, France, Austria and Germany, let alone the United States, analysed in volume 2. Mann would probably agree that the plenipotentiaries gathered at the Congress of Vienna to settle the frontiers and constitutions of European states after 22 years of revolutionary upheaval and warfare represented a diversity of polities at very different stages along Weber's trajectory. For example, Germany (represented by Prussia) and Italy (represented by Austria) remained nation states in waiting. Spain's empire was breaking up and the kingdom was about to disintegrate into decades of civil strife. Portugal continued to survive as a client of England. The Congress reunited the Netherlands into a single kingdom which separated again just fifteen years later. While the Hapsburg and Romanov dynasties ruled over conglomerated and still expanding empires of diverse territories, assets, populations, ethnicities, religions and cultures in ways and at depths of social "penetration" (to use Mann's illuminating concept) that hardly merit being depicted as "co-ordinated" let alone "centralized".

Perhaps the history succeeding 1815 is far more significant for state formation than the run up to the French Revolution? At the Congress only the recently but partially United Kingdom of England, Wales, Scotland and Ireland and perhaps France had constructed states that approximated to an ideal type as conceived by Weber and heuristically extended by Mann's general theory. Even France is a questionable example because although the legal system and administrative apparatus of centralization imposed by the Revolution and Napoleon survived the restoration of monarchy, over the next six decades, the country experienced two revolutions, a coup d'etat and a major invasion by the Prussian army before a widely accepted mode of republican and parliamentary governance provided French citizens with the security, order and national ideology required to qualify as a Weberian state.

Apart from Switzerland and some small Germany princely states, that leaves the United Kingdom as virtually the sole exemplar around at the time of that propitious conjuncture in Europe's geopolitical history of a country ruled by a sovereign state, with the power and resources required to provide its citizens with anything like "Weberian levels" of external security, personal safety, internal order and functional institutions necessary for political stability, economic growth and social welfare.

Nevertheless Mann's insistence that a long run geopolitical dynamic had created conditions and imperatives for the formation of all European states is well nigh incontestible. Furthermore, he validates his core thesis by mobilizing and calibrating data to expose the massive proportions of state expenditures allocated over the centuries before 1815 to support armies and navies and for increasingly expensive engagements in warfare. Historians will agree that the self-same dynamic also promoted the cooption, coordination (and more blatantly over time) the coercion of other sources and centres of power into projects for the defence and expansion of territories, assets and populations under centralizing systems of rule, protection and territorial sovereignty.

Although Mann's highly readable historical narrative illuminates a *process* of interactions between ideological, economic and military power for several centuries across a "single broad based socio-geographical area" his account of why the Hanoverian state moved more rapidly and very much closer to the Weberian ideal than the rest of Europe, seems incomplete. That probably occurred because Mann prefers historical narratives to comparative methods. Yet only Marc Bloch's recommendations (not cited in either volume) could help sociologists and historians to theorize about interactions bounded by and operating within a competitive state system. Interactions between the forms of power cogently specified by Mann were reciprocally conditioned by the evolving positions of states as leaders and laggards, successes (survivors) and failures (extinguished states).

Within Europe and for centuries before the Civil War, the English state remained a follower rather than a front runner in the geopolitical competition for power and profit. The realms, monarchs and ruling elites had shared the ambitions, anxieties and imperatives of other European kings, aristocracies and oligarchies from the Norman conquest onwards. But after more than a hundred years of predatory warfare against France (1336–1453) their armed forces, economy and fiscal base remained too circumscribed to support serious engagement in power politics on the mainland.

According to Mann's model which never downplays the significance of economic power that constraint began to diminish in the 16th century when the scale and structure of the economy moved onto a capitalist trajectory and eventually accelerated into the Industrial Revolution. Mann's economic history continues to deploy those obsolete concepts of capitalism and transitions to capitalism which are subsumed in (more modern literature) into a process encapsulated by the label of "Smithian Growth" which refers to the extension and integration of commodity and factor markets – a process that has, however, been documented as both ubiquitous and virtually comparable across Eurasia from the time of the Sung Dynasty onwards. Furthermore, geography and technology and their connexions to geopolitical as well as economic power play too circumscribed a role throughout the text and particularly in relation to the dominant British case. Mann certainly appreciates that the Island Kingdom possessed clear geopolitical and natural advantages over rivals on the mainland that included: a defendable and economically favourable location at the hub of a rapidly expanding North Sea-Baltic and Atlantic commercial system, navigable rivers, good harbours, fecund soils, abundant and accessible supplies of minerals – especially coal which promoted the development of steam powered engines to pump water from mines. That macro-innovation (the product of European science and British engineering) embodied widespread ramifications for supplying cheap energy to manufacturing industry and transportation.

Geography and technology really mattered for defence of the realm and for Britain's precocious transition to an industrial market economy and also for widening and deepening the fiscal (and contingent financial) base upon which the power of the state rested.

Mann's concentration upon that base is, however, one of his most original and productive insights. It first appeared in an essay published in 1980 and which has subsequently generated a programme of historical research into the rise and decline of fiscal military states. Mann recovered, analysed and quantified the mercantilist conception of fiscal capacity as the "sinews of power". He deployed data to represent expenditures on governance to serve as an indicator of the scale and scope of state activity. These "conceptions", backed by statistics, have allowed him (and a bevy of other historians following his lead) to measure the rise, decline and the relative command exercised by the British and (for shorter periods of time) other European States over an ever increasing volume of fiscal and financial resources – allocated primarily for centuries of intermittent, but persistent, engagement in geopolitical warfare with each other and secondarily to combat, coerce, co-opt and to placate rival claimants for power within their own borders, realms and dominions.

Mann's database constructed for two periods before and after the Napoleonic Wars are certainly commendable, but his pioneering attempt to track and compare the size, scale, scope and functions of five European states over very long time spans by using figures that their governments generated to aggregate their revenues and expenditures is incomplete and underspecified. Serious problems surround both the accuracy of the figures and the categories and definitions used by accounts of the day to report on and measure flows of revenues and expenditures attributable to the decisions and actions of such amorphous and evolving units. For example, what exactly was spent on behalf of a "state" is a matter of definition that changes through time and varied across Europe? Mann has attempted to include regional and local, as well as central government, but he would not pretend that shifts in provisions for governance from feudal to local to regional to central authorities did not complicate the task of quantifying the scale and scope of state activity over the centuries and across polities. Even if total expenditures could be more or less captured, and properly deflated to remove the influence of fluctuations in the prices of goods, services and labour purchased by all governmental authorities serious difficulties of inference remain. For example, comparisons among states (even when expressed as shares of national incomes) are difficult to interpret simply because the purchasing power of their currencies varied. Is it not plausible to suggest that Habsburg emporers could equip and sustain armies recruited from their dominions at a fraction of the costs incurred by Hanoverian monarchs to put troops of comparable efficiency in the field?

Furthermore the inclusion of debt servicing charges (often a considerable share of the recorded totals) in tabulations of aggregated expenditures by states, means the reported figures are an ambiguous indicator of the comparative and evolving capacities of states to exercise "command" over domestic resources required for the implementation of their policies and actions. That occurs because interest on and repayment of debt are simply transfer payments from government revenues to government creditors, whose loans to the state were used for the purchase of goods and services sometime in the near or distant past.

Double counting should be avoided but the inclusion of varying shares of expenditures funded by loans also compromises the inferences that can be safely drawn from these figures as indicators reflecting the "penetrative powers" of states into otherwise private spheres of national and imperial economies and societies over which they claimed sovereignty. For example, the creditors of rulers could have been foreign bankers, merchants and investors. Furthermore, their domestic creditors usually included a rather restricted "coterie of capitalists, financiers, aristocrats and courtiers with the strongest interests in the preservation and expansion of the state". As direct and potentially major beneficiaries of protection and/or aggression they had signed up lend to sovereigns because they anticipated that powerful more centralized states could and would widen and deepen their fiscal bases for the taxation required to amortize and service their debts. "Feudal" cooperation had been monetized and extended – nothing more!

Alas, the "penetrative or infra-structural powers" of states are not easily measured. Perhaps Mann's heuristic concept could be less ambiguously quantified with reference to data which records the total amounts of taxes, assessed, collected and delivered to central governments. Totals assessed refer to imposed/negotiated liabilities for taxation and are estimates made by fiscal departments of the sums that central governments could conceivably collect from taxes levied on goods and services, income and wealth, provided that the proscribed liabilities to sovereign's were actually met. Sums collected invariably fell short (often far short) of the anticipations of governments based upon legal definitions of liabilities, and that gap represents: (a) the administrative capacities of governments to enforce their laws, and (b) the willingness of taxpayers to comply with their liabilities to "sovereigns". It can be presented and compared as proxies for infra-structural powers of states, because it represents gaps between "aspirations" to tax and the "routinized" enforcement of promulgated and/or negotiated fiscal policies.

That other measurable differences between amounts collected and sums delivered to central governments to fund expenditures upon policies that they formulated and sought to implement is also interesting to contemplate. Conceptually this particular and measurable gap proxies the command states exercised over annual flows of tax (and other revenues) that belonged (in theory) to sovereign central authorities, but which in practice and effect had passed as a matter of political expediency and administrative efficiency under the control of other stakeholders in the nominal revenues of sovereigns. Political expediency included bargains that states had been compelled to strike with other claimants to power and resources including: ancient kingdoms, established estates, ecclesiastical authorities, territorial magnates and urban oligarchies in order to assess and collect taxes. Such compromises included both exemptions and agreements over the shares of taxes that had to be spent in the localities in which they were collected.

Apart from the persistence of a path dependant political trajectory towards centralized power, (recognized and elaborated by Mann) for several reasons European sovereigns found it both unavoidable and administratively efficient to refrain from attempts to construct hierarchical fiscal administrations for the assessment, collection and despatch of taxes into their coffers. First such attempts could provoke political resistance or at least weaken the compliance of taxpayers with demands to contribute to the needs of "their" states. Secondly, Europe's decentralized, dispersed medieval and early modern economies of small scale farms, firms and traders could only be effectively taxed by delegating authority to "officials" with local and specialized knowledge. In effect and until well into the 19th century the nature and evolution of most European economies sustained a strong role for private enterprise in all fiscal systems, which involved farming and other contractual arrangements for the assessment, collection and despatch of taxes to the centre. Sovereign property rights to taxes (or demesne rents and other revenues) that could not be effectively enforced except by way of a multiplicity of complex franchising contracts, difficult to monitor and, as historians have revealed, resistant to reform.

Thirdly, in an environment marked fluctuations in harvests, trade and production as well as those more significant and unpredictable relapses into warfare with rival states, few rulers could manage without recourse to inflows of credits and loans in order to sustain normal peacetime government and above all to jack up expenditures to meet the onset of geopolitical crises. In the absence of modern capital markets and banks they resorted to "anticipating" tax and/or demesne rents by borrowing from syndicates of merchants, aristocrats and businessmen, to whom they had delegated responsibility for the assessment and collection of sovereign revenues. Thus, tax farmers evolved inexorably into financiers because they possessed the knowledge required to evaluate the capacity of rulers to service their debts; as well as strategic positions inside fiscal systems which allowed them to deduct interest and amortization payments before delivering *net* flows of revenues to their sovereigns.

Given that data on "Taxes Assessed", "Taxes Collected" and "Taxes Delivered" to central governments are perhaps the most revealing and least ambiguous indicators for any study of the penetrative power of early modern European states the question of how, when and why Britain developed the fiscal and related geopolitical prowess that was clearly on view to European rivals at the Congress of Vienna in 1815 seems to be the central problem to pursue?

In geopolitical terms (and despite Wellington's successes in the Peninsular and as coordinator of allied armies at Waterloo) that superiority continued to reside in naval, not military, power. Yet Britain's fiscal prowess was as widely feared and respected as its ships of the line, even though fiscal power is not as easy to measure or to rank as the scale of armies and navies. But it was surely extraordinary? For example, at the height of the Napoleonic Wars (1810–14) Napoleon spent nearly a billion francs per annum. Most of that money (which had doubled in nominal terms over a decade) the Emperor raised in the form of indemnities and levies from conquered and defeated enemies. One billion francs could, however, have funded purchases of goods and services, sold on British markets, to an estimated value of something like £40 million a year. Over that same span of years the Hanoverian state appropriated £65 million per annum in taxes and borrowed a further £23 million a year in short and long term loans. When we offset the annual amounts for interest and amortization payments transferred to Government creditors the annual *net* amounts borrowed fell to negligible burdens on the national economy of the United Kingdom. Nevertheless, and during those final years of intensified conflict the capacity of the British state to defend the realm and fund military and naval operations in a global geopolitical arena exceeded the fiscal and financial funds made available to the Napoleonic state by a multiplier of 2.2. That multiplier represents much more than an "edge" and it refers, moreover, to a period of time when the population and national product of France were both more than double British levels. Data are not yet to hand, but scattered evidence allows for a conjecture that the fiscal and financial systems of Spain, Austria, Prussia and Russia, let alone other smaller states on the mainland, lacked anything remotely comparable to Britain's "power of the purse".

Medieval historians have suggested that England already possessed a strong fiscal state in the high middle ages, but they offer no comparative data to support the hypothesis. In volume 1 Mann published a run of figures of total revenues collected for the English monarchs at current and constant prices from 1155 to 1688, culled from a range of secondary sources and he tabulated more reliable data for 1695–1820 -covering total expenditures deflated and separated into three allocations: for debt repayment and servicing, for military and for civil and functions. Whether the trends plotted and analysed by Mann to track the long-term rise of an English state can be used to represent an European trajectory looks doubtful. His innovatory exercise has, however, been refined and supplemented by data collected for the European Science Foundation's project on "The Origins of the Modern State in Europe". That enlarged body of evidence confirms Mann's key perception that for centuries before 1815 very high proportions of revenues available to ruling houses and oligarchies throughout Europe were deployed to support military expenditures and to fund the servicing of debt – incurred to an overwhelming degree for frequent and unpredictable engagements in warfare.

Recently published statistical evidence also allows historians to categorize and trace the relative proportions of revenue obtained from different components of the fiscal and financial bases available to a sample of European states. For example, ratios of taxes relative to predatory expropriations and "forced loans"; and to income from demesnes and other property. Furthermore, several different types of taxation can be compared, e.g. ordinary and extraordinary, direct and indirect; levies upon incomes or outlays, direct appropriations based on the measurement of wealth related to assessments upon to regular and monitored declarations of income.

As Mann realized this kind of "classified" statistical information, exemplifies different kinds of connexions and relations between rulers and ruled, government and citizens, and the public and private spheres. Data for taxation can be marshalled in illuminating ways to testify to changes in the penetrative powers of states over time and, for purposes of comparison, across Europe. For example, as Schumpeter pointed out, shifts from domain to tax states implied rulers "no longer lived off their own". Predation inside confederated borders never worked in the long run and gave way to taxation levied by an implicit compact or through some form of "due process" of consultation. "Extraordinary" impositions to meet emergencies or to fund campaigns could be more readily raised than routinized systems of taxation. Assessments based upon approximate nominal and stable indicators of wealth might be more easily negotiated, maintained and monitored than any direct and effective taxation of personal incomes. While indirect taxes on outlays whether levied (preferably) on "foreign" (imported) rather than domestically produced commodities and services maintained space between rulers and ruled; could be represented as "voluntary" (particularly if imposed on luxuries) and generally provoked less resistance than direct taxes, however calibrated to be seen as fair and just.

Naturally the political advantages attending the compliance with ostensibly invisible, voluntary and indirect taxes came to be appreciated by rulers and their fiscal advisers. Unfortunately for their purposes and before national economies became more concentrated in ports, towns and regions and larger scale units of production and networks for exchange, possibilities for extending the range and depth of commodity taxation remained limited. In short, the fiscal (and related) financial bases potentially available to European states for purposes of taxation, debt servicing and borrowing never became a simple function of the size of gross national products, nominally subject to their claims to sovereignty.

Scale certainly mattered and that is why many of Europe's smaller polities disappeared to be absorbed into larger territorial units. Nevertheless the status and success of Europe's enlarged polities depended less upon the size of their gross national products and rather more upon three distinct variables: first, the structure and organization of national economies that they could in theory tax; secondly, the political possibilities open to sovereigns for extensions to taxation; and thirdly, the administrative capacities states could construct and manage in order to assess and collect a variety of taxes designed to tap into those margins of national economies where growth was recurring.

For an appreciation of fiscal development long run chronological perspectives can be heuristic provided states progress through time on some kind of learning curve. That is why medieval history which include Britain's fiscal history down to the conjuncture of the Civil War seems only marginally relevant to the status of the realm's fiscal system on display at the Congress of Vienna. Agreed: the manifest success of that system not merely during the Revolutionary and Napoleonic wars, (1793–1815) but over the entire Second Hundred Years War with France (1689–1815) owed something (but not much) to the political and administrative arrangements for taxation constructed by English kings and their advisers in the high middle ages. But it owed even less to anything accomplished by way of state building during Elton's Revolution in Tudor Government, let alone to the failures of the early Stuarts to do anything to solve the states chronic shortage of revenues.

As an historian Mann favours long chronologies, but recent historical research might convince him that the Civil War can be represented as a "profound conjuncture" in both the political and fiscal history of the state formation in Britain. That conjuncture can, moreover, be validated with reference to recently reconstructed figures for tax revenues collected for central government. Plotted on graphs they convey the impression that over the period, circa 1295 to the end of the First Hundred Years War (1453), English monarchs jacked up and maintained real total revenues from taxation at levels that seem to have been approximately double those obtainable before the reign of Edward I (1272–1307). This period has, moreover, been associated with a shift from a demesne state (when monarchs like Henry II, Richard I, John and Henry III obtained most (up to 80%) of their revenues from rents collected for the use of royal and ecclesiastical property, particularly land, to a tax state. Income from taxes probably peaked in the reign of Henry V, declined down towards 12th century totals during the Wars of the Roses, but regained previous levels during the reign of Henry VII (1485–1509). Throughout Tudor and Early Stuart times the real tax income of English monarchs fluctuated from reign to reign and between periods of war and peace, never reached the £400,000 mark and apart from a "blip" (associated with the wars of Henry VIII – funded by raids on Church property and debasement of the currency – there is no evidence that the constraints imposed by the fiscal system on the ambitions of English rulers changed much (if at all) before the Restoration. In real terms, taxes per capita remained roughly constant for more than two centuries after 1485. Some incremental growth in total revenues occurred, but hardly enough to fund active participation in geopolitics and insufficient (as Charles I discovered) to circumvent a serious fiscal crisis of the State in the 1640s.

Fiscal data displays two other statistically visible tendencies which mark out two centuries of early modern fiscal pressures promoting a cautious withdrawal by the English state from more extensive and costly engagements with great power politics and geopolitical conflicts beyond the borders of the realm. First, the share of total revenues appropriated or expenditures covered by taxation declined below the eighty per cent mark of the high middle ages. English kings compelled to "live more off their own" became predatory towards the wealth of other property owners, particularly the church but also the estates of "treasonable" aristocrats. Secondly, the share of revenues from indirect taxes – principally the levy on exported wool which had featured prominently in the uplift in taxation from 1295–1453 – ceased to go up. Before the reign of Charles II the proportions of total tax revenue obtained from indirect taxes showed no tendency to move above a fifty per cent threshold. Tudors and Early Stuarts continued to depend upon traditional forms of direct taxation – imposed upon the personal incomes and wealth of their subjects. Compared to the high middle ages England's fiscal system became altogether more resistant towards royal ambitions to construct a more powerful state.

That lack of compliance occurred for reasons that appear commonplace throughout Europe. Everywhere rulers tried without success to assess the incomes and wealth of their subjects in accordance with equitable and sustainable criteria for estimating variations in the abilities of taxpayers to contribute to the needs of states. In several polities, rulers failed for political reasons to include aristocratic families and established corporate bodies, estates and other privilege in the net. More generally (even in England where universal taxation was at least accepted in principle) prospects for maintaining reasonably accurate and up-to-date records of income and/or wealth for purposes of regular direct taxation proved to be way beyond administrative capacities of early modern states. Nearly all attempts by ambitious Chancellors and fiscal adviser to construct realistic valuation of the King's base for taxation provoked serious resistance and turned out to be impossible to use on a routine basis. Compromises in the form of stereotyped valuations, rigid local and regional quotas and virtual self-assessment particularly by the rich and powerful, usually prevailed, ensured monarchs of some acceptable "modicum" of income from direct taxes and testified to the altogether weak and limited penetrative powers of governments until well into the 19th century.

When, how and why the British state led the way out of the "cage" of these widespread restrictions (that effectively restrained the powers of its Tudor and Stuart regimes for more than two centuries after the Wars of the Roses (1455–85)) requires both a narrative and synchronic comparisons with other European states, that also remained "caged" for decades before and after the Congress of Vienna.

That narrative should begin with England's more famous Civil War (1642–51) (occasioned by a fiscal crisis of the state) but which can be represented as a conjuncture in the realm's history when the prospects and potential for the construction of an effective fiscal state became politically feasible. The trauma of civil war, followed by an interregnum of republican rule, and innovations in centralized governance led on to something of a consensus among the nation's ruling and economic elites that the internal order and external security of the realm combined with its growing interests overseas required a larger, better funded state. That view was consolidated during the Restoration when a ruling oligarchy (consisting of a monarch with a coterie of aristocratic ministers (operating through, but circumventing a divided and divisive Parliament) began to construct the organizational, administrative and fiscal foundations for a state that would carry a unifying kingdom and loyal nation of "Britons" through nine wars to that position of geopolitical, imperial and economic hegemony it occupied at the Congress of Vienna.

Against a memory evolving into a culture of deep political apprehension of lapses into internal disorder, a royal and aristocratic oligarchy managed Parliament, drew upon the experiments of the interregnum, recruited a body of talented bureaucrats to help them reconstruct two organizations of fundamental significance for the rise of the British state. First and foremost was the Royal Navy, a distinctive arm of geopolitical power appreciated but not analysed in the depth its merits by Mann. Even though he observed that "from the mid-1660s for the next two hundred years, the navy was the largest item in the English state expenditures". And he added that "the permanent war state arrived in England in two stages.

Although Tudor garrisons were its harbingers, Pepys" navy constituted its main thrust?

Mann also recognized those mutually reinforcing linkages
between the navy on the one hand and commercial expansion,
colonization overseas and compliance with mounting demands for
taxes on the other. Rising tax burdens were accepted by the most
mercantilistic of European societies as necessary for the security of
the realm and profitable for the growth of the domestic economy
and its overseas trade. Although the history of the Royal Navy from
1660–1815 can be represented as an extraordinary record of
growth with increased efficiency, Mann's analysis of naval power
seems insufficiently elaborated for a theory that lays so much
stress on geopolitical contexts and interactions for the development
of Weberian states. British success from 1660 through to 1815 over
rival navies – also backing the commercial, colonial and maritime
ambitions of other powers (particularly France and Spain, but
including Venice, Portugal, the Dutch Republic, Sweden, Denmark,
Russia and the United States) – really deserves systematic comparisons. To understand British superiority historians need to
appreciate the sizes of national fleets; the variety, speed and fire-
power of battleships; supplies of skilled officers and seamen available to admiralties; the efficiency of onshore facilities, private and
public, for the construction and maintenance of ships; and above
the quality of the hierarchical bureaucracies set up by states to
mobilize, manage and coordinate their navies.

Again geography combined with history so that the Island kingdom's prior and long commitments to seaborne transportation,
fishing and trade certainly complemented the massive investments
by its state in naval power. While the weakness of military threats
emanating from across frontiers with rival states (apart from Scotland) certainly allowed Britain's rulers to concentrate resources,
revenues and strategies for external security on the Navy and to
promote policies that widened and added to the flows of benefits
accruing from investment in naval power. Nevertheless, the capital
and skills required to defend the realm, protect its seaborne commerce and to inflict damage upon the navies, merchant marines
and maritime potential of rivals had to be accumulated, maintained
and mobilized over no less than nine wars that preceded the final
triumph of Trafalgar – a victory which ushered in a century of
national security and hegemony at sea.

In short, the Royal Navy fashioned and led Britain's trajectory
towards a Weberian state. Geography certainly conditioned the
Island's prospects for naval success. Strategy and effective coordination and organization counted for a great deal, but navies
became steadily more expensive to construct, maintain and run.

Without sustained support from the most efficient fiscal and financial system in Europe, hegemony at sea that prevailed for two centuries after 1713 could never have been sustained.

Mann's concentration on money as the central "sinew of power" is innovatory but his elaboration of the British history is incomplete and the British case needs to be contextualized in the arena geopolitics within which it competed with rival European states. For example, a destructive Civil War, an interregnum of republication experiments (including the establishment of military rule against a tradition of resistance to standing armies) as well as two decades of Restoration and reconstruction to create the political conditions and administrative infrastructure required for the rise of a fiscal naval state all need to be appreciated.

Nine years of civil war followed with governance by a strong army under the Commonwealth and Protectorate provided nearly three decades of experience necessary to convince British elites of the case for a strong and enlarged state based on naval, not military, force. That conviction hardened when Cromwell's navy revived memories of the Armada by preventing a royalist inspired invasion of England from the mainland of Europe.

Taxes increased sharply during and remained high "after the Civil War" when both Parliamentary and Royalist governments resorted to the imposition of a wider and more effectively collected range of internal duties, levied upon domestically produced goods and services. That temporary expedient effectively breached traditional antipathies to excises which remained in place under the Commonwealth and Protectorate and matured during the Restoration to become in the words of Charles II, "the best and easiest tax". The royal quotation recognized the obvious political advantages of indirect taxes (tariffs as well as excises). Kings knew their incidence appeared in the form of higher prices and (provided the necessities of the poor continued to be exempt) taxes on commodities could be presented as "voluntary" and "avoidable". Their disadvantages resided in the high costs of assessing liabilities and collecting cash from producers, merchants, importers and shopkeepers who manufactured, supplied or sold goods and services (never simple to define in law) but often easy enough to conceal and distribute through illegal channels at tax free prices to consumers.

Throughout Europe States had contained potential losses of revenues from indirect taxes by resorting for centuries to franchising responsibility for their assessment and collection to private individuals, syndicates and firms under contracts of extraordinary diversity and complexity and for durations that varied from virtual alienation of a sovereign's property rights to annual renewable leases.

Privatization served multiple purposes. First and foremost farms and farmers (terms redolent of landed estates) promised to provide higher and more stable levels of income than could be secured by constructing bureaucracies and departments of state charged to manage taxation. In any case and for political reasons that option was not often open to rulers negotiating with magnates, merchants, urban oligarchies, and estates, over rights to impose taxes that affected private and local interests. As with direct taxes on wealth and income, rival claimants to "power" over production and trade in commodities and services could be "placated" by leaving assessment and collection in their hands which also assuaged their anxieties about the dangers inherent in the extension of royal bureaucracies.

Thirdly, tax farms and tax farmers provided European rulers with indispensable access to lump sums up front, loans and credits secured on delegated powers to assess, collect and remit taxes on behalf of sovereigns. During those centuries of geopolitical conflict, mercantilist rivalry and wars of religion that succeeded the French invasion of Italy in 1494, but which continued at lower levels of intensity between the Peace of Westphalia (1648), and the Treaty of Vienna (1815), nearly all states came under pressure to deepen the scale and scope of their fiscal and financial bases by raising and extending taxes (particularly indirect taxes) which then allowed them to utilize rising proportions of revenues from taxation to accumulate and service debt. Almost no European polity remained immune from the fiscal fallout emanating from geopolitical competition, the military revolution and mercantilism. Some (Denmark, Prussia, Switzerland and Britain) engaged less actively than other powers (Spain, France, Sweden and Austria, as well as Portugal, Venice, Tuscany and several German princely states).

By that decade of "lull" which spanned the Treaty of Munster (1649) and the Peace of the Pyrenees (1659) the fiscal and financial systems of many governments on the mainland exhibited symptoms of disarray, exhaustion and diminishing returns. For example, in embracing the services of private contractors, tax farmers and rent seekers of all kinds, rulers had with difficulty managed to extend the net beyond direct taxes and to impose "duties" upon an astonishing range and variety of assets, goods and services produced within their territories. That unavoidable embrace turned out to be both costly and restrictive. Rewards (rents) accruing to holders of private franchises in sovereign revenues (from demesnes as well as taxes) had risen sharply. Above all the proportions of annual income transferred as interest and debt servicing charges to Government creditors rose war after war to reach unsustainable levels. Sequences of fiscal crises, marked by defaults and the rescheduling of debts, occurred frequently which enhanced the risks and raised the costs of future borrowing for the Spanish, French, Austrian, Swedish and several other monarchies.

Although Henry VIII and Charles I tried, they failed to deepen and widen their fiscal and financial bases in order to engage more actively in European geopolitics and imperial ventures overseas. Politically the fiscal constraint which confronted both monarchs on the size and shape of their "tax take" loosened up, as the outcome of the Civil War. Not enough, however, to satisfy the geopolitical ambitions of the restored Stuart monarchy, its aristocratic advisers and England's rising mercantile and mercantilist economic elites. Yet despite pressures for fiscal expansion for something like a quarter of a century the restored regime cautiously avoided provocative meddling with the stereotyped system of direct taxation and concentrated on the rules and administration for the assessment and collection of indirect taxes, but at a propitious time when overseas commerce and several proto-industries displayed visible signs of economic expansion.

In 1670 ministers moved to abolish tax farming and to bring the King's revenue from tariffs on imports under direct hierarchical, but not conspicuously efficient control. Thirteen years later they repeated the move and transformed responsibility for the assessment of excise duties to a new and more effectively constructed and closely monitored department of state. By the time James II took a series of politically inept steps towards religious toleration the dependence of the English state on direct forms of taxation had been seriously reduced and the fiscal system was ready to appropriate more and more revenue from customs and excise duties.

At that juncture no other state on the mainland, particularly England's Bourbon rivals, France and Spain, could conceivably depend on any comparable measure of support from their fiscal systems. Nearly two centuries of persistent geopolitical conflict (1494–1689) had already led to a widespread extension of indirect taxes into internal and external trade, urban commerce and services and manufacturing and had proceeded inexorably towards frontiers of diminishing returns – where further increases in the rates and range of taxes generated no extra revenue. The road to those frontiers had been paved and facilitated by tax farming and tax farmers whose control over and vested interest in the assessment, collection and remittance of sovereign revenues became naturally very costly, but resistant to and politically dangerous to reform.

On the offshore island and for more than two centuries before the Dutch coup d'etat of 1688 radically changed their foreign and strategic policies, English monarchs felt less pressure to extend the frontiers of taxation to include unpopular excises. They not only enjoyed substantial income from customs duties, (supposedly paid by foreigners and readily available to rulers of a nation actively engaged in foreign commerce) but as a trade off for representation and consultation, their powerful and richer subjects had conceded rights to their sovereigns to impose taxes that applied *without exemptions* across the territories, wealth assets and incomes located within the kingdom. That established English tradition of no "representation without taxation" (extended with difficulty to Wales, Scotland, Ireland and the border counties, but successfully resisted by the Thirteen colonies in America) implied that the imposition of any English tax (direct or indirect) would in principal be and would become in effect "universal".

Elsewhere in Europe even the principle remained negotiable. Systems to monitor franchised contracts rarely worked for long and the formation of hierarchically organised departments of state to assess and collect taxes on a universal basis could not be replicated on the mainland even in Holland – and despite the best efforts of a famous line of ministers of state to reform Europe's exhausted inefficient, but immobile fiscal systems. In 1688 William III took over an economy with an obvious potential to carry higher burdens of taxation, a fiscal system prepared to assess, collect and deliver rising amounts of acceptable customs and excise duties and an established political consensus poised to support high levels of expenditure on naval power to defend the realm and to protect expanding national interests overseas. He also found a society grateful for his defence of the protestant succession and a Whig oligarchy prepared to be vigorous in the use of coercion and active in the propagation of an ideology of virulent nationalism, conducive to the conversion of taxpayers into compliance with rising burdens of taxation that became necessary to fund the nation's aggressive geopolitical and imperial policies overseas.

Everything, except a set of financial institutions, to mobilize credits and loans secured on anticipated flows of taxes seems to have been in place to support what Michael Mann has delineated as a massive and sustained upswing in real expenditures (on naval and military) power that came in the wake the Glorious Revolution. With a history of European techniques, experiments, successes and failures in borrowing to guide them, and Dutch advisers at their disposal, nothing particularly innovatory or English attended the construction of a framework of institutions to meet the Orange and Hanoverian regimes incessant demands for loans and credits. Finance (borrowing) stablilized expenditures from year to year and more significantly jacked up allocations of funds to the forces of the crown at the outbreak of every war. Since the costs of renegotiating, defaulting or rescheduling debt must have been entirely familiar to

English statesmen of the period, prudential Parliamentary governments became as famous as their Dutch predecessors for honour-
ing their commitments to the states creditors.

Thus, the outcomes of the Glorious Revolution resided less in
another "reassertion" of the rights and powers of Parliament.
English Parliaments had very rarely refused to accede to demands
from monarchs and their ministers for "supplies" to defend the
realm and wage war. There is no record of any serious revisions to
such demands after 1688. Furthermore, the tradition of probity
towards creditors represents realistic behaviour from a state
funding 70–80% of all the extra income raised to fight more than a
century of wars from loans and accumulation of a "national" debt
that rose from something like 5% of the national income under
James II to 270% of that aggregate for 1819.

Britain's quite extraordinary rate of debt accumulation absorbed
rising proportions of all the taxation raised between 1689 and
1815. That "critical" debt servicing ratio which had long constrained the capacity of Britain's rivals to match the realm's fiscal
and naval achievements rose from 24% during the peaceful inter-
lude of 1698–1702 to reach 62% immediately after the Napoleonic
War when the roll back of fiscal state and protracted demise of an
ancien regime became unavoidable. Meanwhile the rise of the
English state to the status it occupied at the Congress of Vienna
had cost "English" taxpayers a great deal of money. In real terms
the realm's taxes rose nearly fifteen times between 1688 and 1815
and the shares of the national income appropriated as taxes
increased from around 3% in the reign of James II to reach 20%
when Wellington coordinated European armies to ensure the final
defeat of France at Waterloo. Although an effective and innovatory
income tax came on stream during the most expensive phase of the
conflict with Napoleon, most of the extra taxation required to
service debt and fund the forces of the Crown came from indirect
taxes, particularly excises.

To conclude this long conversation with Michael Mann: between
1641–88 a painfully reconstructed English state moved the realm
onto a path that carried the nation and its mercantilist ambitions
through nine wars to reach pinnacles of power and prosperity
which the by then United Kingdom enjoyed throughout a golden
age of Victorian and Edwardian liberal and imperial capitalism. In
retrospect, most of the elements of an explanation offered here for
Britain's precocious and peculiar trajectory towards a Weberian
state have emerged as path dependent. In this narrative, they
flowed from geographical endowments, an island location, the
detachment of Tudor and Stuart regimes from geopolitics on the
mainland and the advantages of arriving as a latecomer and free

rider to colonization and commerce with the Americas. Further-more, and to return to Marc Bloch's recommendations, fiscal and financial sclerosis afflicted Britain's rivals on the mainland from 1648–1815 and severely constrained their abilities to take on a well funded Royal Navy in the service of the most aggressively mercan-tilist power in Europe. Fortunately, the inexorable onset of that very same sclerosis that clearly infected the United Kingdom's fiscal and financial system for several decades after Waterloo did not compro-mise the imperial states exercise of hegemony until its rivals had completed their own more protracted and particular transitions to Weberian states. Most European polities and for reasons closely connected to fiscal and financial capacity completed that transition well after Britain. As Michael Mann's second volume illuminates, French, German, Austrian, Italian, Spanish and other European trajectories can be written and represented as separable national narratives coming on stream after, rather than before, the French Revolution.

One final point, once Asian, Middle Eastern and African experi-ence is brought into the frame we may, as Weber anticipated, be able to demarcate a European path and pattern of state formation. We will need Michael Mann to tell us how that might be incorpo-rated into a general theory.

**Note**

[1] This paper was originally written for inclusion in J. Hall and R. Schroeder (eds.) *An Anatomy of Power: the Social Theory of Michael Mann.* The paper was accidentally omitted due to some miscommunication prob-lems. The *Journal of Historical Sociology* is very pleased to publish this paper along with Michael Mann's response.

**Bibliography**

G. Ardant, *Histoire de l'impot*, 2 vols (Paris 1971–2)
V.R. Berghahn, *Imperial Germany 1871–1914. Economy, Society, Culture and Politics* (Oxford, 1994)
J. Black, *Eighteenth Century Europe 1700–89* (Basingstoke, 1990)
J. Black (ed.), *War in the Early Modern World 1450–1815* (London, 1998)
J. Black, *War and World, Military Power and the Fate of Continents 1450–2000* (New Haven, 1998)
R. Bonney, *The European Dynastic State* (Oxford, 1991)
R. Bonney (ed.), *Economic Systems and State Finance* (Oxford, 1995)
———, *The Rise of the Fiscal State in Europe c. 1200–1815* (Oxford, 1999)
M.J. Braddick, *The Nerves of State: Taxation and the Financing of the English State, 1558–1714* (Manchester, 1996)
J. Breuilly, *Nationalism and the State* (Manchester, 1982)
J. Brewer, *The Sinews of Power. War, Money and the English State, 1688–1783* (London, 1989)

C.D. Chandaman, *The English Public Revenue, 1660–88* (Oxford, 1975)

J.C.D. Clark, *English Society 1688–1832. Ideology, Social Structure and Political Practice during the Ancien Regime* (Cambridge, 2000)

L. Colley, *Britons. Forging the Nation* (London, 1992)

F. Comin et al. (eds.), *The Formation and Efficiency of Fiscal States in Europe and Asia* (forthcoming, Cambridge University Press)

P. Contamine (ed.), *War and Competition Between States* (Oxford, 2000)

F. Crouzet, *A History of the European Economy* (Charlottesville, 2001)

H.T. Dickinson (ed.), *Britain and the French Revolution* (Basingstoke, 1989)

P.M.G. Dickson, *The Financial Revolution in England: A Study in the Development of Public Credit, 1688–1756* (Aldershot, 1993)

W. Doyle, *Venality. The Sale of Offices in 18$^{th}$ Century France* (Oxford, 1996)

K.H.F. Dyson, *The State Tradition in Western Europe. A Study of an Idea and an Institution* (Oxford, 1980)

S.R. Epstein, *Freedom and Growth. Markets and States in Pre-Modern Europe* (London, 2002)

T. Ertman, *Birth of the Leviathan. Building States and Regimes in Medieval and Early Modern Europe* (Cambridge, 1997)

N. Ferguson, *The Cash Nexus. Money and Power in the Modern World 1700–2000* (London, 2001)

A. Gunder Frank, *Re Orient. Global Economy in the Asian Age* (Berkeley, 1998)

J. Glete, *War and the State in Early Modern Europe* (London, 2002)

P. Goubert, *The Course of French History* (London, 1991)

N. Henshall, *The Myth of Absolutism. Change and Continuity in Early Modern Europe* (Oxford, 1992)

E.J. Hobsbawm, *Nations and Nationalism since 1780* (Cambridge, 1990)

P.T. Hoffman and K. Norberg (eds.), *Fiscal Crises, Liberty and Representative Government* (Stamford, 1994)

K.J. Holsti, *The State, War and the State of War* (Cambridge, 1997)

R. Lachmann, *Capitalists in Spite of Themselves. Elite Conflict and Economic Transitions in Early Modern Europe* (Oxford, 2000)

D. Levine, *At the Dawn of Modernity. Biology, Culture and Material Life in Europe after the year 1000* (Berkeley, 2001)

R. Magraw, *France 1815–1914. The Bourgeois Century* (Oxford, 1983)

P. Mandler and P. Harling, "From Fiscal Military State to Laissez-Faire State", *Journal of British Studies* 32 (1993), pp. 44–70

D.C. North and B. Weingast, "Constitutions and Commitment: Evolution of Institutions Governing Public Choice in Seventeenth Century England", *Journal of Economic History* 49 (1989), pp. 803–32

P.K. O'Brien, "The Political Economy of British Taxation, 1660–1815", *Economic History Review*, Vol. XLI (February 1988), pp. 1–32

P.K. O'Brien, "The Rise of a Fiscal State in England 1485–1815", in *Bulletin of the Institute of Historical Research*, No. 160 (June, 1993), pp. 129–168

P.K. O'Brien and P. Hunt, "Excises and the Rise of a Fiscal State in England, 1586–1688", in M. Ormrod et al (eds.), Crises, Revolutions and Self-Sustained Growth. Essays in *European Fiscal History* (Stamford, 1999)

F. O'Gorman (ed.), "Britain and Europe" in special issue of *Diplomacy and Statecraft* 8 (1997), pp. 1–164

K. Pomeranz, *Great Divergence. China, Europe and the Making of the Modern World Economy* (Princeton, 2000)

D. Quataert, *The Ottoman Empire 1700–1922* (Cambridge, 2000)

W. Reinhard (ed.), *Power, Elites and State Building* (Oxford, 1996)

H. Roseveare, *The Financial Revolution 1660–1760* (London, 1991)

S. Sogner (ed.), *Making Sense of Global History* (Oslo, 2001)

L. Stone (ed.), *An Imperial State at War. Britain, 1689–1815* (London, 1994)

B. Stuchtey and E. Fuchs (eds.), *Writing World History 1800–2000* (Oxford, 2002)

A. Teichova and H. Matis (eds.), *Nation, State and the Economy in History* (Cambridge, 2003)

M. T'Hart, "Warfare and Capitalism. The Impact of the Economy on State Making in Northwestern Europe, 17th and 18th Centuries", *Fernand Braudel Centre Working Papers* 23 (2000), pp. 209–28

C.H. Tilly (ed.), *The Formation of National States in Western Europe* (Princeton, 1975)

C.H. Tilly, *Coercion, Capital and European States, 990–1990* (Oxford, 1990)

P.H.H. Vries, "Governing Growth. A Comparative Analysis of the Role of the State in the Rise of the West", *Journal of World History* 13 (2002), pp. 28–60

C. Weber and A. Wildawsky, *A History of Taxation and Expenditure in the Western World* (New York, 1986)

D. Winch and P.K. O'Brien (eds.), *The Political Economy of British Historical Experience, 1688–1914* (Oxford, 2002)

R. Bin Wong, *China Transformed. Historical Change and the Limits of European Experience* (Ithaca, 1997)

# Putting the Weberian State in its Social, Geopolitical and Militaristic Context: A Response to Patrick O'Brien

## MICHAEL MANN

*****

I have the greatest respect for Patrick O'Brien. I read his work and I look forward to the papers and articles he sends me. He is definitely my kind of economic historian – skeptical of orthodoxy, striving toward his own grand generalizations, yet only on the basis of detailed empirical data given thorough methodological scrutiny. He is someone whose opinions are to be taken seriously and he is well worth having a conversation with.

Though his present essay does discuss my work, it also presents his own explanation of the rise of the "Weberian state" – that type of stable, secure, sovereign and reasonably efficient state Weber termed "the modern state". I see this as essentially a growth of "infrastructural power" – the power to routinely implement decisions across a realm. O'Brien locates this capacity specifically in the British state of the late 17th to early 19th centuries, and he is quite keen to deny it to other states of the period. He attributes British success to its "fiscal-military" core – more particularly to its "fiscal-naval" core, as his recent work has been emphasizing (O'Brien, 2001, 2005). As will become obvious below, I think he is essentially correct in this.

So instead of argument I will expand our conversation in three main if necessarily brief ways. First I seek to relate the development of the modern state to its social background (for I am a sociologist). I focus here for the sake of simplicity on class structure. Second, I seek to bring more geopolitics into the argument, to situate English development amid a particular geopolitical environment. Third, I ask a rather fundamental yet neglected question: why European states had such a pronounced military-fiscal core, since this has not been a universal feature of state systems.

Though O'Brien is generous about my work, he makes some criticisms, some of which I accept. I do not accept his view that the notion of a transition from feudalism to capitalism is "obsolete", though that is not an argument for here. But the first two volumes of *The Sources of Social Power* (1986, 1993) did progressively narrow their focus to Europe and the United States, and to the single case of England/Britain. On that narrow basis – while conspicuously ignoring Asia – my ability to generalize about the development of the modern state was rather constricted. Volume III of *Sources* will correct this, at least in the modern period. It will discuss the world and specifically focus on China and Japan. I will also make brief comparative references concerning war in this paper. O'Brien is also correct to say that I wrote too much about armies, and not enough about navies. Finally, my compilation of statistical data on state finances (though perhaps an original contribution in the mid 1980s) looks rudimentary now, superseded by the recent labors of an army (or perhaps a fleet) of European historians. Nonetheless, it is good to note that these superior data-sets have substantially confirmed my findings, and not just concerning the domination of state finances by war-making. I also described a doubling of English state finances from the 1270s to the mid 15$^{th}$ century, followed by a collapse and then by two centuries of poor data but, I guessed, zero-growth, with spectacular growth beginning again from 1688. This is exactly what O'Brien confirms, using much better data than I had.

His account of the modern state focuses even more than I did on its finances. Indeed he sometimes seem to stray beyond using state finances merely as a convenient quantitative measure of state development and to see them as the main cause of state development. Yet some aspects of "Weberian" growth have been independent of finances. In *Sources* I discussed trends toward what I called more "organic" state administrations in which the dominant classes of a country were drawn into more regular, routinized political relations with the central (usually monarchical) state. Close relations between state elite and dominant classes was the key to the exercise of infrastructural power. It was also key to English development.

O'Brien likes to downplay the powers of the early English state. He says it remained "a follower rather than a front-runner" in Europe right up to the Civil War. There is some truth in this. Yet the medieval English state had been uniquely founded on a single episode of wholesale conquest, followed by a longer period of mutual assimilation between Norman and Anglo-Saxon aristocrats and clerics. This combination made both the Anglo-Norman state and the Anglo-Normans themselves the most homogenous ruling class in Europe, with the most uniform and centralized administrative structures (counties, shire-reeves, courts etc.). Anglo-Norman expansion into the Celtic periphery was also more state-led than, for example, were the French or German expansions into their peripheries (Davies, 1990; Bartlett, 1994). It particularly integrated Wales into that administrative structure. In the first period of fiscal expansion emphasized by O'Brien, from the reign of Edward I to Henry V, this state waged generally successful warfare against the Scottish and the French kings, despite the logistical difficulties involved in fighting abroad. The Angevin Empire was more impressive than he suggests – and so was the conquest of most of the British Isles.

There was, of course, regression in the Wars of the Roses as aristocratic/monarchical solidarity fell apart, though recovery came with the Tudors. But though the Tudor and early Stuart periods were in fiscal terms zero-growth centuries, they saw consolidation and reform of centralized institutions, as parliament replaced the court and council as the central agency co-ordinating monarch and dominant classes (merchants too, of course). Again they fell apart in the early 17th century over religion and the constitution, resulting in a bloody Civil War. But that produced the solution emphasized by O'Brien. As he himself shows for England and Scotland, the post-Civil War compromise enabled higher legitimate levels of taxation to be achieved through Parliament. O'Brien suggests that the dominant classes got their act together for two reasons. One was that the Civil War experience had made them fear revolution from below; the other was a common determination to defend the Protestant Constitution against Catholic Powers – a fear presumably shared across the classes. I would have liked more discussion of these two factors, since there was obviously some tension between them. But in his account the importance of Parliament is obvious. Moreover, the navy whose role he emphasizes was considered a distinctively parliamentary institution, as opposed to the supposedly royal army (Rodger, 2004).

O'Brien suggests that state fiscal powers were geopolitically decisive once the constitutional formula of "the king in parliament" was established, from the reign of William III onward. Through the 18th century it was very effective in developing a legitimate taxation system and a fairly foreign and commercial policy which was supported by most of the dominant classes. As he says, fiscal strength particularly enabled the construction of a great navy. Navies are capital-intensive – "capital ships" required large amounts of capital up front, before they were even launched. Other Powers did not choose to or could not rival the British Navy because they lacked interest in overseas rather than land expansion and perhaps they also lacked Britain's fiscal capacity to provide massive amounts of capital up front to finance a building program which took years to launch a squadron.

But the other Powers with large populations could build up alternative military forces. They could raise labor-intensive armies cheaply with the help of compliant aristocratic officers and forced conscription of soldiers. Against them on land, the British army possessed no special advantage. It was better to use British resources to provide subsidies to other European Powers threatened by the French. Then the allies would do most of the land fighting against the French. O'Brien suggests that Napoleon lost because he was overspent 2.2 to 1 by the British. This is an impressive statistic, but we must not overdo British triumphalism. Britain subsidized allies who already wanted to resist French domination. French attempts at hegemony were defeated less by British fiscal strength than by alliances of Powers "balancing" against the would-be French hegemon. The allies were not frightened of Britain because British military power on the continent was negligible. In the final victories over Napoleon Russian forces probably proved more important than British forces. Yet Britain got a far bigger reward as its navy was able to grab most of the French overseas empire – to acquire the Great but somewhat Accidental British Empire. Britain had required a rather peculiar geopolitical context to become Great. The main overseas imperial rival was also the would-be hegemon in Europe whom the other European Powers would gladly fight, helped by subsidies, but without much expectation of overseas gain. A geopolitical power vacuum had unexpectedly opened up in the world and the British sailed happily right into it.

I wonder if historians are nowadays overdoing the fiscal. Most accounts of French finances of the 17th or 18th centuries tell of desperate expedients, rapacious tax-farmers and chaotic treasuries. The French state sounds a disaster. Yet somehow or other France launched two attempts at European hegemony. French army size managed to double during the 16th century and it trebled in the 17th century. It levelled off in the 18th century, but then doubled again in the French Revolutionary Wars (Lynn, 1997: 55–8). France also developed the world's second navy. War financing did weaken and eventually bring down the French monarchy, but it was ultimately the attempt at hegemony and the consequent power-balancing that brought down France (both Bourbon and Napoleonic) – as it was later twice to bring down a Germany which was by then a thoroughly organic, modern state. Geopolitics mattered.

In Volume II of *Sources* (1993) I contrasted two relatively efficient "organic" states of the late 18th century with two relatively inefficient, inorganic ones. One of the organic pair was indeed Britain, but the other was Prussia. I argued that the Prussian equivalent of the organic formula of "the king in parliament" was "the aristocracy in bureaucracy", ie the Prussian aristocracy was brought inside the civilian and military administration of the kingdom, providing a degree of cohesion to a smallish state with a rather backward economy. It differed from France and Habsburg Austria with their more decentralized, less cohesive states. Britain proved not to be the only model for the modern state. The Prussian "authoritarian-bureaucratic" model developed further in the 19th century, and was then borrowed from by Japan among others, just as its intensification during World War I was borrowed from by the Soviet Union. Not only the British state was "Weberian".

States cannot be reduced to their finances or indeed to any merely internal logic of development. Their fiscal powers derive most fundamentally from the ability of the state elite to co-ordinate the energies of dominant classes amid the challenges presented by other states and their classes. This can be done in a variety of ways. For example, starting from my concept of infrastructural power, John Hobson and Linda Weiss have shown that the "late development" states of East Asia were successful since the 1960s in rivalling the Western Powers not because they contained strong state riding roughshod over civil society but because their states enabled "governed inter-dependence" of a half-authoritarian kind between state and major business organizations (*zaibatsu* in Japan, *chaebol* in Korea). They also benefitted from considerable American aid amid the Cold War. Again, state, classes and geopolitics entwining in unique ways.

Now to my third argument. It is remarkable that in the large literature devoted to the fiscal-military core of European states almost nobody has asked **why** fighting wars was so important to Europeans. Nor did I. We failed to pursue sufficient comparative research (as O'Brien says). Had we done so, we might have noticed that Europeans made war with greater enthusiasm over a longer space of time than almost anyone else. The Chinese "Spring and Autumn" and Warring States periods, from 771 BC to 220 BC, probably came the closest, with as many wars and comparable casualties over half-a-millennium – though the Europeans went at it for a whole millennium. Comparative data-sets (inadequate as they are) would suggest that Europeans have made war with greater frequency and lethality (eg Lemke, 2002). Europeans are not from Venus, as the American neo-conservative Robert Kaplan has suggested (contrasting them to Americans who he says are from Mars). Europeans are from Mars, though since 1945 most of them have been briefly holidaying in Venus. Why were they so martial?

How did Europeans **begin** their love-affair with war? Five main causes were rooted in medieval social structures.

(1) As the Western Roman Empire fell, accompanied and succeeded by multiple barbarian invasions, the population of Europe

declined by about 50%. The Frankish Empire (Northern France, Germany west of the Elbe, and Northern Italy) contained fertile land and the state most capable of defending it. Economic and population recovery began there and not until the 14th century did expansion produce a "Malthusian crisis" of over-population. There was initially a large surplus of unused or lightly-used land which could support a larger population. But if land was plentiful, labor was scarce. As in Africa through much of its history, this tended to generate free peasant communities, yet it also created an incentive for armed groups to enserf or enslave them – if they could.

(2) "Feudal" social relations arose between lords and peasants. The military institutions arising in the core centered on lords building stone castles garrisoned by small contingents of heavy cavalry, "knights". These were not a response to outside threats since the Viking and Saracen raids had already ceased. The primary use of military power was to conquer peasant communities, revoke their "allodial" freedoms and hold them in serfdom. The main "conquest" was of the peasants (Poly & Bournazel, 1991: 26–33, 238, 352). The key to wealth and power became the serf tied legally to the lord's manor and held there by force so overwhelming that it need not be routinely applied. It slipped gradually into "customary law". Military power became an intrinsic part of the reproduction of class relations (Brenner, 2006). Thus there was an economic incentive for wars of **conquest**, seizing and ruling land and its inhabitants.

(3) Feudalism also involved relations among lords. Land was granted by lords as a "fief" in return for military service by their vassals, who thus had an incentive to help conquer new land and enserf more peasants. Their bonds were reinforced by a growth of lineage solidarity among lords and vassals aimed at keeping family inheritance intact through primogeniture. This deprived younger sons of substantial inheritance, but they were trained in the military arts from childhood. The *juvenes* had an incentive to pursue military careers in which service to a lord might be rewarded by wages or a fiefdom. The heirs of great lords thus tended to develop entourages of young men spoiling for war (Poly & Bournazel, 1991: 107–113; Davies, 1990).

(4) Medieval Europe consisted of an advanced core, originally the lands of the Frankish Empire, and a large periphery of smaller and weaker states and self-governing peasant communities. The lords, vassals and younger sons of the core had the incentive and the military power to conquer, settle and colonize their peripheries. Bartlett (1994) showed that this process of imperial

"cellular replication" of core institutions lasted over a 400 year period, from 950 to 1350, as the core swallowed up free communities and minnow states in the periphery, so creating the early modern kingdoms of France, England, Spain etc. which later became Europe's Great Powers.

(5) The main ideology of the core was Latin Christianity, while most of the periphery was pagan, Muslim or Eastern Orthodox Christian. This increased the ideological power of the colonizers who saw Christianization of the periphery as morally desirable. It also generated clerical colonists (often also younger sons) whose mission was to save souls, if necessary by force.

These five features of early medieval social structure ensured the imperial expansion across Europe itself of militarized elites. Victory meant real gains in land, income and even supposed moral virtue. They could secure this through their military and political superiority over (a) the common people of the core and (b) the population of the periphery. Militarism worked for its practitioners who survived. Of course, militarism is a risky business, killing many of its practitioners. Thus a further medieval ideology developed, legitimizing the knightly way of life which might end in an honorable, sacrificial death, rewarded in heavenly afterlife.

The expansion of the system meant that war was not as costly for its practitioners as war normally is. Militarists of the core gained at the expense of peasants and the periphery; younger sons were willing to take risks for enormous potential benefits which could not be otherwise obtained; and elder sons were getting rid of their troublesome siblings. These conditions in medieval Europe were not found routinely across the world (though most were present in "Spring and Autumn" China, helping account for its high level of fiscal-military state-building). The success of European militarism meant that its institutions and culture kept being reproduced. This brought some "path-dependency": later wars were partly determined by paths already taken. War was normal, "natural" in Europe, and it seemed to work over a very long period of time.

This first phase of militarism produced a mostly colonized Europe divided into several hundred sovereign or half-sovereign states varying greatly in size and power. So after Bartlett's phase of imperial "cellular replication" came a second inter-state phase lasting several more centuries whereby most of the minnow states were swallowed by the bigger ones. Though wars often seemed to pit the great Powers against each other, they generally enabled them to take territories not from each other but from their minnow allies. Gradually, the number of states declined and the cost of war increased. It might still seem more profitable than pacifism, for that invited invasion and destruction. It is not a necessary feature of multi-state systems that they proliferate inter-state wars – witness the few wars in the two centuries of Latin American independence or the fifty years of African independence (Centeno, 2002; Lemke, 2002). But with so much militarism built into its state institutions and its dominant class culture, it was difficult for Europe to break with its traditions. In any case, two further boosts to militarism were now felt: a revival of ideological war in the Wars of Religion and the possibility of expansion outside of Europe. O'Brien refers to them both, but here I focus on the latter.

The Europeans became history's greatest empire-builders. Across the entire planet only Turkey, Japan, China and Ethiopia stayed out of their clutches. Though their empires did not last very long, their explosive burst of imperialism from within a single civilization was historically unprecedented. Imperialism was multiple, involving not just one or two European states, but almost all of them. Russia and the Habsburgs struck out eastward and southeastward across land (Russia reaching to the Pacific), while Portugal, Spain, Holland, France and Britain founded large empires overseas. Denmark, Germany, Italy and even Belgium joined in. By the 20th century Europeans and their settler descendants dominated the earth.

One important reason Europeans were so successful in these imperial ventures was their growing military power. Through repeated wars inside the continent, Europeans had become skilled at a particular style of warfare. European states and armies remained quite small by global standards. But they had refined forms of organization by which quite small forces on land and sea could pour intensive fire-power onto the enemy. Their superiority grew especially at sea, where the "military revolution" proceeded from Portuguese naval cannon, to quick-firing Dutch, French and British naval squadrons able to sail smoothly against the wind. 17th century navies began to use "line-ahead" tactics, able to pour cannon-shot in unbroken sequence from each ship in turn into enemy ships and ports. By now Europeans were clearly superior in open seas, while naval guns and *trace italienne* fortresses made their coastal trading-ports almost invulnerable. They could levy "protection rents" and monopolies over trade and establish a degree of "informal empire" over broader regions. The early centuries of expansion were profitable for most of the European merchants and states involved in it. Even when there were deleterious effects on European economies, as in the case of the massive quantities of gold and silver bullion imported into Spain, this was not evident at the time. By 1815, the Europeans – and especially the British – had every reason to believe they had become richer, more urbanized, and more industrialized as a result of their overseas expansion, as O'Brien has demonstrated (O'Brien, 1999: 26; O'Brien & Leandro Prados de la Escosura, 1998). Some also gloried in the Christianizing and civilizing of the natives. They had every incentive to continue their imperial wars overseas.

Such military power had organizational preconditions hinging most crucially upon the efficient conversion of economic surpluses into trained professional soldiers and sailors, supplied with ample materiel. By the mid 18$^{th}$ century shifting economic power obviously mattered, especially for Britain, now becoming more productive than any rival European or Asian empires. But, as O'Brien suggests, it was probably the linkages between state finances and armed commerce – plus a geopolitical vacuum – that helped give the British a military edge overseas.

In this short response I have generalized freely, and with very little data. I am not sure how much Patrick O'Brien might disagree with me. There might be more differences of emphasis than head-on disagreement. But disputation has not been my main objective. Instead I have sought to provide some more sociological ballast to the data of the economic historian, emphasizing the class structure, the geopolitical rivalries and the underlying militarism of Europe which entwined in sometimes accidental ways with the fiscal-military nexus to generate a Weberian state in Britain and elsewhere, as well as a brief period of great British power in the world.

## Bibliography

Bartlett, Robert 1994 *The Making of Europe. Conquest, Colonization and Cultural Change, 950–1350*. Princeton, NJ: Princeton University Press.

Brenner, Robert 2006 "From theory to history: 'The European Dynamic' or feudalism to capitalism?" in John Hall & Ralph Schroeder (eds.), *An Anatomy of Power: The Social Theory of Michael Mann*. Cambridge: Cambridge University Press.

Centeno, Miguel 2002 *Blood and Debt: War and the Nation-State in Latin America*. College Park, PA: Penn State University Press.

Davies, Rees 1990 *Domination and Conquest. The Experience of Ireland, Scotland and Wales 1100–1300*. Cambridge: Cambridge University Press.

Lemke, Douglas 2002 *Regions of War and Peace*. Cambridge: Cambridge University Press.

Lynn, John 1997 *Giant of the Grand Siècle: The French Army 1610–1715*. New York, Cambridge University Press.

Mann, Michael 1986 & 1993 *The Sources of Social Power*. Cambridge: Cambridge University Press, Vols. I & II.

O'Brien, Patrick 1999 "Balance-sheets for the acquisition, retention and loss of European empires overseas", *Itinerario*, Vol 23, 25–52.

———— 2001 "Inseparable Connections: Trade, Economy, Fiscal State and the Expansion of Empire, 1688–1815", in *The Oxford History of the British Empire*, Vol II, op. cit.

———— 2005 "Fiscal and financial preconditions for the rise of British naval hegemony 1485–1815", LSE Department of Economic History, *Working Papers of the Global Economic History Network*, No. 91/05.

O'Brien, Patrick & Leandro Prados de la Escosura (eds.) 1998 "The costs and benefits for Europeans from their Empires Overseas", special issue of *Revista de Historia Economica*, i: 29–92.

Poly, Jean-Pierre & Eric Bournazel 1991 *The Feudal Transformation, 900–1200*. New York: Holmes & Meier.

Rodger, N.A.M. 2004 *The Command of the Ocean: A Naval History of Britain Vol II 1649–1815*. London: Allen Lane.

Weiss, Linda & John Hobson 1995 *States and Economic Development*. Oxford: Polity Press.